Spectrum Guide to
UGANDA

Camerapix Publishers International

NAIROBI

Spectrum Guide to Uganda

First published 1998 by
Camerapix Publishers International,
P.O. Box 45048,
Nairobi, Kenya

ISBN 1 874041 73 3

This book was designed and produced by
Camerapix Publishers International,
P.O. Box 45048,
Nairobi, Kenya
Tel: (254-2) 448923/4/5
Fax: (254-2) 448926/7
E-mail: info@camerapix. com
Website: http//www. camerapix. com

The **Spectrum Guides** series provides a comprehensive and detailed description of each country it covers, together with all the essential data that tourists, business visitors, or potential investors are likely to require.

Spectrum Guides in print:
African Wildlife Safaris
Eritrea
Ethiopia
India
Jordan
Kenya
Madagascar
Maldives
Mauritius
Namibia
Nepal
Pakistan
Seychelles
South Africa
Sri Lanka
Tanzania
United Arab Emirates
Zambia
Zimbabwe

Color separations by Universal Graphics, Singapore.
Printed and bound by Tien Wah Press, Singapore.

Publisher and Chief Executive:
Mohamed Amin
Editorial Director: Brian Tetley
Picture Editor: Duncan Willetts
Art Editor: Calvin McKenzie
Projects Director: Rukhsana Haq
Chief Editor: Barbara Balletto
Editors: Helen van Houten and Gail Porter
Production Editor: Roger Barnard
Graphics: Lilly Macharia and Harinder Kalsi
Typesetter: Rachel Musyimi
Picture Research: Abdul Rehman

Editorial Board

Uganda is a spectacular country rapidly recovering from decades of anarchy and civil strife. Today Winston Churchill's Pearl of Africa shines again.

In *Spectrum Guide to Uganda*, another in the continuing series of internationally acclaimed *Spectrum Guides*, the lustre that is Uganda spreads through every page, thanks to the breathtaking photography of **Paul Joynson-Hicks**, who has lived in the country for many years, and **David Beatty**, whose passion for photography and skills grew out of a long, pioneering overland trek by four-wheel-drive across the whole of Africa in the early 1970s. In the years since, Beatty has earned a worldwide reputation for his multi-faceted talents as a lensman — and has contributed the pictorial portfolios for a great number of best-selling travel guides and books.

A concept from the three-man travel book team of world-renowned photographer and cameraman **Mohamed Amin**, Chief Executive; equally renowned **Duncan Willetts**, who is Picture Editor; and Editorial Director **Brian Tetley** — all based in Kenya — *Spectrum Guides* have grown so rapidly that today teams of specialists are at work all over the world preparing new titles.

As Chief Editor, American **Barbara Balletto** spent many long hours planning and coordinating the contents of *Spectrum Guide to Uganda*, worked diligently to refine the text and, indeed, made many contributions to it herself. A writer and editor based in Kenya since 1986, she has travelled extensively throughout the region.

The team of editors — which included American **Helen van Houten** and Briton **Gail Porter**, both based in Kenya — worked long and hard to edit the text and were also responsible for maintaining the *Spectrum Guides* in-house style.

Ugandan **Professor Phares M Mutibwa** contributed the entire text for Part One: History, Geography, and People. A professor of history, he has taught at Makerere University, the University of Nairobi, and the University of Swaziland.

A large portion of the book — including the Business section — was written by Ugandan **David Musoke**, the Business Editor of the *New Vision* newspaper in Kampala.

The articles on Uganda's birds, flora, and rainforests were the work of Belgian **Jean Pierre Vande weghe**, a medical doctor who has been involved in the fields of ornithology and nature conservation in various African countries for more than 30 years. He is currently managing director of Uganda Nature Safaris based in Kampala.

American **Craig Sholley** was responsible for the article on Uganda's mountain gorillas. He is currently Director of Conservation and Education for the American-based International Expeditions. He began working with gorillas in Volcano National Park at the celebrated Karisoke Research Centre with Dian Fossey, and later went on to become director of Rwanda's Mountain Gorilla Project. He has acted as scientific adviser on several mountain gorilla film documentaries, including the award-winning IMAX film 'Mountain Gorilla'.

The article on camping was provided by **Avril** and **Chris MacDonald**, who run the Nairobi-based Rafiki Africa, which offers camping and primate trekking in Uganda and elsewhere on the continent.

Numismatist **Roberto Andreeta**, Ndere Troupe director **Stephen Rwangyezi**, and sports writer **Wangwe Mulakha** — all based in Kampala — contributed articles relating to their particular expertise.

5

TABLE OF CONTENTS

IN BRIEF

LISTINGS

MAPS

Half-title: Sunset over Lake Edward. Title: Vast blue sky and waters of Lake Victoria surround the Ssese Islands. Previous pages: Primate playmates: endangered mountain gorillas. Overleaf: Dawn silhouette in the foothills of Mount Elgon. Pages 12–13: The skyline of Kampala, changing rapidly during the 1990s. Pages 14–15: Hippos battle it out in Queen Elizabeth National Park's Kazinga Channel. Page 16: Elephants are returning to Uganda's national parks.

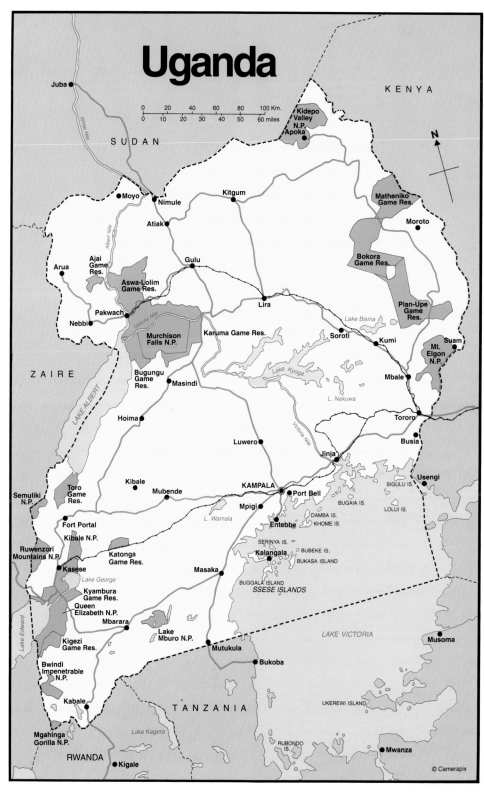

Uganda

KENYA

Juba

0 20 40 60 80 100 Km.
0 10 20 30 40 50 60 miles

SUDAN

Kidepo
Valley
N.P.
Apoka

N

Moyo
Nimule
Kitgum
Matheniko
Game Res.

Atiak
Moroto

Arua
Ajai
Game
Res.
Gulu
Bokora
Game Res.

Aswa-Lolim
Game Res.

Pakwach
Lira
Pian-Upe
Game
Res.

Nebbi
Murchison
Falls N.P.
Karuma Game Res.
Lake Bisina
Soroti
Kumi
Suam
Mt.
Elgon
N.P.

ZAIRE
Bugungu
Game
Res.
Masindi
Lake Kyoga
L. Nakuwa
Mbale

LAKE ALBERT
Victoria Nile

Hoima
Tororo

Luwero
Victoria Nile
Busia

Jinja

Kibale
Mubende
KAMPALA
Port Bell
Usengi
SIGULU IS.

Semuliki
N.P.
Toro
Game
Res.
Mpigi
BUGAIA IS.
LOLUI IS.

Fort Portal
L. Wamala
DAMBA IS.
Entebbe
KHOME IS.

Kibale N.P.
SERINYA IS.

Ruwenzori
Mountains N.P.
Katonga
Game Res.
Kalangala
BUBEKE IS.
BUKASA ISLAND

Kasese
Lake George
Masaka
BUGGALA ISLAND
SSESE ISLANDS

Kyambura
Game Res.
Queen
Elizabeth N.P.
Mbarara
LAKE VICTORIA
Musoma

Kigezi
Game Res.
Lake
Mburo N.P.
Mutukula

Bwindi
Impenetrable
N.P.
Bukoba

Kabale
TANZANIA
UKEREWI ISLAND

Mgahinga
Gorilla N.P.
Lake Kagera
RUBONDO
IS.
Mwanza

RWANDA
Kigale
© Camerapix

Lake Edward

White Nile

Albert Nile

17

The Ugandan Experience

'For magnificence, for variety of form and colour, for profusion of brilliant life — plant, bird, insect, reptile, beast — for vast scale . . . Uganda is truly the pearl of Africa.' So wrote Sir Winston Churchill in his book *My African Journey* in the early 1900s, little knowing what tumultuous events were to come that would dull the lustre of his beautiful pearl.

Those later events brought the worst of the country's first post-independence elected leader, Milton Obote, to light and revealed the atrocities of Uganda's infamous head of state, Idi Amin.

Stability returned to Uganda under Yoweri Museveni and the National Resistance Movement. High on the government's agenda was to restore the tourism industry, and a 10-year plan was drawn up that recommends the type and level of development that should take place to ensure sustainable growth.

The changes are noticeable. The roads, once potholed and decrepit, are being maintained. The ubiquitous *matatu*, one of the main forms of public transportation for much of the population, are not the overcrowded, wildly careering vehicles they used to be. Corruption and bribery are nowhere near the levels they are in other African countries, particularly at the lower levels. Most importantly, in 1996 Uganda's economy was developing rapidly.

Visitors, beginning to hear that the pearl is starting to shine once again, are coming back, along with the wildlife, which was decimated during the Amin era. True, you won't find the vast herds of game that typify Uganda's neighbouring countries of Kenya and Tanzania, but the variety of wildlife (more than 50 large mammal species) and the settings in which it is found are superb. And the birdlife is incomparable; many consider Uganda to be the finest birding country in Africa, with about 1,000 species of birds recorded in the country.

If it is primates you're interested in, Uganda won't disappoint. The country is also home to the endangered mountain gorilla, the chimpanzee, and more than 10 other types of primate, including the tiny and charming wide-eyed bushbaby.

Few things beat the thrill of hiking through a forest, deep in the heart of Africa, and suddenly coming upon a family of the fascinating mountain gorilla. Uganda allows the visitor access to these special primates and, in fact, is one of only three countries in Africa to do so.

For a truly unbeatable experience, take the launch trip down the Nile in Murchison Falls National Park — referred to by many as one of the most exciting wildlife experiences Africa has to offer. Hippos and crocodiles abound; the scenery is spectacular.

History buffs will find Uganda's story an interesting one, and will delight in exploring the relics of the country's four unique kingdoms. In particular, the Kasubi Tombs, near Kampala, are well worth a visit.

But one of the prime attractions of Uganda is its people. Although they still bear the scars of their past — a backfiring car in the streets of Kampala still sends passers-by running for cover — they are quick to laugh, smile, extend an outstretched hand, and offer assistance, ever proud of the country they have helped to rebuild. And they are clearly ready to show it off as one of Africa's miraculous beauties.

Welcome.

Opposite (clockwise from top left): Muganda boy enjoys his homemade toy; Wise and friendly face of a Kampala matriarch; Langi elder in Arua pauses for a rest; Colourful Kampala market vendor. Overleaf: Jubilant women perform a Uganda traditional dance.

Travel Brief and Social Advisory

Some dos and don'ts to make your visit more enjoyable:

A country blessed

Landlocked Uganda, astride the equator in East Africa, is 236,580 square kilometres (91,344 square miles) of beautiful, serene, green plateau situated between the eastern and western branches of the Great Rift Valley. It is truly a country blessed. More than 2,000 millimetres (80 inches) of rain falls on its ever-fertile lands each year, and this on a continent often struggling against drought and famine. Lakes, rivers, and streams — including Lake Victoria, the world's second-largest freshwater lake, and the legendary Nile River — cover 25 per cent of its surface. Its lush rainforests, savannah, and semi-desert areas are home to a splendid array of wildlife, birdlife, and flora. The biggest blessing of all, perhaps, is that it is populated with friendly, hardy folk who have somehow withstood a brutal, humiliating and devastating civil war for almost two decades and have come out on top.

As Uganda continues to enjoy peace and security, it is fast regaining its past glory as a tourist haven — although, thankfully, the tourists do not yet come in the droves that so often spoil the wildlife spectacle in other parts of East Africa. Thousands of Asians and foreigners who were expelled from the country in the early 1970s have been allowed to return and repossess their properties, estates, factories and shops. New foreign investors from all over the world have descended on Uganda to benefit from the new opportunities available; Ugandans, too, are reaping the benefits.

As a result, you'll find the facilities of modern living available almost everywhere in the urban areas: telecommunications, health services, and frequent road, rail and air links. And — again, unlike many other African countries — the services generally work, although telecommunications outside Kampala are none too proven yet.

Uganda now boasts one of the widest ranges of accommodation found anywhere on the continent — from posh, luxurious international hotels like the Kampala Sheraton to self-service cottages and campsites. The country offers comfort for every kind of visitor, be they a budget-conscious backpacker or a 'no-expenses-spared' executive.

While Uganda undergoes its socio-economic and political transformation, the government jealously guards the country's natural heritage. The laws regarding the preservation of forests, rivers and lakes, wild animals, and sites of historical importance are strictly enforced so that both visitors and citizens can enjoy them — now and in the future.

Getting there

Because of the discounted fares offered, many travellers find Nairobi the best gateway in and out of East Africa. It is a relatively simple matter to get from Nairobi to Entebbe (where Uganda's international airport is located, about a half-hour's drive from Kampala) or Kampala, travelling either by air (but book in advance, as flights are often crowded), road, or train. So consider the Nairobi connection first.

Uganda Airlines, the national carrier, flies Boeing 737s directly from Entebbe International Airport once or twice a day to Nairobi. It also flies to Kigali four times a week; Dubai three times a week; Lusaka and Johannesburg twice a week; and Dar es Salaam, Kilimanjaro and Harare (via Lusaka) once a week. They offer both business and economy class.

Other airlines flying in and out of Entebbe include Kenya Airways six times a week; Air Rwanda and Sabena four times a week; Air Burundi, British Airways, and Ethiopian Airlines three times a week; Air France, Air Tanzania, Alliance, Gulf Air, and InterAir twice a week; and Air India,

Egyptair, and Royal Swazi once a week.

Landlocked Uganda can also be reached on all sides by road, but check first before you try coming in via the Rwanda or Sudan borders, as the political and security situation in those countries may make crossing virtually impossible — and sometimes dangerous. At the time of writing, both borders were open. From Kenya, Uganda can be entered at the two main border posts of Malaba and Busia. There are also border points at Suam (near Mount Elgon), Karita, and Amudat, although they are rarely used and there is not much transport on the other side after you cross. The Tanzania border crossings are at Mutukula and Kikagati.

The two main crossing points from Zaire are at Bunagana (between Rutshuru and Kisoro) and Kasindi (between Beni and Katwe) in the south, although the Ishasha border post is also open. Farther north, there are crossing points at Goli and Vurra, although they are little used and it is advisable to check on the security situation in the north of Uganda before attempting to cross: rogue elements still roam this area and trouble occasionally flares up.

If your budget doesn't allow you to fly from Nairobi to Entebbe, consider the bus. Buses run daily between Nairobi and the Uganda border at very reasonable cost. Head for the most convenient border post, Malaba, where you can then get a *matatu* (a type of commuter taxi; often a minibus) to Tororo, which takes about 20 minutes, and then onward from there into Kampala.

An even better bet is the relatively new shuttle bus, a smaller, much more comfortable service that runs between Kampala and Nairobi and back again three times a week. The shuttle bus can be booked through either New Lines Limited in Kampala or Huzara Travel in Nairobi and costs the local currency equivalent of about US$ 40 one way, which includes lunch and refreshments during the trip.

For the more adventurous, an interesting method of two-wheeled 'public transport' has developed at the Kenya–Uganda border:

the *boda boda* 'taxi', so named because it originates at the country's borders. It is actually a cyclist, who will take you on the carrier at the back of his bicycle to points some 10 to 20 kilometres (six to 12 miles) inside the border. Ugandan residents returning from a visit across the border in Kenya like this form of transport, as they can travel along even small paths that would not accommodate even the hardiest four-wheel-drive vehicle. Even during the rainy seasons, when some of the roads are impassable, the boda boda will reach its destination. As time goes by, the bicycles are being replaced by motorcycles or motor scooters — but the bicycles live on, going deeper into the countryside, giving affordable service where it is required.

If you like to travel by rail, you can take the Nairobi–Kampala train (every Tuesday) or the twice-weekly train from Nairobi to Malaba. With the renewal of ties between the East African countries, plans are to continue to expand this line, and it is hoped that soon travel by rail will be possible all the way from Mombasa to Kasese.

Although there are no passenger boat connections between Uganda and Kenya these days, it is possible to travel across Lake Victoria from Tanzania, using the Port Bell ferry, which connects Mwanza to Port Bell (Kampala) on its regular once-a-week service.

Nationals of the following countries do not need visas to enter Uganda: Antigua and Barbuda, Angola, Australia, Austria, Bahamas, Bahrain, Barbados, Belgium, Belize, Botswana, Burundi, Canada, Comoros, Cyprus, Denmark, Djibouti, Eritrea, Ethiopia, Fiji, Finland, France, Gambia, Germany, Greece, Grenada, Hong Kong, Ireland, Israel, Italy, Jamaica, Japan, Kenya, Kuwait, Lesotho, Libya, Luxembourg, Madagascar, Malawi, Malaysia, Malta, Mauritius, Mozambique, Namibia, Netherlands, New Zealand, Norway, Oman, Portugal, Rwanda, Saudi Arabia, Seychelles, Sierra Leone, Singapore, Solomon Islands, Somalia, South Korea, Spain, St Lucia, St Vincent

Opposite: Passenger balances precariously on a *boda boda* 'taxi' as it prepares to take off.

Above: The country's national carrier, Uganda Airlines, operates from Entebbe International Airport.

and Grenadines, Sudan, Swaziland, Sweden, Switzerland, Taiwan, Tanzania, Tonga, Tuvalu, United Arab Emirates, United Kingdom, USA, Vanuatu, Zambia, and Zimbabwe.

Nationals of countries other than those listed above should contact their nearest Ugandan embassy to obtain visas in advance of their visit; otherwise, visas are also obtainable when entering the country.

Getting around

By road

Driving in Uganda can be enjoyable and is really the best way to enjoy the glorious scenery, vegetation, and wildlife. And finding your way around the country should present no problem at all.

Uganda's ordinance maps, obtainable from the Department of the Surveyor General in Entebbe and the Uganda Tourist Board in Kampala, are good and kept constantly updated. You can obtain maps of the whole country or specific regions, as well as street maps of the major cities and towns.

The Uganda Motorists Association also produces an excellent map detailing all the major roads and distances between major centres.

Driving is on the left. If you have a recognized and valid licence you can drive up to 90 days without applying for an international or Ugandan licence.

Uganda has one of the longest tarmacked road systems in East Africa — about 6,230 kilometres (3,870 miles) — and the government is always busy repairing the roads, recognizing the importance of linking the countryside to the major towns and cities. Some 22,100 kilometres (13,730 miles) of secondary and dirt roads are in relatively good condition as well. Be warned: during the rainy seasons (generally March-April and October-November, although there are regional variations) many of the dirt roads become impassable — only four-wheel-drive vehicles will be lucky enough to extricate themselves from the mud.

Above: The road passing through Queen Elizabeth National Park to Kasese, with the Ruwenzori Mountains in the background. Uganda has one of the longest tarmacked road systems in East Africa.

Signposting is frequent (at least on main roads) and often includes distances. Along the main routes, a distance marker is placed every kilometre on either side of the road, so whichever direction you travel you will know how far you have gone and how far you have to go. In an effort to promote their products (and provide a service), several tobacco and beer companies have put up road signposts, indicating street names, and distance signs on some major routes.

Whatever your destination, you are generally never far from contact with people (who are always happy to help) or some method of communication.

Generally, the standard of driving reflects the quality of the roads: as they are in much better shape than those in Kenya, for instance, the accident rate is much lower. Fatal accidents do occur, however: watch out in particular for long-distance *matatus*, which tend to speed. And be careful when dealing with matatu drivers — they can be rough and impolite.

It must also be remembered that, as a landlocked country, Uganda is a major transit route for heavy-laden trucks going — provided borders are open — to and from Rwanda, Burundi, Zaire, Sudan, and sometimes even northern Tanzania. If you come upon a convoy of these trucks, be very cautious when overtaking: they're bigger than you are and often don't see you. Make sure you've got lots of clear road ahead.

When in national parks and game sanctuaries, or in extremely remote areas, four-wheel-drive is really the only way to get around — particularly during or just after the rains. Most tour organizations provide experienced drivers and well-maintained vehicles — let them handle the driving.

For the independent and budget-minded traveller, major towns are linked by frequent and — by Western standards — extremely cheap scheduled 'luxury' bus services. In addition, private (but licensed) small taxis are found in all cities and towns around every corner. They may not have meters — if they don't, make sure you negotiate the

Above: Kampala Railway Station.

fare before you board. The rates should be reasonable, if you're a hard bargainer.

Should you have an accident, Ugandans are always ready to assist. You can also get temporary cover with the Kenya-based Africa Air Rescue or Medivac, which have offices in Kampala. For a small fee, you are guaranteed quick rescue and transportation to any nearby competent hospital.

By air

Uganda has a well-developed domestic air network. Although Uganda Airways does not currently fly domestic routes, three air charter companies operate domestic flights to almost any part of the country from Entebbe International Airport. Bel Air, Eagle Aviation and Take Air all have offices at Entebbe Airport. Other carriers located in Kampala include Air Uganda, CEI Aviation, Speedbird and Tropical Charters and Tours.

By train

Uganda boasts approximately 1,300 kilometres (810 miles) of railway track, once considered to be one of the best rail services in Africa. However, the rail network is

not being rehabilitated as quickly as the road network. Currently the Uganda Railways Corporation operates one passenger train a week to western Uganda up to Kasese and three a week from Tororo north-west to Pakwach via Mbale, Soroti, Lira, and Gulu. If you don't care about time or comfort, this is the way to go; but expect frequent delays, breakdowns, and spartan carriages.

The cargo train service, however, has been restored to almost 90 per cent efficiency to cater for exports and imports through the ports of Mombasa in Kenya and Dar es Salaam in Tanzania.

On foot

There is little need to explore Uganda on foot, although the walking safaris offered by many tour operators in Uganda are a superb experience. A considerable amount of hiking is involved if you want to see the chimpanzees or mountain gorillas in the dense forests of south-western Uganda. Hiking and climbing in Ruwenzori Mountains National Park, on the fabled Mountains of the Moon, is also

Above: Full of joy, boys from Kampala's Buganda Road Primary School celebrate the rebirth of freedom.

an unforgettable adventure. Make sure to bring your own hiking boots or shoes — you won't be able to buy them once you're in the country.

The people

Ugandans are warm, friendly, and full of humour — despite the traumatic period of wars and great suffering they went through. They are anxious to make friends with visitors and are continually asking guests whether they are comfortable and enjoying themselves. If the answer is 'no', they will go to any length to please and assist in any way possible. In a way, they seem to be reciprocating the warm reception many of them got from countries near and far when they were forced into exile. One of the proverbs in many of the Bantu dialects is *'Omusajja gyagenda gyasanga banne'*, literally meaning 'Wherever a man goes he will find friendly people'.

A large number of people speak English, which was introduced into the country in the 1880s, when what is now Uganda was under British administration. Some Ugandans speak the 'Queen's English' much better than the native English people do. Although English and Swahili have been recognized as the country's official languages by the National Constitution, promulgated in November 1995, English is the only true *lingua franca*, as Swahili is seldom spoken. Ugandans — particularly those who have never received any formal education — also speak some 30 indigenous languages, largely in the rural areas. The two main indigenous languages spoken in the country are Luganda and Luo.

English is the main language of instruction in most schools and colleges. Swahili is rarely spoken anywhere except in the market-places and by the country's armed forces, including the regular police and army. Although you might expect Swahili to be more widely spoken and be a unifying factor among the three main East African nations of Tanzania, Kenya, and Uganda, it still evokes bad memories for many people in Uganda, whose property was looted by some undisciplined Tanzanian soldiers back in the late 1970s, who

Above: Many Ugandans shop at colourful, open-air markets.

were meant to assist with the country's reconstruction (see History, Part One).

Ordinarily, all of the country's ethnic groups study, work, and play together everywhere, despite their differences. Unity in diversity is slowly but surely emerging. Nepotism or 'brotherization' — employing people of the same tribe, even if they have no other qualification — is, however, still accepted and tolerated.

Uganda's police, modelled in the British mould, are smart, disciplined, courteous, and always helpful to visitors in need of direction or advice. However, because of the relatively low wages they receive, some policemen (particularly traffic police) are prone to demanding *chai* — literally meaning 'tea' in Swahili, the word has evolved into Swahili slang for a bribe. But keep in mind that offering a bribe is a criminal offence.

In recent years, a number of street children and beggars have begun to take up positions in the country's larger cities and towns, particularly Kampala, but not to the extent found in most other African coun-

tries. They are the unfortunate victims of Uganda's recent past.

Although there is an air of cooperation and amicability (and the past, if not forgotten, is forgiven), the European, Asian, and African communities tend to maintain the social barriers that have divided them for so long. The return of expropriated properties, estates, and shops to their former owners — including Asians and Europeans who had been expelled by Amin's regime — is resented by some Ugandans who profited from this exodus. The majority, however, have welcomed the return of Asians and Europeans, who are rehabilitating their properties, providing employment, and restoring services that had become extinct.

Keep in mind that, as in most developing countries, the head of state commands a great deal more respect than his counterparts in the West — an attitude particularly inherent in African paternalistic cultures. Cultural leaders or monarchies are also regarded with great esteem and respect, including prostrating oneself before them to demonstrate one's loyalty. Unless visitors

Above: Barefoot youngsters enjoy a spontaneous game of soccer, which has long been Uganda's national sport.

want to become involved in a political brouhaha, they should refrain from criticizing either the president or any of the kings, for instance.

Though strongly conservative in attitudes, social habits, and dress, there remains a remarkable air of freedom about this newly liberated society. Ugandans speak their mind easily on whatever they consider are the ills affecting their country. After the restoration of peace and tranquillity and human rights, a number of newspapers and publications have sprung up, with all sorts of shades of opinion. While the government has exhibited tolerance and given licence to constructive criticism, there have been cases where newsmen have been taken to court when the government felt they were reporting 'utter lies'.

Ugandans have suffered immensely from civil wars, and are all united in their determination to avoid any circumstance that could lead to another conflict. For virtually two decades, the country's neighbours developed their economies and societies, leaving Uganda sadly lagging behind. Ugandans are now working hard to catch up, and they welcome anyone who comes to assist them — particularly tourists.

Safety
Although peace and stability — and the rule of law — have been restored, crime does exist. In isolated areas on the country's borders disgruntled rebel groups commit acts of thuggery. In particular, check the security situation before you travel anywhere north of Murchison Falls National Park and Karamoja. Uganda, however, is much better policed than it was a few years back, and visitors observing sensible precautions should enjoy a trouble-free holiday.

Do not leave valuables in your car (if you do, lock them away, out of sight, in the boot or glove compartment).

Walking at night in all major centres is reasonably safe. There have been a few instances of handbags and wristwatches being snatched, and occasional muggings, so be sensible about what you wear (don't flaunt gold jewellery) and keep your eyes open — just as you would in any major city.

Above: Clouds build up over Lake Victoria, the world's second-largest freshwater lake and the source of the Nile.

Weather

Nature has endowed Uganda with one of the most pleasant climates in the world. Situated as it is around Lake Victoria; traversed with innumerable other lakes and rivers, including the mighty Nile; and featuring an interesting combination of mountains, semi-desert, rainforest, and savannah, Uganda actually has a variety of climates: if you don't like one, you won't have to travel far to find one you *do* like.

The area within an 80- to 100-kilometre (50- to 60-mile) radius of Lake Victoria sees rain fall almost every day, but in general there are two major rainfalls in the year. The main long rains start late in February and end in April, while the short rains start falling in October and run until about the middle of December. (Some people believe that there must always be a shower to bless Christmas.) Thereafter, there is much heat from the sun beating down from a cloudless sky. Humidity is generally low.

As you move away from Lake Victoria, the rains become less and less, and the countryside more arid.

South-west Uganda, with its mountainous regions around Kigezi, has been dubbed 'The Switzerland of Africa', with a pleasant, slightly cooler, climate. Not far away rise the Ruwenzori Mountains, known as the Mountains of the Moon, which, although they lie just north of the equator, have snow-capped peaks.

Throughout the year sunshine averages about 6 to 10 hours a day, with the least amount naturally coming during the rainy season. The weather is usually summer-like, with no big contrasts. Day temperatures range between 25° and 34°C (77°–93°F). In January, the hottest month, temperatures may be in the region of 35°C (95°F). Even during the rainy seasons, the temperatures can be very high, which causes heavy tropical thunderstorms. It is considerably warmer all year round in the remote northern and north-eastern parts of the country.

Clothes

Lightweight and casual clothing is ideal for most of the year. In areas of higher altitude, or anywhere during the rainy seasons in

Above: On safari, elephants have the right of way.

the evenings, light woollen clothing may be needed to keep warm.

Despite the year-round warm weather, conservative Ugandan civil servants and technocrats are used to going to the office in a suit and tie. If visitors intend to call on anyone in an office for a business deal or a social outing, they should carry some good, more formal clothes to keep up with the local standards.

Women will find that it is more the norm in the major cities of Kampala or Entebbe to wear skirts and dresses, or lightweight trousers, when walking about, rather than jeans or shorts. Dress modestly. Men, too, would be better off wearing trousers when in town, and should never walk around shirtless in public places.

Remember that the sun on the equator is intense — bring and wear a hat whenever possible, and use sunscreen lotion.

What to take

Imported goods are becoming more widely available, but at a price. It is best to come as self-sufficient as possible, at least when it comes to your photographic equipment and film, contact lenses and supplies, and the like. If you wear glasses, bring a spare pair. Also bring any special medications you may need.

If you come to Uganda, you are more than likely going to be doing a bit of game and bird viewing, so it is best to bring along a good pair of binoculars to increase your enjoyment of your safari.

Health

Visitors from areas infected with yellow fever and cholera require certificates of inoculation against these diseases.

Malaria and bilharzia are endemic. All visitors are advised to take an antimalarial prophylactic beginning two weeks before their arrival and continuing for six weeks after their departure. However, don't assume that will do the trick. Many strains of malaria are resistant to prophylaxis. The best precaution is to prevent being bitten at all. Use mosquito repellant; wear long trousers, thick socks, and long-sleeved shirts in the evenings; and sleep under mosquito nets where possible.

Above: Traditional fishing canoe on Lake Mburo, one of Uganda's many lakes.

Remember that the symptoms of malaria (severe headache, fever, flu-like aches and pains) will not show up until 10 to 14 days or more after you've been bitten. If you're still in Uganda, local doctors are quick to recognize the symptoms and know the treatments well, so take their advice.

If you're already back at home, alert your doctor that you've been in a malarial area and insist that a blood check for malaria be done. And don't wait too long — malaria is generally easily treated if caught early but can be fatal if left untreated.

To avoid bilharzia (caused by an infectious worm found in still or slowly moving, well-oxygenated, well-vegetated fresh water), simply avoid swimming or bathing in streams, rivers, and lakes (although fast-flowing mountain streams are of low risk).

Doctors also recommend visitors to take sensible precautions against tetanus, polio, cholera, typhoid, and paratyphoid. A gamma globulin injection provides some protection against possible infection by hepatitis and is well worth taking. That said, the incidence of these diseases and infections is not high. But prevention is better than cure.

There is prostitution in Uganda, especially in the two major cities of Kampala and Jinja, and there is also evidence of drug trafficking and addiction. Only a fool would ignore the widespread existence of AIDS. The government estimates that at least two million Ugandans may be HIV positive. All blood donations, however, are HIV-tested, and sterilizing needles is normal medical procedure. There is a very high level of AIDS-awareness in the country, including an AIDS commission that, together with UNICEF, monitors the disease and improves awareness and precautions in schools.

Tap water in all urban areas, whether from reservoirs or boreholes, is treated and said to be safe to drink. However, visitors, being prone to travellers' diarrhoea as they are, would probably be better off to at least boil the water. If this is not possible, bottled, treated mineral water should be used, which is available in the major towns. Safari operators carry sufficient supplies of water for bush travel, but if you are travelling

Above: Dusty safari trail in Queen Elizabeth National Park.

in remote areas on your own, it is advisable to carry your own bottled water, or water purification apparatus or pills.

Uganda has reasonable health services, with some good government and private hospitals and clinics in the major cities. There are some first-class private or missionary-run hospitals in Kampala and Jinja with resident specialists and surgeons. There are also excellent dentists and opticians. Medical treatment, however, is expensive. Visitors would be advised to take out medical insurance cover before they leave home. This can be obtained in Uganda, but usually at a higher premium than you would pay in Europe or North America.

Visitors may wish to get temporary health cover from the Kenyan-based Africa Air Rescue or Medivac, which have offices in Kampala. This guarantees you quick rescue and transportation to any nearby competent hospital.

There is no shortage of chemists or drug stores in Uganda, all staffed by qualified pharmacists. If you are taking medication, however, it is recommended that you carry sufficient quantities to cover the duration of your stay. Most drugs are available, but many will have unfamiliar brand names. If your specific prescription is unavailable, the pharmacist or doctor will often prescribe a suitable alternative.

Pharmacies are open during normal weekday shopping hours, from about 0900 to 1700 (some, but not all, close for lunch). Selected pharmacies in the main centres of Kampala and Jinja also offer a night service.

Photography

Film is expensive and visitors are advised to carry all the film they estimate that they will need. Remember that this is one of the most photogenic countries in the world. Stock up with plenty of film in reserve so that you will not be disappointed. Also keep in mind that higher speed films (800/1600 ASA) are needed in the heavily forested areas, such as where the mountain gorillas and chimpanzees are found. Make sure to bring extra batteries for your camera, too — and a spare lens cap.

There are plenty of photo processing shops in the major centres of Uganda, such

Above: Photographic opportunities in Uganda are limitless.

as Kampala and Jinja, but the processing is generally costly and of poor quality. Plan on doing your developing at home.

Areas where photography is restricted or forbidden are clearly marked. Obey the rules. It is also inadvisable to photograph government buildings and other installations. In addition, it is not a good idea to take a photograph of a policeman or a soldier without prior permission — and that goes for members of the general public, as well. It is simply good manners: ask first.

Communications

From Kampala, international postal, telephone, and fax services are good, but don't expect them to be so in the rest of the country. If you make an international call from a hotel, remember that it will generally tack on at least another 50 per cent to the cost of the call. Internal telephone connections are also reasonably good, and greatly improved in the last few years. Computer-based digital technologies, satellite systems, and wireless communications are beginning to transform Uganda.

Callers can also now make local and international calls from Kampala pay phones by using prepaid phone cards, and the company providing that service is also licensed to provide leased voice and data lines, Internet access, and e-mail services.

Sending a letter or postcard from Uganda is cheap and pretty reliable, but takes time. The main post office does maintain a poste restante system, but it is chaotic, disorganized, bureaucratic, and terribly time consuming. It is said, however, that you *do* get your post in the end, so if you've got a lot of patience, it's probably worth it.

When to go

As Uganda has a summer-like climate throughout the year, it is ideal to visit at any time. Be aware, however, that during the rainy seasons the upcountry roads — especially those to the more remote game parks — may be quite muddy and challenging to negotiate, although the four-wheel-drive vehicles used by most safari companies should be able to get through.

If you're planning on hiking or camping in the Ruwenzoris, try to avoid the rains, which occur in April–May and October–

Above: Two male lions laze on a rock in Kidepo Valley National Park.

November. Otherwise, the rainy season can be as pleasant a time to visit as any other, with the temperatures slightly cooler after a shower and the sun still shining on and off each day.

On safari

Uganda is beginning to develop an excellent tourist infrastructure, with first-rate (for Africa) roads and communication facilities. Although these were neglected and some even destroyed during the wars, it is remarkable how the government, in collaboration with the private sector, has moved quickly to restore and rehabilitate them. Virtually everything is now in place to welcome the visitor.

If you are travelling alone in the remote areas of the country, particularly the thickly forested regions, it is a good idea to carry some money in small notes in case of emergency, such as paying helpers to push you out of mud holes.

Always carry essential spare parts with you, as well as a useful number of tools. For more detailed advice, consult the excellent Uganda Motorist Association, which maintains offices in both Kampala and Jinja.

Uganda's national game, forest, and recreational parks are indeed some of the spectacular showpieces Africa has to offer. They do have regulations regarding off-the-road driving, game watching, and so on, which are clearly stated at the entrance gates of the parks or on leaflets supplied by the tourist offices. Please observe these regulations for the sake of your own safety and an enjoyable safari.

Always remember that although some animals have become accustomed to the presence of people and appear friendly, they are still wild animals and not fully domesticated. You are asked not to feed the wild animals from the window of your vehicle, let alone the window of your lodge in the middle of the park.

Neither should you make a lot of noise to attract their attention.

Never deviate from designated routes for that closer camera shot, and never get out of your vehicle except at designated points. Close all windows and zippers when you leave your room or tent: you

Above: The beautiful, unspoilt Ssese Islands, green gems in the waters of Lake Victoria.

would not like to find unwanted guests had paid you a visit when you return.

Many visitors believe that their enjoyment is related to the number of species they can see within the shortest possible time. As an alternative, spend time observing them and learning their habits and characteristic behaviour. Chances are you will find this much more exciting and rewarding.

Mountaineering safaris to the Ruwenzori Mountains (Mountains of the Moon) in the western Rift Valley are now becoming a favourite Ugandan expedition. Similar safaris can also be organized to climb Mount Elgon in the east, sharing the border with Kenya.

Apart from national parks set up to protect wildlife, Uganda has gazetted forest and other natural areas into national parks for the preservation of the vegetation and even insects — such as the country's many rare, beautiful butterflies — that abound in them.

There are islands in Lake Victoria where humans have not yet spoiled the natural habitats of rare birds and wildlife. Visitors who want to discover these simply have to take the boat ride from Bukakata port, near Masaka town, to the Ssese Islands. Some of the islands have never even been occupied by humans; they are ready to explore.

Wildlife aside, any trip to Uganda should include a look into the ancient cultures of the Buganda kingdom by visiting the burial grounds of the *kabakas* (kings) of Buganda at Kasubi Tombs on the outskirts of Kampala. You can also attend the king's court at Bulange and observe the rich royal etiquette — a unique African experience.

Above all, always keep your camera loaded and ready for action. Uganda is full of photogenic surprises just waiting to happen before your eyes.

Where to stay

Uganda's accommodation ranges anywhere from five-star hotels down to simple hostels with a mat on the floor and a bucket for a shower — and everything in between.

The Kampala Sheraton, the Grand Imperial, and the Nile Hotel, all in the nation's capital, are by far the best (but they are naturally also the most expensive). There

Above: Verdant fairway on the shores of Lake Victoria.

are many other less expensive, but quite nice, hotels in the city as well.

Outside Kampala, most towns also have a variety of moderately priced and budget hotels. Even the tiniest village will usually be able to provide you with somewhere to spend the night, but don't expect even two-star accommodation.

Almost all the country's upper-range hotels outside Kampala were once 'official tourist hotels' run by Uganda Hotels Ltd. Considerably run down, they are now privately run enterprises, whose owners say they intend to improve the properties. Prices vary considerably, depending on which part of the country you're in and how much tourism there is in a particular area.

Camping is also an option, both in and outside of the national parks (see Camping in Uganda, Part Four, and Listings).

National bird
For a nation with kings, it is appropriate that the beautiful crowned crane, *Balearica regulorum*, with its distinctive straw-coloured upright crest, is Uganda's national bird. Its distinctive, loud call — similar to the honking of a Canadian goose — can be heard in many parts of the country, particularly around the marshes and swamps it prefers as habitat.

National anthem
Oh Uganda! May God uphold thee
We lay our future in thy hand
United, free
For liberty
Together we'll always stand.

Oh Uganda! the land of freedom
Our love and labour we give
And with neighbours all
At our country's call
In peace and friendship we'll live.

Oh Uganda! The land that feeds us
By sun and fertile soil grown
For our own dear land
We'll always stand
The Pearl of Africa's crown.

Above: The beautiful crowned crane, *Balearica regulorum*, is Uganda's national bird.

National dress

Although technically there is no common national dress, as each of Uganda's many tribes has its own traditional clothing, the most often seen is that of the largest ethnic group in the country, the Baganda. Baganda men wear a long-sleeved *kanzu*, a long, white, floor-length tunic, worn with a long-sleeved jacket, while the women wear a *gomesi*, a long dress with a multicoloured cloth tied around it at the waist. The two forms of dress originated in the Buganda kingdom and have been adopted in many parts of the country. This traditional dress is worn on important cultural occasions, particularly at an audience with the king, a wedding, a burial ceremony, or the formal introduction of a potential bridegroom at the home of his bride-to-be.

National flag

The colourful flag of the Republic of Uganda features the country's national bird, the crowned crane, in a white circle on a background of broad black, yellow, and red stripes: black representing the people of the country, yellow the sunshine that blesses the land, and red the blood spilled in the fight for independence.

Above: Uganda's national flag, proud symbol of a now-peaceful country.
Opposite: Ugandan women wearing their colourful traditional dress.

PART ONE: HISTORY, GEOGRAPHY, AND PEOPLE

Top: One of the first illustrations of Murchison Falls.
Above: Early illustration of Mutesa I, the first *kabaka* to receive the white explorers.
Opposite: Moonrise over the beautiful Kidepo Valley National Park.

Land of kings — and a troublesome past

Uganda, the 'Pearl of Africa', is almost the same size as Britain and sits astride the equator on Lake Victoria, the second-largest freshwater lake in the world. With a population of over 17 million, and endowed with good climate, flora, and fauna, the country has great potential for development — and has at last begun to restore its reputation as one of Africa's richest and most beautiful countries.

Uganda did not come into political existence until the beginning of this century. Before the people of Uganda were brought into contact with the 'modern' world, each of the tribes living in the region was independent, striving to earn a livelihood and contending with foreign (often hostile) forces as best it could. Towards the end of the 18th century, a few centralized states began to emerge in the Lake Victoria region. These were Buganda, Ankole, Bunyoro-Kitara, and Busoga. Initially Bunyoro-Kitara — of which the others could be considered to have been offshoots — was the strongest. However, by the mid-19th century Buganda had emerged as the most powerful.

Religious wars

It was Buganda, in fact, to which the European explorers, coming into the interior of Africa to trade and to propagate their religions, were attracted. The Baganda were, therefore, among the first to embrace Islam and later Christianity, a process that got its people drawn into religious wars, which often spilled into the neighbouring states. The British trading community in the Buganda capital used these religious wars to entrench themselves in Buganda and became arbiters of Buganda politics. These manoeuvres compromised Buganda's sovereignty and led to the declaration of a protectorate over Buganda in 1894 — a protectorate that was consolidated with the conclusion of the Buganda Agreement in 1900.

What followed was the extension of the British protectorate to what is now Uganda, the final boundaries of which were drawn in 1926.

British Colonialism in Uganda has been condemned by numerous nationalists. Undoubtedly it did destroy many of the traditions Ugandans had always held dear to their hearts. But this is not to say that colonialism was all negative. There are elderly Ugandans today who look back with nostalgia to the 'good old days' when the white men were there; Uganda's late Professor Samwiri Karugire once quoted a Zairean peasant, who asked when 'this independence' would come to an end. Many changes were initiated during the colonial period, changes to which the Uganda people themselves contributed. Independence came in 1962 when the British authorities handed over political power to Ugandan nationalists.

As everyone knows, Uganda has had a sad and tortuous history, and most of the first three decades of its independence were traumatic. It is not difficult to identify the culprits, upon whose heads it is easy to heap all the blame for the shortcomings of so many others. It is safer to say that, in one way or another, all Ugandans have been responsible for their country's woes.

Obote and Amin

In 1966, Milton Obote, the country's first prime minister following independence, abolished the 1962 constitution, which had given many federal powers to Buganda. Indeed, 1966 became a turning point in Uganda's history, after Obote had appointed himself the president of Uganda and had forced Sir Edward Mutesa, the kabaka of Buganda and the first president of Uganda, into exile in London, where he died in poverty and distress three years later. But Obote's reign did not last long. He was overthrown on 25 January 1971 by Idi Amin, the semi-literate army general he had promoted after the two had joined hands in dismembering Buganda and destroying constitutionalism and the rule of law in Uganda.

Amin ruled Uganda with more than the proverbial iron hand until he himself was removed after eight years of brutal rule. His overthrow in 1979, which was hailed by all Ugandans, soon became a nightmare through the machiavellian manner in which the Uganda People's Congress manipulated politics, leading to the return to power by Obote — the so-called Obote II regime.

A new era

Obote, however, was never allowed a chance to settle down; for no sooner had he engineered his return to power than a guerrilla movement was raised and a war unleashed upon him by Yoweri Museveni and his 30 or so initial adherents. This movement set the scene for the events that led first to Obote's ouster from power in July 1985 and then to the overthrow of the Uganda National Liberation Army with the two Okellos (Tito and Bazilio) in charge.

In his swearing in on the steps of the Parliament Building on 26 January 1986, Museveni referred to the National Resistance Movement's (NRM) victory not as 'a mere change of guards, but a fundamental change'.

A great deal has been introduced that has changed the Uganda political scene: peace exists in most parts of the country; participatory democracy — based on the system of Resistance Committees and Councils (RCs) — has been introduced and taken root; and, perhaps most important of all, a new national constitution, based on the views of the people of Uganda, has been debated, enacted, and promulgated. These are fundamental changes beyond dispute.

In the realm of economics, the NRM administration has embraced the economic medicine prescribed by the IMF and the World Bank, based on the total liberalization of the economy and the full reorientation of that economy toward free-market forces — a strategy which, the NRM leadership assures Ugandans, will transform Uganda from a peasant to an entrepreneurial society. This is, perhaps, the area that will prove critical in the assessment of President Museveni's regime. The diagnosis and the medicine prescribed are there to be seen, but — so far — the future, or the survival of, the patient for whom all that is being done remains in the balance. The economic policies now in place are another example of fundamental changes being introduced.

Above: A young Yoweri Museveni being sworn in as the new head of state of Uganda on 26 January 1986.

It appears the people of Uganda approve of the changes instituted by Museveni and the NRM: in May 1996 the president was sworn in for a five-year term after a sweeping victory in the country's first direct presidential election. President Museveni has now been in power for a longer tenure of office than any previous leader in Uganda.

The prayer of many Ugandans is that peace and stability continue to prevail, as the road trodden by the country's people since independence in 1962 has been rough. There appears to be some light at the end of the tunnel; Ugandans hope that whatever lies ahead enables them to enjoy peace, tranquillity, and a bit more prosperity. All this will benefit not only Ugandans, but also their friends abroad, to whom the country has now opened its doors, for them to visit as tourists or conduct business as investors. In this way the Pearl of Africa is beginning to shine again.

43

History: An Ancient and Turbulent Past

Written in the soil and the fossils on the floor of the western Rift Valley, where the Acheulian culture is well established on the shores of Lake Albert and in the Semuliki and Kagera river valleys, is evidence of human presence in Uganda, beginning to emerge around 500,000 years ago.

By around 50,000 years ago the people living in the land now known as Uganda had discovered fire, which enabled them to move into the more forested areas around the margins of Lake Victoria. Some 40,000 years later they had conquered most of the regions of Uganda and were living throughout the land, from the Ruwenzori Mountains to Mount Elgon; from the Lake Victoria Basin to Karamoja.

Up to 500 BC it is not easy to put a label on the communities living in Uganda. Although human speech had been developing for a long time before this, it is not possible to identify specific language groups or tribes. All we know is that Uganda was inhabited by negroid peoples living in very small communities.

Ugandans speak Bantu languages in the west, south, and, to a large extent, in the east; Sudanic languages in the north-west; and Nilotic languages in the rest of the north. The Bantu languages are closely related and mutually understood.

The Bantu-speaking people of Uganda are associated with the beginnings of agriculture and iron working. Agricultural practices began around 5000 BC and were augmented by the establishment of an iron-working industry between 600 BC and 300 BC and the introduction of south-eastern Asian crops — such as yams and bananas — around AD 500. By AD 1000, the agricultural Bantu were well established in western and southern Uganda and were organized in small political units, of which the clan was the norm. Also settling the grassland regions of western and southern Uganda during the late first millenium AD were the pastoralists associated with the Sanga (long-horned and big-humped) cattle. The Sanga originated in Ethiopia

and had spread as far south as Zimbabwe by the seventh century AD. These pastoralists — formerly speakers of Cushitic languages — adopted the Bantu languages as they settled among them. By the beginning of the second millennium AD these pastoralists — now the Bahima and Bahuma of western Uganda — were solidly establishing themselves between the Kafu and Kagera rivers. It was as a result of the fusion of these pastoralists and Bantu agriculturalists that pastoral aristocracies — such as the Bachwezi and the Bahinda — emerged in western and central Uganda.

The Sudanic and Nilotic linguistic groups were firmly established in northern Uganda — as well as southern Sudan and south-western Ethiopia — by the first millennium BC but were largely concentrated in the southern Sudan. During the first millennium AD a Sudanic people, the Madi, moved south into the largely Bantu region of Bunyoro and established one of the earliest recognizable dynasties in Bunyoro, the Batembuzi. The western Nilotic speakers from the Sudan began to move southwards into northern Uganda in the 15th century and into eastern Uganda in the following century.

Migrations

According to oral history, major movements of people are recorded criss-crossing the length and breadth of Uganda between 1500 and 1850, mainly the western Nilotes (specifically the Luo), the plains or eastern Nilotes (the Karimojong and Ateso), and the Bantu.

The original home of the Luo was the confluence of the Bahr-el Ghazel and the Nile rivers in southern Sudan, where they lived up to the end of the 15th century. For the next three and a half centuries, the Luo moved into other parts of the Sudan, as well as to Ethiopia, Zaire, northern Uganda, and the coasts of Lake Victoria in Uganda, Kenya, and Tanzania. In northern Uganda the major offshoots of the Luo are the Acholi, Alur, Pawir (Chope) and Jo-Pahdola people.

Above: Ancient rock paintings at Nyero testify to early human presence in Uganda.

Among the major accomplishments of the Luo was the establishment of their hegemony over Bunyoro by the Jo-bito clan, who established the Babiito dynasty (which was removed in 1967 and reinstated in 1993), as well as many kingdoms in Acholi, northern Busoga, and Kooki. Early in the 16th century the Plains Nilotes (the Karimojong and the Ateso) lived to the north and south-west of Mount Moroto respectively. For the next two and a half centuries, the Ateso moved back and forth between Mount Napak and Lake Bisina. The eventual fusion of the western Nilotes and Plains Nilotes created the Lango and the Kumam, who adopted Luo as their language.

By AD 1000 the Bantu were settled in small communities all over western, southern, and eastern Uganda, with concentrations in the Semuliki River Valley in the west and Samia Hills in Bukedi in the east. The major Bantu movements took place largely between the Ruwenzori Mountains and the Semuliki River Valley eastwards towards the present Bantu heartlands of Buganda and Bunyoro, and from Mount Elgon and Samia Hills towards the Lake Victoria

Basin. There were also minor movements of Bantu from the islands of Lake Victoria, especially from the Ssese archipelago, to the northern shores of Lake Victoria and to the Buganda mainland.

The Bantu also moved from Bunyoro into Buganda following the establishment of the Jo-bito hegemony in Bunyoro in the 16th century. The movements of the Bantu from Mount Elgon and Samia Hills westwards is associated with the Kintu and started as early as the 13th century AD into southern Busoga, where many chiefdoms were established by clans involved with this movement.

When they moved into Buganda in the 14th century, the Kintu wave displaced the Bemba chiefdom and established a Kintu dynasty, which was, in turn, replaced by the Kimera dynasty from Bunyoro in the 16th century.

The first wave of Bantu immigrants began in the 11th century from the Ruwenzori/Semuliki Valley region eastwards into central and southern Uganda. The Basoga clan, which has the grasshopper as its totem, figured prominently in these movements, according to the traditions of Bunyoro, Nkore, and Buganda. The Basoga moved into Bwera with their herds of cattle and were the substratum upon which the Bachwezi and the Bahinda built their pastoral aristocracies between the Kafu and the Kagera rivers.

State formation

Before the 15th century the most important state to emerge in Uganda was the Kitara empire of the Bachwezi, which embraced most of central and western Uganda and had a spiritual influence as far as modern north-western Tanzania and Zaire. This state flourished between 1350 and 1500, and the states that replaced it — Bunyoro-Kitara of the Babiito and Nkore of the Bahinda — acknowledge their Bachwezi origins.

Most of the precolonial states of Uganda developed between the 15th and 18th centuries. The centralized kingdoms of Buganda, Bunyoro, Kooki, Mpororo, and Nkore emerged in the south and west of the country, while in Busoga in the east and Acholi in the north a myriad of chiefdoms and kingdoms based on the unity of a few clans also came into being.

Elsewhere in Uganda governance was highly decentralized, and power lay in the hands of elders who practised a form of democratic government comparable to that of the Greek *polis* in the days of Plato.

Between the early 16th and mid-18th centuries the Babiito kingdom of Bunyoro-Kitara was the dominant state in the entire interlacustrine region, drawing tribute from a vast area of southern and western Uganda, northern Busoga, and even from north-western Tanzania.

Because of internal weaknesses and the administrative unwieldiness of the state, Bunyoro-Kitara's dominant position was lost to the more cohesive, carefully administered, and outward-looking Buganda to the south.

The kingdom of Buganda continued to expand and consolidate its gains and maintained its dominant position in the region from the mid-18th century up to the European colonization of Uganda in the late 19th century.

Early contacts with the outside world

In the late 18th century the Nyamwezi traders of modern Tanzania reached Buganda and exchanged cloth and domestic utensils for ivory and slaves. They were followed, in the 1840s, by the Arabs, who introduced guns and Islam, among other things. It was the well-beaten paths of these traders that the British explorers Grant and Speke followed in the 1860s and 'discovered' the Nile, to be followed in the 1870s by Anglican missionaries of the Church Missionary Society and Catholic missionaries of the White Fathers. It was the same trade route, too, that various other adventurers and colonialists followed in the 1880s and 1890s, leading to the official declaration of the Uganda Protectorate in 1894 by Britain.

The Egyptians had, since the time of the pharoahs, been keen to discover the source of the Nile. When the Nile was discovered in the 1860s by Speke, the Khedive of Egypt, Ismail, was very keen to incorporate the whole of the Nile into the Egyptian empire, which had included the Sudan since the early 1820s, for fear that the source of the Nile could fall into hostile hands and jeopardize the lifeblood of Egypt. Traders from Khartoum also began doing business with northern Uganda and Bunyoro, introducing guns and taking out ivory. The attempts to incorporate the source of the Nile into Equatoria Province of the Sudan were thwarted by the indomitable Kabalega and Mutesa I, who defeated armies and agents like Samuel Baker (who was later knighted) and Agar Nuer, both dispatched by Egyptian authority for the purpose. The final blow to this Egyptian scheme was delivered by the Mahdist revolt in the Sudan, which effectively blocked Egyptian advances into Uganda. There were also diplomatic wrangles between Egypt and Zanzibar over the interlacustrine region of East Africa, which Zanzibar claimed as its own. The matters were arbitrated by the British, who actually took control of Egypt in 1881.

Colonization

At the Berlin Conference of 1884, the northern basin of Lake Victoria was

Above: John Hanning Speke 'discovered' the source of the Nile in the 1860s.

Above: Daudi Chwa II, one of the four Buganda kings now buried in Kasubi Tombs, Kampala.

recognized as being in the British sphere of influence, thanks to the activities of British missionaries in Buganda. Since the source of the Nile was in the same area, it was also recognized as having strategic value with regard to the control of Egypt and the sea route to India. Missionaries also trumpeted the economic potentialities of the region. France and Britain contested the area because it was considered essential for the control of Egypt. After a series of treaties in the 1880s between the British and the Germans, who also had a major stake in East Africa, the Germans recognized the British claims to Buganda and its environs, and the British made short work of the local authorities — largely through fraudulent treaties and, where necessary, the gun.

Kabalega of Bunyoro and Mutesa I of Buganda, in the 1890s, resisted the imposition of colonial rule, but the British, through their local collaborators, defeated, captured, and deported them to the Seychelles Islands in the Indian Ocean at the end of the 19th century.

Because the British were short-handed and did not have enough money to run the protectorate, they resorted to indirect rule — ruling through the prevailing indigenous authorities. This was an easy task in those parts of Uganda where authority was traditionally centralized, such as in the kingdoms of Buganda, Bunyoro, Nkore, and Toro. Where there was no central or recognized authority, Buganda chiefs were used as agents and local chiefs were created. The agency system caused a lot of resentment outside Buganda and the inequities of the Buganda agents have been neither forgotten nor forgiven. This has created and continues to create political problems for Uganda.

The rise of nationalism

Nationalism in Uganda first expressed itself as economic nationalism. Beginning in the 1920s, Africans wished to get involved in trade and the ginning of cotton, which were controlled exclusively by the British and the Asians. They expressed themselves through a very

47

active press in Buganda. The peasants also wished to be liberated from feudalism. These various strands of nationalism manifested themselves in bloody riots in 1945 and 1949 in Buganda. The revolutionaries of 1945 and 1949 demanded to appoint the chiefs; they also insisted on ginning their own cotton and processing their coffee. In addition, they wanted a democratically elected *lukiiko* (Buganda parliament). The revolutionaries were defeated, but the riots shocked the British into the democratization of local government and the entry of Africans into the cotton ginning and coffee processing businesses. Memories of the riots also sped up the decolonization process in the 1950s.

The main political developments in the 1950s were the approval of a new agreement (constitution) to Buganda in 1955 and the participation of Africans in the legislative and even executive arms of the colonial government. National political parties were also founded during this period.

Buganda precipitated a crisis in 1953 by ostensibly reacting negatively to a proposal to the federation of East Africa by the British colonial secretary. In fact, Buganda had demanded a set timetable for its independence separate from Uganda, but Sir Andrew Cohen, the governor, was determined to deliver Uganda as one independent nation. It was for this reason that Kabaka Mutesa II was deported to Britain in November 1953. Following protracted negotiations leading to a new agreement between Britain and Buganda, giving Buganda greater local autonomy and making the kabaka a constitutional monarch, Mutesa II returned to Uganda in October 1955.

The first national party, the Uganda National Congress (UNC), was formed in 1952 by Ignatius Musaazi. Its goal was to work for the independence of the country. This was followed by the Democratic Party (DP) in 1954 as a Catholic response to the hegemony the Protestants had enjoyed in administration since the protectorate was established in 1894. The Protestants responded to this challenge by forming the Progressive Party in 1955.

In 1959 some members of the Legislative Council, opposed to the special privileges which Buganda was purported to enjoy, formed a non-Buganda party, the Uganda People's Union, which, in 1960, joined the Obote wing of the UNC to form the Uganda People's Congress (UPC). The UPC formed an alliance with a Buganda Party — the *Kabaka Yekka* (King Only) — and it is this alliance that won the elections of April 1962 and ushered Uganda into independence on 9 October 1962.

Post-independence

The birth of Uganda's independence was not without many pangs. Until Uganda's independence flag was hoisted at midnight on 9 October 1962, it had never been certain that the various ethnic groups which make up Uganda — particularly the seemingly reluctant and secessionist kingdom of Buganda — would agree to come together and forge a new nation. Indeed, the independence negotiations that were held in London had been marked more by differences than uniformity of views.

The 1962 Independence Constitution

The major characteristic of the 1962 constitution — or Lancaster House constitution, as it is generally referred to today — was the entrenchment of Buganda and its kabaka in the affairs of Uganda. In short, Buganda was given a privileged position, making it appear to be a state within the state. This position attracted envy (and later hatred) from non-Baganda who, although they accepted that political arrangement, were by no means in favour of it.

First and foremost, this 1962 constitution provided one full federal state (Buganda), four semi-federal states (Ankole, Bunyoro, Toro, and the Territory of Busoga) and 10 unitary districts for the rest of Uganda.

Opposite: Sir Edward Mutesa II, who was deported to Britain in 1953.

Above: Apolo Milton Obote.

Lastly, as a final bow to the superiority of federal states, the National Assembly had no power to alter the constitutions of the four kingdoms and the territory of Busoga.

The 1966 constitutional crisis

The Independence Constitution, so well elaborated at Lancaster House in London, lasted no more than three years. In retrospect, it is not surprising. For the first two years of Uganda's independence, Apolo Milton Obote, the executive head of government, presided over a country that was striving to be a nation, with at least one political centre to which all other parts of the country should pay their loyalties. It was not easy, and trouble came mainly from three sources.

The first was the disagreements that arose within the ruling alliance of UPC and Kabaka Yekka (KY), which had been formed in 1961 and had ushered Uganda into independence. The core of the difference between UPC and KY was the so-called Lost Counties, two of which were soon torn from Buganda and given to Bunyoro. The alliance formally snapped in August 1964.

The second source of political difference — which, in fact, was a direct result of the first — was the open quarrel between the central government of Obote and the Buganda government headed by Kabaka Mutesa II. The scenario was complicated by the fact that in October 1963 Sir Edward Mutesa, kabaka of Buganda, had been elected the first president of Uganda. So, in the end, the UPC–Buganda quarrel turned into a quarrel between the president of Uganda and his prime minister, Obote.

The third — and what turned out to be the last straw — was the split within the ruling party, UPC, into two factions: one led mostly by northerners, at the head of which stood Obote, and the other led by a Bantu group headed by Grace Ibingira and enjoying the full support of the president of Uganda and the Buganda government at Mengo. This was the background to the 1966 constitutional crisis, which swept away the kingdom of Buganda, led to Kabaka Mutesa's exile and subsequent death in London in November 1969, and paved the way for the introduction of

Secondly, it provided for a National Assembly of directly elected members, with the proviso that Buganda (again being singled out) could nominate its representatives through the *lukiiko* (Buganda's parliament) acting as an electoral college.

Thirdly, by virtue of the fact that Her Majesty the Queen of Great Britain was the head of state represented by her chosen governor-general, Uganda remained a monarchy. To some Ugandan politicians this monarchism did not ring well in their ears, as it reminded them of the Buganda monarchy's domination of Ugandan politics.

Fourthly, the constitution gave more financial independence to federal states, at the expense of those districts in unitary relationship with the country's political centre. To add insult to injury — with the benefit of hindsight on the part of those who did not relish the entrenchment of federalism — the 1962 constitution provided for high courts for Buganda (at par with the Uganda High Court) both of which were to be presided over by the same high court judges.

republicanism and the 1967 constitution — which, to the amazement of many, survived, although with some amendments, up to the promulgation of a completely new constitution in 1995.

In crude terms, the 1966 constitutional crisis was really about politics and power. It was a power struggle between the centre and the federal state of Buganda, with the internal conflict between Obote's faction of UPC and those who opposed and wanted to oust him from power providing the necessary ammunition for the constitutional conflict. The net result was the constitutional crisis of 1966, which was the turning point in Uganda's recent political history. Those who survived the 1966 crisis were Obote and his supporters within UPC.

There was, however, another important entrant into the political scene — Major General Idi Amin, who became the new army commander. Obote and Amin cooperated closely in the disposal of the Buganda monarchy, of its head, Mutesa II, and of those within UPC who had opposed Obote.

For the next five years there was an alliance between the civilian rulers (led by Obote) and the military (headed by Idi Amin); but, as is almost always the case, once Obote had elevated Amin to run the army — and as the civilian administration came to rely more and more on the army in administering a country deeply divided — Amin's thirst for power grew to such an extent that he had to acquire more if he was to survive. In January 1971 he ousted Obote from power. A new chapter of brutal rule was ushered in.

Idi Amin regime

The reason Amin sent Obote reeling out of politics in the 1970s was because he himself was about to be removed by Obote. Amin received much support from Ugandans opposed to Obote, especially from the Baganda, and this partly explains why Amin survived when he was so vulnerable — for the alternative was the return of the hated Obote. Amin also received support from the British, the Israelis, and other Western powers to whom his ulterior motives were at first unknown. However, it was not long before the Israelis — and

Above: In January 1971 Major General Idi Amin began his reign of terror over Uganda.

later the Asians — were all expelled from Uganda. This, together with the general appropriation of Asian property and foreign firms — mostly British — led to what became known, in Amin's words, as an 'economic war'.

The manner in which Asians — including those of Ugandan citizenship — were bundled out of Uganda remains testimony to a Hitler-like crime. In the end, however, even the Ugandans who had earlier rejoiced in looting and appropriating the property of the fleeing Asians suffered the wrath of the military dictator. There followed a reign of terror that institutionalized violence as a system of governance, a violence that clearly surpassed any witnessed during the 1966 crisis. Indeed, what is remembered of Amin is the sheer ability of a ruler to inflict so much suffering on a civilian society. Today, Amin's rule has become a litmus test for Uganda's politics; any subsequent leader's term has always been judged against the record of violence and insanity that Amin bequeathed to Uganda. In the end, in March 1979, Amin was swept out of power

Above: Idi Amin announces his historic 'Get out' order to leaders of the Asian community.

by the combined forces of Tanzania People's Defence Forces and the Ugandan exiles, who returned to Uganda as the liberators under the banner of the Uganda National Liberation Front (UNLF/UNLA) led by Professor Yusuf Kironde Lule.

The return of Obote
Virtually brought to power by Julius Nyerere's army, the UNLF failed to unite the country that had suffered so much. Although Ugandans, particularly the exiles who returned to rule the country, were agreed on the removal of dictator Amin, they failed to govern Uganda once Amin was out of the way.

The three regimes that followed one another in a space of only 20 months — from March 1979, when UNLF came to power, to December 1980, when Obote and his old UPC returned to power — all collapsed. Lule was accused of dictatorial tendencies. But Godfrey Lukongwa Binaisa, his surprise replacement, did not last long. In May 1980, Paulo Muwanga, the old veteran of Ugandan politics, emerged on the scene as the strongman,

apparently with a hidden mandate — some say endorsed by UPC's supporters in Dar es Salaam — to return UPC to power and install Obote in the State House once again. The old Democratic Party, now under Paul Kawanga Ssemogerere, tried to revive its fortune, but the smarter UPC machine was virtually ensured of victory in the general elections that took place in December 1980.

A new party, called the Uganda Patriotic Movement (UPM), under the leadership of the then young and intellectual freedom fighter Yoweri Museveni was of little consequence during the 1980 elections. It was, however, to emerge as a major force as it spearheaded the civil war against Obote's regime, which led to the subsequent defeat of the Uganda National Liberation Army and the assumption of power by the National Resistance Movement (NRM/NRA) in January 1986.

The significance of Milton Obote's return to power for the second time in December 1980 should not be underestimated. During the 1980 elections, Obote disorganized his opponent so completely that he stepped into the State House, incorrectly believing that the whole country welcomed him as its liberator. And, indeed, he started his second presidency as if he were the liberator, the one who had returned, as the others had done before him, to pick up from where he had left off in 1971. The result was his inability to deal with the civil war which was started, on a very small scale, in February 1981, by Yoweri Museveni and 27 other young soldiers. The war left over 300,000 people dead in Buganda alone, with the atrocities committed by Obote's army on the civilian population contributing a great deal to the death toll.

The NRM, led on the political front by Yusuf Lule, who had been removed in June 1979 and even detained by Julius Nyerere for some time in Dar es Salaam, took up arms against Obote on the pretext that the 1980 elections had been rigged. The Liberation War, as it came to be called, devastated a large part of the country, especially the Luwero Triangle, where most of the initial fighting took place. It was Buganda that bore the brunt of the war and, despite the denials so often heard these days, it was the young Baganda fighters who provided the thrust for the NRM. In the end, Obote fell out with his military commanders, who, in a coup in July 1985, removed him from power. This time Obote flew to Zambia, where he was still in political asylum in 1996, a forgotten and embittered old man still deluded by power and writing letters on paper headed 'Office of the President'.

Towards NRM victory

Obote's ouster was his army commander, General Tito Lutwa Okello, but the man behind the coup was Lutwa's deputy, another Okello, whose first name was Bazilio. The two Okellos, hailing from Acholiland in the north, tried to establish an alliance with the DP, buttressed by the Baganda, who were at first jubilant that Obote, their traditional enemy, had been removed once more. The Okellos did receive support from Paul Ssemogerere and his DP remnants who, since independence, had remained in the political wilderness. They gave support to a regime that precipitated

Above: Obote's army commander, General Tito Okello, took over the reins of power in July 1985 but remained head of state for only six months.
Below: Former president Yusuf Lule.

Above: Elected in May 1996 to serve as Uganda's president for another five years, Yoweri Museveni planned to continue his path of positive change for his country.

a wave of violence as soon as it came into power. Members of UPM (like Bidandi-Ssali and his ilk) joined a regime that their comrades-in-arms (Museveni and others who had been of the same party) were still fighting. Other political lightweights — such as J Mayanja-Nkangi, the leader of the small and ineffective Conservative Party (the successor, it is said, to the old KY) — also joined the Lutwa junta. The junta had no political programme of its own beyond vague promises to return the country to civilian rule. Museveni's NRM/NRA refused to join the military junta and intensified the war. At the end of January 1986, the two Okellos, like Obote before them, were bundled up and driven out of the country. The NRM administration had begun.

The assumption of power by NRM/ NRA, particularly by the young and committed soldiers who promised a new and real change, was greeted with the wildest of jubilation by many Ugandans. Naturally, the greatest joy was witnessed in the south and west of the country; by contrast, a feeling of doomsday descended upon the north and east. The reasons for this are not difficult to fathom. For the first time in Uganda's history, an armed group of people, without any foreign support, had fought and defeated a legally constituted government. More significantly, those who had won were people who, from the British colonialists to Obote, Amin, and the Okellos, were always considered to be non-martial, incapable of fighting wars, and referred to as 'small *matoke*-eaters'. In contrast, those from the north and east, who had formed the Ugandan army right from the inception of the state of Uganda early in the century, had been defeated and humiliated.

This explains why there were almost instant armed rebellions in the north and east after the Liberation War was over.

The NRM administration attempted to reverse the decline of the country in many spheres of national development. It introduced popular democracy, based on the system of Resistance Committees and Councils (RCs), where every Ugandan can

Above: The people of Uganda look forward to a bright future.

participate in the decision-making and implementation of its policy. And it introduced the concept of accountability in political behaviour, in that commissions of inquiry into the violation of human rights have become part of the political system in the country. An attempt to heal the wounds of the past was made through a policy of reconciliation and accommodation, by which a broadly-based government incorporating all of the political forces and groupings in the country — including, it must be emphasized, those groups such as UPC, which the NRM had fought for over five years — was formed.

The NRM also attempted to revive the economy which, before it came to power, registered a recession of unbelievable magnitude. But perhaps the major task the NRC set itself was the creation of a new constitution. The process effectively began in February 1989 with the appointment of the Uganda Constitutional Commission, which, after almost four years of deliberations, produced a draft constitution which was debated for more than a year by an elected Constituent Assembly. The new constitution was finally promulgated in July 1995.

The next hurdles facing the people were the presidential and parliamentary elections of mid-1996. After vigorous campaigning by President Museveni and his two opponents, Paul Ssemogerere and Mohamed Mayanja, the president won a resounding victory, capturing 74.2 per cent of the votes in the country's first direct presidential poll. Ssemogerere and Mayanja boycotted the subsequent parliamentary elections, charging that the presidential election was rigged — despite the fact that international monitors reported that the result had appropriately reflected the vote in the largely trouble-free poll.

Addressing an estimated 50,000 supporters after being sworn in as president for five years, Museveni promised to stick with the reforms that have turned Uganda into one of Africa's fastest growing economies.

With the completion of the constitutional programme for returning the country to constitutionalism and the rule of law, in 1996 Ugandans hoped that a new era of optimism and prosperity lay ahead.

The Land: Water, Water Everywhere

Uganda, as so many authors including Winston Churchill noted, is blessed with a great variety of nature's endowments such as rarely exist within any one country's boundaries. Uganda's remarkable beauty is derived from its geographical diversity which, in turn, influences the distribution of flora and fauna.

The geography and the geology

Uganda is a compact country, with an area of 236,580 square kilometres (91,344 square miles) — roughly the size of Great Britain or the American state of Oregon. It is located on the equator, within the eastern plateau region of the African continent and between the eastern and the western ridges of the Great Rift Valley. The central plateau averages 1,050 metres (3,450 feet) above sea level and displays a large expanse of planed-down land surfaces, within which are flat-topped hills and rocky inselbergs. Near the borders several mountain masses stand out strikingly from the plateaux.

Near the western border lies the highest point in the country — at 5,109 metres (16,762 feet) — the Margherita peak of the Ruwenzori range. The mountains were known to early Arab traders as the Mountains of the Moon, and the name remains to this day. The Ruwenzoris, where the interesting phenomenon of snow on the equator is found, are a landmark of physical beauty. The mountains also mark the boundary between Uganda and Zaire. The Ruwenzoris, formed during the formation of the Rift Valley, rise sharply from the level of adjoining plateau and extend for 100 kilometres (60 miles) along the base of the range, traversing the districts of Kasese, Kabarole, and Bundibugyo. The Ruwenzori range, the highest non-volcanic mountain range in Africa, has beautiful and extensive glaciers. At its base are a copper mine, salt lakes, and the renowned Queen Elizabeth National Park.

North of the Ruwenzoris is Lake Albert, through which the boundary of Uganda and Zaire passes in the western Rift Valley depression of Hoima and Masindi districts. To the extreme south-west corner of Uganda are three extinct volcanic mountains that are part of the range that extends southwards into the Virunga Mountains of Zaire. The three mountains, from east to west, are Muhabura, Gahinga, and Sabyinyo. At 4,127 metres (13,540 feet), Muhabura, the highest of them, consists of an impressive single cone, at the top of which is a small crater lake.

Gahinga, the smallest of the three, also has a single cone. Its abundant bamboo stands and lush vegetation are home to the rare mountain gorilla, a prime tourist attraction. The third mountain, Sabyinyo, is a double cone. On its extreme western cone the boundaries of Uganda, Rwanda, and Zaire converge, with those of Uganda and Rwanda having run along the summits of Muhabura and Gahinga. The dissected plateau to the north-east of the volcanic mountains resembles in many ways the Scottish or Swiss mountains and has been named the Switzerland of Africa. These mountains, in Kisoro and Kabale districts, rise to over 2,000 metres (6,560 feet) in places and extend into the neighbouring districts of Bushenyi, Mbarara, and Rakai.

Important drainage features developed during the latter part of the Rift Valley formation in this western area. The tremendous upward thrust of the land surface resulted in changes in drainage, making rivers such as the Katonga, Rwizi, and Kagera flow towards the Lake Victoria depression. During the same period, many crater lakes in the Rift Valley region were formed. Lake formations as a result of lava flows and deposits of volcanic ash left many beautiful lakes in the area, such as Mutanda, Muhele, Chahafi, and Kayumbu in Kisoro District,

Opposite: Solitary fisherman on beautiful Lake Mburo.
Overleaf: Grand expanse of the mythical Mountains of the Moon: Uganda's Ruwenzoris.

Above: The mighty Nile carves its way through much of Uganda from its origin at Lake Victoria.

and Bunyonyi in Kabale District. The crater lakes in the hills of Bushenyi District, overlooking Queen Elizabeth National Park in Kasese District, are adjacent to lakes George and Edward, which are joined by the Kazinga Channel and abound with a great variety of wildlife.

The central region of Uganda is dominated by the saucer-like depression of Lake Victoria, which is the second-largest freshwater lake in the world. Within it, the boundaries of Uganda, Tanzania, and Kenya converge. The Nile River emerges from Lake Victoria at 1,240 metres (4,070 feet) above sea level, offering its potential for hydroelectric power, long predicted by explorers and colonial administrators.

The Owen Falls Dam, constructed in the early 1950s at the source of the Nile from Lake Victoria in Jinja, provides large amounts of hydroelectricity, which are transmitted to Kenya and northern Tanzania. Another dam is being constructed nearby to generate more hydroelectric power for the ever-growing demand for energy in the region.

From its origin at Lake Victoria, the great Nile flows northwards, traversing the districts of the Buganda region to the swampy valley of Lake Kyoga and, from there, capturing the tributaries from the eastern plateau of the eastern districts. From Lake Kyoga, the Nile flows towards the northern tip of Lake Albert, which it reaches after crossing the Karuma Falls and funneling further downstream into a very narrow cleft less than six metres (20 feet) in width at the Murchison Falls, where it drops 43 metres (140 feet) to flow along the Rift Valley into Lake Albert. From there it flows in a northerly direction, eventually reaching Sudan at Nimule. The river then continues its course through Sudan and Egypt, ultimately ending in the Mediterranean Sea. From its furthest tributary in Burundi, the Nile traverses over 6,400 kilometres (4,000 miles), making it the longest river in the world.

To the north of Lake Kyoga is a generally flat area covering Apac, Lira, Soroti, Kumi, Gulu, and Kitgum districts, through which the Aswa River follows an old fault line to join the Nile River just beyond the border

Above: Salt extraction at Lake Katwe, near Queen Elizabeth National Park.
Overleaf: The Kabale region of Uganda, often called the Switzerland of Africa.

of Uganda and Sudan after Nimule. The north-western part of Uganda forms the West Nile Plateau — an uplifted block lying on the western side of the Rift — which forms the boundary between Uganda and Zaire.

In eastern Uganda the enormous bulk of Mount Elgon, a large extinct volcano that rises to 4,324 metres (14,186 feet), forms the boundary between Uganda and Kenya. North of Mount Elgon are four smaller volcanic mountains: Karum, Napak, Moroto, and Tororo in the Karamoja region. The landscape in this region is generally flat but rises to mountains that extend into the Turkana escarpment of Kenya, which overlooks the eastern Rift Valley of Kenya. North of the Karamoja region are the Imatong Mountains, which lie mostly in Sudan.

A variety of mineral deposits are known to exist in Uganda, some of which have been mined for centuries, although the economic potential of most of them has yet to be established. Industrial minerals such as graphite, talc, asbestos, garnet, magnesite, vermiculite, dolomite and limestone exist in various parts of the country, with a concentration of limestone in the east and west. Chromite, gold and copper exist in Karamoja, with minor gold centres in the east, west and south-west.

Up until the 1960s, copper was of great importance in the Ruwenzori Mountain region. Tin, tungsten (wolfram), beryllium and iron ore have been mined in small quantities in southern and south-western Uganda, although several million tonnes of high-quality iron ore occur in the Kisoro-Kabale region, providing potential for an iron smelting industry in the country.

Local salt extraction has gone on for a long time in Katwe, south of the Ruwenzoris, and in Kibiro in Hoima District. Glass sands of high quality are available from the Lake Victoria region. In 1996, it was planned to drill for oil on the shores of Lake Albert, and it is believed that there could be other deposits in the central region around Lake Wamala, but the area has yet to be explored.

Above: Maize and coffee: two of many crops that do well in the country's fertile soils.

The weather

In most regions of Uganda there are quite distinctive wet and dry seasons. In much of the southern half, rainfall occurs around March to May and September to November, with the period of June–July and December–January being relatively dry. In northern Uganda the two rainy seasons run together, in effect extending from April to October. In most of Uganda rain falls in the afternoons — although early morning and evening rains do occur at times. However, in parts of western Uganda, the rainfall is predominantly in the form of thunderstorms, and severe hailstorms are frequent, damaging crops and soil cover.

The region surrounding Lake Victoria — sometimes called the Lake Victoria crescent — receives well-distributed rainfall throughout the year, with a relatively dry season between December and March and in June–July. The afternoon rains common in the region clear away after a few hours and the land dries up rapidly when the sun appears.

The north-eastern part of Uganda (the Karamoja region) is drier than the rest of the country, partly as a result of the influence of the passage of wind from Somalia (the water vapour content is low by the time the winds reach the region after passing through the Ethiopian and Kenyan highlands).

The rainy season in the north-east is April to August, with a marked minimum in June and marked peaks in May and July.

The hilly areas attract more rains, but they are generally heavy and brief, causing sheet erosion and carrying everything down in the seasonal stream and river valleys miles beyond where they originated.

The mean temperature over the whole of Uganda shows little variation, save for the mountainous districts of western Uganda and around Mount Elgon. In west 4°C (39°F) and rise to 21°C (70°F) in Kabale District, whereas in Mbarara District it can climb as high as 29.5°C (85°F), with drastic daily variations. In Karamoja, temperatures can reach 35°C (95°F) during the dry season and 26.6°C (80°F) during the wet months.

The land

Uganda is blessed with fertile soils that support a wide variety of vegetation. This includes high-altitude moorland and heath on tops of mountains, characterized by patches of ferns, reeds and sedges, tree heathers, mosses and liverworts, and everlasting flowers and tree heather as found on Elgon, Muhabura, Sabyinyo, and the Ruwenzori Mountains.

Forests abound in the mountains, valleys, and plateaux. Semi-deciduous forests with large-leaved and soft-leaved species occur in the mountain areas of Elgon, Ruwenzori, and the south-west (Kigezi and Kisoro), and mountain bamboos can be found in pure stands towering to 20 metres (66 feet) on these mountains. Moist evergreen and semi-deciduous forests are found in well-watered areas to the north of Lake Victoria and in eastern and western Uganda. The forests are the home of hardwoods, used for making high-quality and long-lasting furniture. Areas of tall elephant grass create forest-savannah 'mosaics', indicating a wider forest cover in the past, which has been reduced by clearing, repeated cultivation, and burning. Wooded savannahs are scattered throughout the high grassland areas of most of Uganda. Grass savannah abounds in many parts of Uganda, whereas swampy marshy areas are a common feature of central Uganda.

The great variety of flora and fauna in Uganda is important for a tourist industry linked to the diversity of ecological communities. In the extreme west there are the rare mountain gorillas and forest elephants. A variety of plains-dwelling species — such as zebra, hartebeest, topi, Uganda kob, buffalo, hippo and elephant — thrive. The fauna include more than 40 different species of primates, ungulates, carnivores and large mammals. In the drier north-east, fauna of the low rainfall areas include oryx, gazelle, kudu and cheetah. Most game areas have been safeguarded by the establishment of national parks, game reserves, sanctuaries and controlled hunting areas.

Uganda's fertile soils support a wide variety of food and export crops, both annual and perennial. Agriculture is the

Above: Harvesting coffee.

dominant sector of Uganda's economy. It contributes about 70 per cent of the gross domestic product (GDP), more than 90 per cent of the country's foreign earnings, and provides a livelihood for about 90 per cent of the population.

Agriculture is primarily carried out by smallholders, who account for over 90 per cent of the total agricultural output. The major traditional export crops are coffee, cotton, tea, tobacco and sugar cane, while groundnuts, maize, beans, sorghum, and millet have emerged in recent years as cash crops for the peasant farmers. Cereals, legumes, tubers and plantains (*matoke*) are important staple foodstuffs. A variety of tropical fruit trees are grown in the lower plateau areas, while the upland areas grow a range of temperate crops, such as Irish potatoes, wheat and barley.

Most of the livestock is kept by smallholder farmers, although the Karimojong in the north-east and the Bahima in the south-west are important traditional cattle keepers.

The People: Diverse and United

More than 40 languages are spoken in Uganda, although the indigenous population may be classified into four major language groupings: Bantu, Nilotic (western Nilotes), Nilo-Hamitic (eastern Nilotes), and Sudanic. There are differences within each group, and the social background is complex and varies from tribe to tribe, rendering it difficult to generalize as a whole. The Bantu groups occupy most of the southern half of Uganda. The Nilotic (Luo) speaking groups occupy the central section of northern Uganda, while the Nilo-Hamites live in the north-east and the Sudanic in the north-west.

There are 17 Bantu tribes: Bafumbira, Baganda, Bagisu, Bagwe, Bagwere, Bakenyi, Bakiga, Bakonjo, Bamba, Banyankole, Banyarwanda, Banyoro, Banyuli, Basoga, Batoro, Batwa, and Samia. The Nilotic include Acholi, Alur, Jonam, Langi, Luo, and Padhola. The Nilo-Hamites comprise the Iteso, Kakwa, Karimojong, Kumam, Labwor, Sebei Pokot (Suk), and Tepeth. The Lendu, Lugbara, and Madi make up the Sudanic group.

The official language in Uganda is English. Swahili is spoken and understood by some but has not been accepted as the *lingua franca*, and Luo has been introduced as a degree language course at Makerere University, giving it semi-official status.

As a result of colonial rule, new religions, modernization, and education, cultural practices have undergone some changes, and adherence to tradition is not as strong as it once was. However, traditions in marriage, dress, and diet still hold. Settlement is generally dispersed — that is, the people live in family homesteads surrounded by their gardens and fields. In some cases in northern Uganda, the settlements are nucleated and plots are a few miles from home. Where a husband has more than one wife, each wife has a separate house, with her own plot to cultivate.

The cattle-herding people are the Bahima in the south-west and the Karimojong in the north-east. They live in groups around their cattle kraals and move with their herds, looking for pasture and water. Their diet is mainly milk, blood, and meat.

The crop-growing communities prepare special delicacies at ceremonies based on the crops and vegetables they grow. In the central region, banana, groundnuts, and greens are available at almost every meal — and all taste sweeter when steamed in banana leaves. Millet bread is a delicacy in the north, east, and west of Uganda and forms a major dish at ceremonies.

Long robes and dresses are worn at ceremonies and on days of prayer. On most occasions in Buganda men wear the *kanzu*, a long robe with long sleeves, over which a coat is worn, making the attire smart and attractive. The women don colourful long robes known as *gomesi* or *busuti*, with a large length of cloth tied around the *gomesi* at the waist. Originally worn at ceremonies in Buganda, the *gomesi* has been adopted in most parts of the country. Among the Banyankole, Batoro, and Banyoro women, colourful dresses are adorned with beautiful lengths of cloth.

The major religions in Uganda are Christianity, to which about 85 per cent of the people nominally belong, and Islam, of which about 11 per cent are followers. Those who do not fall into these two broad categories practise either the traditional (animist) religions or are atheists.

Among the people of Uganda, descent, succession, and inheritance follow the paternal line. Bride-wealth is paid by the bridegroom's father and is high in some places, usually in the form of cattle or money. Intertribal marriages occur, but

Opposite (clockwise from top left): Elderly tobacco seller; Schoolgirls at Kampala's Buganda Road. Primary School; Young banana seller on the capital's streets; Nubian woman carries a heavy load. Overleaf: Happy bridal parties pose for pictures at Namirembe Cathedral, Kampala.

Above: Baganda men play *mweso* on the outskirts of Entebbe.
Opposite: Many Ugandan traditions are still passed on from old to young.

they remain comparatively few. A man generally prefers a wife to be of his tribe, familiar with the same customs, and speaking the same language. This is slowly changing, however, as a result of greater interaction through education and migration.

Traditionally, all property belongs to the man, and when he dies it is divided among all the sons (in practice in the south-west) or to one of the sons — for instance, the eldest son — as among the Acholi, Langi, and Baganda people. The son is then responsible for providing bride-wealth and education for his younger brothers. In many areas, girls traditionally inherit little of worth — like land or property — from their parents. But, as with most cultures in the modern and more educated world, these traditions are fading.

Some traditions last longer than others, however. Among the Bagisu, male circumcision ceremonies take place every other year, while female circumcision is still practised by the Sebei people.

Ugandan traditional society developed a system of non-formal education for imparting skills in pottery, crafts, and iron smelting. However, these were largely neglected with the introduction of formal education.

Uganda's school system is well developed. There are large numbers of educational institutions, and more than half of the school-age children are enrolled in primary school. The country is striving to achieve universal primary education in the first decade of the next century. Primary school education is backed up by secondary education based on a centralized system of syllabus and examination.

Tertiary institutions and universities have been established; foremost among them is Makerere University, long famous for its contribution to the high-level development of the workforce in East Africa.

PART TWO: PLACES AND TRAVEL

Above: Signpost in Queen Elizabeth National Park.
Opposite: Sunset over Lake Mburo, one of Uganda's many beautiful national parks.

The South-west: Gorilla Country

A trip to Uganda's deep south-west, where the borders of Rwanda, Zaire, and Uganda meet, is a trip not soon to be forgotten. For it is there that the visitor will meet — if they choose to make the trek — the rare and endangered mountain gorilla.

There are only two mountain gorilla populations in the world — both in this region of Africa — and the gorillas number fewer than 600 all told. There are only four national parks where you can see them, two of which are in Uganda: Mgahinga Gorilla National Park and Bwindi Impenetrable National Park.

Although viewing the gorillas is certainly the culmination of any visit to Uganda's south-west, it is by no means all there is to see.

The region also boasts a number of beautiful lakes and waterfalls, particularly Lake Nabugabo near Masaka, Lake Mburo National Park, a haven for acacia-associated birds and a good variety of wildlife, and Lake Bunyonyi near Kabale. Lake Bunyonyi is in Kabale District, which, together with neighbouring Rukungiri and Kisoro districts, is known as the Switzerland of Africa, largely because of the cooler climate and beautiful mountain scenery found there. Gorillas aside, this part of the country offers some spectacular walks and hikes.

Ssese Islands

The way to the deep south-west passes close to Lake Victoria and the offshore Ssese (sometimes spelled Sese) Islands. Truly a slice of unspoilt Africa, the 84 islands, east of Masaka, are a refuge of peace and friendliness, offering relaxing days admiring the views, watching birds, or going boating — traditional style.

Getting there
Kalangala, the principal town on Buggala

Island (one of the Ssese Islands), as the crow flies, is about 30 kilometres (19 miles) from Bukakata on the mainland and some 75 kilometres (47 miles) from Port Bell, near Kampala. Ferries ply from both Bukakata (about a two-and-a-half-hour trip to Luku on the westernmost tip of Buggala Island) and Port Bell (a 10-hour trip to Kalangala) to the islands, but it is far better to hire a private outboard in Bukakata, which will take you to Luku in about 90 minutes.

When to go
The Ssese Islands are blessed with rain all year round. But they are even wetter — and the ferry trip may be even more choppy — during the rainy seasons around April–May and October–November, so you may prefer to visit at a different time.

Where to stay
There are some simple but comfortable and clean places to stay. In Kalangala, try the Malaanga Ssese Safari Lodge (also known as Andronico's Lodge) or the Church of Uganda's Ssese Guest House. In Luku, the Ssese Scorpion Lodge. On Bukasa Island, Agnes's Guest House. There are other lodges and guesthouses in the other main towns on the islands. Camping is also possible on all of the islands. See Listings.

Sightseeing
The most common starting point for any trip to the south-west — or anywhere else in the country, for that matter — is from Kampala. From the **roundabout** near the **bus and taxi parks** and **Nakivubo Stadium**, head **west** on **Namirembe Road** (being careful to keep right towards the old Kampala Fort and the Sports Ground) for about 1.5 kilometres (one mile) until it ends at the junction with **Natete Road.** Turn **left** and head out of town on Natete Road, following the signs to Masaka. This tarmacked road, which in 1996 was in excellent condition all the way to Kabale in the extreme south-west, is part of the

Above: Woman enjoys *matoke* at one of Uganda's many roadside markets.

Northern African Highway — the gateway to the sea for the landlocked countries of Uganda, Rwanda, Burundi, and parts of eastern Zaire.

Soon after leaving Kampala you begin to see open countryside, dotted with villages and *shambas* (cultivated plots).

The staple food in the south-west belt of the country is steamed bananas, known as *matoke*, and around every homestead in this region there is a cluster of the unmistakable banana trees. To a typical Muganda man (a member of the main ethnic group in the kingdom of Buganda), a meal is not a meal unless matoke is served. It is as important to him as bread is to a European.

This type of banana is eaten when green. Commonly, after peeling the fruit, the banana itself is wrapped in a banana leaf and boiled in water. Meat or groundnut sauce may be added and boiled together with the bananas in the same pot. After about half an hour, the matoke is ready to eat — using the fingers, while seated on colourful mats.

As you drive towards Masaka, you'll see heaps and heaps of matoke bananas being sold by the roadside, or awaiting transport to outlying districts. Huge banana plantations cover the hills and valleys in every direction as far as the eye can see.

You'll also see a bounty of other fruits for sale on the roadside, such as mango and pineapple, which, after being purchased, can be sliced and eaten straight away — a great on-the-road healthy snack.

Many local travellers break their journey at **Mbizinnya roadside market,** about 30 kilometres (19 miles) from Kampala, to sample a tasty chicken leg or small pieces of beef or goat meat, which have been pierced, kebab-style, on a small stick and nicely roasted on a charcoal grill, washed down by a choice of cold drinks — such as beer, soda, or mineral water — stored in paraffin-driven refrigerators.

There is also an abundance of fruit, vegetables, and other produce on offer. Even if you don't want to buy anything, a stop at any local market promises to be a colourful and enjoyable experience, with plenty of photo opportunities. (But ask permission before you take anyone's picture, as a matter of courtesy.)

Mpanga Forest Reserve

About 40 kilometres (25 miles) along the Masaka road from Kampala, you come to the **turnoff** for **Mpigi**, the headquarters of Mpigi District. About three kilometres (two miles) beyond the turnoff, the main road passes through a **dip**. Immediately past the dip to the **right** is an unmarked **track** leading — after about 500 metres (1,640 feet) — to the **forest station** of the **Mpanga Forest Reserve**, a 450-hectare (1,110-acre) medium-altitude rainforest, typical of that which once covered much of this region.

The reserve was created in the 1950s, essentially for research purposes. There is an extensive network of **paths** within its borders, from which visitors can view the few species of **wildlife** — mainly monkeys, such as the black-and-white **colobus** and the **vervet** — and the prolific birdlife that make this forest their home. **Butterflies** are abundant and beautiful.

Entrance to the reserve is free, but check at the forest station before venturing into the forest. The ranger can provide information about the forest's flora, and you may also be able to obtain a map showing the main paths through the forest. If you want to make the most of your visit in a short time, ask for a guide to accompany you: besides knowing the trails, his eyes are more accustomed to searching out the more elusive wildlife and birdlife in the heavy forest cover.

There is a lovely **campsite**, where you can camp for free, about 100 metres (110 yards) from the forest station. But there are no facilities, so you have to be self-sufficient, which includes bringing your own tent and food. Water and firewood may be organized at the forest station. Take note, however, that you need written permission from the Forestry Department in Kampala before you camp there. Basic lodgings are available in nearby Mpigi as well.

Nearby is **Mpambire village**, the home of the **Royal Drum Makers**. All along the roadsides in this area you can watch traditional drums being crafted using methods passed down through the generations. Most **roadside stalls** sell the drums. You can bargain for the one you like. Drums have been used in Africa since time immemorial for communicating and calling people to festive occasions, and Ugandan drums are particularly well crafted. Today, drums are used extensively in traditional music and dance, and make excellent souvenirs.

From the Mpigi turnoff, it is another 40 kilometres (25 miles) or so before you reach the **equator**, where you can stop to take the obligatory photo by the circular white **equator signpost**, with your legs straddling both hemispheres, if you like. Shops and stalls nearby sell souvenirs.

Masaka

From the equator, it is approximately another 40 kilometres (25 miles) to **Masaka**. The town is the headquarters for the Masaka District and is attractively situated but otherwise has no real endearing traits.

In the late 1970s the town was wrecked by Tanzanian soldiers at the close of the war that ousted Idi Amin, and the main road is lined by the shells of bombed-out government buildings. The streets of Masaka also have huge potholes; take care when driving.

For most visitors, Masaka is just an overnight stop en route to the Ssese Islands or Tanzania, and there is little to do. There is some decent accommodation, however, including the Hotel La Nova and the Laston Hotel. If you're on a tight budget, try the Iqbal Hotel, the Victoria End Rest House, or the Kadoda Guest House. (See Listings.)

The next step towards the Ssese Islands is to find the **road** to Bukakata from Masaka, which isn't all that easy. Head downhill (**east**) out of the centre of Masaka town, cross over the **river bridge** and take the first **right turn** (there is a **sign** for the Church of Uganda Holiday and Conference Centre). From there, go **straight** across the first **junction** and then turn **left** at the next

Above: Roadside drum maker practises his centuries-old craft.
Overleaf: Port Bell ferry arrives at Buggala Island, one of the Ssese Islands in Lake Victoria.

T-junction. There is **another turning** for Lake Nabugabo about 10 kilometres (six miles) before you reach Masaka, on the **east** side of the road, which is **signposted**. If you prefer, you can follow this road until you reach a **T-junction**, where you turn **right**. After a few more kilometres, turn **right** again to get to the lake.

Lake Nabugabo

About 20 kilometres (12 miles) along the Masaka–Bukakata road you come to the **Church of Uganda Holiday and Conference Centre**, about four kilometres (2.5 miles) off the main road (the **turnoff** is clearly **signposted**). This beautiful resort, situated on the shores of **Lake Nabugabo,** has a few **bandas** to rent, as well as a **dormitory** and **campsites**.

If you want to cook for yourself, take what you need — except firewood, which is available. What you should not carry is alcohol, including beer, out of respect for the Church of Uganda's Christian beliefs and rules.

Lake Nabugabo itself is a wonderful place to spend a day or two. The area around the lake can be explored on any one of a number of **roads** and **footpaths**. You may see some small **animals** and the glorious **birdlife** in the area. In particular, keep an eye open for the **broad-billed roller**, **Ross's turaco**, and a myriad of **sunbirds**, **weavers**, and **hornbills**. The lake, which is separated from Lake Victoria by a thin, forested sand bar, is said to be free from bilharzia, so swimming is possible.

Retrace your steps to the main Masaka–Bukakata road and turn **right**, where, after about 16 kilometres (10 miles), you'll come to **Bukakata** town. There you can catch the **ferry** to the Ssese Islands, or hire an outboard, which is more reliable).

If you travel by public transport, the easiest option is to take the bus, which leaves Masaka at 1400 and connects with the ferry to Luku on the islands and then continues on to Kalangala, which is the principal town.

On to the islands

Although seldom visited by travellers, the 84 Ssese Islands are an interesting and very different side to Uganda. With no civil war scars, they remain quite unspoiled.

They are inhabited by the Basese people — a distinct ethnic group with their own language, culture, and folklore. Primarily fishermen, the Basese also farm coffee, sweet potato, cassava, yams, and bananas. They are extremely friendly people, particularly to tourists, as so few visit the islands.

There are no dangers whatsoever in walking around the islands, which is actually the best way to explore them.

Don't go there expecting lots of action: this is a place to relax, unwind, enjoy the beautiful views, and explore. It's an easy matter to convince a local fisherman to take you out on his boat, and swimming is possible (but avoid the reedy areas where the snails that carry the bilharzia parasite live).

You should, however, report to the Kalangala police station on arrival (a straightforward and friendly procedure). Note also that these islands are reputed to have the highest AIDS rate in Uganda, so use common sense; and dress modestly (swim with a T-shirt on) to avoid offending the islanders, who have complained about women, in particular, walking around in shorts.

The islands are lush and well watered, with an average rainfall of more than 2,000 millimetres (80 inches) a year. The main islands of **Buggala**, **Bufumira**, **Bukasa**, **Bubeke**, and **Kkome** are hilly and forested (in areas where they are not cultivated) with a large variety of trees.

Buggala, where the ferry stops of Luku and Kalangala are located, is the most accessible island. It is 43 kilometres (27 miles long) and has about 50 kilometres (30 miles) of roads.

There is little organized transport on the islands, save for the bus from Kampala/Masaka, which runs between Luku and Kalangala on alternate days. There are also ferries between the larger islands, and it is not difficult to hire a boat to get from one island to the other. By far the best way of getting around is on foot or by bicycle (which can be hired from Andronico's Lodge in Kalangala).

In addition to the delightful **views** that greet you as you explore in any direction from Kalangala, a walk through the forests will probably bring to light a number of **monkeys**, some **antelope**, brilliant **butterflies**, and an overwhelming selection of water and forest **birds**.

In particular, expect to see **hornbills**, **barbets**, **turacos**, **weavers**, and **paradise flycatchers**.

If you like to cycle, go to **Mutambala Beach** off the Kalangala–Luku road. The place is said to be free of bilharzia, and many people go there to swim.

It is worth exploring the other islands, too: Andronico's Lodge in Kalangala can arrange a day trip to Bufumira Island. Bukasa Island (the second largest in the group) is often rated as more attractive than Buggala.

It is extensively forested, with plenty of wildlife and birdlife, a road network for easy foot exploration, two lovely beaches, a plunge pool surrounded by forest, and a waterfall.

To continue your journey to Uganda's south-west, return to Masaka. If you're heading into Tanzania, take the tarmac road **south** from Masaka to the **Mutukula** border point, and continue to the Tanzanian village of **Kyaka**, where a turn to the **east** leads to the more major town of **Bukoba**.

There is a basic **guesthouse** on the Ugandan side of the border but nowhere to stay on the Tanzanian side. The road to the border was in good condition in 1996, but once you cross into Tanzania it deteriorates rapidly.

To head for Uganda's gorilla country, however, take the main tarmac road from Masaka to the **south-west**, in the direction of Mbarara and Kabale. But before you reach these you come to one of Uganda's most low-profile, but still beautiful, national parks, Lake Mburo.

Lake Mburo National Park

Gazetted in 1982, this 260-square-kilometre (100-square-mile) park encompasses not only Lake Mburo but also four other smaller lakes. Its easy accessibility from Kampala (about a three-hour drive on a good road to the park turnoff) makes it a favourite weekend getaway for the capital's residents. Mainly savannah with scattered acacia trees, the park features rolling hills, open grass valleys, thickets, woodlands, and rich wetlands. It is home to a wide variety of wildlife and birdlife; it is also outstanding in that it has a strong community extension component, trying to work closely with the local people to conserve the wildlife and other natural resources both inside and outside the park.

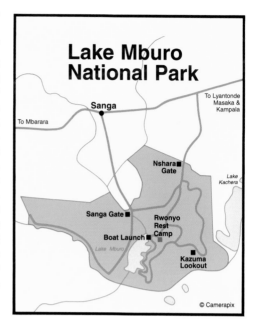

Getting there

The main turnoff to Lake Mburo National Park's Nshara gate is approximately 110 kilometres (68 miles) from Masaka, 219 kilometres (136 miles) from Kampala, and 35 kilometres (22 miles) from Mbarara. It is served by the good tarmac Kampala–Kabale road, although there is a 24-kilometre (15-mile) stretch of dirt road to the park gate. Four-wheel-drive is necessary during the rainy seasons, but at other times of the year two-wheel-drive is reliable.

When to go

The park is enjoyable at any time but is particularly green and fresh just after the April–May and October–November rains.

Where to stay

The Rwonyo Rest Camp at the park headquarters has several bandas with bedding and mosquito nets, and a communal shower. The park also has three campsites (at Nshara gate, near the Interpretation Centre, and on the lakeshore). Meals can be provided by the park staff at Rwonyo, but campers should bring their own food. Firewood is available. Book both accommodation and meals at the Uganda National Parks Headquarters in Kampala. In 1996, a Kampala-based safari company was building a lodge in the park.

Sightseeing

Head **south-west** on the **main road** from Masaka, where 77 kilometres (48 miles) further on, you'll come to the town of **Lyantonde**, where there is petrol and a police station. If you are at all interested in African history and archaeology, you may at this point want to divert from the route to Lake Mburo.

Turn **right** (north) on a **dirt road** from Lyantonde that leads to the town of **Ntusi**, 61 kilometres (38 miles) off the main road. Although a modern village, Ntusi lies on the site of what is thought to be the most ancient large **settlement** in Uganda. Strong evidence suggests that the people who once lived there gave rise to the legendary and mysterious Batembuzi gods, who play a central role in Ugandan folklore.

Legend has it that the first empire in what is now western Uganda was that of the Batembuzi. Oral history places the Batembuzi empire at between AD 1100 and 1350, and evidence in the Ntusi region confirms that a highly centralized society existed there as early as the 11th century.

Most modern Ugandan kingdoms trace their ancestry to the Bachwezi kingdom, and some oral history suggests that the Bachwezi descended directly from the Batembuzi. However, it is thought more

Above: Mist-shrouded acacia tree at Lake Mburo.

likely that they were Cushitic-speaking herdsmen who migrated into Uganda from Ethiopia. Religious cults based around Bachwezi leaders have been using places such as Masaka Hill, near Ntusi, as sites of worship for centuries. Many are still active today. There are interesting displays relating to the Ntusi region in the Uganda Museum in Kampala. See Listings.

The ancient town is thought to have been the largest settlement in sub-Saharan Africa when it reached its pinnacle in the 12th and 13th centuries. It is believed to have been the capital of an empire stretching all the way to Lake Albert in the north and thought by some to be the source of the Batembuzi legends. Evidence of iron smelting and ivory and wood carving has been found there by archaeologists.

The word *ntusi* means mound: the prominent features of Ntusi are two huge **mounds**, known by the local people as the 'male' and 'female' mounds. They are basically 300-year-old waste dumps, containing piles of bones, pottery fragments, and other refuse material. There are also several non-natural **depressions** around the village, the largest of which is thought to have once been a dam linked to an extensive irrigation system. The mounds and depressions are all located within a 1-square-kilometre radius around the **Ntusi District Headquarters** and can be visited on foot from the village.

There are two other archaeological sites of interest in the area. The first is **Bigo Bya Mugenyi** (Mugenyi's Fort), which can be reached by travelling about 10 kilometres (six miles) **north** from Ntusi to **Makole**, where a **turnoff** to the **right** (east) leads to Bigo, another 10 kilometres (six miles) from the turnoff.

Bigo Bya Mugenyi is the largest and most important of the several **earthworks** built by the Bachwezi and related kingdoms. It is thought that Bigo was a fort built to protect the southern extreme of the Bachwezi kingdom. There are two concentric sets of earthworks: an outer ditch and an inner **royal enclosure** built on a small hill. Local people regard the earthworks as having supernatural powers, and they are regarded with reverence.

On the **north bank** of the **Katonga**

Above: View of Lake Mburo National Park from the Interpretation Centre near park headquarters.
Overleaf: Rwonyo fishing village at Lake Mburo.

River, 18 kilometres (11 miles) upstream from Bigo, **Masaka Hill** is thought to have been the site of the last capital of the Bachwezi leader Wamara. For centuries, it has been used as a place of cult worship and pilgrimage. On top of the hill a circular **grove** of ancient **fig trees** is thought to have ritual significance. To get there, cross the Katonga River at **Lubale station**, where you board a **canoe** which takes you across for a nominal charge. Masaka Hill is about two kilometres (1.2 miles) **west** of **Nkonge** and the Ntusi–Mubende road.

On to the lake

From Lyantonde on the main Masaka–Kabale road, continue to head **south-west**. In just 13 kilometres (8 miles) — at the 50-kilometre **marker** — you'll see a **signpost** for the first **turnoff** to **Lake Mburo National Park's Nshara gate**. The drive from the main road to the park headquarters is 24 kilometres (15 miles). There is a **second turnoff**, leading to the **Sanga gate**, 15 kilmetres (9 miles) farther along the main road, at the **Sanga Trading Centre**. It is a

21-kilometre (13-mile) drive from the Sanga Trading Centre to the park headquarters. Four-wheel-drive vehicles are recommended, particularly during the rainy season, but two-wheel-drive vehicles can sometimes make it through.

As this is a national park, there are, of course, fees to pay, and there is a different structure for non-residents, foreign residents, and Uganda citizens. Check with the Uganda National Parks Headquarters in Kampala for up-to-date fees, but in mid-1996 non-residents paid US$ 23. There is also a minimal charge for vehicles.

The most straightforward route to the **park headquarters** (and the **Rwonyo Rest Camp**) is the second main **turnoff** on the **left** from the Nshara gate entrance, which leads towards the **lake** and the **boat launch**.

The **east** side of the park features undulating, low hills broken by rocky outcrops, while in the **west** a series of rugged hills overlook flat-bottomed, open valleys. These grassy valleys offer the best game-viewing opportunities, with

83

impala being the most remarkable species there, as it is found nowhere else in Uganda. Herds of **buffalo, zebra**, and the shy but magnificent **eland** can also be found, particularly by the waterholes during the drier seasons. **Oribi** and **topi**, seen in pairs and small groups, are abundant and easily approached. You'll also spot families of the comical **warthog**, and occasionally **reedbuck**, which hide in the grass.

The acacia and olive woodland harbour shy **bush duikers**, as well as **waterbuck, vervet monkeys**, and **baboons**. Keep an eye out for elusive **klipspringers** and **rock hyrax** on the granite outcrops in the west of the park, and in the rocky hills in the east.

The five **lakes** in the park — and several others that lie just outside the southern park boundary — are home to **crocodiles** and to **hippos**, which can be seen grazing out of the water on cool mornings. The surrounding papyrus swamps hide the beautiful **sitatunga**, which has narrow, elongated hooves that allow it to move easily over marshy, unstable ground.

Predators are rarely seen in the park, which is why it is possible to walk anywhere within the park borders, provided you are accompanied by a ranger. Lion were hunted out in the 1970s, but **jackal, spotted hyena**, and **leopard** still remain — although the latter is very difficult to spot. You can walk alone on the one-kilometre (half-mile) stretch of road between the park headquarters and the lake, but keep your eyes open for hippo and buffalo — particularly in early morning and around dusk. Either full- or half-day **walking safaris**, a wonderful African experience, can be arranged at the park headquarters.

Bird enthusiasts will delight in this park, which offers a wide variety of water and dry-land species, including the rare **shoebill stork**, the **Abyssinian ground hornbill**, and the **saddlebill stork**. The forested areas of the park are home to the beautiful **Narina's trogon**.

As well as the walking safaris and the more traditional **game drives**, the park also offers a self-guided **nature trail** and an **Interpretation Centre** to help visitors learn more about the park, its wildlife, and its ecosystems. The centre is located 1 kilometre (half a mile) from Rwonyo, and the nature trail begins and ends there. Brochures about the nature trail are available at a small fee.

For a first-hand view of Lake Mburo, you can hire a guide and a wooden Ssese canoe, which seats up to six people, for a two-hour tour of the lake — perfect for searching out birds, such as **kingfishers** and **herons**, at the water's edge, watching animals come down to the water to drink, and getting an 'eyeball-to-eyeball' look at hippos and crocs, which may surface nearby. Don't worry, your guide will ensure you keep a safe distance!

Facilities are constantly being improved by the Lake Mburo National Park Community Conservation Project, which is part of the African Wildlife Foundation project. The project is based on the concept that if people view natural resources as belonging to them and benefiting them, they will take a more active role in caring for them. As a result, the local communities are slowly beginning to change their attitudes towards the park: it is becoming less and less 'government property' and more and more their own asset. Locally made **crafts** are for sale at the park headquarters, and a percentage of the park's income goes to support community development projects, such as schools and clinics.

The people in the area bordering the park are the traditional, pastoral Bahima people, known for their famous long-horned Ankole cattle (see Ankole Cattle, Part Four). From time to time, visitors may see a remarkable combination of cattle, impala, and zebra grazing together.

Mbarara

One of Uganda's major towns, Mbarara serves as a good overnight stop for visitors going to the western Mountains of the Moon region or the south-western mountains and forests of Kabale and

Above: Buffalo browsing in the shallows of Lake Mburo.

Kisoro. Although Mbarara suffered considerably during the war to oust Idi Amin, it now bears few scars and is a pleasant, sprawling town with a good range of facilities.

The town has an interesting history. When the Bachwezi kingdom folded around AD 1500, the Ankole kingdom was formed, with Mbarara as its 'capital'. The dynasty of the first Ankole king (*omugabe*), Ruhinda, maintained a strong link to Bachwezi rituals and traditions. But Ankole didn't become a driving political force until after early 18th century, when the 11th omugabe, Ntare IV Kiitabanyoro (meaning 'killer of the Banyoro'), defeated the Banyoro.

Over the next 100 years, the Ankole kingdom grew to the point where it stretched for more than 100 kilometres (60 miles), from an area east of Lake Albert to Katonga River in the north and Kagera River in the south. But in the late 1800s, the kingdom began to crumble, thought to be a result of disease, drought, and the rise of the Bunyoro under Kabalega. Kabalega, in fact, had his sights set on taking over the Ankole kingdom, but the British intervened in the 1890s and put a stop to his designs. Ankole, was disbanded shortly after the country's independence was gained.

When to go

Mbarara can be visited at any time.

Getting there

Mbarara is 283 kilometres (176 miles) from Kampala, 146 kilometres (90 miles) from Masaka, 147 kilometres (91 miles) from Kabale, and 232 kilometres (144 miles) from Fort Portal. It is served by two good tarmac roads (one running from Kampala to Kabale and the other from Fort Portal), and also has an airstrip.

Where to stay

The best place in this area is the Katatumba Resort, 10 kilometres (six miles) outside of Mbarara on the road to Kabale. Its exceptional facilities include saunas, horse-riding, tennis courts, and a television lounge with satellite TV. It has an excellent restaurant, a variety of

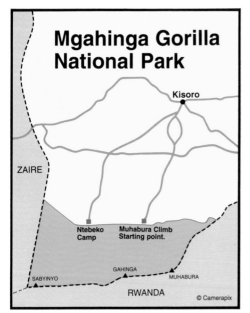

Mgahinga Gorilla National Park

 Kisoro

ZAIRE

Ntebeko Camp

Muhabura Climb Starting point.

GAHINGA

SABYINYO

MUHABURA

RWANDA

© Camerapix

Another Ankole site, the **Nkokonjeru Tomb**, burial place of the last two Ankole kings — Kahaya II and Gasyonga II — can be found four kilometres (2.5 miles) **west** of Mbarara.

Mgahinga Gorilla National Park

At the extreme south-western tip of Uganda, on the borders with Zaire and Rwanda, lies Uganda's smallest national park, 33.7 square kilometres (13 square miles).

The Mgahinga Gorilla National Park, established in 1991, is also one of the country's newest parks. It is an integral part of the Virunga Conservation Area and is contiguous with Parc National des Volcans in Rwanda and Parc National des Virungas in Zaire. There, in this tiny corner of the globe, one-half of the world's remaining mountain gorillas make their home.

Three extinct volcanic mountains lie within the park: Mount Muhabura, at 4,127 metres (13,540 feet); Mount Gahinga at 3,475 metres (11,400 feet); and the 3,645-metre (11,958-foot) Mount Sabyinyo, whose peaks lie along Uganda's border with Rwanda.

Mgahinga is an afro-montane tropical rainforest, and the vegetation is typical of this terrain, with a montane forest belt, a bamboo zone, an ericaceous belt, and an alpine zone. There are three large swamps in the park as well: Rugezi, Kabiranyuma, and Kazibakye.

The park, situated within one of the most densely populated areas in rural Africa, is surrounded by the terraced fields of the Batwa and Bafumbira people. Now agriculturalists, the Batwa lived in the forest as hunters and gatherers more than 20,000 years ago.

Both ethnic groups grow crops such as Irish potatoes, beans, and millet, and rear livestock that includes cattle, goats, sheep, and chickens.

accommodation, and boasts the only camels in Uganda (which wander around the hotel grounds). Closer to Mbarara is the Lake View Hotel (three kilometres — two miles — out of town), and, in the town itself, the Mbarara University Inn and the Pelikan Hotel. Those on a tight budget could try the Church of Uganda Hostel or the Silver Inn. Campers should head for the Sabena Club, three kilometres (two miles) outside the town on the Kasese–Kabale road. Camping is also available at the Katatumba Resort. See Listings.

Sightseeing

From Lake Mburo National Park, head **south-west** once again on the main **tarmac road** to Kabale. Mbarara is 35 kilometres (22 miles) farther on from the **Sanga Trading Centre**. Although it has an impressive history, there is little for travellers to see, save for a couple of Ankole sites just outside the town.

To visit the site of the old Ankole capital, **Kamukazi**, for instance, just head **north** from Mbarara on the **road** to Fort Portal for about two kilometres (1.2 miles). Although most of the buildings are in a rather derelict state, the **drum house** is still standing — but, unfortunately, the royal drum, symbol of Ankole national unity, has disappeared.

Above: Verdant hills surround Lake Bunyonyi in the Kabale area.

Most of the lower forest in the park has been lost as a result of human pressure over the last five decades.

Bamboo and alpine habitat are largely all that remain. The local people, however, benefit from the park, with a portion of the fees going to local development projects.

Getting there
Kisoro, where the Mgahinga Gorilla National Park booking office is located, is 496 kilometres (308 miles) from Kampala, 213 kilometres (132 miles) from Mbarara, and 66 kilometres (41 miles) from Kabale. It is served by a gravel road from Kabale, which is more or less a continuation of the main tarmac road from Kampala to Kabale.

When to go
As a rainforest, the park is always wet, even more so during the rains (April–May and October–November). But, as gorilla tracking permits are hard to come by — for only a limited number of people each day — go when you can.

Where to stay
Overnight camping is available at Ntebeko Camp within the park, but you must be totally self-contained in the way of a tent, cooking equipment, and food (available from Kisoro town). Firewood is available and water is provided. There is also a campsite near the departure point for the climb to Mount Muhabura. In Kisoro, the Mubano Hotel or the Travellers Rest Inn offer adequate accommodation. In Kabale, the White Horse Inn, Highland Hotel, Victoria Inn, Visitours Hotel, or Skyblue Hotel. See Listings.

Sightseeing
From Mbarara, continue towards Kabale on the main **tarmac road** to the **south-west**, through the towns of **Kinoni** and **Ndeija** to **Ntungamo**, the headquarters of Ntungamo District, a 66-kilometre (41-mile) drive from Mbarara.

There the main road heads more directly **south**, through **Rubaare**, **Rushenyi**, and **Bukinda** to **Kabale**, which is 84 kilometres (52 miles) past Ntungamo.

Above: Church atop hill on Bwama Island, the largest of Lake Bunyonyi's islands.

Kabale

Kabale in south-west Uganda is the unofficial capital of the Kigezi region and is a beautiful, mountainous area with steep-sided hills, neatly terraced cultivation, and many small lakes.

At 2,000 metres (6,560 feet), Uganda's highest town is attractive and its citizens friendly. It is situated in an area criss-crossed by numerous **tracks** and **paths** — making it a haven for hikers. A trek down any path yields beautiful vistas and interesting hamlets and farms. In addition to being a sort of springboard from which to visit the gorillas in the nearby national parks, Kabale is a good base to meet other travellers and perhaps take a couple of excursions.

One of the most attractive places is **Lake Bunyonyi**, which is situated over a **ridge** to the **north-west** of Kabale. The **access road** to the lake is a **left** turn approximately one kilometre (half-a-mile) past the **Highlands Hotel** on the road to Kisoro. You can also walk: it's about six

kilometres (3.7 miles) from the town. At the lake's edge there is a **fishing village**, where you can negotiate **canoe** hire. The Visitours or Skyblue hotels in Kabale also organize trips to the lake, with a guide.

Large and irregularly shaped, Lake Bunyonyi features a number of **islands** and is surrounded by heavily cultivated hillsides. A Dutch-built leper colony used to be located on the largest island, **Bwama Island**. It was founded in the late 1940s but was relocated in 1969, after which the buildings were taken over by a community of disabled people producing crafts. There is a **craft shop**, and also a **resthouse** (with a restaurant) where you can stay the night very inexpensively.

There are several other small, uninhabited islands on the lake, where you can camp for free. Again, organize this through the Visitours or Skyblue hotels. It involves renting a canoe and taking all your kit with you, including food.

Other trips from Kabale include a visit to the **Kicumba Swamp** and **hot springs** (where you can swim), about eight kilometres (five miles) **south** of the town

Above: What many visitors to Uganda hope to see: an endangered mountain gorilla.

towards the Rwanda border; the **Kisizi Falls**, a 15-metre (50-foot) waterfall on the **Kyabamba River** near **Kisizi** village. The falls, now a source of hydroelectric power for the nearby Church of Uganda Hospital, were once used to punish unmarried women who became pregnant — by binding their hands and feet and hurling them over the edge.

If you don't have your own transport you can get one of the many *matatus* that make the two-hour run **north** to Kisizi from Kabale approximately every hour.

Kisoro

From Kabale, it is about 66 kilometres (41 miles) via a **gravel road** that first heads **north** and then **south** at the village of **Ikumba**, to **Kisoro**. The road offers spectacular **views** of the peaks of the Virunga mountain range, and takes you past the tip of Lake Bunyonyi.

There isn't much to see or do in Kisoro, an overgrown village (which in 1996 had large numbers of Rwandan refugees), except to wait to see the gorillas. And wait you may. Groups are limited to six, with one group visit a day. Remember, too, that only one gorilla group has been habituated (accustomed to visitors) in Mgahinga Gorilla National Park, and it frequently crosses the border into neighbouring Zaire and cannot be followed. Viewing possibilities are determined on a day-to-day basis.

If you feel like exploring while waiting in Kisoro, you can pay a visit to **lakes Mutanda** and **Muhele** a few kilometres north of town. The **turnoff** is about two kilometres (1.2 miles) out of town on the Kabale road.

Getting to the gorillas

It is best to make reservations to track the gorillas in advance at the Uganda National Park headquarters in Kampala or through a reputable safari company in Kampala or Nairobi, which will handle everything. The National Parks headquarters also give up-to-date information on tracking permit availability, current fees, and other park activities. The gorilla-viewing situation is constantly changing, so the best rule is to check before you go.

In 1996 gorilla tracking cost US$ 120 for non-residents and US$ 90 for foreign residents, while park entry fees were US$ 23 for non-residents and Ush 17,300 for foreign residents. Uganda citizens pay less.

When you reach Kisoro, check in at the Mgahinga Gorilla National Park **booking office** on the **main road** in the centre of town before 1700 on the day before you are due to track the gorillas. Double check that the gorilla group is indeed in the park, confirm your booking, and receive your permit. This is also where to make enquiries about seeing the gorillas, arrange transport to take you there, and pay your fees (if you haven't done so already).

You have to arrive at the **park headquarters** at **Ntebeko Camp** at the foot of the mountain before 0830 the following morning. It is a three-hour hike or a one-hour drive in a four-wheel-drive vehicle to this camp. To get there from Kisoro, turn **left** at the **Travellers Rest Inn** and drive (or walk) 13 kilometres (eight miles) along a very **rough road**, which ends at the camp.

Once there, be prepared for some strenuous walking and scrambling through thick undergrowth. You must be in good physical shape. To protect the gorillas from diseases, children under 15 and people who are ill are not allowed entry. Follow your guide's instructions closely: these animals are capable of killing people.

There are only about 600 mountain gorillas in the world, of which almost half live in the Virunga Conservation Area and the other half in Uganda's Bwindi Impenetrable National Park, about 25 kilometres (15 miles) north of Mgahinga. It is estimated that around 45 gorillas use Mgahinga, but the home ranges of all extend into Rwanda and Zaire, which is why you cannot be guaranteed a sighting at Mgahinga (see Uganda's Mountain Gorillas, Part Four).

If you're taking photographs, remember that no flash is allowed, the gorillas are black, and their habitat is dark. You need 800 or 1600 ASA film for any worthwhile pictures — and don't expect to buy this film in Uganda. Bring it with you.

Many people don't realize it, but there is much more to do in Mgahinga than just view gorillas. So if you miss out on tracking permits, explore other options.

The park supports uniquely adapted plant and animal species, many with a high level of endemism. Mammals recorded — besides the endangered mountain gorilla — include the rare **golden monkey** (whose range is also limited to Uganda, Rwanda, and Zaire), **buffalo, elephant, black-fronted duiker, bushbuck, leopard, giant forest hog, side-striped jackal, Egyptian mongoose, serval cat, golden cat**, and **spotted hyena**.

More than 185 species of **birds** have been recorded in the area as well, including 12 species endemic to the region. These include the **handsome francolin**, the **Ruwenzori turaco** and the **stripe-breasted tit**.

There are a number of exciting **hikes** to take in the park, which showcase Mgahinga's dramatic views, lush vegetation, and interesting wildlife. Visitors may, for example, attempt challenging full-day **climbs** to the tops of **Mount Muhabura** and **Mount Gahinga**, whose summits afford great **views** of Uganda, Rwanda, and Zaire. You'll see lots of unique **alpine vegetation** there, as well as a small **volcanic lake**, hidden away at the top of Muhabura. At Gahinga's summit, a small **wetland** is frequented by **purple-breasted sunbirds, duikers**, and **bushbucks**.

For safety reasons, climbing nearby **Mount Sabyinyo** is not recommended, but you can hike through the beautiful and dramatic **Sabyinyo Gorge**. Steep, lush, tropical slopes surround you on both sides as you climb toward a lovely **waterfall** at the head of the gorge. There you might see **golden monkeys, turacos, sunbirds**, and many other tropical species.

Group size for these hikes is limited to 12, with only one group a day. Children under nine are not allowed to climb the mountains, and there is no overnight camping.

Above: Though seen only rarely, leopard are present in Mgahinga.
Overleaf: Large male mountain gorillas. Mature males are known as 'silverbacks'.

Another outing can be arranged to **Garama Cave**, where humans once sheltered during the late Iron Age. The cave, rumoured to cut through to Rwanda, is about two kilometres (1.2 miles) from Ntebeko Camp. The visit lasts about two to three hours and does not require any special hiking or climbing skills. Bring a torch: cave exploration goes as deep as 300 metres (about 330 yards), and it is dark. Group size is six, with two groups a day.

Mgahinga Gorilla National Park also features a 13-kilometre (8-mile) **nature trail**, providing the opportunity to learn about the ecology and wildlife of this special park. During this walk, you may see **golden monkey, duikers**, and **bushbucks**. Group size is six, with two groups a day.

Another rewarding walk to the **Rugezi Swamp** is particularly good in the early morning or late afternoon. **Elephant, giant forest hog, golden monkey, duiker**, and many species of **birds** are often seen on this excursion.

The trek up Muhabura begins at a special departure point from 0700 to 0815. All other activities begin from Ntebeko Camp at 0815. Both the nature trail walk and the Garama Cave visit also have afternoon trips, which depart at 1300.

You must make bookings and pay for these activities at the Kisoro booking office before heading out to the park, and you must carry proof of payment to the park headquarters at Ntebeko Camp, or you'll be sent back.

For trekking to see the gorillas, or going on any of the organized hikes, good hiking boots or gumboots (Wellingtons), good rainwear, and warm clothing (it is best to layer) are recommended. Long trousers and long-sleeved shirts protect against nettles.

If you're camping, make sure to carry your own tent and food — and a small paraffin stove for cooking.

93

Bwindi Impenetrable National Park

Close to Mgahinga National Park is Bwindi Impenetrable National Park, where you may have an even better chance at seeing the rare mountain gorilla, as two groups are habituated there. As its name — 'impenetrable' — implies, this park is not quite as accessible as Mgahinga, but it is well worth the effort of going there.

Like Mgahinga, Bwindi, which was gazetted in 1991, is one of the country's newest national parks. It covers 331 square kilometres (128 square miles) — the third largest forested park in Uganda — and lies on the Zaire border, adjacent to the Parc National des Virungas of Zaire. Situated on the edge of the western Rift Valley on the highest block of the Rukiga Highlands, it is one of the largest natural forests in East Africa containing both montane and lowland forest vegetation. The species diversity is quite high and the park supports a large number of plants and animals endemic to the region.

Bwindi ranges in altitude between 1,160 and 2,607 metres (3,805 and 8,553 feet). The highlands on which the park sits consist of old (Precambrian) rock, much eroded and altered. Like Mgahinga, much of the vegetation is typical tropical rainforest, with a very dense, thick undergrowth — hence the name 'impenetrable'. Make no mistake about it — tracking gorillas in this area is strenuous work.

An interesting feature of Bwindi is Mubwindi Swamp, which covers an area of about two square kilometres (nearly one square mile). The park also has an extensive stand of bamboo that covers about six square kilometres (2.3 square miles): a rare and beautiful habitat found nowhere else in the park.

Bwindi's 120-plus species of mammals make it one of the richest ecosystems in Africa. Primates are particularly abundant and include the mountain gorilla, chimpanzee, blue monkey, red-tailed monkey, L'Hoest's monkey, black-and-white colobus, baboon, potto, Demidoff's galago and needle-clawed galago.

Elephants are also found there, although they now number fewer than 20 as a result of heavy poaching. They can be found in the south-east of the park around the bamboo zone and the Mubwindi Swamp.

Other mammals present include the bushpig, giant forest hog, black-fronted duiker, clawless otter, golden cat, side-striped jackal, civet, genet, and many species of bats and rodents.

Bird-lovers will take delight in the fact that some 346 species are found there, of which 184 are typical forest species. Seven species are on the endangered list.

In addition, Bwindi is home to more than 14 species of snakes, 27 species of frogs and toad, six chameleons, and 14 lizards, skinks and geckos. You're also bound to notice the incredible variety of butterflies in the park: more than 202 species have been identified so far.

If you're more into flora than fauna, you'll be interested to note that there are more than 163 species of trees in Bwindi — 10 of which occur nowhere else in Uganda and 16 of which show a very limited distribution elsewhere in Uganda.

Two major ethnic groups live on the land surrounding the park: the Bakiga and the Bafumbira, both agriculturalists. The park is under considerable human pressure, as the population in this area is on the increase at the rate of about 5.2 per cent each year. Bwindi is undertaking extensive joint programmes with neighbouring communities to try to ease this 'people pressure' on park resources.

Getting there
Buhoma, from where the gorilla viewing is conducted, is 120 kilometres (75 miles) from Kabale (through Bulema and Butogota), 550 kilometres (342 miles) from Kampala, 267 kilometres (166 miles) from Mbarara, and 418 kilometres (260 miles) from Fort Portal (via Kabale). It is served

Opposite: National park trackers search for gorillas in Bwindi Impenetrable National Park.

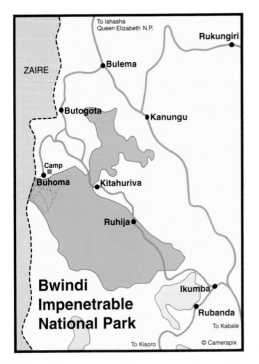

by road — tarmac from Kampala or Fort Portal to Kabale, and then a dirt track from there on.

When to go
Like Mgahinga, Bwindi is a rainforest and thus is wet all year round, although of course the rains increase during the seasons of April–May and October–November. But go when you get tracking permits. As in the case of Mgahinga,´ these are strictly limited.

Where to stay
At Buhoma visitors can stay in simple bandas or camp using their own tents in a community-run campsite. Bandas come with bedding but not much else. Carry your own food, which the camp staff can help prepare, or you can eat at the basic canteen across the road from the camp. Book accommodation there at the Uganda National Parks headquarters in Kampala in advance.

In addition, African Pearl Safaris has a mid-range lodge in Buhoma, and both Mantana Safaris and Abercrombie and Kent run luxury tented camps nearby.

In nearby Butogota, 17 kilometres (10.5 miles) from Buhoma, you could stay at the Travellers Inn, which has basic rooms. Otherwise, you can overnight in Kabale (120 kilometres — 75 miles — away) at the White Horse Inn, Highland Hotel, Victoria Inn, Skyblue Hotel, or Visitours Hotel. See Listings.

Sightseeing
From Kabale, head **north** to where the road forks. The left fork leads to the village of Ikumba (and, later, Kisoro). Take the **right fork** instead and continue **northwards**. After a short distance another road forks right, leading to Kisizi — don't take that. Keep **left** instead, for another 20 kilometres (12 miles) or so, to the village of **Kanungu**. Continue through Kanungu (avoiding the road that turns off to the right, leading to Rukungiri) to **Bulema**, roughly 17 kilometres (10.5 miles) further on.

Turn **left** in Bulema, where the road heads **south** again, to the town of **Butogota**. From Butogota, follow the road **south** as it twists and turns to **Buhoma**, where the **park headquarters** is located.

From Kabale to Buhoma, the drive takes about three hours and may require a four-wheel-drive vehicle.

If you have your own four-wheel-drive vehicle, you may want to consider going to Buhoma via another route from Kabale, which crosses the rugged centre of Bwindi Impenetrable National Park through Ruhija. This will allow you some incredible vistas of deep, undisturbed forest. You can also stop in Ruhija and take the three-hour hike from there to the Mubwindi Swamp.

To take this alternative route, head **north** from Kabale, and take the first **left** fork to **Ikumba** village. There, turn **right** into the national park itself. There is only one road through **Ruhija** and **Kitahuriva**. After Kitahuriva, always keep **left** to get to **Buhoma**, where the road ends. If you turn right at any point, you'll be heading for Butogota. The route cuts off a few kilometres from Kabale to Buhoma, but will probably take you just as long as the going will be. slower — but infinitely more interesting.

If you don't have your own transport,

Above: True African rainforest abounds in Bwindi Impenetrable National Park.

you can hire a vehicle in Kabale, or take a pick-up truck taxi to Butogota. By far the better option is to use the services of one of the reputable safari companies in Kampala or Nairobi. See Listings.

Gorillas and more

Mountain gorilla viewing is the major attraction in Bwindi. There are two groups: Mubare, with 14 animals, and Katendegyere, with six animals. Only the Mubare group is fully habituated, and a maximum of six visitors a day is allowed. For the Katendegyere group, four tourists are allowed to book in advance, with two slots available on a standby basis from Buhoma. Book to see the gorillas at the Uganda National Parks headquarters in Kampala. It is best to book at least three months (but no more than one year) in advance to ensure that requested dates are available. Prices for tracking permits and park entrance fees in early 1996 were the same as for Mgahinga, but please check with the National Parks headquarters for current rates.

Remember, that the gorilla situation changes continuously. There have been many reports of tracking permit bottlenecks confusing the booking system. The best rule of thumb is to book well in advance, and, if you can, use a reputable safari company — preferably one that specializes in gorilla tours — to handle the red tape.

Visits are strictly controlled to ensure the sustainability of the programme. You must strictly adhere to the rules explained to you prior to gorilla tracking to prevent behavioural disturbances and transmission of diseases from human beings to gorillas. Remember, Uganda is understandably concerned that these creatures are not unduly disturbed or harmed (see Uganda's Mountain Gorillas, Part Four).

Hiking

As in Mgahinga, there are other things to see in Buhoma besides gorillas. There are a number of **hiking trails** in the park, but visitors must arrange a day in advance for a guide to accompany them.

Three trails begin in Buhoma, including

Above: Rangers brief a gorilla tracking group on important rules before they set off.
Opposite: Spotting a gorilla family like this one makes the difficult trekking well worthwhile.

the **Munyaga River Trail** — an ideal short walk for visitors with little time to spare.

Alternatively, try the **Waterfall Trail**, which follows the **Munyaga River** upstream as it tumbles down the steep slopes south-east of Buhoma, flowing through a series of **waterfalls** before entering the camp area.

The **Rushuura Trail** will afford you some fantastic **views** across the western Rift Valley floor, with Zaire's **Parc National des Virungas** providing a particularly spectacular backdrop. On rare clear days, **Lake Edward** and the **Ruwenzori Mountains** are visible.

New trails are always being developed. Ask about them when you get to Buhoma.

Buhoma is an ideal place from which to watch **primates** and **birds**. You'll see many **monkeys** along the roads, around the periphery of the park, and at the forest edge. **Chimpanzees**, although difficult to see, inhabit the forest adjacent to the camp and are frequently heard. This is also the richest site for birds in the park, with some 190 species on record.

Of particular interest are the **Kiva ground thrush, white-bellied robin chat, red-throated alethe, collared apalis, short-tailed warbler, yellow-eyed black flycatcher, Rwenzori batis, blue-headed sunbird, strange weaver**, and **Shelley's crimsonwing**.

The **Mubwindi Swamp** in the centre of the park is a three-hour hike from **Ruhija**. The scenic walk passes through a beautiful forest and affords fine **views** of the **Virunga volcanoes**. Keep an eye open for the **Grauer's swamp warbler**, as well as a wealth of other birds.

From Bwindi, you can continue on north to Queen Elizabeth National Park (see The Mountains of the Moon, Part Two) or head back through Kabale on the main tarmac road to Kampala.

The West: Mountains of the Moon

Along with the south-west of the country and its mountain gorillas, the west is one of the most visited regions of Uganda. As their backdrop, lush tea estates and rolling hills have the majestic, snow-capped Mountains of the Moon. The area is also thickly forested and contains three beautiful lakes — Albert, George, and Edward (named after British royalty) — as well as several forest and game reserves and four national parks, comprising one of the oldest, Queen Elizabeth, and three of the newest: Kibale, Semuliki, and Ruwenzori Mountains.

There is often some confusion over the names in this area so make sure you carry an up-to-date map. During Idi Amin's regime, Queen Elizabeth National Park was given the name 'Ruwenzori National Park', but it reverted to its original name in 1991 when the higher slopes of the Ruwenzoris were gazetted under the name of 'Ruwenzori Mountains National Park'.

The two main towns in this region are Fort Portal, which can easily be reached by road from Kampala, and Kasese, about 74 kilometres (46 miles) south of Fort Portal, which can also be reached by road, as well as by the railway from Kampala. Both towns are at the foot of the Ruwenzoris, in beautiful, fertile countryside.

Fort Portal

Considered by many to be one of Uganda's most attractive towns, Fort Portal has been a centre of activity for many years. It is, in effect, the capital of the Toro kingdom, which was set up in the early 1800s by a rebel Banyoro prince named Kaboyo.

The Banyoro leader, Kabalega, recaptured Toro in 1876, but the British expelled Kabalega from his capital in 1891 and installed a new Toro king — Kasagama — in Fort Portal. Although the kingdom was done away with by Obote in 1966, it was reinstated in July 1993 by Museveni.

The fort in Fort Portal is now the site of the town's golf club. Built in the late 1800s, its purpose is presumed to have been to protect Kasagama from Kabalega's attacks. The fort was named after Sir Gerald Portal, the British consul general of Zanzibar, who went to Uganda in 1892 to formalize the protectorate of Uganda. He died of malaria a few months after the fort was completed.

Fort Portal makes a perfect base from which to explore the surrounding area, including Semuliki National Park, Kibale National Park, the Toro Game Reserve, and Lake Albert.

Getting there

Fort Portal is 322 kilometres (200 miles) from Kampala, 74 kilometres (46 miles) from Kasese, and 232 kilometres (144 miles) from Mbarara. It is served by a main road from Kampala, about 150 kilometres (93 miles) of which was rough gravel in 1996 (but under construction to become tarmac), and the rest tarmac. Plan on spending about five to six hours on the road from Kampala. The nearest airstrip is at Kasese to the south.

When to go

The town is fine to visit at any time of the year. The gravel road is an all-weather road, so you should have no difficulty driving on it, even during the rains.

Where to stay

Eight kilometres (5 miles) before Fort Portal, on the Kampala road stands the Ruwenzori Tea Hotel, an old colonial building with landscaped gardens and breathtaking views. In Fort Portal are the Mountains of the Moon Hotel, the Wooden Hotel, and — for the more budget-conscious — the Christian Guest House. See Listings.

Sightseeing

In Kampala, from the **roundabout** near the **bus and taxi parks** and **Nakivubo Stadium**, drive **west** on **Namirembe Road** for about one-and-a-half kilometres (one

Above: Tea pluckers harvest the crop on a lush plantation in western Uganda.

mile) until the junction with **Natete Road**. Turn **left** and head out of town on Natete Road. After a few kilometres there is a **right turn** on a tarmac road to **Mubende**.

Follow this for about 70 kilometres (43 miles) to the prosperous-looking town of **Mityana**. This marks the beginning of the large **tea-growing areas** in the country. Near Mityana town is a region known as **Namutamba**, a small tea-growing area where, in the 1950s, a British missionary named Wilson established a large tea estate and unified the area with 'born-again' Christianity. Many prominent Ugandan families had their homes in Namutamba.

There is an attractive **lake** another eight kilometres (five miles) further along the road near the village of **Naama**, from which it's about a 20-minute walk to the shores of **Lake Wamala**. If you want to explore the large **island** on the lake, hire one of a number of dugout canoes along the shore to row you across.

Archaeological sites

From Mityana, you pass through several small villages on the 92-kilometre (57-mile) drive to the town of **Mubende**. Although pretty, there's not much to see in the town itself, but several interesting **archaeological sites** nearby are worth visiting.

A **dirt road** takes you to **Mubende Hill**, where excavations have led archaeologists to believe that it was occupied about 500 years ago. Oral history connects Mubende Hill with Ndahura, the founder of the legendary Bachwezi kingdom. Since the kingdom collapsed, the hill has drawn a number of Bachwezi-related cults to its slopes, where the 40-metre (130-foot) **high Nakaima Tree** is found.

The tree, believed to contain Ndahura's spirit and thought to be at least 400 years old, is named after Ndahura's wife, renowned for her mystical powers. The Nakaima Tree has been a site of worship for centuries, and was once guarded by a hereditary line of priestesses (also called *nakaima*) of the Basazima clan. The last of these died in 1907, and her regalia is now on display in the National Museum in Kampala — as are two large pots that were unearthed near the tree, apparently once used in religious rituals.

Above: Fort Portal remains a charming, colonial-looking outpost at the foot of the Ruwenzoris.

To visit a couple of other Bachwezi-related sites in the area, head **north** on a **dirt road** from Mubende to the village of **Kakumiro**, about a 35-kilometre (22-mile) drive. The **Munsa Earthworks**, which surround three large interconnected **rock shelters**, is about five kilometres (three miles) from the village, as is an **ancient shrine** reached by stone stairs in a **cave** in **Semwana Hill**. The rock shelters were thought to have been able to hold up to 100 people and are traditionally linked to Kateboha, a Bachwezi prince.

If you're inclined to spend the night in Mubende, about the only place is the Nakaima Hotel.

Continue **west** along the **main road** out of Mubende, which now turns to rough gravel. In mid-1996, this gravel stretch of road to Fort Portal was 'under construction' as a tarmac road. It passes through the small town of **Kyegegwa** (where there is a cheap, pleasant 'cottage' run by the local government, if you wish to stay), **Kakabara**, and **Matiri** before reaching the town of **Kyenjojo**, 112 kilometres (69.5 miles) from Mubende. A right turn there

leads north to Hoima and eventually Murchison Falls National Park.

From Kyenjojo, it is a 49-kilometre (30-mile) drive along a scenic stretch of road that passes through some magnificent forested areas and, later, impressive **tea plantations**, in the midst of which the aptly named **Ruwenzori Tea Hotel** is located, to Fort Portal.

Near Fort Portal, the road follows the course of the **Mpanga River**. When the road ends at a **T-junction**, **turn left** to the centre of town; **right** for the **Mountains of the Moon Hotel** and points north.

A large, circular 'shell' on top of a hill above the town is the **omukama's palace**, built in the 1960s for Toro king Kasagama's son and his successor, Rukidi III. It was destroyed and looted after Obote abolished the old kingdoms, but, with the recent revival of the kingdom of Toro, the rehabilitation of the palace is under way and progressing well.

In the middle of town, on the **east** side of the **main road**, **Kabarole Tours**, a local tour agency, arranges trips to just about anywhere in the vicinity: the Semuliki

Above: Although reduced to ruins, the omukama's palace is now slowly being rehabilitated.

Valley, Kibale National Park, Queen Elizabeth National Park, the Nyakasura Caves, a nearby tea factory, the Toro Game Reserve, a local fishing village, and even a trek across the lower levels of the Ruwenzoris. It is worth paying them a visit if you haven't pre-arranged any trips.

Semuliki National Park

Gazetted only in 1993, Semuliki National Park lies in the Semuliki Valley north-west of Fort Portal — about a two- to three-hour drive along rough roads. Formerly a forest reserve, the 220-square-kilometre (85-square-mile) park is virtually untouched by tourism or development of any sort (although there are plans to develop some sort of tourist accommodation in the Semuliki region soon). It is a great place to spend a few days just relaxing and exploring.

The park shares its unique ecosystem with the Ituri Forest, across the Semuliki River in Zaire. Some researchers say that this area has the most diverse wildlife in East Africa.

Semuliki is the only park in the country primarily made up of tropical lowland forest, which is characterized by a more diverse vegetation than found in other typical tropical forests. It is wetter, and the vegetation is more dense. Anticipate rain during your visit: there is no real 'dry season'.

Local people are the Bamba and Bakonjo ethnic groups, mainly coffee and cocoa growers. There are also about 150 Batwa, traditional forest dwellers who moved out of the forest when it was established as a national park. They continue to gather medicinal plants from within, however. You can experience a good taste of local life by visiting one of the nearby markets, which operate one or two days a week.

Getting there

Sempaya, where the road first meets the park boundary, is roughly 41 kilometres (25 miles) from Fort Portal and thus about 363 kilometres (225 miles) from Kampala. Ntandi, where the park headquarters is located, is a few kilometres further along the same road. Remember, the road is rough and the going slow — but many consider this to be one of

Semuliki National Park

ZAIRE

Hot Springs Office
Sempaya ■
To Fort Portal Kampala.

Park HQ Ntandi ■

● Bundibugyo

To Ngite Falls.

© Camerapix

the most spectacular and scenic drives in East Africa, because of its wonderful views.

When to go
Be prepared for wet weather most of the year. If you're interested in hiking in the area, this is best during the dry season from June through July and December through February. No matter when you go, carry hiking boots and raingear.

Where to stay
It is best to stay the night in Fort Portal and start off for Semuliki National Park the following morning. In Bundibugyo, just south of the park boundary, you can stay at the Union Guest House. There is also a campsite inside the park at the Ntandi head-quarters. Go fully prepared and carry a tent, cooking utensils, and food. The park pro-vides charcoal for cooking and water. In Sempaya, adjacent to the park hot springs office, there is another campsite, run by a pri-vate organization.

Sightseeing
From Fort Portal, head **north-east** out of town on **Lugard Road**, past the **market** and the **post office**, and then **turn left** into **Saka Road**, opposite the **golf course**. Only

eight kilometres (five miles) from town you come to **Lake Saka**, a lovely crater lake. It's safe to **swim**, and there is good **fishing**. If you continue along Saka Road, it curves **west** and eventually joins up with the road that heads towards **Bundibugyo**.

For Semuliki National Park, head **west** out of Fort Portal on **Bwamba Road**, towards Bundibugyo. A four-wheel-drive vehicle is recommended — or at least a vehicle with high clearance. After about 41 kilometres (25 miles), you come to the park's **Hot Springs Office** at **Sempaya**, where the road first meets the Semuliki National Park boundary.

The area represents one of the specialized micro-habitats of the park. The **Sempaya hot springs**, at a temperature of about 106°C (223°F), were created by the same thrust fault responsible for the formation of the nearby Ruwenzori Mountains. There are a number of smaller hot springs, as well as two large ones — one of which has an opening about eight metres (26 feet) wide. The water and the surrounding land are rich in salt and sulphur, which attracts an unusually large population of **shorebirds**. Many of them feed on a strange type of fish — similar to a lungfish — that lives in the mud around the springs. Expect to see **sacred ibis**, in particu-lar. Animals also frequent the hot springs because the area is a natural salt lick.

A short **nature trail** loops around the hot springs from the park hot springs office at Sempaya, and guides are optional. Allow about one or two hours for this hike.

A **trail** is also being cleared from Sempaya to the main park headquarters in **Ntandi**, although at present many visitors take the pleasant hike along the main road, which takes about an hour and passes the beautiful **Mungilo Falls**.

Another, more adventurous, hike from Sempaya leads along the park boundary **north** to the **Semuliki River** and the Zaire border. Take a guide, and expect to have to clear some bush along the way. Many hikers on this route take a tent and food, and camp overnight along the river. It takes about three hours each way from Sempaya to the river.

The Semuliki River provides another of

Above: The hot springs in Semuliki represent one of the park's several micro-habitats..

the park's micro-habitats, with **vervet monkeys** playing along the river banks and larger animals coming to drink. Keep an eye open for **hippos** and **crocodiles**.

Hiking through the park takes you through a variety of habitats, including clearings of grassland; bits of swamp; isolated stands of oil palm, acacia, or ironwood; and glimpses of bamboo swamp.

Animals you see as you hike may include **elephant, buffalo, leopard, civet, scaly-tailed flying squirrel, hippo**, and **crocodile** — as well as eight different species of primates. These include the **bush-baby, black-and-white colobus, red-tailed monkey, baboon,** and **vervet monkey**.

The park is also home to some 400 species of **birds** and 300 different species of **butterflies**. Remember to keep your eyes open and your camera ready as you hike: the dense forest cover makes it easy for the wildlife to hide.

If you enjoy getting off the regular tourist circuit, plan on spending three or four days camping. It will be well worth it. **Nature walks** with guides are easily arranged, as are multiple-day **camping**

trips. It takes about six days for a circuit of the entire park. If you have your own vehicle, consider taking a day trip to the foot of the **Ruwenzoris** and the two spectacular **Ngite Falls** just below the boundary of Ruwenzori Mountains National Park (about a two-hour drive from the Semuliki park headquarters past Bundibugyo). Make arrangements for any of these activities with the park headquarters in Ntandi.

In early 1996, non-residents paid Ush 11,500 (about US$ 11) and Uganda citizens or foreign residents Ush 1,200 (about US$ 1) to enter Semuliki National Park. There are separate rates for camping within the park and for ranger guides. Check with the Uganda National Parks headquarters in Kampala for current prices.

Pygmies

A group of **pygmies** who settled near Ntandi some years ago have turned into a major tourist attraction, but most who see them say it was a most depressing and disturbing experience. There is an 'official' charge to visit their village of some

Above: The lush green expanse of the Semuliki Valley, with the Semuliki River carving a path in the distance.

Ush 1,500 (about US$ 1.5) a person, but they will probably insist on charging you three times that. You will also be under pressure to buy junk 'souvenirs'.

No one describes the Ntandi pygmy situation more frankly than author Philip Briggs, who says 'the Ntandi pygmies are basically a bunch of shorter-than-average people who spend the day hanging around their banana-leaf huts, smoking dope, drinking, and waiting for the next bunch of tourists to arrive . . . they are locked into a cycle of dependency which would now be difficult to break, and their situation offers a short, sharp lesson in the potential consquences of irresponsible cultural voyeurism'.

Toro Game Reserve
North of Fort Portal the Uganda–Zaire border runs through the great expanse of **Lake Albert**.

Kabarole Tours in Fort Portal arrange visits to the lake — and to **Ntoroko** fishing village at its southern tip. To drive there yourself, head **north** out of town on the

road to Semuliki National Park, and, after you pass through the small town of **Itojo**, turn **right** (north-east) onto a **dirt road** through the **Toro Game Reserve**, a 555-square-kilometre (214-square-mile) area protecting large tracts of the **Semuliki Forest** and containing grassy lakeshore flats, swamps, steep forested escarpments, and heavily wooded streams.

The varied wildlife there includes **hippopotamus, bohor reedbuck, giant forest hog, Defassa waterbuck, leopard**, and a few **Uganda kob**.

There are also many species of birds, such as the **African hobby, brown harrier eagle, banded harrier eagle, painted snipe, white-naped pigeon, white-thighed hornbill, wattled black hornbill, pied hornbill, yellow-spotted barbet**, and **Hartlaub's marsh widowbird**.

Visitors will find some interesting places to visit to the south-east of Fort Portal as well. Particularly noteworthy is one of Uganda's newest national parks, Kibale, with its profusion of primates, including the chimpanzee and red colobus.

108

Kibale National Park

Although it is contiguous with Queen Elizabeth National Park to the south-west, the 766-square-kilometre (296-square-mile) Kibale National Park is much wetter and contains a unique moist forest habitat with an extremely high diversity of wildlife and flora.

Gazetted in October 1993, Kibale contains what is probably the most accessible of the country's large forests.

The park includes what used to be the Kibale Forest Corridor Game Reserve, established in 1964 to allow additional habitat for the then large herds of wildlife in Queen Elizabeth National Park.

It also served as an important stop on the migratory route to game reserves — and Murchison Falls National Park — further north for the huge herds of elephant that once roamed Uganda's western frontier.

The altitude ranges from 1,590 metres (5,217 feet) in the north to 1,110 metres (3,642 feet) in the south, and to a large degree is responsible for the differing vegetation within the park. It is a medium-altitude, transitional moist evergreen forest, occurring at elevations between montane forest and mixed tropical deciduous forest.

The ethnic groups who live near the park are the Batoro and the Bakiga, many of whom grow cash crops — such as coffee — and eucalyptus trees for timber. Many local groups are also involved in the tourist industry.

Getting there
Kanyanchu, where the park's visitor centre is located, is 35 kilometres (22 miles) south of Fort Portal, 357 kilometres (222 miles) from Kampala, and six kilometres (four miles) north of Bigodi village. It is served by a dirt road from Fort Portal.

When to go
Kibale National Park can be visited at any time of the year, but expect cool nights, particularly during the rainy seasons of April–May and October–November.

Where to stay
Two private campsites are available near Kanyanchu, each equipped with a tent containing twin beds, bedding, and a hurricane lamp. Three general campsites are also available to visitors who bring their own tent. Carry your own food and cooking utensils no matter where you camp. Firewood is available. You must arrive before 1800.

Basic lodging can be found in Nkingo trading centre immediately outside the park boundary to the south, or in Bigodi, which is further south still. In the latter, try the Mucusu guesthouse or the Safari Hotel and Lodge.

Just to the west of the park is the Crater Valley Kibale Resort Beach, where visitors with their own tents can camp in a beautiful setting looking out over a lake. You can also buy snacks and sodas. See Listings.

Sightseeing
From Fort Portal, head **north-east** on **Lugard Road**, turning **right** on **Kamwenge Road** immediately before you cross over the **Mpanga River**. The Kamwenge Road follows the river in an **easterly** direction for a short stretch before it dips sharply **south**. About 35 kilometres (22 miles) from Fort Portal, after crossing through a section of Kibale National Park, you arrive at the **Kanyanchu Visitor Centre**, which is **signposted** on the **left-hand** side of the road.

Camp there if you can: the surrounding forest is alive with the rustlings of unseen animals, raucous bird calls, and, in the evening, a riotous choir of cicadas.

From Kanyanchu, **guided walks** can be arranged along well-marked **tracks** (about a three-kilometre — 1.8-mile — round trip) in search of the many types of **primates** found there, including **chimpanzees**. Led by knowledgeable field staff, who are also actively involved in the ongoing research there, the forest walks leave from Kanyanchu at 0730 and 1530 daily. The walks last two to three hours and are limited to six people a guide.

You may, for example, see a **crowned crane nesting and feeding site**, climb up to a **treehouse viewing platform**, see the

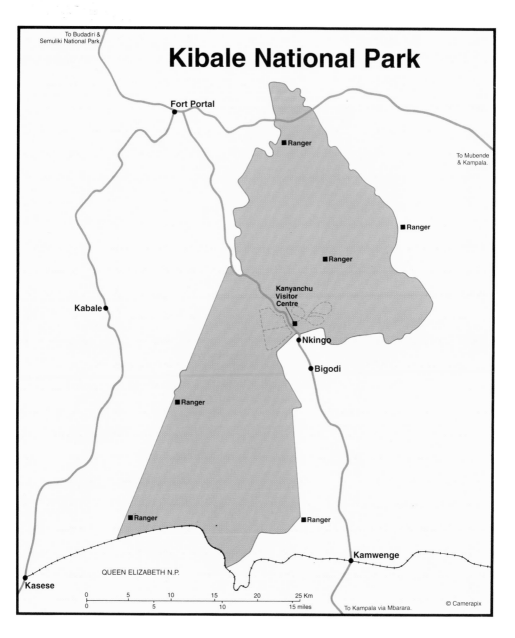

Kibale National Park

To Budadiri &
Semuliki National Park

Fort Portal

To Mubende
& Kampala.

■ Ranger

■ Ranger

■ Ranger

Kanyanchu
Visitor
Centre

Kabale●

●Nkingo

●Bigodi

■ Ranger

■ Ranger

■ Ranger

Kamwenge●

QUEEN ELIZABETH N.P.

●Kasese

| 0 | 5 | 10 | 15 | 20 | 25 Km |
| 0 | | 5 | | 10 | 15 miles |

To Kampala via Mbarara.

© Camerapix

exotic-looking **Dura River screw palms**, or walk along the **Kanyanchu River**. Make sure you carry a pair of good walking shoes, as well as waterproof clothing — and binoculars.

The primates of Kibale have been the object of much research, with the forest supporting the highest number of primates in Uganda — and one of the highest primate densities in the world.

There are 12 species of primate, of which three are nocturnal. **Red colobus monkeys**, as well as **black-and-white colobus**, can be found within the park. The red colobus is a rare species in Uganda, found almost exclusively in Kibale, where it exists at very high density and can usually be seen by visitors on the forest walk from Kanyanchu. Guenons present include **red-tailed, blue**, and **L'Hoest's monkeys**, with the red-tailed most commonly seen in the Kanyanchu area.

Above: Chimpanzees are among the many primates found in Kibale Forest.

L'Hoest's monkeys are normally seen along the main Kibale road. Blue monkeys, although abundant, are rarely seen by tourists, although **mangabey** and **olive baboons** may be observed from time to time.

The most anticipated sighting by visitors to this park, however, is the chimpanzee. Several communities of the fascinating primate have been habituated by researchers and can often be seen — although there is no guarantee.

The park also supports a rich diversity of other wildlife, including **bushbuck, red duiker, blue duiker, bush pig**, and **civet**. **Buffalo** and **giant forest hog** are also present, but rarely seen.

In addition, Kibale now contains the largest population of **forest elephant** in Uganda. These small elephants frequent Kanyanchu for brief periods during the rainy season, but surprisingly are almost never seen — although the telltale signs of their presence are abundant. While walking in the forest, be alert: it is important to avoid these animals, which can be dangerous — particularly if you come upon them unexpectedly.

About 325 species of **birds** are reported in Kibale, a number of which are endemic. In addition, there are more than 144 species of **butterflies** and a large number of **moths** and other **insects**.

The dominant tree species in Kibale include *Parinari, Piptadeniastrum,* and *Cynometra* (ironwood). In valley bottoms, waterlogged soils support swamp forest characterized by lower tree diversity and an abundance of semi-woody plants. Coffee grows wild in the park, as do many medicinal plants.

Hiking

The people who live in the area have become involved in the tourist industry and offer several worthwhile hikes. One of these **guided walks**, led by the **Rwetera Tourism Society**, takes you to the nearby **Bunyuruguru Crater Lake Field** — a chain of some 30 beautiful lakes, each a different shade of blue or green. You can go **boating** on the lakes, the water is safe for **swimming**, and the **birdlife** is prolific. Legend has it that the chain of lakes was created by Ndahura, the first Bachwezi king, when he

Above: Sunset over Kibale Forest.
Opposite: Kibale's chimpanzee population is not easy to see, but it is well worth the effort.

retired to the area after abdicating in favour of his son, Wamara.

Another organization, the **Kibale Association for Rural and Environmental Development**, is involved in conserving the **Magombe Swamp** outside Kibale National Park near Kanyanchu. The group offers guided hikes of the swamp, complete with primate viewing and excellent bird watching. During the walk, which lasts about four hours, keep an eye out for several different species of monkey — **black-and-white colobus, L'Hoest's, red-tailed**, and **blue** — and, as far as birdlife goes, **turacos (Ross's, great blue**, and **black-billed), copper sunbirds, crowned cranes, coucals, kingfishers, finches**, and a myriad of **weavers**.

The fee for the walk — approximately Ush 6,000 (about US$ 6) in 1996 — goes to community development projects such as building schools and bridges, as well as for conservation projects.

The **shop** at the park's Visitor Centre, run by the **Bigodi Women's Group**, sells handicrafts, drinks, snacks and firewood.

In 1996, fees for entering Kibale National Park were US$ 12 for non-residents, Ush 11,500 (about US$ 11) for foreign residents, and Ush 1,200 (just over US$ 1) for Uganda citizens. Campsites and ranger guides cost extra. Check with the Uganda National Parks headquarters in Kampala for current rates and bookings.

Katonga Game Reserve

If you have time, you may want to visit **Katonga Game Reserve**, about 25 kilometres (15 miles) **east** of the national park as the crow flies, and just **north** of the Kampala–Kasese railway. Ask at the Kanyanchu Visitor Centre in Kibale for directions, as no direct roads lead to the reserve.

The **Katonga River** forms the southern boundary of the 208-square-kilometre (80-square-mile) reserve, which is traversed by the river's many tributaries. Because of this plentiful water, flora and fauna are diverse,

113

Above: Whether or not you spy any of Kibale's resident wildlife, hiking in the forest is itself a rewarding experience.

including **waterbuck, bushbuck, bohor reedbuck, buffalo, hippo**, and **warthog** — as well as many bird species.

But to experience and enjoy some of the world's loveliest mountain scenery and plentiful wildlife, return to Fort Portal and head south to the Mountains of the Moon.

Ruwenzori Mountains National Park

It wasn't until 1889 that white people set eyes on the Ruwenzori Mountains, long labelled the 'Mountains of the Moon', which were thought by Roman geographer Ptolemy in AD 150 to be the source of the Nile. Arthur Jephson and Thomas Parke, members of Henry Morton Stanley's cross-continental expedition to rescue the Emin Pasha, were no doubt astounded to behold the snow-covered peaks on the equator. The range was unexplored by Europeans, however, until 1906, when Luigi di Savoia led an expedition to the major peaks.

Everyone from experienced climbers to casual day hikers find the Ruwenzori Mountains National Park a magnificent environment, with its non-volcanic mountains capped with ice and snow, massive ice-rime sculptures, awe-inspiring vegetation, spectacular scenic beauty, and unique fauna. This is truly Rider Haggard's 'Land of Mist': the whole region is perpetually shrouded by mist, making it a somewhat eerie, but still fascinating, destination. The mountains themselves — 120 kilometres (75 miles) long and 48 kilometres (30 miles) wide — were forced up during the creation of the Great Rift Valley. Over time, the eroding forces of rivers and glaciers have carved out — and are still carving out — the wonderful, sculptured land mass seen today.

At the centre of the range are six snow-covered peaks. The highest mountain in the range, Mount Stanley, is the third highest in Africa after Mount Kilimanjaro and Mount Kenya, in neighbouring

Tanzania and Kenya, respectively. Mount Stanley's highest peak, Margherita, rises 5,109 metres (16,762 feet) above sea level. Other high peaks in the range include Alexandria, at 5,083 metres (16,676 feet); Speke, at 4,890 metres (16,043 feet); Emin, at 4,791 metres (15,718 feet); Gessi, at 4,715 metres (15,469 feet); and Luigi di Savoia, at 4,627 metres (15,180 feet).

Interestingly, more people visit the Ruwenzoris to explore and view the fascinating vegetation than to climb the peaks and glaciers. Because of the strange evolutionary pattern, common plants grow to absurd proportions. Lobelias weigh in at 60 kilos (130 lbs), while groundsel plants tower above you and heather shoots up to some 10 metres (33 feet) tall. Equally splendid are the smaller flowers, such as blackberry, cuckoo flower, and the everlastings.

The people on the lower slopes of the Ruwenzori Mountains are the Bakonjo. Strong and energetic, they are well suited to life in the mountains, which are an integral part of their traditional beliefs. Many local men work for the Ruwenzori Mountaineering Services (RMS), which has the exclusive concession to provide guides and porters for tourists in the southern and western areas of the park.

Some 500,000 Ugandans living below the park boundary are dependent on the Ruwenzori watershed for year-round agricultural production. Major crops include coffee, beans, maize, yams, Irish potatoes, bananas, passion fruit, and wheat.

Getting there

Ibanda, the nearest town to the Nyakalengija park headquarters (the starting point for climbing in the mountains), is about 69 kilometres (43 miles) from Fort Portal, 25 kilometres (16 miles) from Kasese, 389 kilometres (242 miles) from Kampala, and about 158 kilometres (98 miles) from Mbarara. It is served by a good tarmac road from both Fort Portal and Kasese, with a dirt road leading to the park headquarters. The nearest large town, Kasese, is also served by rail from Kampala, and public transport is available from Kasese to Ibanda. Kasese also has an airstrip.

When to go

Constant mist covers the mountains all year round. The driest months are usually July and August, and December to February. Visits at any other time may be disappointing.

Where to stay

Along the central hiking circuit, huts are available at convenient stopping points, each accommodating 15 guests. Visitors need to carry enough food for their entire stay as well as simple cooking utensils. Gas stoves or charcoal are available, but it is far better to bring your own paraffin stove.

Accommodation is available in Kasese at the Margherita Hotel, the Saad Hotel and several inexpensive lodges. There is also the Ruwenzori Mountaineering Services Hostel at Nyakalengija (park headquarters), with meals at the Mubuku Valley Restaurant across the road. See Listings.

Sightseeing

Head **south** out of Fort Portal on **Kyembambe Road** towards Kasese. About five kilometres (three miles) out of town, on the **left** side of the road, stand the **Karambi Tombs**, where Toro king Kasagama and his son and successor, Rukidi II, are buried.

There's not much else to see before the Ruwenzori National Park turnoff, but the **scenery** along the way is beautiful, and you pass through several small towns. Some 54 kilometres (34 miles) from Fort Portal, you come to the **turnoff** to **Ibanda** and the Nyakalengija park headquarters on the **right** side of the road. From there, it's another 10 kilometres (six miles) to Ibanda, and then another five kilometres (three miles) through banana and sugar cane plantations to **Nyakalengija**, where the **hiking trails** begin.

A four-wheel-drive vehicle is normally recommended for the last section of road, but two-wheel-drive is usually possible. Vehicles can be left safely at park headquarters. In 1996, park entry charges were US$ 23 for non-residents, Ush 17,250 (about US$ 17) for foreign residents, and Ush 2,300 (about US$ 2) for Uganda citizens. There are extra charges involved

115

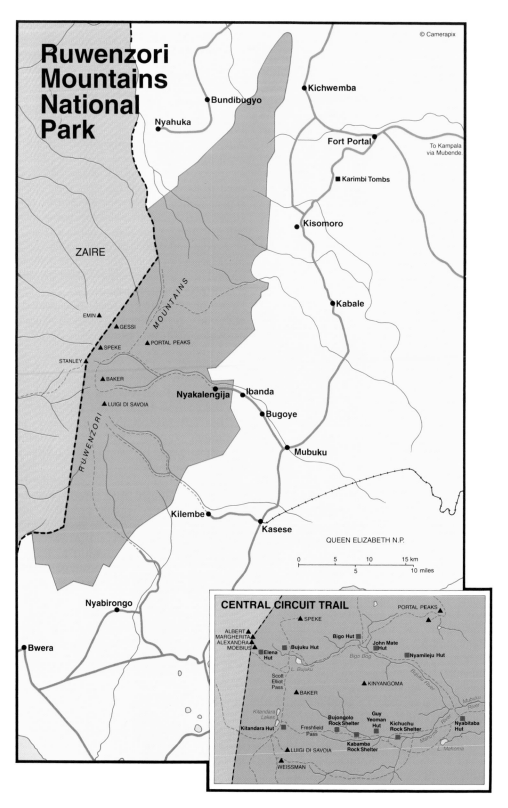

Ruwenzori Mountains National Park

© Camerapix

Kichwemba

Bundibugyo

Nyahuka

Fort Portal

To Kampala
via Mubende

Karimbi Tombs

ZAIRE

Kisomoro

MOUNTAINS

EMIN ▲

▲ GESSI

Kabale

▲ PORTAL PEAKS

SPEKE ▲

STANLEY ▲

▲ BAKER

Nyakalengija   Ibanda

RUWENZORI

▲ LUIGI DI SAVOIA

Bugoye

Mubuku

Kilembe

Kasese

QUEEN ELIZABETH N.P.

0   5   10   15 km

5   10 miles

Nyabirongo

CENTRAL CIRCUIT TRAIL

PORTAL PEAKS

▲ SPEKE

Bwera

ALBERT ▲
MARGHERITA ▲
ALEXANDRA ▲
MOEBIUS

Bigo Hut

John Mate
Hut

Elena
Hut

Bujuku Hut

Bigo Bog

Nyamileju Hut

Bujuku River

Scott
Elliot
Pass

L. Bujuku

▲ KINYANGOMA

Mubuku River

▲ BAKER

Kitandara
Lakes

Bujongolo
Rock Shelter

Guy
Yeoman
Hut

Kichuchu
Rock Shelter

Nyabitaba
Hut

Kitandara Hut

Freshfield
Pass

Mahoma River

▲ LUIGI DI SAVOIA

Kabamba
Rock Shelter

L. Mahoma

▲ WEISSMAN

for camping, guides, and porters, but these vary depending on the length of your stay. Obtain current prices and information from the Uganda National Parks headquarters in Kampala or from the RMS (PO Box 33, tel 0493-4115, Kasese), through whom you can also book trips into the park. The hiring of RMS guides is mandatory, and RMS porters are also considered necessary. It is best to book at least one week in advance if you want to be sure to start a trek on a particular day. Make sure you arrive at Nyakalengija by 1000 on the day you start your trek.

The usual trip to the Ruwenzoris lasts six to seven days, which is just long enough to hike the well-travelled Central Circuit Trail. Shorter trips can also be arranged, but they do not reach the high mountains. It is best to allow a minimum of five days, even for the shorter trips.

No special climbing equipment is necessary unless you attempt one of the summits — although keep in mind that hiking is tough work, usually in poor weather, and should not be undertaken lightly.

It is recommended that you carry food, a paraffin stove, cooking utensils, raingear, a good sleeping bag, warm hat and gloves, heavy socks, woollen clothing, gumboots, sunglasses, sunscreen, a water bottle, a day pack, and a first aid kit. Of course, if a reputable safari company (of which there are several based in Kampala or Nairobi; see Listings) is handling the trip, much of the gear will be provided.

A good map is also essential, even if you have a knowledgeable guide. *Ruwenzori — Map & Guide* by Andrew Wielochowski (1989) is considered by many to be the best. (It's on sale in most Nairobi bookshops for a modest price, otherwise contact the author at 32 Seamill Park Crescent, Worthing BN11 2PN, UK.) The guide carries a large-scale contour map of the mountains, with all the main trails, huts, and camping sites — as well as other features — marked.

Before you attempt a climb or high-altitude hike, make sure you are aware of the dangers and symptoms of mountain, or altitude, sickness, which can be fatal. It usually becomes noticeable above 3,000 metres (about 10,000 feet). Mild symptoms include headaches, mild nausea, and a slight loss of coordination. Severe symptoms include abnormal speech and behaviour, severe nausea and headaches, a marked loss of coordination, and persistant coughing spasms. If you have any of the severe symptoms (if you are in doubt, your guides are trained to recognize these as well), immediately descend to lower altitudes — even if you have to go down in the dark. There is no rhyme or reason as to who gets altitude sickness — fitness, age, and previous high-altitude experience seem to be irrelevant. The only cure is to descend immediately.

Be aware, too, of the dangers of hypothermia. Waterproof everything — and that includes not only matches, but yourself. Hypothermia occurs when the body temperature is lowered, usually caused by a combination of cold and wet. If you've got a mild case, you'll probably just experience uncontrollable shivering; put on some warm, dry clothes and get into a sleeping bag to raise your body temperature. Note that severe symptoms of hypothermia include disorientation, lethargy, mental confusion (you may even feel warm and healthy), and coma. It can be fatal, so look out for its early signs.

The **Central Circuit Trail** is by far the most popular hike or climb. Like the others, it begins at Nyakalengija park headquarters and then takes you to the **Nyabitaba Hut** at 2,651 metres (8,698 feet). It is a fairly easy walk of about four to five hours (10 kilometres — six miles) to this two-roomed hut, which was built in 1987. There is also a good **rock shelter** and a water supply close by.

On the way, you pass through a small **coffee plantation** and a meadow before

Overleaf: Expect stunning scenery and fantastic vegetation around every corner when hiking in the Ruwenzori Mountains.

Above: Porters carry gear along the snowy mountain trail.
Opposite: The Kurt Schafer Bridge on the Circuit Trail in the Ruwenzoris.

hitting the 'bush' and, later, forest. Wear long trousers — the nettles are nasty.

The trout-filled **Mubuku River** is on your **right** towards the start of the journey. You cross a couple of streams and then another river — the **Mahoma** — before climbing the ridge to Nyabitaba. Keep an eye out for some small grass and twig huts about 40 centimetres (16 inches) high in this area, which are **shrines**, usually containing offerings of food, put there by the local Bakonjo before they go hunting or climbing to appease the god Kitasamba, whom they believe lives with his wives amid the peaks of the mountains.

From Nyabitaba, you can tackle the trail in either a clockwise or an anticlockwise direction.

The next day's hike on the anticlockwise circuit is tough, taking a minimum of seven hours before you reach the next night stop, **John Mate Hut**, at 3,505 metres (11,499 feet). The path takes you down through the forest, dropping steeply to the **Mubuku River**, which you cross by the **Kurt Schafer Bridge** (built in 1989).

You then climb steeply up the bank and walk several kilometres through **bamboo**, followed by another arduous ascent, with many rocks on the path. There you begin to enter the moorland zone, and **giant tree heathers** (*Philippia trimera*) are everywhere. **Giant groundsels** (*Senecio admiralis*) also flourish.

A good place to stop for lunch is **Nyamileju Hut**, which is pretty run down, but there is also a **rock shelter** nearby, along with a water supply. **Lichen** and **Spanish moss** ornament the trees around the hut. If the weather is clear, there is a great **view** of mounts Speke and Stanley from the top of the rock.

From Nyamileju it is another two hours or so to John Mate Hut through a **giant heather forest** following the course of the **Bujuku River**. The hut is about 200 metres (220 yards) from the river, from which you can collect water.

An alternative night stop is **Bigo Hut** at 3,445 metres (11,300 feet), another kilometre or so of tough track through a **bog**, which often requires wading through deep mud

Above: The Guy Yeoman Hut on the Central Circuit Trail: one of several possible overnight stops.

or leap from one grassy patch to the next.

From Bigo, the Circuit Trail heads **south-west** but, if you have a guide who knows the way, you can also head north to the Roccati Pass or north-east to the Bukurungu Pass and the little-explored Portal Peaks.

To continue on the Circuit Trail from the John Mate Hut, on the third day you head towards **Bujuku Hut**, at 3,962 metres (12,998 feet). This may take up to five hours, depending on the condition of the **Bigo Bog**, which may be slow going if the mud is deep.

You pass through another **bog** before reaching beautiful **Lake Bujuku**, majestically set against a backdrop of Mount Baker's scree slopes and **affording views** of Mount Speke and Mount Stanley.

There is water 20 metres (20 yards) from Bujuku Hut, which is actually a camp made up of two huts and a **rock shelter**.

If you intend to climb Mount Speke, make this your base, but you have to spend an extra night to do this. To scale the highest point in the Ruwenzoris (Margherita Peak on Mount Stanley), you need to base yourself at Elena Hut, which is about two kilometres (1.2 miles) off the Circuit Trail and a three- to four-hour walk from Bujuku Hut.

From Lake Bujuku, head **south** to **Kitandara** at 4,023 metres (13,198 feet). This takes you to the highest point on the Circuit Trail, **Scott Elliot Pass** at 4,372 metres (14,343 feet). You pass through plenty of **giant groundsel** before you reach boulders and scree and then descend to the two beautiful **Kitandara lakes**.

Kitandara Hut, close to the foot of **Elena Glacier**, is actually two huts, which are pleasantly positioned on the shore of Lake Kitandara, the lower of the two lakes. This idyllic spot is only about a four-hour walk from Lake Bujuku.

The following day you begin your descent to the **east** and head for **Guy Yeoman Hut** at 3,450 metres (11,319 feet). You can also opt to stay the night at the **Kabamba rock shelter**, which you reach first. There is a **bog** between the two.

Plan on about a five-hour hike: first a

Above: The first of two beautiful Kitandara lakes seen from the Central Circuit Trail.

very steep ascent to **Freshfield Pass** and then a drop down to **Bujongolo**, a cliff overhang providing good shelter. Kabamba rock shelter, with its nearby **waterfall**, is a short way past this. After passing through the bog from Kabamba, you come upon the Guy Yeoman Hut, on a ridge above a steep valley.

The next day — which could be your final one on the Circuit Trail — you head down the steep valley (where there is another **rock shelter, Kichuchu**), through **bamboo forests** and **bog**, across the **Mahoma River** (there's no bridge) and two minor **streams**, and through an abundance of tropical **vegetation** before you follow a ridge down to the Nyabitaba Hut.

This part of the journey should take around five hours. From there you can push on for another three hours to the Nyakalengija base.

In addition to the many unusual plants and trees you see on your journey down the Circuit Trail, you also may come upon some of the diverse bird and animal species that make this their home.

Primates and other mammals in the park include the **chimpanzee, Ruwenzori colobus monkey, black-and-white colobus, blue monkeys, elephant, bushbuck, red duiker, yellow-backed duiker, giant forest hog, hyrax** (you'll undoubtedly hear its shrieking call at night), **serval**, and **leopard**. The only ones you're likely to see, however, are the black-and-white colobus and the blue monkey.

Some unique birds are the **Ruwenzori turaco, handsome francolin, olive pigeon**, and **white-necked raven**. About the forest zone, watch for the **alpine swift** and the **scarlet-tufted malachite sunbird**, both of which are restricted to high-altitude habitats in East Africa. Keep a watchful eye out, too, for the weird-looking **three-horned chameleon**, which plays a powerful role in local superstitions. Interesting insects such as **safari ants,** which inflict a bite that is momentarily painful, but otherwise harmless, might also catch your attention.

Above: Trekking in the Ruwenzoris yields superb views of the range's many awesome peaks.

Queen Elizabeth National Park

Established in 1952, Queen Elizabeth National Park is one of Uganda's three oldest national parks, with an area of almost 2,000 square kilometres (770 square miles) of grass savannah, open bush country, riverine forest, lowland rainforest, wetlands, rivers, and lakes. Bordering Lake Edward and Lake George, as well as the Kazinga Channel in the western area of the Great Rift Valley, the park has been designated as a Biosphere Reserve for Humanity under the auspices of UNESCO. Despite some setbacks, it remains one of Uganda's national treasures.

The park has its origins early in the 20th century, after many people fled the area when a wave of sleeping sickness plagued the country. Between 1925 and 1947, these abandoned areas became two game reserves: Lake George and Lake Edward. In 1952, the reserves were merged into Kazinga National Park. Two years later, when Queen Elizabeth of England visited

the park, it was renamed in her honour. During the Idi Amin regime, the park was renamed Ruwenzori National Park, but it regained its original name in 1991, when the Ruwenzori Mountains National Park was gazetted.

One of the richest and best-managed parks in Africa, supporting an astounding density of wildlife, Queen Elizabeth National Park was hard hit by Uganda's wars, when animal populations there and elsewhere in the country were decimated. Now, as peace and stability return to the country, the park is steadily regaining its past grandeur. It remains one of the best places on the continent to see a high concentration of hippos — and often at close quarters, especially when you take the renowned launch trip along the Kazinga Channel.

The park is divided into two sectors: the north, with park headquarters at Mweya, and the south, with its own subheadquarters at Ishasha. Each sector has different ecosystems with their own distinctive attractions.

Unlike Uganda's other national parks,

Queen Elizabeth was created with several enclave villages within its boundaries. These include Katwe, which exists principally to exploit the natural salt production in a highly saline crater lake, and Katunguru, which — along with a few other villages — supports itself mainly through fishing.

Getting there
Mweya, the main park headquarters, is 41 kilometres (25 miles) from Kasese, 115 kilometres (71 miles) from Fort Portal, 144 kilometres (89 miles) from Mbarara, and about 420 kilometres (260 miles) from Kampala (via Masaka and Mbarara). A good tarmac road leads to the main gate turnoff, and from there it's a 20-kilometre (12-mile) drive on a dirt road easily negotiated by two-wheel-drive vehicles. Nearby Kasese is also served by an airstrip and by rail from Kampala. There is also a smaller landing strip near Mweya Safari Lodge for charter aircraft. The drive from Kampala takes about six hours.

When to go
Queen Elizabeth National Park is at its best after the rainy seasons of March–April and October–November. The air is fresh, the grass green, and there is an air of spring-time and renewal.

Where to stay
In Mweya, visitors can choose from the Mweya Safari Lodge, the Uganda Institute of Ecology Hostel, or the Student's Camp. There is also a campsite at Mweya, and another two near the banks of the Kazinga Channel. Campers should travel totally self-sufficient with tent, gear, and, in the case of the campsites near the Kazinga Channel, food and drinks as well. Near Ishasha, in the southern sector of the park, there are basic campsites and some old bandas. Again, carry everything you need.

In nearby Kasese there are the Saad Hotel, the Margherita Hotel, and several less expensive lodges. See Listings.

Sightseeing
From the Ruwenzori National Park turnoff on the main Fort Portal–Kasese road, head south. After 10 kilometres (six miles), you reach Kasese, which is fairly unremarkable but is a good base from which to explore either the Ruwenzori Mountains National Park or Queen Elizabeth National Park. The **Ruwenzori Mountaineering Services** (RMS) maintains offices there. The Margherita Hotel is two kilometres (1.2 miles) out of town on the Kilembe Road to the west and the Saad Hotel is in the town centre.

Kasese escaped the looting and destruction that befell so many other Uganda towns, and remains unblemished. It is the westernmost railhead of Uganda — and was once important to the economy because of the nearby copper mines at Kilembe, which are now closed.

To reach the mines, hire a bicycle from the Saad Hotel and cycle the 11 kilometres (seven miles) or so to the old **copper mine** site. It's a long, gradual uphill climb to get there — but the downhill return is easy. On the way, keep a lookout for a colony of thousands of **fruit bats** along the side of the road.

Once at Kilembe, you can tour the copper mine site and what remains of the surface equipment free of charge, but you are not allowed underground.

From Kasese, drive another 21 kilometres (13 miles) **south** to the **turnoff** to **Mweya** and the north sector of Queen Elizabeth Park, which is to the **west** of the road. From that turnoff, it's another 20 kilometres (12 miles) on a good **dirt road** which is easily negotiated by two-wheel-drive vehicles to Mweya Lodge and **park headquarters**.

Try to arrive or drive in the park before 1930 and after 0630. In 1996, park entry fees were US$ 23 for non-residents, Ush 17,300 (US$ 17) for foreign residents, and Ush 2,300 (about US$ 2) for Uganda citizens. There is also a small daily charge for vehicles.

Much of the park is open savanna dotted with **acacia** and **euphorbia** trees. It is home to a variety of mammals, including **elephant, buffalo, warthog, baboon, lion, leopard, several monkey species, chimpanzee, spotted hyena, Uganda kob**, and **bushbuck**. The

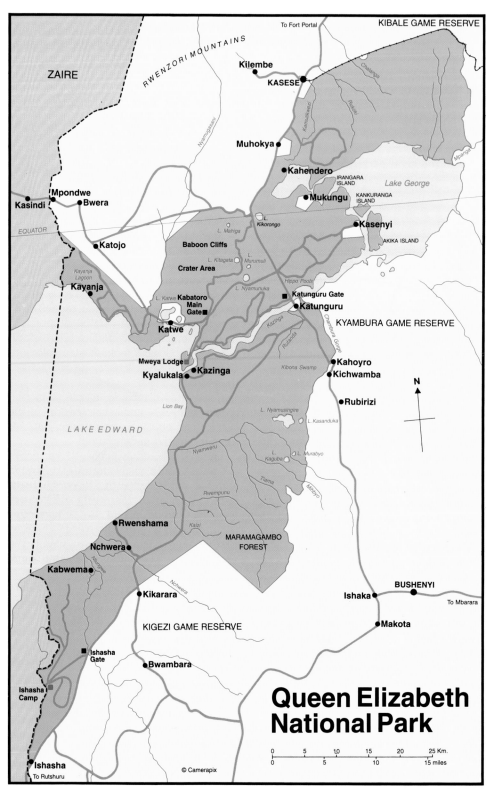

To Fort Portal

KIBALE GAME RESERVE

RWENZORI MOUNTAINS

Kilembe

KASESE

ZAIRE

Muhokya

Kahendero

IRANGARA ISLAND

Lake George

KANKURANGA ISLAND

Mukungu

Mpondwe
Bwera

Kasindi

L. Kikorongo

Kasenyi

EQUATOR

L. Mahiga

AKIKA ISLAND

Katojo

Baboon Cliffs

L. Kitagata   L. Murumuli

Crater Area

Kayanja Lagoon

Kayanja

L. Nyamunuka

Hippo Pools

Katunguru Gate

L. Katwe   Kabatoro Main Gate

Katunguru

Katwe

KYAMBURA GAME RESERVE

Rutanda

Kazinga

Chambura Gorge

Mweya Lodge

Kahoyro

Kyalukala   Kazinga

Kibona Swamp

Kichwamba

Lion Bay

L. Nyamusingire

Rubirizi

L. Kasanduka

N

LAKE EDWARD

Nyamweru

L. Kaguba   L. Murabyo

Tiama

Rwempunu

Minbyo

Rwenshama   Kaizi

Nchwera

MARAMAGAMBO FOREST

Kabwema

Nchwera

BUSHENYI

Kikarara

Ishaka

To Mbarara

KIGEZI GAME RESERVE

Makota

Ishasha Gate

Bwambara

Ishasha Camp

Queen Elizabeth National Park

| 0 | 5 | 10 | 15 | 20 | 25 Km. |
| 0 | | 5 | | 10 | 15 miles |

Ishasha

To Rutshuru

© Camerapix

Above: Mweya Safari Lodge in Queen Elizabeth National Park is spectacularly situated on a peninsula overlooking the Kazinga Channel.

interesting **sitatunga**, a semi-aquatic antelope, is known to live in the papyrus swamps around **Lake George**. More than 550 **bird** species have been recorded, including 50 raptors.

In the **north sector** of the park, the place to stay is the **Mweya Safari Lodge**, one of the most highly rated hotels in Uganda. Surprisingly moderately priced, the hotel is perched on the peninsula overlooking the **Kazinga Channel** and **Lake Edward** and features a bar and good restaurant. On a clear day, you can see across the channel to the glaciers and peaks of the Ruwenzori Mountains — a spectacular sight.

Lake Edward, another of Uganda's large lakes, was 'discovered' in 1889 by Henry Morton Stanley and named after the Prince of Wales, later Edward VII. The Rutshuru River flows into the lake, which covers 4,000 square kilometres (1,500 square miles) and is 80 kilometres (50 miles) long and 50 kilometres (30 miles) wide.

From Mweya, there are a number of well-established **game-viewing circuits**, which allow you to explore in your own

vehicle or in one hired from the park headquarters (at a cost of about US$ 1 a kilometre in 1996).

Hiding in the scrub near Mweya are **bushbuck, Defassa waterbuck, banded mongoose**, and **warthog**, while large herds of the graceful **Uganda kob** — the Uganda National Parks symbol — graze farther along the track. **Elephants** — now staging a comeback after their population was decimated during the Obote and Amin eras — are often seen in small family groups, making their way across the park in their daily search for food and water.

North of the **main gate** is the **crater area**, one of the most scenic parts of the park. Head for **Baboon Cliffs**, which are surrounded by a series of dramatic craters and are home to **buffalo, waterbuck, kob**, and sometimes **lion** and **elephant**.

At **Lake Katwe**, one of the crater lakes in the area, it is possible to see **salt** being **mined** using centuries-old methods.

To the **east** of the **main tarmac road** lie the **wetlands** of **Lake George**, a 'wetland of international importance' protected

Above: One of Uganda's greatest experiences: the launch trip on the Kazinga Channel.

under the Ramsar Convention. Bird watchers will delight in this place, with a large number of species present. You may even see the rare and elusive **shoebill stork**. On the drive out to **Kasenyi** on the shores of Lake George, keep an eye out for **lions** hiding in the tall grass.

Kasenyi, too, is the area where you can find the unique **Uganda kob mating ground:** a defined area specifcally used for challenging, enticing, and mating. Watch for spectacular fights as bucks defend their territories.

One of the major delights of any visit to Queen Elizabeth, however, is the **launch trip** along the **Kazinga Channel** from Mweya. Many who experience it consider it the highlight of their entire African safari. From the relative safety of your boat, you can watch hundreds of **hippos** at close range, observe — from this different point of view — **buffalo**, **waterbuck**, **elephant**, and sometimes even **lion** and **leopard** coming down to drink at the water's edge, and enjoy the tremendous display of **birdlife**.

The many fish in the channel attract a number of waterbirds, such as **pelicans, saddlebill storks, fish eagles, cormorants, skimmers**, and **kingfishers**. Look closely along the shores and you may see prehistoric-looking **monitor lizards** in the grass.

The trip lasts about two hours, and there are three trips each day: at 0800 (the best time to go), 1100, and 1500. Non-resident costs (in 1996), for 10 people or less, are US$ 69 a trip, and for more than 10 people, US$ 7 a person. Foreign residents and Uganda citizens are charged approximately the same prices, but in Uganda shillings. Book at the Mweya park headquarters.

Another unforgettable experience to be enjoyed in the north sector of the park is the **foot safari** through **Chambura Gorge**. As you walk quietly through an enchanting tropical forest along a river, you're likely to see **black-and-white colobus, red-tailed monkeys**, and **chimpanzees**. Walks are limited to four people a day, and advance booking is required.

Visits can be arranged either at Mweya headquarters or via radio from Uganda

Above: Both elephant (top) and hippos are regularly seen features of a launch trip down the famous Kazinga Channel in Queen Elizabeth National Park.
Overleaf: Sunrise over Chambura Gorge.

Above: Foot safaris take visitors into the depths of the Chambura Gorge.

National Parks headquarters in Kampala. Walks depart from Fig Tree Camp every day at 0730 and last from three to five hours. Make sure you have a pair of sturdy walking or hiking shoes.

For those seeking a more individual experience, make your way down to the **south sector** of the park, which has its headquarters at **Ishasha.** The rugged experience of this area is quite a contrast to the relative comforts of Mweya and its surrounding areas but is rewarding in its own way.

The rest camp and game viewing loops are less accessible and more isolated; the topography is basically open grassland with scattered acacia trees — as well as a remarkable **floating fig forest** along the bank of **Lake Albert**.

There are two ways to Ishasha. The first, which would seem the most logical, is not necessarily the easiest. Head **south** on the main Mbarara–Kasese **tarmac road** that cuts through the park. The **turnoff** to Ishasha and the south sector is to the **west** of the road, just south of the Kazinga Channel at **Katunguru**. It is

roughly 100 kilometres (60 miles) of rough road from the turnoff to the **Ishasha rest camp** and is usually impassable in the rainy seasons. Even when conditions are good it takes about four hours to travel from Mweya to Ishasha.

One advantage is that the road traverses the **Maramagambo Forest**, one of the largest in Uganda, and **black-and-white colobus monkeys** and **chimpanzees** are sometimes spotted there. If you have the warden's permission, you can 'visit' (which presumably means 'hike in') the forest around **Lake Nyamusingire**. Check with the Mweya park headquarters about making arrangements.

The other way to the south sector is more promising. Although much longer, it is sometimes passable during the rainy seasons with a four-wheel-drive vehicle or a vehicle with high clearance. To go this route, continue **straight** through **Katunguru** on the **main road** to Mbarara. After about 45 kilometres (28 miles), you come to **Ishaka**, where the main road bends left (east), but you head off

Above: Baboon with baby, one of many species of wildlife that make Queen Elizabeth National Park their home.
Overleaf: The crater area in Queen Elizabeth features many small, sparkling lakes.

straight along a **dirt road** for a short stretch until you come to the small village of **Makota**, where you turn **right**, heading **south-west**. The road leads through the village of **Ruhinda** and then heads directly **south** to the larger village of **Rukungiri**. Turn **right** (west) in Rukungiri on another **dirt road** that eventually leads to a point just north of the town of **Ishasha**, right on the border with Zaire. Turn **right** at the junction, and, after another seven kilometres (four miles) or so, the southern park **entrance gate** is on your **left**.

No matter which route you take, make sure to ask about local conditions before you set off, and find out which route is best at the time you are going.

The Ishasha rest **camp** is near to the entrance gate, and from there you can take a couple of **circuits** to view the wildlife of the area, which includes **hippo**, herds of **buffalo**, many **elephants**, and **topi**. This area is also home to Queen Elizabeth's famous **tree-climbing lions**, which have developed a surprising tendency to lounge in the upper branches of old fig trees — a habit not commonly found in other lion populations. The **Ishasha River Gorge**, technically outside the park and upstream of the camp, is an outstandingly beautiful area. You reach the gorge only on foot from the camp.

To complete your circuit of Uganda's west, get yourself back to **Ishaka.** You may wish to make a slight detour to the **Kitagata Hot Springs**, which many people visit in the hope of being cured of such ailments as arthritis and rheumatism. To get there from Ishaka, head **south** on a **dirt road** for about 17 kilometres (10 miles) to the village of **Kitagata**, where the hot springs are.

To return to Kampala from Ishaka, head east on the **main tarmac road** through **Bushenyi** to **Mbarara**, and from there turn **left** on the **main road** to **Masaka** and on to Kampala (see The South-west: Gorilla Country).

The Lush North-west

Less popular than Uganda's west and south-west, the north-west is nevertheless a beautiful and lush region, containing the many wonders of Murchison Falls National Park.

This area — particularly north of the Nile River which bisects the park — has suffered from rebel activities, continuing even up to mid-1996. The government has stationed many troops throughout the north to quash insurgency. However ask about conditions before travelling to Murchison, and always carry your passport in case of road checks.

One route to this part of the country circles the sprawling expanse of the wandering, large Lake Kyoga, heading north out of Kampala before eventually returning to the capital via Mbale and Jinja. However, many expatriates in Kampala visiting Murchison for the weekend simply head straight up and back using the same route — about a four-hour drive in each direction on decent roads.

Murchison Falls National Park

This beautiful park owes its existence to a serious outbreak of sleeping sickness that decimated Uganda's human population between 1898 and 1915. As the only effective way known to combat this disease was to evacuate the region, between 1907 and 1912 a huge area — some 13,000 square kilometres (5,000 square miles) — was depopulated. Murchison Falls National Park was gazetted in July 1952, a few months after the National Parks Act was passed.

The spectacular, 3,840-square-kilometre (1,483-square-mile) park — the country's largest — is renowned for its scenic beauty and abundant flora and fauna, although it suffered considerably during the late 1970s and early 1980s, which had a disastrous impact on its once-abundant game. However, the park is well on its way to

recovery, with animal populations consistently growing, and Murchison Falls may soon regain its reputation as one of Africa's favourite destinations.

Take note that the park was briefly renamed Kabalega Falls National Park, and remains as such on some maps.

No matter by which name it is known, the park offers some of the wildest and most pristine scenery in Africa. Lush plains are scattered with palms, rich forest, and growing herds of animals.

And, of course, there are the magnificent Murchison Falls, where the mighty 50-metre-wide (160-foot) Victoria Nile squeezes through a six-metre (23-foot) cleft in the rocks to drop 43 metres (141 feet) in a cascading thunder of water forming an inevitable mist and beautiful rainbow.

The Nile, in fact, is the most prominent feature of the park, bisecting it from east to west for some 115 kilometres (70 miles). The northernmost tip of Lake Albert forms the western boundary of the park, so the area is extremely well watered and fertile.

Getting there

Using the most direct route, Paraa, where the sole camp in Murchison Falls is located, is 303 kilometres (188 miles) from Kampala, 86 kilometres (53 miles) from Masindi, 142 kilometres (88 miles) from Hoima, about 243 kilometres (151 miles) from Arua, and 109 kilometres (68 miles) from Gulu. It is served by road from Kampala (most of which is tarmac) and can also be reached by air charter, using the all-weather airstrip at Pakuba, about 10 kilometres (six miles) north-west of Paraa. A four-wheel-drive vehicle is recommended for game drives and for the gravel parts of the route between Masindi and the park.

When to go

The park is lovely at any time of the year, but most visitors choose to avoid the rainy seasons of April–May and October–November.

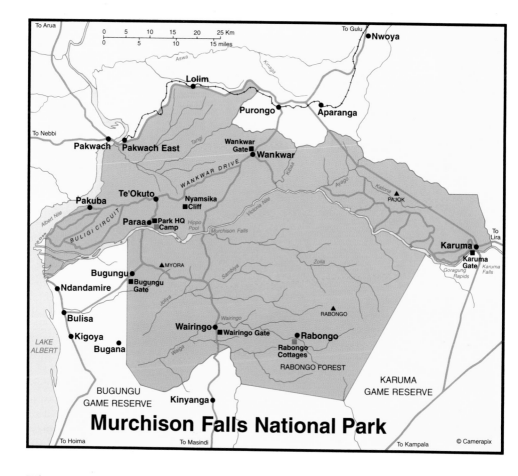

Murchison Falls National Park

© Camerapix

Where to stay

At Paraa, the Paraa Rest Camp has 14 bandas with beds, bedding, mosquito nets, and kerosene lamps, but not much else. You can camp at Paraa as well. The newer Sambiya River Tented Camp is on the south bank of the river not far from Paraa. There are also some rustic campsites near the top of the falls, for which you must be totally self-sufficient. If you travel with a reputable safari company, you willl probably have your own private campsite, with everything laid on.There are also some defunct cottages on the Waringo River, in the less-visited south-east sector of the park, but they are not maintained and extremely hard to reach.

Bombed, burned, and looted during the civil unrest, the two original lodges — Paraa Safari Lodge and Chobe Safari Lodge — are now receiving new life. Paraa Lodge was being refurbished in 1996 by a major Nairobi-based hotel group, while the Madhvani Group had reportedly purchased the Chobe Lodge with similar plans for refurbishment. There is also a new lodge (close to completion in mid-1996) near the Sambiya River Tented Camp. Check with Uganda National Parks headquarters in Kampala for up-to-date information.

Just outside the park is the Inn On The Nile luxury tented camp. Otherwise, the nearest hotel accommodation is in Masindi, at the Masindi Hotel. See Listings.

Sightseeing

From the **Old Kampala Road roundabout** that circumvents the Kampala Old Fort, head **north** on **Boundary Close**, which becomes **Sir Apollo Kaggwa Road.** As you travel out of town on this road (which may be **signposted** to Bombo, Luwero, Gulu or any combination of the three), you pass

137

Above: Colourful local markets can be found near almost every major village on the way into Uganda's north-west.

the extensive grounds of the prestigious **Makerere University** on your **right**.

There is nothing much to see of note along the way, although you pass through numerous small towns, each with its own colourful ambience, particularly on market day. After about 119 kilometres (74 miles) you come to the town of **Nakasongola**, where the main tarmac road veers **left**, following the meandering contours of **Lake Kyoga**.

The Victoria Nile flows northward from Owen Falls Dam into this shallow, papyrus- and water-lily-girt lake, which is 100 kilometres (63 miles) long and covers a total area of 4,427 square kilometres (1,700 square miles). Much of it is swamp; it is one of Africa's greatest wetland ecosystems with prolific bird and lacustrine life. To take a closer look at the lake, you can make a 23-kilometre (14-mile) detour on the **dirt road** that leads **north** of Nakasongola to the lake's edge at **Lwampanga village**.

From Nakasongola it is a 98-kilometre (61-mile) drive **north-west** to Masindi —

but take care: after only 58 kilometres (36 miles) the road forks — just after you cross the **Kafu River** — with a **right fork**, the **main tarmac road**, **north** to **Gulu** and a **left fork** (which is a good **gravel road**) to Masindi.

A worthwhile side trip, only 31 kilometres (19 miles) away, is to take the **right fork** and stay on the **tarmac** until you come to the village of **Rwekunye**, where you turn **right** to the town of **Masindi Port**, on the banks of Victoria Nile where it leaves Lake Kyoga. The town has a colourful open **market**, full of hundreds of friendly villagers.

To reach Masindi, return to the main road and take the **left fork**. You reach **Masindi** some 40 kilometres (25 miles) later. The land to the **west** of Masindi, known as the West Nile region, is Uganda's main **tobacco**-growing area.

While Masindi is nothing much to speak of, it is a base from which to visit the historic sites around Hoima and the Budongo Forest Reserve. The Masindi Hotel, about a kilometre out of town on the road **north** to Murchison Falls, is the only 'upper range' hotel, although there are several guesthouses. Only five kilometres (three miles) out of town is the Bunyoro king's **palace** on **Kihande Hill**, which is worth a visit.

The Hoima historical sites and the Budongo Forest Reserve may be visited separately or as part of a circuit drive. To do the latter, head **south-west** out of Masindi towards Hoima, some 56 kilometres (35 miles) away. About four kilometres (two-and-a-half miles) before you reach Hoima, on the **left** of the road, are the **Mparo Tombs**, where the Bunyoro king Kabalega, who died in 1923, and several of his successors (including his son, Tito Winyi) are buried.

The **burial site** is a large enclosure made of natural materials, while Kabalega's **grave** is housed in a domed construction similar to that of the Kasubi Tombs in Kampala, although much smaller. The grave is surrounded by many of Kabalega's **personal effects**. Outside the main enclosure is a **plaque** marking the spot where Kabalega met the Emin Pasha in 1877. Take off your shoes before entering the main tomb.

It was from Mparo that Kabalega led his raids into the neighbouring kingdoms of Toro and Buganda, although the king was driven from his capital by the British in 1891 and turned to guerrilla warfare. Eventually the British captured him after a series of forts were built in the Lake Albert region in 1894.

You can see the site of the main fort by travelling to **Hoima** town and turning **north** on the road to Butiaba. After only three kilometres (1.8 miles), you come to **Katasiha**, where the **main fort** was.

All that remains today is an eight-metre-deep (26-foot) **trench**, now filled in, and a small **cave** that was used as an arsenal. The fort, like the others the British used in the area, was built by General Colville.

Continue your journey **north** on the **Butiaba road**. About 32 kilometres (20 miles) **west** of the town of **Kigorobya**, on the shores of **Lake Albert**, are the **Kibiro hot springs** and **salt works**, where the traditional methods of extracting salt can be viewed. Ask locally for directions. You can also enquire about hiring a boat for a **tour** of Lake Albert. The lake, particularly the northern tip near Murchison Falls National Park, is a real **fishing centre**, with plentiful **tilapia, tiger fish,** and **Nile perch** (known locally as *mputa*). The perch, in particular, grow to huge sizes, and many anglers have set records there, such as the 102-kilo (225-lb) specimen taken on rod and line from a boat, and some of up to 165 kilos (364 lbs) snared by net fishermen.

Budongo Forest Reserve

The road **north** eventually ends at the town of **Biso**, where you turn **right** (east) on a **dirt road** for some 23 kilometres (14 miles), to the **turnoff** to **the Nyabyeya Forestry College**, which adjoins the **Budongo Forest Reserve**. You can camp there, but it is advisable to carry everything you need, including food.

Budongo Forest, one of the most extensive forests in East Africa, is famous for its **chimpanzees**, which have been studied for several decades. There is a **research station** in the reserve (about five kilometres – three miles – from the college), and there are regular morning and evening departures for **chimp tracking**. Check first with the Forestry Department in Kampala for permission to go there.

Other uncommon animals in the Budongo include the curious **scaly-tailed flying squirrel, tree pangolin, potto, black-fronted duiker, blue duiker, black-and-white colobus, blue monkey** and **giant forest squirrel**. Because the forest was opened up by sawmillers over many years, a network of forest **roads** and **tracks** makes exploring — and bird-watching — easy.

The **birdlife** is extremely rich with many outstanding species, including a number of colourful **turacos, kingfishers, barbets, woodpeckers,** and **sunbirds**. **Butterflies**, also, are stunning and prolific.

Above: Budongo Forest is one of the most extensive forests in East Africa.

From Budongo forest, it is about 30 kilometres (19 miles) **east** to Masindi.

On to the park

There are two routes to Murchison Falls National Park from Masindi, both of which require four-wheel-drive vehicles. The first option, which is considerably shorter than the second, is to head directly **north** on the gravel road from Masindi, through the village of **Kinyanga** before reaching, 86 kilometres (53 miles) later, the park's **Wairingo gate.** Although the route used to be quite rough, the road is now graded and reasonably smooth.

The second option, at 136 kilometres (85 miles), is much longer but considerably smoother and more scenic. Head **west** out of Masindi on the **dirt road** to the **Budongo Forest Reserve** and **Biso**, turning **right** shortly after Biso on a **dirt road** along the shores of **Lake Albert** that heads **north**, through **Bugungu Game Reserve** — a sort of buffer zone to Murchison Falls National Park with similar wildlife and birdlife — to **Bulisa.**

Turn **right** at Bulisa on another **dirt**

road that, after 25 kilometres (15 miles), leads to the **park headquarters** and **Paraa Rest Camp.**

Park entry fees, in 1996, were US$ 23 for non-residents, Ush 17,300 (about US$ 17) for foreign residents, and Ush 2,300 (about US$ 2) for Uganda citizens. There is also a vehicle charge of Ush 4,600 (about US$ 4.50). Additional fee information — such as for the bandas, camping, ranger guides, the Paraa ferry, and fishing — may be obtained from Uganda National Parks headquarters in Kampala.

The Paraa Rest Camp has 14 bandas and is situated near the **ferry launch** on the south bank of the Nile. The bandas are constructed in typical Acholi style, with mud walls and grass roofs, and are kitted out with twin beds, bedding, mosquito nets, and kerosene lamps. A central campfire is provided upon request. You have the option of cooking for yourself or taking advantage of food provided by park staff. Warm water is available for bathing. The bandas need to be booked a week in advance.

The main attraction in Murchison is the fantastic three-hour **launch trip** from Paraa

Above: The exciting Murchison launch trip is a highlight of a visit to the park.
Overleaf: The thundering Murchison Falls, where the mighty Nile is funnelled through a 7-metre (23-foot) cleft in the rocks.

to the foot of the falls. In 1996, this cost non-residents US$ 92 for 10 people or less, or US$ 10 a person if more than 10 people. Charges for foreign residents and Uganda citizens are slightly less. There are two trips each day: one in the morning and another in the afternoon.

As you cruise up this 17-kilometre (10-mile) stretch of the historic Nile, you're likely to see **elephant, hippo, buffalo, waterbuck, Uganda kob, giraffe**, and, of course, the **Nile crocodile**, many of which grow to enormous size.

It is not unusual to see 60 or more bird species on a single launch trip, including the **shoebill** (or **whale-headed**) **stork** in the **papyrus** lining the river banks. Also watch out for the dazzling **red-throated bee-eater, saddlebill stork, Goliath heron, malachite kingfisher, wattled plover, Egyptian goose, pelican, cormorant**, and **hornbill**.

The trip climaxes at the foot of the **falls** and the awesome spectacle of the power of the roaring water. The boat often beaches

at the foot of a **trail** that leads through dense **rainforest** to a natural **viewing platform** of boulders extending into the water near the foot of the falls — a trip well worth doing, allowing you to appreciate the waterfall from the top, where its full force is very evident. The trail continues up a steep incline to a **campsite** and **upper viewpoint**.

In addition to the launch trip, another enjoyable experience is **game driving.** The **Buligi Circuit**, between the Albert Nile and the Victoria Nile, is famous for its open plain dotted with **borassus palm** and wildlife that includes the **Uganda kob, giraffe, lion, oribi**, and **warthog**.

Dominating the plains' horizon is the blue-grey western wall of the Rift Valley and the shimmering waters of Lake Albert.

For a period during Idi Amin's regime, Albert was renamed Lake Mobutu Sese-Seko, but has now reverted to its original name. Discovered' in 1884 by Samuel Baker, the lake is named after Queen Victoria's consort and is quite literally an inland sea

Above: Huge crocodiles line the banks of the Nile at Murchison.
Opposite: Aerial view of the spectacular Murchison Falls.

that dominates the environment about it. The Rift Valley's precipitous walls rise on either side, appearing from the opposite shores as distant blue ranges. But the lake is far too long — 160 kilometres (100 miles) — for one end to be seen from the other. Both the Victoria Nile and the Semuliki River flow into Lake Albert, which covers 6,400 square kilometres (2,500 square miles).

A trip along **Wankwar Drive** may provide close encounters with **Jackson's hartebeest, lion, elephant,** and **buffalo** — and you'll also pass near **kob breeding grounds.** Another interesting locale along this drive is **Nyamsika cliff,** where numerous **kob,** as well as **elephant, leopard,** and a myriad of **birds,** are usually found just below along the stream bank.

In the southern part of the park the **Rabongo Forest** provides shelter for **tropical rainforest** primates, and has a cool, relaxed atmosphere. **Chimpanzee, black-and-white colobus,** and **baboon** are often seen in their natural habitat.

In the eastern sector of the park is another drive, at the beginning of which are the Karuma and Goragung falls. Although tracks are being built to this area from within the park, at the moment it is best approached by leaving the park and re-entering at the eastern Karuma gate.

Overall, the park is dominated by rolling savannah and tall grassland, with increasingly thick bush and woodlands in the higher and wetter areas to the south and east. Closed canopy forest is limited to the Rabongo area — where **ironwood** predominates — and to certain riparian localities along the south bank of the Nile.

The original checklist of mammals in the park includes 55 species. Of these, the white rhinoceros and black rhinoceros were wiped out by organized poaching during the Amin regime. Other animal populations in Murchison, however, are rapidly regaining their numbers and show every sign of increasing to their former abundance.

Murchison's **elephants,** in particular, are staging a remarkable comeback. This

Above: Bridge over the Nile marks the Pakwach 'city limits'.
Opposite: The Uganda kob, one of a variety of wildlife to be found at Murchison.

area once had an astounding elephant population — one of the highest densities in East Africa. In the past few years, there has been a dramatic upsurge, and the elephant is beginning to re-establish itself, with the help of adequate security. The elephant population in the park is now estimated to be nearly a thousand.

Other animals have also been showing a sharp upswing in numbers, **buffalo** and **Rothschild's giraffe** among them. **Uganda kob, hartebeest**, and **waterbuck** are commonly seen, and you may also see **oribi, bushbuck, Bohor reedbuck, sitatunga, bush duiker, warthog**, and **bushpig** as you drive.

There are six species of **primates** present in the park, including the **chimpanzee**, while large carnivores include **lion, leopard**, and **spotted hyena**. The avifauna is also extensive, with 424 **bird species** on record.

Most visitors, at this point, simply retrace their steps to Kampala. However, some may opt to go north around sprawling Lake Kyoga. In 1996 the possibilities of exploring Uganda's north beyond Murchison Falls National Park were limited, largely because of recurring rebel activity in the area, although the government repeatedly said the situation was under control. So before you venture elsewhere, check with the relevant authorities in Kampala or with the park headquarters staff at Murchison.

Arua

If the way is said to be safe, you can reach Arua, the north-easternmost district headquarters, from Murchison by following the **Wankwar Drive** and going out of the park through the **Wankwar gate**, a few kilometres beyond which lies the village of **Purongo**, where the dirt road ends.

A **left turn** onto the **gravel road** there leads along the top edge of the national park and the bottom edge of the little-visited **Aswa-Lolim Game Reserve** for 57 kilometres (35 miles) to **Pakwach**, a small town on the banks of the Albert Nile,

147

Above: Not exactly the crossroads of the world, Gulu signs nevertheless point the way.

where there are basic lodgings. This is also the **railhead** for the Tororo–Gulu–Pakwach line.

From Pakwach, it is 52 kilometres (32 miles) **west** to **Nebbi**, another district headquarters, where you take a **right turn** on the **main gravel road** heading **north** to **Arua**, 68 kilometres (42 miles) away.

There is an **airstrip, police station, hospital**, and the **White Rhino Hotel**. The **border crossing** into neighbouring Zaire is about eight kilometres (five miles) from Arua.

Just before Arua, you can turn **right** at the village of **Olevu** on a **dirt road** through the seldom-visited **Ajai Game Reserve**, about 32 kilometres (20 miles) from Arua. Covering only 158 square kilometres (61 square miles), the reserve was originally gazetted to protect the white rhinoceros, now extinct in Uganda because of poaching.

The scenic reserve is named after a former tribal ruler of the area. During the rainy season the **swamps** in the reserve flood, and attract game that includes **buffalo, hippo, warthog, Jackson's hartebeest, waterbuck**, and **bushbuck**.

Gulu

Back at the village of **Purongo**, just outside the Wankwar gate of Murchison Falls National Park, a **right turn** on the **main gravel road** takes you to the village of **Lalem**, where the road forks. The **left fork**, 64 kilometres (40 miles) beyond, leads to the northern town of **Gulu**, while the right fork cuts across the north-east section of Murchison Falls National Park and eventually joins the tarmac road near the park's Karuma gate, about 53 kilometres (33 miles) from Lalem.

Although most of the area north of Murchison features wide plains and is sparse in population, around the towns of Gulu, Kitgum, and Lira agriculture is well developed, with many small farms growing simsim (sesame), groundnuts, millet, and cotton.

The middle stop on the railway line between Tororo and Pakwach, Gulu is the largest Ugandan town in the north but saw few tourists in the early 1990s because of rebel problems. There is an **airstrip**, a

Above: Typical road leading from Gulu into Uganda's far north.
Overleaf: Rock caves near Kumi.

police station, and several lodgings, including the **Church of Uganda Guest House** and the more up-market **Acholi Inn**. Throughout the town you see and can buy some of the **handicrafts** of the area, including baskets, pottery, and ironwork.

About 30 kilometres (19 miles) **north** of Gulu, at Patiko, is **Baker's Fort**, built by the British in the late 1800s as a base from which to suppress the slave trade. All that now remains is a 700-metre-long (2,300-foot) **defence ditch** and **rampart**, which enclose a stately tree-filled **park**. In the south-western corner of the enclosure is a low **granite hill**, on the highest point of which is a remarkable **vertical slab**.

The **border** with Sudan, at **Nimule on the banks of the Nile**, is 113 kilometres (70 miles) **north** of Gulu via a **gravel road**.

From Gulu, a good tarmac road leads **south**, where, after 60 kilometres (37 miles), you come to the village of **Kamudini**, and the road splits. The turn **right** (west) takes you 18 kilometres (11 miles) to the **Karuma gate** of **Murchison Falls National Park**, which is also at the tip of the **Karuma Game**

Reserve, another of the park buffer zones. Also near this point are the **Karuma Falls**, in the very eastern sector of the national park, where the Nile cascades over 23 kilometres (14 miles) of rapids in a breathtaking maelstrom. Some five kilometres (three miles) downstream are the **Goragung Falls**.

To return to Kampala via the route that runs north of Lake Kyoga, return to **Kamudini** village and head **south** for about 10 kilometres (six miles) on the **tarmac road** to the village of **Aber**. Continue on the tarmac, which takes a sharp turn and heads **east** to **Lira,** some 75 kilometres (46 miles) away. There are several hotels, the most up-market being the **Lira Hotel**, as well as an **airstrip** and a **police station**. The town is also a stop on the Tororo–Pakwach railway line. Directly north of Lira is the northern frontier town of **Kitgum**, some 126 kilometres (78 miles) distant on a dirt road.

The next stretch of road — from Lira to Soroti, 121 kilometres (75 miles) away — is a good **gravel road**. You pass through numerous small towns and

149

Above: Visitors are welcome to come and explore the mysterious Nyero rock paintings near Kumi, created by Uganda's early human residents.

villages along the way, including **Aloi** and **Tiriri**, where you can get petrol.

In **Soroti**, 19 kilometres (12 miles) east of one arm of Lake Kyoga, there is the **Soroti Hotel**, as well as an **airstrip** and a small **museum**.

Nyero rock paintings

From Soroti, the road is **tarmac** again, and you continue **south-east** to **Kumi**, 44 kilometres (27 miles) farther on.

A fascinating side trip from Kumi is to the nearby **Nyero rock paintings**, only 11 kilometres (7 miles) **south-west** of the town just off the **dirt road** to the village of **Ngora.**

The paintings, thought to be about 400 years old, are in three shelters situated close to each other. They are said to be among the finest rock paintings in East Africa, and in particular feature some good examples of geometrical paintings.

Another set of rock paintings — the

Kakoro rock paintings — may be seen about 10 kilometres (6 miles) **south-west** of the main **Kumi–Mbale road**. The nearest village is **Nakaloke** on the main road, where you can ask for specific directions. Although the paintings, which are located on a **koppie**, are nothing spectacular, they are worth seeing. In addition, there is an **ancient rock gong** near the paintings that is quite unusual. Make sure you wear long trousers, as the koppie is quite overgrown, and out of courtesy ask permission from the nearest homeowner to climb it.

From Kumi, it is 53 kilometres (33 miles) to **Mbale**, at the foot of Mount Elgon, where the main tarmac road heads **south** to **Tororo** on the Kenya border and then turns towards the **west** and **Kampala**. The capital is some 250 kilometres (155 miles) from Mbale. (See The North-east: Remote and Wild.)

The North-east: Remote and Wild

By road, the way to Uganda's remote north-east travels through the industrial city of Jinja and on to Mbale and the beautiful and fertile slopes of Mount Elgon, which straddles the Uganda–Kenya border. However in 1996 the road further north, which eventually leads to the country's most remote — and in some ways finest — national park, Kidepo Valley, was not the safest way, particularly with ongoing rebel activity. Therefore it is important that you check with relevant and knowledgeable authorities in Kampala before attempting this trip on your own. A far safer way to visit Kidepo Valley is by air charter, but that is more expensive.

If the route is considered safe, you will have the pleasure of discovering some of the least-visited places in Uganda: places still virtually untouched and unexplored and sure to make your trip memorable.

For the first leg of the journey, there is no need to worry. Head out with confidence on a good tarmac road to one of the country's most recent national parks: Mount Elgon.

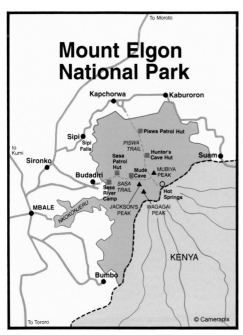

Mount Elgon National Park

Known as *Masaba* by the local people, Mount Elgon is an extinct volcano that first erupted about 24 million years ago and had its last major eruption some 10 million years ago. The mountain's volcanic past is evident in the hot springs that still bubble out of the caldera floor.

Some scientists, judging from Mount Elgon's 50-kilometre (30-mile) diameter, reckon it may once have been higher than Africa's highest mountain, Kilimanjaro. Elgon's highest peak, Wagagai, reaches 4,321 metres (14,176 feet) above sea level.

Besides volcanic forces, many other geological events have shaped Mount Elgon. The many crater lakes in the mountain's caldera were formed by glaciers, which extended from the summits down to about 3,500 metres (11,483 feet) during the Pleistocene era. The same glaciers gouged a deep gash out of the eastern wall, creating what is now the Suam Gorge. Rock falls and landslides, in addition to the growth of astounding vegetation, have enhanced the fascinating, tumbled landscape.

Jutting westwards from the main mountain is the Nkonkonjeru peninsula, a 2,350-metre (7,710-foot) ridge extending for about 20 kilometres (12 miles).

Years of land-use practices and a growing population have had their effect on the area, which is one of the reasons the park was created. Gazetted in October 1993, the 1,145-square-kilometre (442-square-mile) Mount Elgon National Park is primarily concerned with conserving and restoring the original forest that once covered the slopes, enabling the mountain to continue its essential role as a major watershed.

The area around the park is largely occupied by the Bagisu people, one of the few ethnic groups in Uganda who still practise traditional circumcision and believe strongly in magic and witchcraft.

Mainly agriculturalists, they grow crops

153

Above: Watchful pied kingfisher surveys its domain.

that include coffee, *matoke* (bananas), millet, potatoes, beans and peas. Their terraced coffee plantations can be seen throughout the area. The Bagisu also rear some cattle, sheep, and goats, and use the donkey as a beast of burden.

With the friendly people in the area, and its waterfalls, caves, hot springs, mountain vegetation, peaks, the Suam Gorge, and the fascinating caldera itself, Mount Elgon is an exciting place to explore.

Getting there
Mbale, where the Mount Elgon National Park headquarters is located, is 250 kilometres (155 miles) from Kampala, 97 kilometres (60 miles) from Soroti, 45 kilometres (28 miles) from Tororo to the south, and 224 kilometres (139 miles) from Moroto to the north. It is served by excellent tarmac roads from Kampala, Tororo, and Soroti, and a gravel road from Moroto. The nearest airstrip is in Tororo.

When to go
The best time to visit is during the dry season, from June to August and December to March, with the latter preferable. However, even at other times of the year, it is manageable, although it can rain at any time and you should be prepared for it.

Where to stay
Inside the park, campsites are available. In Mbale, the Mount Elgon Hotel is the best, although there are several reasonable budget hotels as well. There is also very basic accommodation in the small towns bordering the park — Budadiri, Sipi, Kapchorwa, and Suam — but options are limited. See Listings.

Sightseeing
It takes about four hours by road from Kampala to Mbale. To get there, head **west** out of the capital on the **Jinja Road**, which takes you past the **Lugogo Indoor Stadium**, through the middle of the **KCC Sports Ground** before you pass through an **industrial area** on your way out of the capital.

After 80 kilometres (50 miles), you come to Uganda's second largest town, **Jinja**, the location of the **source of the Nile** and

Above: Tororo Rock, a volcanic plug, dominates Tororo's skyline.

home to the **Owen Falls Dam** (see The Capital and the Cities, Part Three).

From Jinja, stay on the **main tarmac road** heading **east** to **Tororo**, which is 125 kilometres (77 miles) away. On the way, you pass some fairly major towns and villages, including **Bugembe** and **Iganga**.

Tororo, only 14 kilometres (nine miles) from the Kenya border, is a busy but not very appealing place, with an **airstrip, police station**, and several **hotels**, including the Crystal Hotel and the Rock Hotel. The latter gets its name from **Tororo Rock**, a small but steep volcanic plug that dominates the town's skyline. If the weather is clear it affords some good **views** across to Lake Victoria. You can also board a **train** at Tororo and take it as far north as Pakwach at the edge of Murchison Falls National Park, through Mbale, Lira, and Gulu. But it is not recommended for visitors: it is slow, unreliable, and uncomfortable.

It's a 45-kilometre (28-mile) drive **north** from Tororo on the **main tarmac road** to **Mbale**, where the **headquarters** of **Mount Elgon National Park** is located. Although an attractive town, Mbale itself does not have much of interest. The 30-minute **walk** from the **Mount Elgon Hotel** — the best place to stay in Mbale, with its peaceful atmosphere and lovely gardens — to the town centre is pleasant.

To reach the national park headquarters from the centre of Mbale, take the **road south-east** (towards Mount Elgon) from the **clock tower (Republic Street)** into **Masaba Road.** The office is about one-and-a-half kilometres (one mile) from town in a large yellow building on the **left** opposite the Mount Elgon Hotel.

In 1996, park entrance fees were US$ 12 for non-residents, Ush 11,500 (about US$ 11) for foreign residents, and Ush 1,200 (about US$ 1) for Uganda citizens. There are additional charges for camping and park ranger escorts. Charges for porters and guides are negotiable, but in 1996 Uganda National Parks said they were to become fixed. The price then was about Ush 6,000 (US$ 6) a day for a guide and Ush 5,000 (US$ 5) a day for a porter. Food is an additional Ush 2,000 (US$ 2) a day for each guide and porter.

Above: The town of Mbale, where the Mount Elgon National Park headquarters is located.

Mount Elgon is ideal for climbers seeking a less strenuous alternative to the Ruwenzori Mountains, as scaling Elgon requires no technical climbing skills, and all major summits are accessible to hikers. The beautifully wooded slopes, smaller scale, and milder climate make Mount Elgon a wonderful wilderness experience that is often overlooked by tourists.

Guides, porters, and park rangers are highly recommended, but optional. An armed ranger is required in the caldera for safety reasons. It is helpful to have a guide within the park and from Budadiri to the park boundary, as the route may be confusing.

Visitors can organize their trip at park headquarters in Mbale or in Budadiri, where a **visitor centre** was soon to be established in 1996. At either of these places, you can book guides and porters, pay the entry fees, and discuss your route. Although you can also book a visit in advance by radio message from Uganda National Parks headquarters in Kampala, advance reservations are not necessary.

Before you begin your trek, make sure you have food, tent, warm sleeping bag, hiking boots or good walking shoes, waterproof gear, backpack, hat, wool clothing, gloves, sunglasses, torch, water bottle, simple cooking utensils, small paraffin stove, first aid kit, and map. Some camping equipment and a vehicle are available for rental from the Salem Brotherhood, which is located about nine kilometres (six miles) from Mbale on the Kumi Road.

There are two main **trails** in the park: the **Sasa** and the **Piswa**, and any combination of the two trails is possible, depending on your fitness, interests, and time available. Ideally, you should allow at least four days for a normal trip — which includes climbing the highest peak, Wagagai — but a six-day trip is more comprehensive, also allowing you to visit the caldera and climb Jackson's Point, the second highest peak.

Visitors beginning with the **Sasa trail** should travel on to **Budadiri** to pick up guides and porters. The village is reached by first heading out of Mbale on the

Above: The beautiful Sipi Falls, on the way to Mount Elgon.

tarmacked **Kumi Road** and then, not far along, turning **right** on a **gravel road**, which forks shortly after you turn. Take the **right fork** to Budadiri. Several *matatus* make daily runs between Mbale and Budadiri.

Sipi Falls

If you choose to start off with the **Piswa trail**, drive as if you were going to Budadiri, but where the road forks, **keep left**. (A four-wheel-drive vehicle is recommended for this route.) You pass through **Siroko**, and, after about six kilometres (four miles), take a **right turn**, to **Sipi**. The village, in fact, is a lovely place to spend a couple of days. For accommodation, there is the **Sipi Rest House**, originally built as a governor's residence in the 1950s.

The **views** across the plains around Lake Kyoga are breathtaking, and there are numerous **footpaths** and roads around Sipi worth exploring. The most rewarding walk is the one to the base of the pretty **Sipi Falls**, where the **Sipi River** gushes down a steep 50-metre (160-foot) cliff. The **path** to the falls starts in the village behind the **post office**. You can continue your walk from the falls to the **caves** on the opposite side of the river.

To get to the Piswa trailhead, continue on the **dirt road** from Sipi to **Kapchorwa**, where you turn **right** to Kamnarkut after a short journey. (If you continue straight along this road through Kapchorwa, you eventually come to the Kenya border post at Suam.)

One itinerary that Uganda National Parks recommends is to ascend Mount Elgon via the Sasa trail and descend via the Piswa trail, allowing six days for your trek. Make an early start on the day of departure, for the first day is a long one.

You go from Budadiri to trailhead, which takes about four hours, and then continue to the **Sasa River Camp** (another two hours). The second day, you hike for two hours to the **Sasa Patrol Hut**, and then another hour to the **Mude Cave campsite**. Strong walkers may choose to leave their bags at Mude and continue on to **Jackson's**

157

Above: The foothills of Mount Elgon.
Opposite: Elephant, for many years only known to live on the Kenya side of the mountain, are making a return to Uganda's half of Mount Elgon, but they are still rarely seen by hikers.

Point summit — 4,192 metres (13,753 feet) — which should take another two hours, and then spend the night at Mude Cave.

With Mude Cave as your base, the next day plan to climb the 4,321-metre-high (14,176-foot) **Wagagai Peak**, which should take around four hours, and then return to Mude for a second night.

On the fourth day of your exploration of Mount Elgon, you'll trek from Mude Cave to the **caldera** and **hot springs**, a journey of about four hours. From the caldera continue to **Hunter's Cave Camp** — a three-hour trek. Day five is spent hiking from Hunter's Cave Camp to the **Piswa Patrol Hut**, and the last day from the hut to Kamnarkut and on to Kapchorwa.

As you hike through the park, keep in mind the four altitudinal belts on the mountain, which are common to afro-montane systems. In descending order, these include the afro-alpine zone, the sub-alpine or heath zone, the bamboo zone, and the montane forest.

The largest number of plant and animal species exist in the montane forest, but the high elevation areas have much to offer as well. The vegetation there has adapted to the extreme weather conditions in bizarre ways, as you'll clearly observe when you see the **giant groundsel, giant lobelia**, and **giant heather** common in the area. Two types of giant groundsel — *Senecio barbatipes* and *Senecio elgonensis* — are endemic to the area. **Bamboo forests** grow in the southern and western parts of the park, with shoots growing up to 15 metres (50 feet) tall. There are also many beautiful **wildflowers** in the park.

Although many animals are present on Mount Elgon, past harassment by poachers has made them extremely shy. You may be lucky and spot **buffalo, bushbuck, black-fronted duiker, tree hyrax**, and **bush pig**. **Leopard** and **hyena** also reside there, and **elephant**, once confined to the Kenyan side of the mountain, are beginning to return. Primates include the **baboon, blue monkey**, and **black-and-white colobus**.

Birds, of course, are prolific, and

Above: Uganda's north-east is largely inhabited by the pastoralist Karimojong people.

include the interesting **Ross's turaco, casqued hornbill, gregarious hornbill, crowned eagle**, and **lammergeyer**.

After Mount Elgon, a trip to the next, and last, Uganda national park, Kidepo Valley, is a startling and wonderful contrast.

Kidepo Valley National Park

The vast, semi-arid plains of Uganda's remote north-east are home to one of the country's real treasures: Kidepo Valley National Park. Indeed, part of the park's appeal is its remoteness — guaranteeing that the visitor won't be fighting off minibuses in an attempt to see wildlife. Gazetted in 1962, Kidepo Valley National Park is truly one of Uganda's most spectacular parks, offering some of the wildest and most magnificent scenery to be found in East Africa, relatively unspoilt by development.

The Kidepo Basin lies in mountainous country at an altitude of between 900 and 1,200 metres (3,000 and 4,000 feet) and is encircled by wooded hills. It is dominated by 2,750-metre (9,022-foot) Mount Morongole on its eastern flank, and by the forested Lotuke in Sudan, with peaks rising to more than 2,700 metres (9,000 feet).

The park, covering 1,442 square kilometres (556 square miles), is in the far north-eastern horn of the country; it borders on Sudan and is very near to Kenya. This part of the country is generally referred to as the Karamoja district (although not now officially named as such), where the famous pastoralists, the Karimojong, graze their cattle across the plains.

There are actually about six different groups of Karimojong in Uganda: the Jie, Ik, Nyangia, Napore, Teuso, and Dodoth. The Napore and the Nyangia have become more involved in agriculture over recent years, while the Teuso are hunter-gatherers, speaking a different dialect from the other Karimojong. The Dodoth, however, still maintain their strong pastoralist way of life.

Above: The unpredictable buffalo — one of the most dangerous animals in Africa.

Getting there

The ideal way to Apoka, where the park headquarters and rest camp are located, is by air charter (it takes about two hours) — but this is, of course, rather expensive, although air charter prices to this park are generally a 'package deal' that includes accommodation and meals.

Apoka can also be reached by road, although it may be a dangerous journey because of bandits and is not recommended.

Apoka is about 504 kilometres (313 miles) from Kampala (a two-day drive), 162 kilometres (100 miles) from Kitgum, and 255 kilometres (158 miles) from Moroto. Four-wheel-drive is recommended.

When to go

The best time to visit Kidepo is during the dry season, between December and early April. During the Kidepo rainy season — from April to September — travel is not easy and game is difficult to locate because of the long grass.

Where to stay

There are 20 excellent bandas, each containing two beds, solar lighting, and mosquito nets, at Apoka Rest Camp. Park staff also provide bedding and hurricane

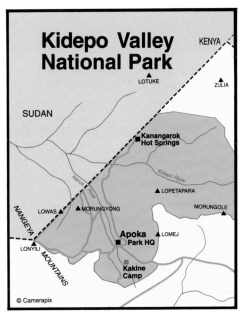

161

Above: Rock bluff near Mount Elgon dominates the surrounding landscape.
Overleaf: Large herd of elephants in the Narus Valley, Kidepo Valley National Park.

lamps, but guests must take their own food. There is also a simple campsite at nearby Kakine, where firewood and water are provided, but nothing else.

Sightseeing

From **Mbale**, head out of town on the **Kumi Road**. You can take a couple of side trips along this road to see the **rock paintings** at **Kakoro** and **Nyero** (see The Lush North-west). But to drive to Kidepo, turn **right** a few kilometres out of town on the **main gravel road** heading **north**.

Remember, it is very important that you check with Uganda National Parks headquarters in Kampala — or other relevant authorities — as to the present conditions and safety of this road before you embark on a road journey to Kidepo.

After the turnoff, you pass through the village of **Siroko** and, soon afterwards, the turnoff to Sipi. After about 50 kilometres (30 miles), you come to the village of **Chepsikunya**. Shortly after this, the road passes through the lower part of the **Pian-Upe Game Reserve**, one of three large,

adjoining reserves in Uganda's north-east. The 2,314 square kilometres (893 square miles) of rolling plains of black cotton soil run from the Greek River in the south to Mount Napak on the boundary of Bokora Game Reserve in the north. The area which includes Pian-Upe, Matheniko and Bokora reserves is known as the Bokora Corridor.

From Chepsikunya village, it is about 140 kilometres (87 miles) before the **Moroto turnoff**, which is 10 kilometres (six miles) **east** of the main road. There is an **airstrip** there, as well as **petrol, police**, a **hospital**, and the **Mount Moroto Hotel** — making it a good place to break your journey.

Back on the **main road** at the Moroto turnoff, head **north** once again. After about

30 kilometres (20 miles), you pass through **Lokichar**, and shortly thereafter the road travels directly across the corridor linking the **Matheniko Game Reserve** and the Bokora Game Reserve. The Matheniko, to the **right** of the road, covers some 1,605 square kilometres (620 square miles), but there is not much — if any — game left. To the **left** of the road is the tip of the huge — 2,056-square-kilometre (794-square-mile) — **Bokora Game Reserve**, a large, dry, flat plain where several species of **antelope** may still roam. **Birdlife** is abundant and varied.

From Lokichar, it is about 55 kilometres (34 miles) to the town of **Kotido**, where there is a **police station**, and another 41 kilometres (25 miles) before the main road takes a **sharp bend** to the **west**. Shortly after this bend (which is really a T-junction, as a minor dirt road heads off east at this point as well), you come to the village of **Koputh**, where you turn **right** to continue **north** on the **main gravel road**. After 24 kilometres (15 miles), you pass through **Kaabong** town, and then, 69 kilometres (43 miles) later, eventually reach your destination: **Apoka**.

In 1996, entrance fees to Kidepo were US$ 23 for non-residents, Ush 17,300 (about US$ 17) for foreign residents, and Ush 2,300 (about US$ 2) for Uganda citizens. There is also a vehicle entry charge of Ush 4,600 (US$ 4.50). There are separate charges for bandas, camping, and vehicle hire. There is also an aircraft landing fee of Ush 20,500 (US$ 20) for a single-engined plane, and Ush 27,400 (US$ 27) for a twin-engined plane.

The park consists of two shallow valley systems, with rugged, dry, mountain terrain. The area's remarkable variation in altitude has created a profusion of habitats within the park, including montane forest, grassy plains, open tree savannah, dry thorn bush, thick woodlands, borassus palm forest, and koppies (rocky outcrops).

During the six dry months of the year in Kidepo, wildlife is attracted to the water sources that remain in the Narus Valley in the south-west of the park. There is a great diversity of wildlife: 80 species, more than in any other Ugandan park.

Above: Kidepo ranger relaxes, seemingly oblivious to the lions lazing on the nearby rock.
Opposite: Burchell's zebra find the ideal grazing grounds in Kidepo Valley National Park.

You can expect to see **zebra**, large herds of **elephant, eland, lesser kudu, dik-dik**, and **buffalo**. **Oribi** are also abundant, as is the almost-tame **Apoka waterbuck**. Surprsingly, 28 of the species resident there do not exist in any other parks in the country, including **cheetah, greater kudu**, and **Bright's gazelle**.

Kidepo is also an ornithologist's delight. The official checklist includes 462 species, with the park's koppies and forest patches providing very good habitats for unusual species. Two birds found there not in other Ugandan parks are the **ostrich** and the **kori bustard**. There are five species of **hornbill**, including the giant **ground hornbill**. Birds of prey include **Verreaux's eagle, lammergeyer**, and **Egyptian vulture**.

Visitors can get a good look at this bountiful wildlife and birdlife from several **game-viewing loops** close to the main rest camp at Apoka in the Narus Valley, where most of the game is concentrated. Visitors can also take the drive north to the **Kanangarok hot springs**, crossing the **Kidepo River**, with its sandy beaches and borassus palm forest.

In addition, the park **nature exhibit** at the Apoka headquarters is open to visitors and contains specimens of lion skins, giraffe skulls, butterflies, scorpions, and photographs of a rare albino buffalo.

If you're interested in a taste of local life, you may arrange to visit **Karimojong** *manyattas* (homesteads) in the area to see the traditional clothing, stools, spears, headdresses, knives, bows and arrows, and jewellery. Ask about attending one of their **traditional dances** — such as the *emuya* and *ekaharo* — for a memorable experience. It is best to arrange any visits with the local people at least two days in advance from the Apoka park headquarters or by radioing ahead from Uganda National Parks headquarters in Kampala.

If you are travelling by road, you can return via the same route or, alternatively, at the village of Koputh (south of the park on the route back), turn **west** to **Kitgum** and then on to **Gulu**, but this route is much longer and the road is not as good as the one leading south.

PART THREE: THE CAPITAL AND THE CITIES

Above: Twilight at Kibuli Mosque, situated at the top of one of Kampala's many hills.
Opposite: Kampala's fast-growing skyline reflects Uganda's dynamic growth.

Kampala: The Capital of Antelopes

Uganda's capital city, Kampala, derives its name from the Luganda *Kasozi ka Impala*, or 'Hill of Antelopes', and was so named because 19th-century Buganda kings once grazed impala on the slopes of a hill near Mengo Palace. The area had long been a centre of Baganda activity, with Kabaka Mutesa having his capital at Kasubi Hill and Kabaka Mwanga establishing his at nearby Mengo Hill. The name Kasozi ka Impala was given specifically to the hill on which a British explorer and adventurer, Captain Fredrick Lord Lugard, established his fort in December 1890.

At this little fort and administrative post, Lugard hoisted the Imperial British East African Company flag, which was to be replaced by the Union Jack three years later. The fort at Kampala Hill, as it was later to be called (it is now known as Old Kampala Hill) attracted hundreds of people, who formed a small township, out of which modern Kampala developed.

Like the legendary city of Rome, Kampala was originally built on seven hills, around which was an appealing mixture of delightful valleys, green swamplands, and flowing streams. The seven historical hills on which the city was founded are Lubaga, Namirembe (Mengo), Makerere, Kololo, Kibuli, Kampala (Old Kampala), and Mulago.

Soon traders erected shops at the foot of the hill by the fort. By 1909 the confines of the fort had become too small for administrative purposes, and it was decided to move the colonial offices and government residences to Nakasero Hill, another nearby hill. The shops and other commercial premises followed suit.

Kampala's hills all similarly developed their own identities in the ensuing years. Lubaga, Namirembe, and Kibuli became the headquarters of Uganda's three main religious groups: the Roman Catholics of the order of the White Fathers, the Protestants of the British Church Missionary Society, and the Muslims. Nakasero and Kololo became prime sites for administrative offices and residential areas for senior government civil service staff. Makerere (much later) evolved into a university campus, and Mulago developed into a site for health institutions. Kampala Hill remained a fort, with a small administrative centre. Now, years later, the hills all still have those same basic identities.

Mengo Hill — where the palace (*lubiri*) of the king (*kabaka*) of Buganda was situated — remained separate as the capital of the Buganda kingdom. White missionaries, before proceeding to their respective hills, were first required to report at Mengo.

When you stand on any of the original seven hills, at some 1,200 metres (3,800 feet), you are disarmed by the unexpected greenness of the capital, which is broken by red-tiled villas, green-roofed bungalows and their whitewashed walls, and modern buildings of the city centre. Despite almost two decades of civil wars, political turmoil, gross mismanagement, and sheer neglect, Kampala still retains its charm and remains one of the greenest cities in Africa, with a beauty giving way to a still more attractive countryside.

The city is traversed by streams and small rivers, features a small lake (the Kabaka's Lake), and lies in the fertile Lake Basin region, all of which assure Kampala of abundant fresh water for both industrial and domestic use.

Since the return of peace and stability to the country in 1986, Kampala has extended onto more than 20 green, gently rounded hills in the area. The city's pleasant climate and temperatures — which are improved by the night lake breezes off Africa's largest lake, Victoria — have attracted thousands of people to work, build, and settle in the city. In 1991, Kampala's official population was given as 774,261, but now is estimated to be somewhere near one million, and comprises about 90 per cent Africans and 10 per cent Asians, Europeans, and people of mixed race (known locally as

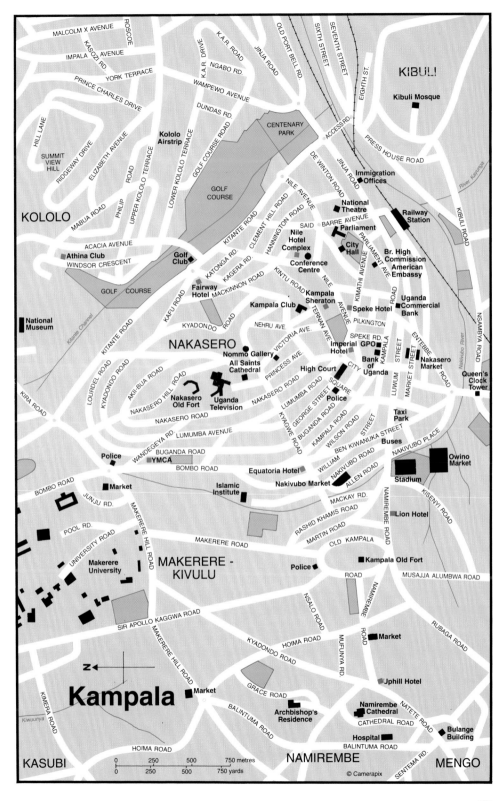

Above: Striking monument in the heart of Kampala commemorates Uganda's independence.

chotaras). The city — one of the fastest growing districts in the country — now covers more than 300 square kilometres (116 square miles), with the Greater Kampala planning area having a radius of about 20 kilometres (12 miles).

The city's centennial was celebrated quietly in 1990, with the majority of the people perhaps just thankful they had anything to celebrate at all. Yet until 20 years earlier, Kampala was a legendary city, a beautiful city — filled with open, generous, and hospitable people who were always ready to smile. The city had become a major rendezvous and was frequently the favoured site of numerous international conferences and meetings.

That all changed on 26 January 1971, when a military coup ushered in neglect, mismanagement, and intermittent war and destruction, which turned Kampala into one of the ugliest cities of the world. When, in 1972, Idi Amin decided to expel some 80,000 Asians and foreign investors — who had been dominating the country's commerce and industry at the time — the city turned into a shadow of its former

majesty almost overnight.

After the restoration of peace and stability in most parts of the country, including the capital, in 1986, the problem of the restoration of Kampala — and other districts as well — started to be addressed. A popularly elected new city administration (the Kampala Resistance Council), with a new mayor, concentrated on rebuilding the city's potholed roads, schools, and clinics, and streamlining the administration and financial management of the capital.

In 1989 a second city administration, based on the popularly elected grassroots Resistance Committees (RCs), continued with the rehabilitation started by their predecessors three years earlier. New plans and policies were implemented that dealt with city land management, market management, and administration. Kampala slowly began to return to normal.

Now, after waiting and watching from afar for many years, the once-expelled Asians and foreign investors were encouraged to come back and

Above: Despite the constant building, Kampala remains green and inviting.

reclaim their property, shops, factories, and other estates. Some 10,000 Asians and Europeans took up the offer and set about cleaning out 20 years of war debris from their shops and workplaces. Where possible, some rehabilitated, renovated, and put on new coats of paint; others pulled their old buildings down and started from scratch, adding a taste of new and modern architecture to the city's skyline.

In the 1990s Kampala truly underwent a facelift almost daily, with the building industry one of the fastest growing enterprises in the city. Places of worship replaced old, rundown cinema halls. New restaurants and 'take-away' establishments popped up on every street corner. Much of the new building was being done by foreign investors, who were given generous incentives to come to Uganda and actively participate in this new era of development.

Residents, too, were involved with the rebuilding of Kampala. Each month, the city's inhabitants — and many visitors — enthusiastically took part in a 'Keep

Kampala Clean' campaign, complementing the city administration's efforts to improve the general cleanliness of the capital. A new public park — to be known as Centenary Park — was put in motion and already features a centenary monument to mark the 100th anniversary of the city's founding.

Because of this constant change, Kampala in the late 1990s is an intriguing place to explore. Unlike some other major cities in Africa, it's safe to walk around at any time of the day or night. The city is attractive, green, and full of friendly people.

Although the city is built on many hills, you'll undoubtedly spend most of your time on just one of them: Nakasero, where the city centre is located. The top half of the hill is filled with pretty, tree-lined streets, up-market private houses, embassies, aid organizations, the better hotels, and some government buildings.

The city's dividing line is busy Kampala Road where you will find most of the banks, the railway station, and a few decent hotels and restaurants.

Above: For that latest trendy look, Ugandans visit their nearest suburban hair salon.
Opposite: The Pride Theatre in Kampala, where many colourful productions are staged.

The area below Kampala Road is the 'seedier' section of town, but it is filled with colourful local life, if that is what you are looking for. The streets there are potholed, congested, and lined with people, overflowing garbage dumps, street markets, kiosks selling everything under the sun, and innumerable hustlers.

Symbols of the new Kampala include sprawling suburbs with large trading centres, a wealth of theatres featuring local music and dance, and many entertaining nightspots. Thanks to the government's trade and foreign exchange liberalization policies, the city's shops are full of the latest local — as well as imported — goods. (Make sure you bargain when you shop; it's all part of the shopping experience.)

If it's conventional sightseeing you are after, don't miss the Kasubi Tombs and the Uganda National Museum. However, just meandering around the city is an adventure in itself.

When to go
The city is pleasant all year round.

Getting there
Kampala, 34 kilometres (21 miles) from Entebbe, 80 kilometres (50 miles) from Jinja, 205 kilometres (127 miles) from Tororo, and 346 kilometres (215 miles) from Gulu, is well served by many international flights into Entebbe International Airport. Domestic and regional air, rail, and road services link it with major centres in Uganda and central and eastern Africa. By road, it is 667 kilometres (417 miles) from Nairobi, Kenya.

Where to stay
The Kampala Sheraton, Nile Hotel Complex, Fairway, Equatoria, Grand Imperial, Speke, and Diplomate are some of the better choices. There are many other hotels with various degrees of quality and service, and many guest houses. See Listings.

Sightseeing
As you head into town from Entebbe International Airport (about a 40-minute drive away), one of the first things you come to is the **roundabout** where Mengo Hill,

175

Queen's Way, and Nsambya roads all intersect. In the middle of the roundabout is the **Queen's Clock Tower**, which is often used as a landmark when you ask directions. Apart from reminding commuters of the correct time, it is remembered as the place where Amin's regime executed 21 presumed enemies of the state by firing squad in 1978.

Immediately **west** of the clock tower is a **monument** commemorating African liberation, built in 1995 by the Pan African Congress.

Just before the clock tower roundabout, on the **right** side of the road, is a large former cricket ground that has become known as a **'religious freedom square'**. Protestants, Catholics, Muslim fundamentalists, and other sects alternatively preach their doctrines from the cricket field. Area residents have complained to the authorities about the loud noise made by the faithful, but no action has been taken as the government does not want to interfere in religious freedom, happy that the many religious sects that had been banned by the Amin regime and expelled from the country have been resurrected.

At the very next roundabout, keep **right** and turn onto **Entebbe Road** to head into the city centre. On your **left** as you travel along this road is one of the city's major markets — the **Nakasero Market** — where farmers and their agents bring their goods for sale to the general public. In addition to finding plenty of Uganda's staple food, *matoke*, you'll find a wealth of other foodstuffs, such as sweet potatoes, Irish potatoes, cassava, yams, and various fruits and vegetables, including oranges, onions, tomatoes, cabbages, kale, and spinach. There are also stalls for beef, fish, pork, goat meat, and lamb. Maize flour, rice, wheat flour, sugar, salt, milk, and other essentials are sold at nearby trading centres.

There is a **traffic light** at the **T-junction** where Entebbe Road joins up with the city's main thoroughfare, alternatively known as **Kampala Road** or **Jinja Road**, depending on where you're standing.

If you turn **left**, you go down Kampala Road's **'bank row'**, where all the major financial institutions and **foreign exchange bureaux** are located. (If you're hungry, a turn to the **right** on **Pilkington Road** will take you to one of the capital's best and oldest Chinese restaurants, the **China Palace**.) Back on Kampala Road and heading west, just after passing the junction of **Speke Road** on your **right**, you'll find the **General Post Office** and, next to that on the same side of the street, the **Bank of Uganda**. Opposite this is the state-run **Uganda Investment Authority**, a one-stop shop for investors.

You'll notice several empty and undeveloped plots along this stretch of Kampala Road, once the sites of structures destroyed during the 1979 civil war that saw the toppling of dictator Idi Amin's regime. More aching reminders of this strife than the empty plots, however, are the derelict buildings still standing empty and forgotten. The plots on which these buildings stand, however, were allocated to prospective developers, and in the not-too-distant future some new, modern buildings should replace these scars of a time that everyone wants to forget. One of the plots was allocated to the Anglican Church of Uganda, who planned a multi-storeyed church building in front of Stanbic Bank. But until they can raise enough money for this ambitious project, the plot has turned into a temporary car park.

After passing Stanbic Bank you come to **City Square** on the **right**, another legacy of the Amin era, but this one more pleasant, as it has been turned into an open-air meeting place used by many groups of people every day. In the square stands a World War II monument. Just behind City Square, along Buganda Road, are the **Uganda High Court** buildings and the **Central Police Station**.

If you're in the mood for a burger, go across the road and try the **Kembobazi Burger Queen**, which is located on the first floor of an office building overlooking City Square. It's a great place to sit and watch the world go by and be entertained by the shouting *matatu* drivers on the

Opposite: Vegetables piled high in a Kampala market.

Above: The main building of Makerere University in Kampala, one of East Africa's finest institutes of higher learning.

street below. In addition to excellent burgers, the restaurant serves several fish and meat dishes, and prices are reasonable.

Just across Kampala Road from City Square is **Pioneer Mall**, the city's first shopping mall, of which the residents are extremely proud. The small, compact shopping centre, completed a few years ago by a British developer, features a wide variety of goods for sale, including high-quality — and expensive — imported products. There is a tiled parking area for its customers.

Until this mall was completed, many Ugandans did not know what shopping malls looked like. However, since the launching of Pioneer Mall, several other developers in the area have converted their properties into supermarket complexes, which they have conveniently dubbed 'shopping malls'.

There are also some nice **restaurants** along this stretch of Kampala Road. Not far past City Square on the same side of the street the **Curry Pot**, a popular Indian

Makerere University

After the YMCA you come to a **major roundabout**. Go **left** there onto **Makerere Hill Road** and then make a **right** turn onto **University Road** to visit the sprawling campus of **Makerere University**.

East Africa's oldest institution of higher learning, the university sits on one of the original seven hills of the capital. It was founded in 1922, originally as a technical school, training artisans such as carpenters, plumbers, painters, and welders for the country's growing industrial needs. But it grew to become the leading university in the region and became part of what was then known as the University of East Africa which, besides Makerere, comprised the university colleges of Nairobi, Kenya, and Dar es Salaam, Tanzania. Before awarding University of East Africa degrees, it was awarding London University degrees.

Under the regional arrangement, Makerere University College specialized in human medicine and education, Nairobi University College specialized in commerce and Dar es Salaam specialized in law.

The University of East Africa broke up when the East African Community dissolved in the 1970s, although, realizing that there was still a necessity for the three universities to maintain links, an Inter-University Council for East Africa was created in the same year, with its headquarters in Kampala.

As each country began to set up its own independent and fully fledged university, each had to work hard to build from scratch those academic disciplines it did not have previously.

Unfortunately, the dissolution of the University of East Africa came in the middle of Uganda's worst period of civil strife. As a result, Makerere University's development stagnated, with most of its academic staff fleeing into neighbouring countries and even further afield to seek employment. No meaningful research or academic journals were forthcoming because of the lack of funding.

While Makerere seemingly stood still, its sister universities in Nairobi and Dar es Salaam flourished. Uganda's premier university finally came out of its slumber

restaurant, serves good curries and stews at reasonable prices.

Continue **west** on Kampala Road to the junction of **Kyagwe Road**, where a **left turn** leads to the **Equatoria Hotel** a little further along on the **right** side of the road.

After crossing Kyagwe Road, Kampala Road joins up with **Bombo Road** (the southern part of which is known as Ben Kiwanuka Street, after the first premier of Uganda). Head **north** on Bombo Road and, after about 550 metres (600 yards), the **Bat Valley Disco** is on the **left**, one of Kampala's more popular discos, and, next to it, the **Sitar Restaurant**, which serves an array of tasty Indian dishes. A little further along Bombo Road on the **right** is the **YMCA**.

179

in 1986, when the new government was ushered in and, together with other donors, injected some much-needed money into Makerere for rehabilitation.

In recent years the government has come to realize that it cannot entirely fund the activities of the university and has requested parents or guardians who can afford to sponsor their children at the university to do so. The government has also asked parents to become involved in a cost-sharing arrangement with them so that the growing costs of university education can be met.

This cost-sharing idea did not go down well with many parents and students and rsulted in student riots in 1991 and 1992 as a protest against the new measures. Government authorities were forced to send armed police onto the campus to protect public property against vandalism. During the riots, two students were shot dead, which led to a temporary closure of the university.

Despite this, by 1996 Makerere University was doing well. It boasted more than 8,000 students in its 14 faculties of agriculture, arts, social sciences, commerce, law, education, technology (engineering), medicine, science, veterinary medicine, fine art, pharmacy, architecture, and nursing — as well as in its five schools and institutions, which include the Centre for Adult Education and Studies, Librarianship, Statistics and Applied Economics, Institute of Social Research, and the Postgraduate Studies School. The faculties were being encouraged to offer evening courses for non-boarders and part-time students from the city.

The public are often invited to lectures in the **Main Hall** of the imposing university administrative block, with its so-called ivory tower. In addition, the School of Fine Arts on the campus features the modern **Margaret Trowell Art Gallery**, named after the school's founder and mentor.

The public is welcome to view the many fine paintings, sculptures, and other works of art on display in this gallery, some of which are for sale.

Bahai temple

To explore other areas in this northern part of the capital, return to the **major roundabout** where Makerere Hill Road and Bombo Road meet. At a corner of the roundabout is a branch of the popular **Bimbo's ice cream parlour**. Continue **north** on **Bombo Road** past the **College Inn** on your **right**, which is popular with budget-minded travellers and which has a **restaurant**.

At the next **roundabout**, Bombo Road veers left, but keep heading **north** on **Gayaza Road** to **Kikaya Hill**, where the majestic **Bahai Temple**, the Mother Temple of Africa, is situated, about six kilometres (four miles) from the city centre. Work on this, the only temple of this religious sect found in Africa, began in May 1957 and it was opened to the public in January 1961. From its compound, there is a superb **panoramic view** of Kampala and the surrounding green countryside.

Now return to the major **Bombo Road roundabout** and head **north-east** on **Mulago Hill Road**. Just after the next **roundabout**, the road becomes **Kira Road**. A turn **left** on **Upper Mulago Hill Road** (just past the roundabout) leads into the grounds of the **Mulago Hospital** and the respected **Makerere University Hospital** and **medical school**.

To reach Uganda's history-packed **National Museum**, however, keep on **Kira Road**, and after a long **bend** to the **right** (where another road, Tufnell Drive, forks left), you'll see the museum on the **right** side of the road.

National treasure

The Uganda National Museum has displays on the **Nakaima Tree, Ntusi, Bigo Bya Mugenyi**, and many other aspects of Ugandan history. There are also good **ethnological exhibits** covering **hunting, agriculture, war, religion**, and **witchcraft** (known locally as *juju*), as well as **natural history** displays.

One of the museum's most enjoyable features is its collection of **traditional**

Opposite: The beautiful Bahai Temple is perched atop yet another of Kampala's many hills.

Above: Bugisu clay drum, one of many artefacts on display in the Uganda National Museum.

musical instruments, which visitors are allowed to play.

There are English-speaking guides at the museum, some of whom have been working there for 10 to 20 years and are full of fascinating information about the exhibits — and about Uganda itself. The National Museum is open all day from Mondays to Saturdays and in the afternoon on Sundays.

There is also an office of the East African Wildlife Society at the museum.

Not far away, on Kanjokya Street in Kamwokya, is the Uganda National Parks headquarters. There you can obtain up-to-date information on where to go and stay in the country's national parks and reserves, as well as make bookings for gorilla treks and the like.

This area of the city, known as Kololo Hill, is residential, featuring winding, tree-lined streets evoking memories of colonial days with names such as Elizabeth Avenue, Philip Road, and Prince Charles Drive (which, rather incongruously, connects with Malcolm X Avenue).

Turn right as you leave the museum

and continue along Kira Road, and a right turn onto Acacia Avenue and then a left onto Kololo Hill Drive will eventually lead you to one of the highest points in the city, at 1,312 metres (4,304 feet), where a Uganda Television mast now stands sentry. Known as Summit View Hill, it was once a popular place for visitors to admire the views of the city, but an army post now established there has put a stop to uninvited guests.

Backtrack to Acacia Avenue and head south, turning right onto Mabua Road and then left onto Windsor Crescent, which brings you to the Athina Club — not only a great place to stay but a great place to eat, with authentic and delicious Greek Cypriot food.

Further south Windsor Crescent ends at the Kitante (or Kampala) Golf Club, where you can turn left (east) onto Lower Kololo Terrace Road. An immediate right turn at this point will put you back on Acacia Avenue heading south, right through the golf course and past the clubhouse itself. Although a members' club, it is open to visitors on introduction.

Above: Golfer tries his skill on the lush fairways of the Kampala golf course.

Kololo airstrip

Straight on along Lower Kololo Terrace Road is the **Kololo Airstrip**, where small aircraft can take off and land easily. The airstrip is where the British Duke of Kent, representing Queen Elizabeth II, officially handed over the instruments of political independence to Dr Milton Obote on the night of 9 October 1962, thus ending British administration of Uganda. Since that day, the annual independence anniversary celebrations have — more often than not — been staged there, as well as other national festivities.

At one end of the Kololo Airstrip is a **national cemetery** where some of the country's leaders and heroes are buried, among them former President **Yusuf Lule**, who governed the country for 68 days after the toppling of dictator Idi Amin's regime. There are permanent guards in the area, mainly to protect the graves from vandals.

Just after the airstrip, turn **right** on **Wampewo Avenue** back towards the city centre. After you pass **Golf Course Road**, you'll see a **new hotel complex** on your right, which in 1996 already had an operative **sports centre** with professional masseurs on hand to work on any muscular ailments that you may have developed playing a round on the nearby golf course.

Shortly after the hotel complex, Wampewo Avenue ends at one of the two major **Jinja Road roundabouts**, where you turn **right** (south-west) for **Centenary Park**. At the next **roundabout**, a **left** turn on **Access Road** leads to **Kibuli Hill**, where the **Kibuli Mosque**, one of the centres of worship for the city's Muslim population, stands.

Back on Jinja Road, however, continue **south-west** towards the city centre, past the **Immigration Offices** on your **left**, to the junction of Siad Barre Avenue, where you find the main branch of **Bimbo's ice cream parlour**, which serves up full meals and a variety of cakes and bread as well as its popular ice cream. Opposite is the **Oriental Pearl** restaurant, which serves a variety of Chinese, Indian, and Western dishes.

As you continue along Jinja Road the

Above: From its position atop Kibuli Hill, Kibuli mosque affords excellent views of the city.

Tropicana 2000 disco is on your **right** after crossing Siad Barre Avenue. Although somewhat sleazier than its competitor, Bat Valley, it remains one of Kampala's most popular nightspots.

Virtually opposite the road from the Tropicana is the **railway station** and, shortly past that on the same side of the road, the city's first modern **casino**, which is constructed of intricately decorated glass and also features a **shopping centre**. Opposite is the famous **City Bar**, where expatriates and tourists congregate.

A stone's throw away on the same side of the road is **Uganda House**, the multi-storey headquarters of the former ruling political party, Milton Obote's Uganda People's Congress (UPC). The imposing white building accommodates the UPC national secretariat, several government ministries, a shopping centre, as well as expensive apartments. On the ground floor is the **Nile Grill**, an outdoor bar and restaurant popular with travellers, expats, and political activists, who often meet there to exchange ideas on the latest issues

over a cup of coffee or a beer. Opposite the Nile Grill is the **Great Wall Restaurant**, which serves a variety of Indian and European dishes as well as the standard Chinese fare.

Adjacent to Uganda House is the multi-storey headquarters of the state-owned **Uganda Commercial Bank**. From Uganda House, head up Parliament Avenue to the **British High Commission** on the left, next to which is the Aga Khan-owned **International Promotion Services**, a tall glass building.

Behind the British High Commission, with its entrance on **Kimathi Avenue**, is the **American Embassy** and, within walking distance on the same avenue, are two **casinos**. A few steps across the road from the casinos is the **'White House'**, the name given to the home of the **Kampala City Council** (KCC) and the **offices** of the **Mayor of Kampala**. The spacious White House was completed in the early 1970s and also features a **Town Hall**, where people's representatives often gather to deliberate on civic and political issues. The old City Council offices still stand next to the new offices.

Above: 'The White House', home of the Kampala City Council.
Overleaf: The imposing entrance of Uganda's Parliament Buildings.

Parliament Avenue ends at the junction with Siad Barre Avenue where, directly in front of you, is Uganda's **National Theatre**. The theatre has a regular programme of events and offers performances in English as well as vernacular languages. One of the more popular groups performing there regularly is the **Ndere Troupe**, a company composed of members of Uganda's many ethnic groups, who have gained worldwide acclaim for their excellent traditional dance, music, and drama shows. The troupe has an office at the museum, where director Stephen Rwangyezi will be happy to let you know about the troupe's upcoming performances (see 'Uganda's Music and Dance', Part Four).

The National Theatre itself is a rewarding place to wander around, as work of local artists is often displayed on the walls. In addition, in the museum grounds you'll find a sort of temporary **artist's village**, where Ugandan **arts and crafts** of all types are for sale in a number of colourful kiosks. Take the time to ask the people staffing the kiosks about the crafts and their use: many

of them are very knowledgeable and interesting to talk to.

On the large plot of land lying between Parliament Avenue, Siad Barre Avenue, Colville Avenue, and Kimathi Avenue are the impressive-looking **white Parliament Buildings**, where the democratically elected and military-backed juntas meet — a link in the historical chain of Uganda's colonization dating from the 1880s up to today. The Parliament Buildings share borders with the White House of the Kampala City Council.

Opposite the Parliament Buildings on Nile Avenue is the **Nile Hotel Complex** and the **Uganda International Conference Centre,** which is connected to the hotel by a covered walkway. The ultra-modern 4-star hotel has 50 rooms, including deluxe, executive, and presidential suites, and features a wide expanse of manicured lawn and many flower-filled gardens.

Both facilities were built in 1971 for the Organization of African Unity (OAU) Heads of States and Leaders Summit meeting in Kampala. That meeting, in fact, never

Above: The Sheraton Kampala, one of the capital city's landmarks.

took place, as the country experienced its first military coup in January 1971, which saw President Milton Obote's government replaced by a military junta led by former army commander Idi Amin, starting a chain of events that was not only to ruin Uganda, but also to cause the break-up of the exemplary East African Community.

Amin did manage to host the OAU summit in 1974, however. No sooner did the illustrious visitors depart than he turned the international conference centre into a centre of interrogation, torture, and killing.

Since President Museveni took over the reigns of political power in 1986, however, the Uganda International Conference Centre has regained its status as a premier meeting place. Several years ago, the president himself opened an office at the centre to enable him to easily tend to important state matters and meet with visiting dignitaries.

Around the corner from the Nile Hotel complex, with its main entrance on Ternan Avenue, is the **Sheraton Kampala Hotel,** a 5-star property set in expansive gardens. It

is a city landmark, as it stands on an elevated site and can be seen from nearly everywhere in town.

Although the Sheraton opened in October 1987, this spot has been an important hotel site since 1967, when the newly established (and 100 per cent government-owned) Apolo Hotel Corporation built a hotel on the property with the help of an Israeli construction firm. It featured the same central 12-storey tower and two large wings (which house the bedrooms) that you see in today's Sheraton.

In 1971 the hotel was renamed the Kampala International Hotel and served as a top hotel during Amin's regime, but as the political situation grew more unstable the hotel deteriorated and, by 1980, had to be closed down.

In 1987, the new government contracted an international firm to renovate the hotel to first-class standard, at a total cost of US$ 29.3 million, and contracted with ITT Sheraton for its management.

The hotel boasts 251 bedrooms, 10 junior suites, and two presidential suites, as well as flats for long-term rental. It also features a huge, circular **swimming pool**, **squash and tennis courts**, a **business centre**, a **health centre**, a **shopping arcade**, a large selection of top-class **restaurants** and **bars**, and a number of **banqueting and meeting rooms**.

The Sheraton is particularly known for its support of local artists. There are **art exhibitions** held every week, but most noticeable is the permanent exhibition found in the entrance hall of the Ruwenzori Ballroom and in the shopping arcade, where artists can display their works free of charge. In the Ruwenzori Bar foyer there is a desk staffed by a representative of the Uganda Artists Association to attend to inquiries from art collectors. In addition, in the gardens of the hotel, there are small **kiosks** from which a number of artists work and sell their products.

Just outside the grounds of the Sheraton is the striking **Independence Monument**, and, around the corner, the new 5-star Grand Imperial Hotel, with its impressive entrance.

In contrast to the modern Sheraton and Grand Imperial, but appealing in its own way, is the charming, colonial **Speke Hotel**, located on nearby Nile Avenue, close to where it intersects with Kimathi Avenue. The hotel, recently renovated and attractively decorated, features 30 rooms and a good **restaurant**.

When you reach the **roundabout** at the bottom of Nile Avenue, turn **right** on **Speke Road**, and then, at the next **roundabout**, take another **right** onto **Ternan Avenue**. A little further up the road is the members-only **Kampala Club**, where the Shanghai Chinese restaurant, open to the public, is located.

From Kampala Club, backtrack a little to the road that runs alongside it and turn **right**, heading **north-west**. When you reach the **T-junction**, turn **left** onto **Nehru Avenue** and then **right** onto **Victoria Avenue**, where, a little farther along on the **left** side of the road, you find the **Nommo Gallery**, the only gallery in Kampala devoted to the promotion of local art. This small, humble gallery, situated in flower-filled, large gardens, regularly hosts **art**

exhibitions and shows by both well-known and little-known Ugandan artists. Many of the items on display, which include **sculptures**, are for sale.

Across from the gallery is **Nakasero State Lodge**, one of the residences of the head of state (photography is not allowed.) Next to the State Lodge is the former Uganda Club which is now the NRA headquarters.

Continue up Victoria Avenue, crossing the intersection with **Kyagwe Road.** There, on the **left**, is **All Saints Cathedral**, the cathedral of the Anglican Church of Uganda, located on the top of **Nakasero Hill.** Until independence in October 1962 it was a small parish church for exclusive use by the white expatriates residing in the Nakasero Hill area, but after independence, when the white community dwindled, the well-to-do Ugandan Christians — who had taken over the whites' jobs and residences — also took over the church.

However, when the Baganda Christians refused to let a non-Muganda archbishop turn nearby Namirembe Cathedral into the church headquarters, Nakasero church was expanded physically and was promoted to cathedral status and the seat of the Uganda archbishop. Because of the structures added during this time, the cathedral has a rather awkward shape.

All Saints is open daily, but the big day, of course, is Sunday, when there are four or more services — all of which are filled to capacity, with many people spilling out onto the lawns and forced to listen to the sermons via outside loudspeakers.

Kikuubo

To see how the average person lives, works, and spends time, return to the main **Entebbe Road roundabout** and head **north-west** on **Ben Kiwanuka Street**. All along there, you'll see heavy-duty trucks and trailers, loaded with merchandise imported from neighbouring Kenya and Tanzania. They all converge in this busy and heavily congested area, known locally as the *Kikuubo*, where they offload their goods onto the many smaller trucks, which are waiting to transport essential commodities to all corners of the country.

Above: A busy, bustling world of its own: the Kampala Taxi Park.

The Kikuubo opens early in the morning and closes late in the evening, and much money changes hands.

Near the Kikuubo, buzzing with overcrowded and overworked minibuses, is the old **Kampala Taxi Park** which is estimated to handle more than a million people every day. At the back of the Kikuubo is the *Baasi za Baganda*, meaning the parking area for up-country buses — an equally congested place.

To lessen the congestion at the Kampala Taxi Park, the KCC built a second **taxi park** across the banks of the **Nakivubo River**. The new park, inaugurated in early 1994, is for use by commuter taxis going out of the capital city. The old taxi park has been left to those wanting to travel within the city and its suburbs.

If you are wandering about in this area, take care against pickpockets and conmen, particularly in the taxi parks. Also be prepared for the unorthodox behaviour of the *bulokas*, the brokers or guides that call out to passengers to entice them to board waiting taxis or buses. As they are paid a commission for each full load, these bulokas sometimes fight over passengers to fill their quota.

Nearby, where **Nakivubo Place** and **Namirembe Road** meet, is the **Nakivubo World War II Memorial Stadium**, where soccer matches, motorcycle racing, and other sporting events are held regularly throughout the year. Perhaps the biggest crowd puller, however, is the annual Buganda Clans Football Competition, in which the 52 clans of the Buganda kingdom fight it out with each other on the pitch on a knock-out basis.

On the first day, hundreds and thousands of Baganda men and women, dressed smartly in their traditional tribal clothes, gather at the stadium.

Led by a colourful motorcade, the kabaka drives into the stadium in an open-roofed vehicle, cheered on by his loyal subjects. The winners of the competition, which spans a four-month period, are awarded a shield by the kabaka.

Behind the stadium is the large, open-air **Owino Market**. When liberalization of foreign exchange dealings began to be effective, black marketeers in forex (foreign

Above: Local soccer matches are always a crowd puller at Nakivubo Stadium.

exchange) — locally called 'Kibanda Boys' — used their savings to put up makeshift shops made of iron and steel containers. They first established their container shopping centre in the empty spaces on the edge of the city's bank district, doing roaring business in cheap fabrics and garments.

The KCC, however, decided a few years back to allocate the Kibanda Boys a zone near Owino Market. There you'll find hundreds of **open containers**, fixed on the ground by cemented supports and bursting with all sorts of merchandise.

Be prepared to drive a hard bargain: the young men and women are good at selling, and will not want to let you go until you've bought something.

Also along Nakivubo Place, you'll see many small **kiosks** selling commodities until late in the evening. Many of these small businesses are operated by civil service and parastatal workers, who find they have to supplement their meagre official incomes. The kiosks do plenty of business, regularly visited by workers returning from the city to their homes in the evenings.

Kasubi Tombs

A number of Kampala's most interesting attractions to visitors are actually located outside the city centre, although not far away. By far the most impressive of these are the royal tombs of the ancient Buganda kingdom, the Kabaka's or Kasubi Tombs, located on Kasubi Hill some five kilometres (three miles) north-west of the city centre.

Start from the main **Entebbe Road roundabout**, turning **north-west** onto **Nakivubo Place**, passing Nakivubo Stadium and then turning **left** onto **Namirembe Road**. After a short distance, as you come to the hill where **Kampala Old Fort** is situated, the road **splits** off in three directions: Rubaga Road to the left, Namirembe Road in the **middle**, and Old Kampala Road to the right. Keep on **Namirembe Road**, then turn right on Hoima Road.

But to see the impressive **Namirembe Cathedral** on the top of **Namirembe Hill**, keep on Namirembe Road until the **T-junction** at **Natete/Kyadondo Road**. Turn **right** there, and then **left** on **Willis Road.** After a short distance, turn **left** onto **Cathedral Road**, which leads to the cathedral itself.

Namirembe Cathedral, also known as St Paul's, is Uganda's oldest cathedral. The first representatives of the Church Missionary Society — who arrived in Uganda in 1877 at the invitation of Kabaka Mutesa's letter printed in the British newspaper *The Daily Telegraph* — erected the first church building on Namirembe Hill in March 1890. *Namirembe*, the name by which both the hill and the cathedral have come to be known, means 'the mother of peace and tranquillity' in the Luganda language.

When this first grass-thatched church was completed, it coincided with the murder of Bishop Hannington in Busoga, allegedly done in error when the kabaka's orders, given in Luganda, were misinterpreted. The kabaka had ordered that the bishop be freed — *mute* in Luganda — but his overzealous aides understood it to mean kill — *mutte* — him. During the same year, hundreds of Christian converts were burnt to death. Despite such setbacks, only four years after these terrible events, some 1,000 worshippers thronged the new Namirembe church at Christmas in defiance.

Namirembe Cathedral, like the countryside around it, has undergone tremendous changes over the years. Now a huge, impressive edifice with fine **views** of the city from its grounds, the cathedral betrays no outward signs of its chequered history. The congregation continues to flock to its services, called to worship by the beating of drums. An artistically illustrated guide to St Paul's Cathedral, Namirembe, written by Karen Moon, tells of this fascinating history, although copies are difficult to come by.

Many other religions have imposing headquarters on the outskirts of the city: those of the Roman Catholic Church are at Lubaga Hill, south-west of Namirembe; the Orthodox Church headquarters is located at Namungona Hill, five kilometres (two-and-a-half miles) north-west of Kampala on the Hoima Road; and the minority Seventh Day Adventists can be found four kilometres (two-and-a-half miles) south of Kampala on the Entebbe Road. To get to the Kasubi Tombs from Namirembe, take **Cathedral Road** back to **Willis Road** and turn **left**, continuing along Willis Road until you reach the next major **intersection**, where you'll turn **right** on **Balintuma Road**. When you come to a major **roundabout** (which Makerere Hill Road joins), turn **left** onto **Hoima Road**. After about one kilometre (half a mile), turn **left** on **Masiro Road**, and the tombs will be on the **left** side of the road a short distance after the turn.

The Kasubi Tombs, constructed in traditional fashion with thatch, poles, and reeds, is a huge domed structure that houses the remains of four former Buganda kings: Mutesa I, Mwanga II, Daudi Chwa II, and Edward Mutesa II. Still maintained and guarded by Baganda tribespeople, the tombs also hold a variety of **artefacts** that belonged to the kings, including **musical instruments** (such as drums), **weapons**, **fetishes** — and a **stuffed leopard** once kept as a pet by Mutesa I.

Entry to the shrine is through two reed fences: an outer fence and the inner fence. The gate to the shrine is a two-door edifice that once served as a gate for the king.

The tombs are open seven days a week, from 0900 to 1800. Visitors are requested to remove their shoes before entering the dome as a sign of respect and reverence. English-speaking guides narrate the history of the Buganda kingdom. There is an entrance fee of Ush 1,000 (about US$ 1), but an extra small tip to the guide is always welcome.

Kasubi Hill was established by Kabaka Mutesa as the capital of Buganda in 1881, and the **Kabaka's Palace** is also still nearby, but it is closed to the public.

Another interesting reminder of the kabakas of old is the **Kabaka's Lake**, reached by travelling down **Mengo Hill Road** from the **clock tower** and then turning **right** onto **Ring Road**, which circles around until you'll eventually see the lake on your **right**. The lake is reported to have been dug out on the orders of Kabaka Mwanga in the 1880s so that he could use it as an 'escape corridor' to Lake Victoria,

Opposite: Bride-to-be prepares to enter Namirembe Cathedral for her wedding ceremony.
Overleaf: The Buganda kingdom's most important cultural monument, the Kasubi Tombs.

but the actual link to the big lake was never achieved, as the kabaka was driven from his capital by Muslim dissenters.

Martyrs' shrine

Another important religious and historical site related to the Buganda kingdom is the Namugongo Martyrs' Shrine, situated about 12 kilometres (7.5 miles) north-east of Kampala off the Jinja Road.

To get there, head out of the capital on the **Jinja Road**. At the **second main roundabout** on Jinja Road, near **Centenary Park**, there is a **right turn** to **Port Bell**, some five kilometres (three miles) away on the shores of Lake Victoria. Uganda Railways Corporation uses the town as its base from which to operate the country's second route to the Indian Ocean by utilizing wagon ferries between Port Bell and the northern Tanzanian lake port of Mwanza, where traffic is connected by railway to the Indian Ocean port of Dar es Salaam.

In the 1990s this important operation suffered, however — as did the local fishing industry — when water hyacinth, a floating weed, completely blocked the port. Work and research were going on to fight this rapidly spreading plant, which threatens the livelihood of many millions of people around Lake Victoria.

To continue to the shrine, return to the Jinja Road and head **north-east,** past the **Uganda Management Institute** on your **left** before you come to the huge **Lugogo sports complex.** The **Lugogo Stadium** features an impeccably green **cricket pitch,** at which both local and international competitions take place. Every year, several Ugandan schools and colleges take part in a national cricket week hosted at the stadium, during which they compete on a points system.

The **Lugogo Indoor Stadium** also located there is a huge hall with amphitheatre-like seating. There, national boxing champion-ships — as well as regional competitions be-tween Uganda, Tanzania, and Kenya — are held each year. The complex also has lawn **tennis courts**. Nearby is the newly established **Lugogo Permanent Show Grounds**, belonging to the ambitious Uganda Manufacturers Association. In mid-October every year, a show of goods produced by the country's emerging manu-facturers is held there. Lugogo is scattered with small, custom-built individualistic buildings of various architectural styles where companies display their products. Exhibition buildings with stalls are also available for hire by visiting foreign exhibitors.

The Lugogo Permanent Show Grounds are located near the heavily populated shanty estates of **Nakawa** and **Naguru,** originally built by the Kampala City Council (KCC) for rental to its low-income workers, as well as to the general public. In the 1990s the two sprawling estates were condemned by the KCC and scheduled for demolition. The council planned to sell off the plots, and required prospective buyers to erect simple but modern units of approved architectural design. However, there was political resistance, as many people living in the condemned houses could not afford to buy the plots — let alone put up new units of a required modern standard.

Not far from the controversial Naguru and Nakawa estates on the Kampala–Jinja highway is the **industrial area** of **Nakawa** and **Kyambogo**. New structures were springing up there every day in the marshy area during the 1990s, competing fiercely for the limited land available.

As you descend to the industrial area, on the **right** is the home of the state-run **Uganda Revenue Authority** (URA) and the yard for containerized cargo. The road leading to the URA headquarters is often clogged with queues of heavy trailers laden with containers waiting to be checked and offloaded.

Uganda's only **drive-in cinema** is nearby – closed since the 1970s. Beyond it is the fast-growing **Ntinda** village, with modern private property developments.

Further along the Jinja Road, about 11 kilometres (7 miles) outside the city centre,

Opposite: The peaceful inner sanctum of the Kasubi Tombs displays artefacts from many of the Buganda kings.

Above: Large painting at Namugongo Martyrs' Shrine tells the story of the Christian massacre.
Opposite: Monument marking the 100th anniversary of Kampala's founding stands in the city's new Centenary Park.

in 1996 Chinese contractors were busy constructing a US$ 28.6 million giant **sports centre** and **stadium** at **Namboole** village, a short distance behind **Kireka** trading centre. In an effort to promote sports in Africa, the Chinese government granted the Uganda government an interest-free loan to build the complex. The sports centre was scheduled for completion in 1997 and in anticipation, private developers were already busy erecting a modern **hotel** nearby.

The stadium has been named Mandela Stadium, in honour of South African President Nelson Mandela, who laid the foundation stone.

Not far beyond the new sports centre is the **Namugongo Martyrs' Shrine, o**n this spot where in 1886 more than 20 newly converted Ugandan Christians were burnt alive by command of Kabaka Mwanga II, who had ordered them to renounce the white man's religion.

A beautiful steel structure, in traditional style, stands at the scene of the atrocity.

Artistic work depicting the scenes of this historic Christian episode grace the interior wall of the circular **church** that stands on the site. In the centre of the church, preserved in glass, are some **remains** of one of the Roman Catholic martyrs, Kaloli Lwanga.

The shrine was visited and consecrated by Pope Paul V during his first visit to Uganda and the African continent in 1969.

Anglicans as well as Catholics were among the martyrs and, to commemorate their suffering, the Anglican Church of Uganda has built a **seminary** at the spot.

Every year, on 3 June, the country observes Martyrs Day as a public holiday. During the day, thousands of the faithful make a religious pilgrimage to Namugongo in remembrance of the martyrs.

Lakeside excursion
For a trip to the shores of Lake Victoria, head **south** out of Kampala on **Entebbe Road** and turn **left** (east) at the **Queen's Clock Tower** on **Nsambya Road**, which after a short while takes a sharp **turn** to the

199

south-east. After a **sports ground** on your **right**, take the **left fork** onto **Gaba Road, which** is tarmacked all the way to the lake.

The first hill you come to as you leave the capital is **Muyenga Hill**, often referred to as Tank Hill because a huge **tank** that holds most of the city's water supply is located there. Just before you reach this hill, you'll see **Le Chateau restaurant, considered by many in 1996 to be** the city's best restaurant.

As you climb Muyenga Hill, you pass the city's most famous **social drinking clubs** at the **Kabalagala trading centre**, about seven kilometres (four miles) outside the city centre. Retail shops in the suburbs with off-licences (allowed to sell liquor for take-away) often convert their shops into these clubs, which extend onto the verandas and courtyards at the fronts of their establishments. Although in the strict sense these drinking places are illegal, the KCC enforcement department has come to accept them.

Muyenga is one of the most heavily built-up areas of Kampala, with some of the most elegant and expensive homes in the country on its slopes, although it is often referred to as an expensive slum area because of its unplanned nature. But at the top of Muyenga Hill, in addition to the water tank, is the **Hotel Diplomate**, a medium-priced hotel with **panoramic views** of the city. The rooms are decent, the service friendly and efficient.

Continuing **south** on **Gaba Road** to Lake Victoria, you come to the popular **Half London** restaurant and bar, which is usually quite evident by the large number of cars parked on either side of the road towards evening. Get there early if you want to park anywhere near the place. There's **live music** — a combination of African and Western — every night of the week. Partially open-air and partially enclosed, its ambience is friendly and boisterous, with a multiracial crowd thoroughly enjoying the band that never seems to stop playing.

Gaba Road ends at Gaba port. Not far from there is **Munyonyo port**, where, even before the British explorers arrived in Uganda in the 1860s, the ancient Buganda kingdom used to organize an annual **royal regatta**. Competing teams comprising various clans would vie for victory in dugout canoes, using oars. The kabaka of Buganda and his entourage — consisting of ministers, princes, princesses, and other dignitaries — would be in attendance. The annual royal regatta was suspended indefinitely when in 1966 the Obote regime forced Kabaka Edward Mutesa II into exile in the United Kingdom, where he died. The regatta was resumed in 1994, however, when President Museveni's administration agreed to amend the constitution and allow the revival of the kingdoms.

If you head **east** on a **dirt road** from Munyonyo along the lake shoreline, you will come to the former resort of **Jajja Villas**, which was developed by a private entrepreneur during the 1970s. However, Idi Amin's gun-toting soldiers killed the developer and Amin turned the resort into his lakeside State Lodge, where he entertained the high and mighty.

When Amin hosted the OAU Heads of State Summit in 1974, he invited his colleagues to Jajja Villas, where he arranged a display of military gunships and fighter planes, which demonstrated how they would launch an attack on the then racist South African regime. Several of the fighter planes missed their targets — but no local newspaper dared report this truth.

After Amin was ousted in 1979, in 1996 Jajja Villas was bought by a Ugandan tycoon, who built a private residence on the plot.

A few kilometres from Jajja Villas, a property developer was constructing a **hotel** on the lakeshore. He built a large platform at **KK Beach Gaba**, where musicians perform every weekend to large crowds. Weddings and other functions were held at the site. The developer also had a number of **steamers** that took customers for pleasure cruises on the lake.

More resorts were planned or were in various stages of construction along the lakeshore from Gaba towards Entebbe, as the area has enormous potential.

Opposite: View of Kampala's sprawling suburbs from Muyenga, or 'Tank', Hill.

Jinja: Source of the Nile

Around 1870, John Hanning Speke, an English soldier and explorer, arrived on the west bank of a river, opposite a village known locally as Ejjinja, and confirmed for the world that the Nile flows out of Lake Victoria at this point to start its 6,400-kilometre-long (4,000-mile) journey to the Mediterranean Sea. The starting point of the great river — on which Sudan and Egypt have always depended for their livelihood and sheer existence — had puzzled many people of great vision for centuries.

Today, now that most of the world has been mapped and surveyed, it seems surprising that geographers should have argued so much over what, in the eyes of local people, was actually there all along. The people who lived nearby knew only that the river Kiyira (the local name for the Nile, which describes its roar as it drops into the big gorge there) flowed from the lake — although they naturally did not know where it eventually led, nor of its ages-long significance for humanity.

Speke described his 'discovery' thus: 'We were well rewarded, for the "stones", as the Waganda call the falls, was by far the most interesting sight I had seen in Africa.'

At the village overlooking the river at this point there was (and still is) a large stone, or, in Luganda, *ejjinja*, from which the place obviously got its name. Speke named the falls that he saw Ripon Falls, after the president of the Royal Geographical Society in London, but they are now no more, having disappeared in 1947 when work began on the giant Owen Falls Dam.

Then, however, the sight of the falls attracted Speke for hours. He later wrote: 'the roar of the waters, the thousands of passenger fish, leaping at the falls with all their might, the Wasoga and Waganda fishermen coming out in boats and taking posts on all the rocks with rod and hook, hippopotami and cattle, driven down to drink and the margin of the lake, made, in all, with the pretty nature of the countryside . . . as interesting a picture as one could wish to see.'

There were canoes on the west bank of the river, which crossed the Nile from Busoga into the neighbouring kingdom of Buganda at Jinja, but Speke did not make the trip. It was actually Henry Morton Stanley who became the first European to set foot in the town in 1875, during his voyage around Lake Victoria.

By 1890 the Napoleon Gulf — as the bay through which the waters of the lake funnel into the Nile is called — was becoming of increasing importance as the main ferry on the route from Kampala to the Kenyan shores of Lake Victoria.

In 1901 the administrator of the colonial protectorate government in Busoga moved his headquarters from Iganga — 32 kilometres (20 miles) away in the east — to Jinja. The same year saw the railway line from Mombasa reach Kisumu, on the Kenyan side of the lake east of Jinja, and a steamer service was established to serve the different parts of the lake. For the first few years Jinja developed slowly as the Busoga District headquarters. The only item traded with the coast was ivory. Though cotton was introduced in Buganda in 1903 and was soon being grown in the eastern province, it was not to grow in this part of the country in quantities sufficient to stimulate trade for some years.

But the promise that Jinja held out to the industrialist and investor was recognized early on. In 1908, Sir Winston Churchill, who called Uganda the 'Pearl of Africa', wrote: 'Jinja is destined to become a very important place in the future of central Africa . . . in years to come the shores of this splendid bay may be crowned with long rows of tropical villas and imposing offices and the gorge of the River Nile crowded with factories and warehouses.' In the years that followed, that prophecy became a reality.

The earliest industries in Jinja were

Opposite: Wide, tree-lined streets and colonial buildings still characterize the lakeside town of Jinja.

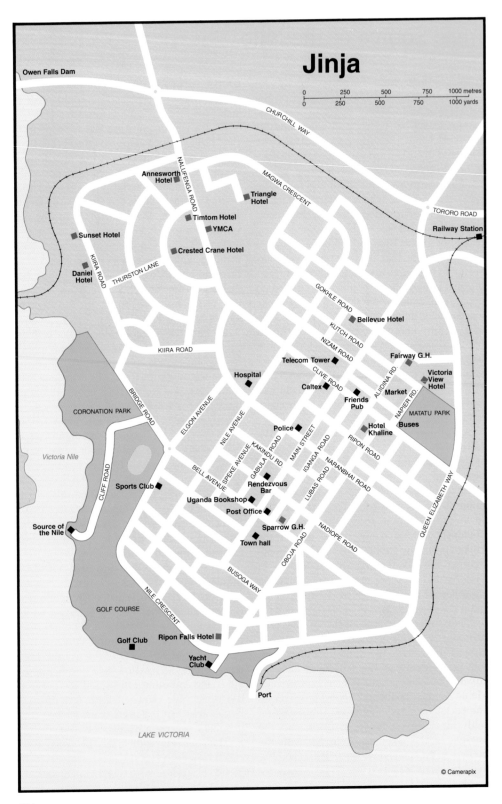

Jinja

Owen Falls Dam

| 0 | 250 | 500 | 750 | 1000 metres |
| 0 | 250 | 500 | 750 | 1000 yards |

CHURCHILL WAY

NALUFENGA ROAD

MAGWA CRESCENT

Annesworth Hotel

Triangle Hotel

Timtom Hotel

YMCA

Sunset Hotel

Crested Crane Hotel

TORORO ROAD

Railway Station

Daniel Hotel

KIIRA ROAD

THURSTON LANE

GOKHLE ROAD

KUTCH ROAD

Bellevue Hotel

NIZAM ROAD

KIIRA ROAD

Fairway G.H.

Telecom Tower

CLIVE ROAD

Hospital

Caltex

Victoria View Hotel

ALIIDINA RD

Market

NAPIER RD

Friends Pub

CORONATION PARK

BRIDGE ROAD

ELGON AVENUE

NILE AVENUE

Police

MAIN STREET

KAKINDU ROAD

IGANGA ROAD

RIPON ROAD

Hotel Khaline

MATATU PARK

Buses

Victoria Nile

CLIFF ROAD

SPEKE AVENUE

GABULA ROAD

NARANBHAI ROAD

QUEEN ELIZABETH WAY

BELL AVENUE

Sports Club

Rendezvous Bar

LUBAS ROAD

Uganda Bookshop

Post Office

Source of the Nile

Sparrow G.H.

Town hall

NADIOPE ROAD

OBOJA ROAD

BUSOGA WAY

NILE CRESCENT

GOLF COURSE

Golf Club

Ripon Falls Hotel

Yacht Club

Port

LAKE VICTORIA

© Camerapix

204

Above: The late Jayant Muljibhai Madhvani, a leading entrepreneur, was born at Jinja.

based primarily on agricultural production in Busoga District, particularly cotton, sugar, timber, and their by-products. By 1910 Busoga and some areas north of Lake Kyoga were growing so much cotton as a cash crop that it became necessary to construct a railway from Jinja northwards to Namasagali, on which the cotton could be shipped to Jinja and then transported by steamer to Kisumu.

A direct railway line — from Nakuru, in Kenya, to Jinja — was completed in 1928.

The Asian workers who had come to East Africa to work on the Uganda Railway in the last decade of the last century fell in love with the region and embarked on the pioneering work of building agricultural and industrial enterprises. The more adventurous ones — such as Nanji Kalidas Mehta and Muljibhai Madhvani, whose names have since become synonymous with Jinja — through hard work, perseverance, and entrepreneurial spirit, built empires that dominated the economic heights of the region.

Mehta actually started the sugar industry in Uganda and, although the name is principally associated with the sugar estate at Lugazi, about 40 kilometres (25 miles) west of Jinja, the group developed widespread interests elsewhere in Uganda and overseas.

The Muljibhai Madhvani group of companies, which had similar interests, developed a massive sugar estate at Kakira, about 16 kilometres (10 miles) east of Jinja on the Tororo Road, as well as a steel smelter and rolling mill in Jinja itself — one of the biggest in East Africa. The mill was started in 1963 by the Madhvani group in association with a state-owned holding company known as the Uganda Development Corporation.

Another Madhvani project was the Jinja-based Mulco Textiles, which went into production in 1965 and employed about 1,400 people.

It was no surprise, therefore, in the 1970s, when the Amin regime gave 90-day marching orders to the Mehtas, the Madhvanis, and well over 80,000 other Asians and foreign investors, it unravelled the very social and economic fabric of the

Above: Despite its small-town appearance, Jinja is the second largest city in Uganda.

country. The Asian industrialists and shopkeepers not only dominated the urban areas and trading centres, but went deep into the countryside to buy cotton, coffee, and other produce from the farmers, paying them cash on the spot, providing credit facilities, and exchanging the farmer's products with essential commodities. When the Asians left so abruptly, the ˙huge vacuum could not easily be filled by the inexperienced, unmotivated, indigenous Ugandans. The seven years' absence of the Asian sugar, tea, coffee, and cotton estate owners dealt a big blow to Jinja's promising future, as it did to the rest of the country.

And conversely, the return of Asians and foreigners in the 1980s, which allowed them to repossess their expropriated property, has greatly contributed to the revival of Jinja's industrial base.

Now Uganda's largest town after the capital city of Kampala, Jinja, situated at the source of the legendary River Nile, is once again a principal East African industrial centre. With a population in 1991 of 65,169, Jinja is now estimated to have some 80,000 residents.

On the shores of Africa's largest freshwater body, Lake Victoria, Jinja is conveniently situated from an industrial point of view — only 80 kilometres (50 miles) from Kampala and 125 kilometres (78 miles) from the town of Tororo on the border with neighbouring Kenya.

The construction of the Owen Falls hydroelectric dam at the source of the Nile in 1954 gave Jinja a tremendous advantage in attracting industry. The provincial city has, in fact, become home to almost the entire range of the country's manufacturers. Jinja has everything an industrialist desires: plenty of water, power, and land, cheap labour, good communication facilities; and good transportation links to neighbouring countries by air, road, and lake ferry.

The principal town of what is still known as the Busoga region (despite what recent maps say), Jinja also remains an agricultural centre, with the potential of producing more than 90,000 bales of cotton a year — more than all the rest of Uganda. Other crops grown here include sugar, coffee, and nutritious groundnuts. Lying north of the equator at an altitude of 1,143 metres (3,750 feet), the town enjoys a pleasant climate, with temperatures ranging from 17° to 28°C (63° to 82°F). The municipality itself, which has strong links with the neighbouring township of Njeru on the western bank of the Nile, covers an area of 30 square kilometres (11.5 square miles).

For tourist and resident alike, Jinja offers a variety of recreational activities, from sailing on the lake to swimming, golf, tennis, and many team sports. In addition to the obvious attraction of seeing the source of the Nile, a trip to the Bujagali Falls, a few kilometres downstream, is also a favourite activity, particularly for picnickers.

For evening entertainment, the visitor will find three cinemas in the town and a first-class and energetic amateur dramatic group, the Nile Players, which stages frequent productions.

There are Christian churches of several denominations, as well as mosques and temples. In one of the Hindu temples is a plaque commemorating the ceremony in 1948 when some of the Mahatma Gandhi's ashes were scattered on the Nile.

Getting there
Jinja, 80 kilometres (50 miles) from Kampala, 125 kilometres (78 miles) from Tororo, 114 kilometres (71 miles) from Entebbe, and 587 kilometres (367 miles) from Nairobi, is well served by air, road, and rail, linking it with major centres in Uganda and east and central Africa.

When to go
Jinja is pleasant at any time of the year.

Where to stay
The Sunset, Crested Crane, Timtom, Annesworth, and Triangle hotels all offer good accommodation, with the Sunset surpassing the others by way of its great location (overlooking the Owen Falls Dam) and pleasant gardens. There are also a number of guesthouses and budget hotels with various degrees of quality. See Listings. Camping is allowed at the Jinja Golf Club and at the Timtom Hotel, but you need to take your own tent.

Sightseeing
As you travel along the main road from Kampala, there is no mistaking the mighty **Owen Falls Dam** and the **railway bridge** across the Nile, which mark the entrance to Jinja. A tribute to modern engineering, the dam was opened by Princess Elizabeth of Great Britain in 1952 to harness the waters of the Nile to generate electricity for not only Uganda, but Kenya, Tanzania, and Rwanda as well.

Drive slowly as you go over the dam, and if you believe — as some locals do — that the Nile was given birth by a human mother, toss in some coins as you cross to appease the 'mother spirit'. Residents of the area allege that at midday, when the sun is directly above your head, Mother Nile, dressed in white robes, can be seen seated quietly on one of the surviving rocks in the middle of the river. More recent events have added to its spiritual associations: several people have committed suicide by throwing themselves over the edge of the dam into the churning waters below.

The water, escaping from the lake at high speed, enters the spectacular dam's gates and turns the turbines, creating the hydroelectric power. Two or three of the dam's gates (or sluices), depending on the amount of water in the artificial lake, are opened daily, causing water to gush out in a wide arc, which, on a sunny day, creates brilliant rainbows.

During the years of insecurity, armed soldiers used to be stationed at the observation platform. At that time, photographers were not allowed to take snaps of the dam — although, if they wished, visitors could buy postcards bearing a photo of the dam from any bookshop in town. Today, taking photographs is no problem.

With assistance from the British government and the Commonwealth Development Corporation, the Owen Falls Dam underwent a thorough overhaul, and its generating capacity was increased. The

Overleaf: Construction of the Owen Falls Dam changed the face of Jinja forever.

Above: The railway bridge spanning the Nile was opened in 1931.

World Bank and other donors extended credit for the construction of a second power project extending the Owen Falls Dam. Hundreds of Chinese workers came to the country to carry out the work, and the once empty fields — east of the now condemned police post near the dam — became a housing estate where the new power station workers stayed. The project was expected to take two to three years to complete and would make fundamental changes to the landscape near the river.

The Madhvani Group also concluded an agreement with the government to establish another power station — at a cost of some US$ 400 million — at Bujagali Falls, a few kilometres downstream. These new developments inevitably saw Jinja playing an even more important role in Uganda's social and economic future.

A few metres up on the **western** bank of the river, **Nile Breweries Limited** — who brew beer using the waters of the Nile, a unique marketing point — in 1996 were planning to set up a modern settlement on the city's agricultural showground called an **'African Village'**, overlooking both the Owen Falls Dam and the railway bridge. Traditional musical groups would be permanently stationed at the village to entertain visitors.

From the dam you have a good view of the Nile railway bridge, which, when opened in 1931, allowed the railway to extend to Kampala.

After you cross the dam, turn **right** at the first **roundabout** into **Nalufenya Road**, which further on becomes Clive Road. Unlike other cities in Uganda, Jinja does not have many roundabouts. The city, built on the flat banks of Lake Victoria and the River Nile, has been neatly laid out, with long, straight streets in what appears to be a preplanned manner, and it is easy to get your bearings.

After a **railway bridge**, turn **right** at **Kiira Road**, which heads **south-west** and then turns sharply **south-east**. Soon after the road turns, on your right you can see both the **Daniel Hotel** (popular with expatriates) and, a little further along, the **Sunset Hotel**. The Sunset overlooks the dam and has pleasant gardens. A couple of streets back towards Nalufenya Road you find a cluster

Above: Whitewashed walls and neatly manicured lawn of the Jinja post office.

of other hotels, including the **Crested Crane**, **Timtom**, and **Triangle**.

Continue **south-east** on Nalufenya Road, which turns into **Clive Road**, to the city centre. To the **north** of Clive Road there is the **Belle View Hotel**. To get there, turn **left** onto **Main Street** and then, three blocks or so later, turn **left** again on **Gokhle Road**, and the hotel is on the **left**. There is also **Friend's Pub**, on Clive Road on your **left** just past the **intersection** with **Main Street**, where you can get a friendly drink and a cheap but good meal in a run-down English pub-type atmosphere. The city **market**, always good for a splash of local colour, is also a block or so **north** of Clive Road, between **Alidina** and **Napier** roads, and adjacent to the **bus station** and *matatu* **park**.

To explore the **southern** section of town, turn **right** from Clive Road onto **Main Street**. The **police station** will soon be on your **right**, at the junction of **Ripon Road**. A little further down, but also on your **right**, between **Naranbhai** and **Kakindu** roads, is the popular **Rendezvous Bar and Restaurant** which serves a variety of

Western dishes. At the next **intersection** with **Bell Avenue**, you'll find the **Uganda Bookshop** on your **right**, with the **post office** on the other side of the street.

Across from the post office on Bell Avenue, near where it intersects with Iganga Road, is the **Town Hall**, where the administration of the Jinja Municipal Council is housed. Officially opened in 1958, the Town Hall building has a spacious council chamber where the mayor of the city presides over a popularly elected council. In addition to the management of the municipality, the council's powers include the administration of primary schools and certain health services, as well as control, management, and development of leased land and housing estates.

The council, in addition to running the usual health inspectorate under the medical officer of health, also operates an up-to-date health and maternity centre at its housing estate at nearby Walukuba, the largest estate of its kind in Uganda.

Continue down Bell Avenue past the Town Hall, turn **right** on **Oboja Road**, and take it all the way to the end to get

Above: Golfers enjoy 18 holes at the scenic Jinja Golf Club.

to the **Jinja Sailing Club**, where there is a nine-month racing season for two main classes of boats, Ospreys and Enterprises. You can get meals and drinks at the club, which is located at a pretty spot on the water's edge, and there is a popular **disco** on Friday and Saturday nights. Only 200 metres (220 yards) to the east is the town's **port**.

Just to the west of the Sailing Club is the **Jinja Golf Club** which, in addition to a nine-hole **golf course**, has facilities for **tennis, cricket, football** and **hockey**. It also has a fine **swimming pool**. Visitors to Jinja are welcome at the club without formality, and for those staying several days, temporary membership can easily be arranged for a small fee.

In addition to the usual hazards, Jinja's golf course, which overlooks the Nile and Lake Victoria, has another that has become a topic of conversation in clubhouses all over the world: the **hippo footprint**. Hippos regularly wander around the golf course area after dark, and it is not unusual for a player the next day to be confronted by a large footprint on the green — and a three-

ton hippo is not particularly light of foot. To deal with this hazard, one of the club's rules states: If a hippo footmark or an old hole interferes with the lie of the ball or line of putt, the ball may be lifted and placed not nearer the hole, on ground that avoids these conditions. Another hazard is the **kites** in the area, who have developed a rather annoying habit of picking up nice white golf balls along the fairways and depositing them with a splash into the waters of the Napoleon Gulf, opposite the eighth fairway of the course.

Sporting enthusiasts can also enjoy the many facilities offered at the **Amber Court Club**, which has a **swimming pool**. This club was founded during the influx of expatriates to work on the Owen Falls Dam.

Cricket is one of the most popular sports in Jinja, particularly among members of the Asian community, and there are about a dozen different clubs in town catering for this sport. Rugby, football, and hockey are also widely played.

As Jinja is on the lake, angling of course has its devotees: there is spinning

Above: Plaque makes known to all that this is the long-sought-after source of the Nile.

for **barbel** in the rough water below the dam, while float-fishing for **tilapia** takes place in the quieter waters. And, of course, there are huge catches to be made of the famous giant **Nile perch**.

Near the golf club is the **agricultural showground**, originally part of Coronation Park, bordered by **Bridge Street**. Once used as a multi-sectoral showground, the plot was allocated to the Uganda Farmers Association a few years back for the staging of an annual show by farmers and agro-industrialists.

But of course what most visitors to Jinja want to see is the **source of the Nile** itself. To get there, take **Nile Crescent Road** from the golf club in a **northerly** direction Then, go **left** at the **round-about** onto **Bridge Road**, and then **left** again at **Cliff Road**, which comes to a dead end at the **picnic site. There you'll find** a **plaque** marking the spot where the mighty Nile leaves Lake Victoria. This was once the site of the Ripon Falls, before they became inundated by the waters of the Owen Falls Dam. You can still make out where the falls once were,

however, by the turbulence in the water, and the spot affords a good view of the railway bridge across the Nile.

The plaque once commemorated Speke's 'discovery' of the source of the Nile. However, now it reads: 'This spot marks the point where the Nile starts its journey of 6,400 kilometres through Sudan and Egypt to the Mediterranean Sea'. The change was made at the insistence of the late Thomas Sankara of Burkino Faso who, when on a visit to the site, said he could not believe the claims that Speke was the first person to discover the source of the Nile. He argued that the indigenous Africans knew the source of the river hundreds of years before Speke visited the spot, and that the plaque should be changed to reflect the true facts.

For those who feel that Speke was slighted, take heart: on the **opposite bank**, near **Njeru** town, within view of the Jinja site, stands an **obelisk** that marks the spot where Speke stood and gazed in wonder at the sight before him.

It was once free to visit the source of the

Nile but after President Yoweri Museveni advised the Jinja Municipality Council to charge a fee to everyone who wanted to follow in the footsteps of explorer Speke, a small entry fee has been charged since December 1994. During the past couple of years, the number of visitors to the site has doubled, considerably boosting the council's revenue from the attraction. And the revenue has been put to good use: there are no longer knife-wielding bag-snatchers to look out for, as the council provides security guards. The adjacent **gardens**, bordering the Jinja golf course, are regularly tended and kept neat and tidy. Toilet facilities have been revamped and makeshift **kiosks** selling **handicrafts** and other gift items erected.

And don't think that VIPs get away without paying to visit the site: even the country's most important man coughs up. 'The policy here now is that even the president, his relatives, and visitors pay to enter the place,' a guide collecting the fees explains. 'When the president receives VIPs wishing to see the source of the Nile, he sends us a cheque — meaning he loves to see the area transformed into a better spot for all visitors.'

At one time there were many wildlife sanctuaries around Jinja, but these have been replaced with modern housing and parks. However, the **hippopotamus** still remains and has almost become a symbol of the town. Small schools float off the Bugungu shore and come right into the heart of town to graze each night. Many are the tales of encounters with hippo in streets and gardens, so beware if you're out for an evening stroll.

Only 70 years ago, Jinja residents used to hear lion roaring around nearby Bugungu Hill, but they have now moved far away — as have the elephant and buffalo that once roamed the area. What remains are a few **waterbuck** and **wild pig**, which wander in the papyrus marshlands near the edges of the lake, and **monitor lizards**, which are frequently seen sunning themselves along the river's edge. The waters of the gulf and the river banks were once thick with **crocodiles**, but intensive trapping and control have made

this reptile uncommon, and the local fishermen can wade safely along the shores of the lake. But don't take any chances. In 1995, an unsuspecting motorist driving out of Jinja on the road over the dam had a shock when he saw a huge crocodile crossing the road in front of him.

Industry

On the **eastern** side of town, outside the city centre, there are a number of fascinating places to see for those interested in local industry. In addition to the large steel rolling mill and the major sugar operations, industries represented in Jinja include textile producers, a flour mill, a paper bag manufacturer, a modern printing works, a cigarette and match manufacturer, a soap and oil producer, a sawmill, a furniture maker, and a steel tubing manufacturer. Several multinational companies represented here include Dunlop, who have a tyre and tube factory in Jinja; the Chillington Tool Company of Wolverhampton, England; and the British-American Tobacco Company (BAT).

To explore the industrial aspect of Jinja from the city centre, take the **Jinja main road** to the roundabout, **turn left** on **Tobacco Road**, and then **turn right**. After the railway crossing, you will see the huge grain storage facilities of the **Uganda Grain Milling Company** on your **left** and, on the **opposite side** of the road, the **BAT factory.** Just a few steps away is the sprawling **Walukuba Housing Estate.**

Continue along Tobacco Road and you will come to the **Masese fish-landing port**, where fishermen and fishmongers gather every morning to conduct their smelly business. Near the port is the government-owned **Uganda Fish Enterprises Limited factory**, which was set up in the 1980s to process fish for export — just one of more than 10 factories located on the shores of Lake Victoria involved in processing and the export of fish.

At the end of the **tarmac road** after the Masese port is the giant **East African Steel Corporation**, owned and managed by the Madhvani Group of Companies. This **steel smelter and rolling mill,** one of the largest in East Africa, has a capacity to produce

Above: Jinja steel rolling mill, just one of many important industries located around the town.

more than 24,000 metric tonnes of finished steel a year.

To explore another area outside the city centre, take **Clive Road** to **Main Street** and turn **left**. You will soon come to the **junction** with **Milton Obote Way**, where you turn **left** again, cross over the **railroad tracks**, and come to the **roundabout** marking the city's eastern gateway, where you turn **right** on the **Jinja–Tororo Road**. After half a kilometre, you come to the **Jinja Railway Station** — the first in the country. There is a weekly passenger train service to Nairobi and on to the Kenya coast in one direction, and to Kampala and western Uganda in the other.

Continue along the **Tororo Road** and, after about a kilometre (half-a-mile), you come to another **roundabout.** A turn to the **north** takes you onto the tarmacked **Kamuli Road**, leading to the countryside in Kamuli District. About 3.5 kilometres (two miles) out of the Jinja city centre, on a **hill** east of Kamuli Road, stands a **memorial** to a British administrator of the early 1900s. It is a small **cairn** of stones, topped by a **marble slab** that reads (in the Luganda

vernacular), 'This pile of stones is to commemorate Mr F Spire, CMG, the Provincial Commissioner of our country, Busoga, who helped us from 1909 to 1918, as recorded by us in his memento book.' The inscription is followed by the names of the nine Busoga chiefs who erected the memorial.

Spire, who died in England in 1951 at the age of 87, entered the Uganda Protectorate service in 1893, formerly having been batman to a military officer serving in East Africa. A remarkable man, Spire overcame the class consciousness of his time and rose through the ranks in the service until 1909, when, as acting provincial commissioner, he took up residence in Jinja.

A turn to the **east** at the **roundabout** will put you on **Tororo Road**, leading to **Bugembe Hill**, which has political, cultural, recreational, and religious importance to the people of the area. A relatively small sports centre, **Bugembe Stadium**, enclosed within a concrete wall, can be seen on the edge of the hill near the main road. Soccer matches are regularly played there, including the national super league competition. School children from the surrounding regions also use the stadium for athletics competitions.

A short distance away, on the eastern edge of Bugembe Hill, is the controversial **Bugembe Cathedral**, supposedly built by Christians of the Anglican diocese of Busoga, comprising the districts of Jinja, Iganga, and Kamuli.

However, around 1992, one faction, opposed to the leadership of Bishop Cyprian Bamwoze as Bishop of Busoga Diocese, took control of the cathedral and ejected the bishop and his supporters. All sorts of accusations have been made. The controlling faction, claiming it has lost confidence in Bishop Bamwoze, has requested the archbishop of the Church of Uganda to send a replacement. Several commissions of inquiry have been appointed to look into the dispute, and a number of recommendations have been made, but the two warring parties seem not yet ready for reconciliation.

Near the controversial cathedral there was once the palace of the kyabazinga (paramount ruler) of Busoga. The palace, or *lubiri*, was later transferred to the top of the highest hill in Bugembe. Unlike other kingdoms in other parts of the country, the kyabazingaship in Busoga was elective among the royal clans from all eight counties, and was meant to rotate among them. In the past, there was no overall ruler of Busoga region. The 'president of Busoga' was a creation of the British colonialists in the 1940s.

Bugembe is the administrative headquarters of Busoga, with a council chamber and official residences of the cabinet ministers and top officials of Busoga region.

If you stand on **Bugembe Hill** and face **westwards**, you see many new **industrial buildings** that have mushroomed on nearby **Masese Hill**, which include a **steel rolling mill** and modern **grain stores** built by the Produce Marketing Board, a parastatal.

On your **left**, closer to the shores of Lake Victoria, you can see a long **chimney** and built-up area belonging to the government-owned **Kilembe Mines Ltd**,

which is responsible for the exploration, processing, and exporting of minerals like copper and cobalt. Kilembe Mines, on **Walukuba Hill**, has been silent since 1977, when copper smelting was halted.

Busoga boasts the longest dual carriage highway in the country, stretching for about 20 kilometres (12 miles) from Jinja to Kakira, and it is completely lined with street lights — although none worked in 1996.

The first and largest **sugar estate** and factory in the whole of east and central Africa was built in Kakira by the Madhvani family. The factory went into operation in 1930, producing about 15 metric tonnes of sugar a day. Since then, it has steadily progressed, with the addition of more modern machinery. Kakira Sugar Works is the main industrial venture of the Madhvani Group of Companies and is a joint venture between the Uganda government and East Africa Holdings Limited.

It will soon increase its production to 70,000 tonnes of white sugar a year, which will save the country more than US$ 50 million in foreign exchange at 1996 import parity prices. An expansion programme was planned to produce 120,000 tonnes of sugar a year, saving the country more than US$ 80 million at 1996 levels.

There are over 8,000 hectares (20,000 acres) of **sugar cane** under cultivation at Kakira, giving employment to more than 10,000 field and factory workers, most of whom are housed on the estate.

During the 1960s and early 1970s, Kakira Sugar Works was a net exporter of sugar, earning the country a substantial amount of foreign exchange. However, sugar exports stopped in 1977, when the Amin regime expelled Asian investors from the country — including the Kakira owners. During the 10 years of misrule and mismanagement of the economy, sugar production stopped completely.

The Madhvanis and other expelled Asians were invited to return and repossess their businesses in 1980, after Amin was removed from power. Since then, the Madhvanis have returned and have been busy rehabilitating their sugar empire. In addition to sugar, the family have invested

Above: Harvesting sugar cane at Kakira Sugar Works near Jinja.

in sugar-allied industries, textiles, beer, steel rolling, insurance, tea, soap, edible oil, and packaging. They have even gone into television broadcasting: their Channel Television transmits programmes to some parts of the country.

A number of hills in the vicinity of Bugembe are still untouched, covered with long, green grass and bush. **Wanyange, Mwiri**, and **Butiki hills** have **missionary schools** located on their summits.

The oldest school started by the Church Missionary Society is **Busoga College Mwiri**, which has produced most of the leaders in Busoga — as well as the entire country, including the country's first president, Milton Obote. The hill has a panoramic **view** of Lake Victoria and the green Kakira sugar estates on its eastern side. In 1996 the Anglican Busoga Diocese was planning to build a Christian university on one side of the large hill.

Bujagali Falls
To get to the Bujagali Falls, drive out of Jinja on **Nalufenya Road, around** the **roundabout** at the Kampala–Tororo Road

junction, and then straight on. About 10 kilometres (six miles) further on, a **sign** on the **left** points the way to the falls, which are about a kilometre off the main road.

Actually more rapids than falls, the place is pleasant and popular with picnickers. Keep an eye open for the legendary 'Mr Bujagali' (a spirit), who is occasionally seen floating on the river on a barkcloth.

The Madhvani group plans to tap the falls, which are about a kilometre long, with a power station project.

Another enjoyable nature break you might consider while in Jinja is to visit the **Mabira Forest**, about 17 kilometres (10 miles) outside the city towards Kampala. There in sunny open glades, particularly after the rains, you will see hundreds and hundreds of Uganda's beautiful and world famous **butterflies**, as well as an abundance of **birdlife**.

Entebbe: Gateway to Uganda

Visitors to Uganda by air land at Entebbe International Airport, the country's sole international airport. The town of Entebbe is 34 kilometres (21 miles) south of the capital, Kampala, on the shores of Lake Victoria. Entebbe was initially the capital of Uganda, but, after independence in 1962, the capital was moved to Kampala.

In the Luganda language, the word *entebbe* means 'a chair'. The city of Entebbe derives its name from a legend about Mugula, head of the local Mamba (lungfish) clan. The legend asserts that Mugula used to command his dominion from a royal enclosure not far from the present Entebbe International Airport, seated on a chair carved out of rock.

Eventually, the seat was submerged in the waters of Lake Victoria, but the legend lived on when the colonial town nearby was named Entebbe.

The beginnings of present-day Entebbe go back to the 19th century, when colonialists built a major administrative centre there. Today, a number of government offices are still located in the town.

Sitting 1,158 metres (3,800 feet) above sea level and almost entirely surrounded by the cool waters of Lake Victoria, Entebbe has a comforting and comfortable climate throughout the year — so much so that several senior civil servants choose to live in old colonial residences there and commute every day to and from Kampala.

The traffic on Entebbe Road leading to the capital moves very fast, making the 34-kilometre (21-mile journey) in only about 20 minutes — particularly if the vehicle carries a passenger hurrying to catch a plane. The result, however, is a number of nasty accidents, so take care.

At weekends, many Kampala residents escape the bustle of the capital and visit Entebbe, relaxing at its beach resorts and botanical gardens. The city has excellent hotel facilities and restaurants, which offer a wide range of services, depending on your pocket and preference.

Entebbe is a delightful mix of old and new, with unusual and interesting buildings of the 1930s and 1940s mixing with imposing new residences built by retired civil servants along lovely tree-lined avenues.

Much of Uganda's history has been made at State House, Entebbe, where colonial governors and independent Uganda rulers have conferred with local and foreign leaders on matters of international importance. Apart from being the official residence of Uganda's head of state, the building is used as a meeting place for weekly cabinet encounters, at which government ministers debate and decide on national issues under the chairmanship of the president, away from the hustle and bustle of the capital city.

Entebbe International Airport earned a chapter for itself in the world's history books in 1976, when armed Israeli commandos flew into the airport under the cover of darkness and successfully rescued a group of Israeli travellers who were being held hostage by Palestinian terrorists. The Israeli nationals were travelling in a Lufthansa passenger plane when it was hijacked and forced to fly to Entebbe, where they were held hostage against the demand that a number of the hijackers' compatriots, who had been arrested and imprisoned in Israeli jails, be freed. The terrorists also demanded ransom money.

Although during the hijack, dictator Idi Amin pretended to play a mediating role between the Israeli government and the hijackers, his involvement — and his allegiance — soon became apparent, and the negotiations became protracted.

At the time of the hijack, Amin was a close ally and supporter of the Arab cause (he became a close friend of several Arab leaders, including Gaddafi of Libya and the king of Saudi Arabia). A few years back, he had expelled Israeli military advisers — who had been giving technical assistance to the Uganda Air Force — from the country (despite the fact that Amin had himself

Above: Fishermen on the shores of Lake Victoria.

received military training in Israel). His dislike for the Israelis was evident.

The Israeli reaction to the deadlock was to send a group of paratroopers in to storm the airport in a daring surprise raid that resulted in virtually all the hostages being freed. The unanticipated successful rescue of the hostages was a great embarrassment to Amin's regime and, in effect was the end of the already shaky East African Community as, in retaliation, Amin broke off relations with Kenya, which had given the Israelis air clearance.

A senior Uganda army officer, suspected of prior knowledge of the rescue plans but who did not alert authorities, was sacked. In revenge for the raid, members of the army took an Israeli hostage — 75-year-old Dora Bloch — from Mulago Hospital, where she had been rushed after choking on her food, and presumably killed her, for she was never seen again.

The entire episode of the Entebbe raid was made into a film some years ago called *Ninety Minutes at Entebbe*, which was shown around the world.

Dora Bloch's relatives are now reported to be seeking permission from the Ugandan authorities to build a memorial at Entebbe in her honour.

Since the days of the raid, a new airport has been constructed at Entebbe, and the nearby Old Entebbe Airport, where the rescue mission took place, has been turned into a military base, where no photographs are allowed, and corrugated iron sheets obscure any possible view a passer-by might have of the old facility.

In 1994, Uganda resumed diplomatic relations with Israel, and nationals of either country are free to travel to each other's capital. (Before then, Ugandan passports were officially stamped 'No travel to Israel'.)

Although most people who live in Entebbe — which is, in reality, only a one-street 'township' five kilometres (three miles) north of the airport — work and shop in Kampala, there is a fairly well-developed sporting community, and activities like golf, swimming, sailing, and lawn and table tennis are popular.

Getting there

Entebbe, 34 kilometres (21 miles) from Kampala, 114 kilometres (71 miles) from Jinja, 239 kilometres (148 miles) from Tororo, and 704 kilometres (437 miles) from Nairobi, is well served by air and road services. Domestic and regional flights, as well as bus and taxi services, link it with major centres in Uganda and the rest of eastern and central Africa.

When to go

Entebbe is pleasant all year round, although perhaps wetter than other parts at times because of its proximity to Lake Victoria.

Where to stay

Windsor Lake Victoria Hotel, the Botanical Beach Hotel, and the Victoria Inn, as well as several budget guesthouses. There are bandas and campsites at the Entebbe Resort on the Lake Victoria shore. See Listings.

Sightseeing

For most people, a tour of Entebbe begins at the **Entebbe International Airport**, on the shores of Lake Victoria, which until 1992, was in a very sorry state after being damaged extensively during the country's civil wars. With a Spanish loan of some US$ 26 million, the airport is now completely rehabilitated and renovated. In 1991, the government, with assistance from the United Nations Development Programme, established an independent Civil Aviation Authority to oversee the rehabilitation at Entebbe and also plan and manage the affairs of the country's air transport industry.

Entebbe International Airport now boasts a newly refurbished passenger terminal, which was officially commissioned in December 1994, as well as modern air facilities meeting international standards. From 1991 to 1996, the number of international scheduled airlines landing at Entebbe increased from eight to 16. At the moment the state-owned Uganda Airlines is the handling agent for the bigger airlines that serve Uganda two to five times weekly.

The positive developments in Uganda's air transport industry have had an effect not only on the airline companies, who are realizing profits, but also on the country's economy as a whole. The increasing number of airlines touching down at Entebbe means an increased volume of cargo of exports and imports going through the gateway, an increased number of tourists visiting Uganda, and more revenue for the government in handling charges and taxes.

Although the airport is capable of handling four million passengers a year, in 1996 it was handling less than 10 per cent of that figure. The flow of cargo through Entebbe increased by 14.8 per cent between 1986 and 1991 and by 59.3 per cent each year between 1991 and 1994. In 1986 the airport handled 4,526 metric tonnes of cargo, compared with 7,886 tonnes in 1991 and 21,916 tonnes in 1994. The volume of export cargo — especially cut flowers — was expected to increase as more and more farmers turned to commercial production of roses.

The future of Uganda's air transport is bright. The Danish International Development Agency has signed an agreement with the government to extend a grant worth US$ 28 million for rehabilitation work on the runways at both the new airport and the old (now renamed East Airport). The funds are to be used to resurface the main runway, associated runways, and apron, as well as to put in a new runway lighting system and navigational aids, re-equip the airport control tower, and build new fire and rescue stations. In addition, funds provided by the United States Agency for International Development and the Civil Aviation Authority will soon see cold storage facilities erected, with an American company also granted the concession licence to develop another cold storage facility that will contain 68,000 cubic metres (2.4 million cubic feet) of storage containment space at the East Airport.

As the volume of passengers and cargo increases, larger airlines such as Lufthansa, KLM, and SAS were eyeing Entebbe with interest. In early 1996, Air France began flying into the airport twice a week.

The airport earned some unexpected

Above: Ceremonial drummers welcome guests at Entebbe international airport.
Overleaf: Evoking memories of a colonial past, the Windsor Lake Victoria Hotel is considered one of the best in the country.

profits in 1995 when the US government decided to use Entebbe as an operations centre for their huge humanitarian rescue mission to Uganda's embattled neighbour to the south, Rwanda. The windfall is expected to be utilised for further developments of the air transport industry in the country, including the rehabilitation of upcountry aerodromes.

Since more and more passengers have started coming through Entebbe, several **duty-free shops** have been established at the airport. Private **foreign exchange bureaux** are also opening up shop there, making it easier for passengers to change money at competitive rates.

From the airport, the township of Entebbe is only five kilometres (three miles) up the **main road** towards Kampala. As you enter the town, you will see the budget-priced **Kidepo Hotel** on your **left**, followed shortly afterwards by the **market** and **bus station**; always beehives of activity.

The **Windsor Lake Victoria Hotel**, with its colonial and tropical atmosphere, is just a little further along the main road on your **right**. One of the best hotels in the country, it is situated in attractive grounds overlooking the lake; it has 99 guest rooms, a **swimming pool**, **health centre**, three **restaurants** and **bars**, a **coffee shop** and a **conference room** seating up to 150 people.

Just past the Windsor Lake Victoria Hotel is a road that, if you turn **right**, leads to the **Entebbe Resort**, which has a **beach** for swimming (but beware of bilharzia in these waters), a **bar** and **restaurant**, and a **disco** on Saturdays. There are self-contained double bandas for accommodation, or you can pitch your tent at the quiet and attractive **campsite. Birdlife** is abundant, especially **pied kingfishers.**

Back on the **main road**, just past the turnoff to the Entebbe Resort, you'll come to the **Entebbe Club** on your **right**, which overlooks the 18-hole golf course. The club welcomes visiting golfers from all over the world — just contact the club manager to arrange your games. See Listings.

Further along the main road from

Entebbe Club, a small **grid** of **streets** could be termed the town centre. There, mostly to the **right** off the **main road**, are many of Uganda's central government offices, including the Statistics and Census Department of the Ministry of Finance and Economic Planning; the Ministry of Works, Transport, and Communications; the Ministry of Agriculture, Animal Industry, and Fisheries; the Ministry of Health; and the Government Printer. The only government offices of interest to tourists would be the **Maps and Surveys Department** of the Ministry of Lands, Housing, and Urban Development, which provides up-to-date maps of many parts of the country, and the **Game Department** of the Ministry of Tourism, Wildlife, and Antiquities, which is away from the town centre near the lakeshore and the botanical gardens.

Botanical Gardens

From the town centre, almost any road to the **right** off the **main road** leads to the well-known **Entebbe Botanical Gardens**, also on the lakeshore. Started in 1898 by Mr A Whyte, the first curator of the country's National Museum, the gardens were originally a natural forest used as a research ground for the introduction of various exotic fruits and ornamental plants to Uganda. Indigenous trees that were already there when the gardens were started are still in place today, as are many of the introduced exotic trees and plants, most of which are marked with their common and scientific names.

The gardens, which spread over 2.6 square kilometres (one square mile), are not fenced off, although there is one entry point for motor vehicles at which you must pay a small fee, which goes into maintaining the gardens. Over weekends and on major religious holidays like Christmas, Easter, and Idd-el-Fitr, hundreds of families drive into the gardens for all-day picnics. Visitors are advised to vacate the gardens before darkness, as there are no lights in the area.

In addition to the obvious **flora**, there is also abundant **wildlife** in the gardens, particularly **black-and-white colobus monkeys** and **squirrels**. **Birdlife**, too, is prolific and includes some species especially noted in the Lake Victoria region — such as the **yellow-throated leaflove** and **slender-billed weaver** — as well as the more common **fish eagle** and **palmnut vulture**. Forest birds include the **great blue turaco** and **black-and-white casqued hornbill**.

If you want to see more wildlife still, there is a sort of **zoo** near the gardens, known as the **Entebbe Wildlife Education Centre**. Originally started as an animal orphanage in the 1920s, the zoo gradually grew to be a showplace of many animal species, including **buffalo, zebra, chimpanzees, monkeys, lion,** various **antelopes, crocodiles,** and **hyenas**. **Birdlife** at the zoo also abounds, with **crowned cranes, weaver birds, shoebill storks, pelicans, parrots,** and **ostrich**.

There is also a **pier**, where canoes and motorboats take passengers to some of the lake's islands or just for pleasure cruises on the lake. Nearby is a huge sandy **beach** and shallow waters, where hundreds swim.

Near the Wildlife Education Centre is a large, rolling **sports ground**, which is actually part of the golf course. Close to the road is a **church** belonging to the Anglican Church of Uganda, where the president usually attends Sunday services. Opposite, in the bend of the main road, is a **World War II mortar gun**, which was abandoned in the area when it went out of action many years ago.

Five kilometres (three miles) off the Airport Road is the **Kigungu Landing Site**, the place where the first Catholic missionaries, Reverend Father Simon Lourdel and Brother Amans of the

Opposite: A path cuts through the lush flora of the Entebbe Botanical Gardens.
Overleaf: A former research ground, the Entebbe Botanical Gardens feature an amazing array of both indigenous and introduced flora.

Above: Fisherman casts his net into the blue waters of Lake Victoria.

Society of White Fathers, came ashore on 17 February 1879. A small brick-walled **church** was erected on this site and still stands next to a **memorial plaque**.

In the village there, you can also witness **traditional fishing methods**, as well as go on a **boat excursion** into the lake. At another nearby fishing village, **Kasenyi** — six kilometres (four miles) off the main Entebbe–Kampala Road — both traditional and modern fishing methods are used to catch the giant Nile perch, tilapia, and various other species of fish that abound in the lake. A **fish market** dominates the area and, as a result, a branch of the state-owned Uganda Commercial Bank has been opened at Kasenyi to cater for the growing business. **Boats** can also be hired there to any of the **islands** in the lake.

About 10 kilometres (six miles) outside Entebbe on the road to Kampala is the newly opened Garuga Golf and Country Club, which features an 18-hole **golf course** and a **restaurant**, and a proposed major hotel complex. The club is on the lakeside and also offers boat excursions on Lake Victoria.

Above: Fruit of the lake: tilapia drying in the sun.
Opposite: Sun goes down over Lake Victoria.

PART FOUR: SPECIAL FEATURES

Above: Colourful woven basket is functional as well as beautiful.
Opposite: Male silverback mountain gorilla stands guard.

Wildlife: A Dramatic Comeback

Although not as plentiful as that of its neighbours, Kenya and Tanzania, Uganda's wildlife is in remarkably good shape, particularly in view of the country's many years of civil strife and unrest, when poaching was uncontrolled. And, as far as diversity goes, Uganda may have the edge over its neighbouring countries. Its marvellous rainforests protect a wealth of wildlife, including an astonishing number of primate species found in few other places.

It is Uganda's primates, in fact, that many visitors come to see. In the southwest of the country are two of only four national parks in the world — Mgahinga Gorilla and Bwindi Impenetrable — where you can see the endangered **mountain gorilla.**

But no one said it will be easy: permits to go gorilla tracking are expensive, hard to come by, and, once you do get them, there's no guarantee you'll even see the few gorillas there are in those parks. But if you should be one of the lucky few, you'll know that the trouble was well worth it (see Uganda's Mountain Gorillas).

Uganda is also one of the top places in the world to see the **chimpanzee**, more closely related to humans than to any other ape. One of the best places in the country to see this primate is in the Kibale Forest National Park, but they may also be seen in the Budongo Forest and the Chambura River Gorge in Queen Elizabeth National Park. An island sanctuary for chimpanzees has also been set up in Queen Elizabeth National Park, where they can be seen more easily.

All the monkeys found in the country belong to the family Cercopithecidae. They include the **yellow baboon**, with its doglike head; the savannah-dwelling **patas monkey**; four races of the **vervet monkey**; the **blue monkey**, common in most of Uganda's forests; the **red-tailed monkey**, also a forest-dweller; the extremely localized **de Brazza's monkey**; **L'Hoest's monkey**, most likely to be seen in Kibale Forest National Park; **Wolf's guenon**, a race of the mona monkey; the **owl-faced monkey**, or Hamlyn's guenon; the **grey-cheeked mangabey**, also common in the Kibale Forest; the widespread and often seen **black-and-white colobus**; and two races of the **red colobus.** Other primates are the wide-eyed **greater bushbaby** and its smaller relative, the **lesser bushbaby** — more often heard than seen.

The Big Five

It is said that all the Big Five — elephant, buffalo, lion, leopard, and rhinoceros — still exist in the country, although whether any rhinos remain is questionable. It is thought that a few **black rhino** may be clinging to existence in the north in Kidepo Valley National Park, and there is said to be a privately protected herd of **white rhino** near Pakwach in Uganda's northwest, but no accurate numbers exist.

The largest land animal in the world, the **elephant**, has surprisingly managed to hang on, despite massive poaching, and its numbers are once again climbing. Two races are recognized in the country: the savannah elephant and the forest elephant, and the two are thought to interbreed in parts of western Uganda. Particularly large herds exist in the Kidepo Valley National Park, but elephant can also be seen in Murchison Falls, Queen Elizabeth, and Kibale Forest national parks.

You shouldn't have any trouble at all in seeing at least one of the Big Five on any Ugandan safari: the **African buffalo**. This hardy and adaptable animal is found in virtually all the national parks and forests, often in large herds. You may even spot a mixed breed of savannah buffalo and the West African red buffalo in Queen Elizabeth National Park.

Heavy poaching has made Africa's largest cat, the **lion**, scarce; nevertheless it does continue to exist. Your best chance of seeing this impressive predator is in Kidepo Valley National Park, but it is also present

Above: The black-and-white colobus monkey is common throughout Uganda.

in Murchison Falls and Queen Elizabeth national parks.

Although rarely seen because of its nocturnal and secretive nature, the **leopard** is also found in virtually all Uganda's national parks and forests, as well as in areas close to human habitation. It has rosette-shaped spots and is more stockily built than the streamlined **cheetah**, which in Uganda is found only in Kidepo Valley National Park.

Other members of the cat family present in Uganda are the **caracal** and the **serval**, although both are rarely seen as they are nocturnal. Also nocturnal are the catlike **civet** and **genet**, which are widespread throughout the country. While the genet may often be spotted slinking around campsites at night, the civet is seldom seen.

Of the other predators resident in Uganda, the most likely to be seen is the **spotted hyena**, which is surprisingly more closely related to the mongoose and the cat than it is to the dog, which it more closely resembles. Living in clans dominated by females, the hyena is widespread and common throughout the country, although it prefers savannah and woodland habitats.

The **African hunting dog** is a ferocious and successful hunter, but it is on the brink of extinction because of its susceptibility to canine disease. This highly social animal, many of whose characteristics resemble those of the domestic dog, is said to be present in Queen Elizabeth National Park, but its numbers are few.

Two races of another member of the dog family reside in the country: the **black-backed jackal** and the **side-striped jackal**. Both are present in many of Uganda's national parks, although the latter is the one most likely to be seen.

Another predator found throughout Uganda — but rarely seen — is the **ratel**, or honey badger, which has an amazing symbiotic relationship with the greater honeyguide. The bird, wanting honey, will lead the ratel to a beehive. The ratel then obligingly tears the hive open, eating what it wants, leaving the rest for the honeyguide.

Antelopes

Antelopes of all shapes and sizes exist in Uganda in fairly large numbers. One most often associated with the country (often referred to as its 'national antelope') is the **Uganda kob**, a stocky, russet-coloured animal about half the size of a waterbuck, to which it is related. Preferring moist, savannah-like habitats, the Uganda kob (also known as Thomas's kob) can be easily seen in Lake Mburo, Murchison Falls, and Queen Elizabeth national parks. In Queen Elizabeth, in particular, it is worth spending time at the kob mating ground, which is demarcated with signs, to observe some of the interesting habits of this animal.

Another, much smaller, antelope is endemic to Uganda: **Bate's pigmy antelope**, weighing only three kilos (seven lbs). The smallest ungulate in East Africa, it inhabits the country's western forests, but is rarely seen as it prefers thick cover and is very shy.

Africa's largest antelope, the eland, is also found in the country. The rare **giant**, or **Lord Derby's**, **eland** — the male of which could weigh up to 900 kilos (2,000 lbs) — was once found in northern Uganda west of the Albert Nile, but it is doubtful that any remain.

The smaller **common eland**, weighing in at around 700 kilos (1,500 lbs), occurs in Kidepo Valley National Park in the north and Lake Mburo National Park in the south of the country. Both species feature long, spiraled horns and large dewlaps.

Kidepo Valley National Park is also home to two other beautiful, spiral-horned antelope, the **greater kudu** and the **lesser kudu**. Although, true to its name, the lesser kudu is about half the size of the greater, both varieties having light brown coats and delicate white stripes down the sides of their bodies. Only the males have horns.

Two species of the awkward-looking hartebeest, with its long, mournful face, exist in Uganda. Most common is **Jackson's hartebeest**, found in Kidepo and Lake Mburo national parks, while the **lelwel hartebeest** occurs west of the Nile. The hartebeest's darker cousin, the topi, is frequently seen in the Ishasha sector of Queen Elizabeth National Park.

Any visitor is pretty sure to see the shaggy-looking waterbuck while on safari in Uganda, as it occurs throughout the country, often grazing near water. The variety that occurs there is the **Defassa waterbuck**, which has a solid white rump. (Its relative, the common waterbuck, found further to the east, has a white ring on its rump.)

The handsome **roan antelope** is a reddish-brown animal with short, backward-curving horns and a small mane on the back of its neck. Although said to be present in Lake Mburo and Kidepo Valley national parks, it must be few in number, as sightings are rare.

The rapier-horned, gregarious **Beisa oryx**, weighing over 200 kilos (440 lbs), is a truly desert-adapted species that makes its home in Uganda in the drier parts of Kidepo Valley National Park.

Another species preferring the arid lands found in Kidepo is the delicate **Grant's gazelle**, a light brown animal with lyre-shaped horns. Although herds can number up to 400, it is more common to see 20 to 40 of these gazelles grazing together on the plains.

Although quite common elsewhere in East Africa, the chestnut-coloured **impala** is found in Uganda only in Lake Mburo National Park. Only the males have horns. Impala are tremendous jumpers, and it is a fantastic sight to see a herd, white tails flashing, leaping over bushes and rocks, often seemingly just for the sheer joy of it.

Top: Elephants, their numbers depleted by heavy poaching, are now making a comeback in Uganda.
Above: The Uganda kob is considered the country's 'national antelope'.

Above: The male bushbuck is considerably darker than its female companion.
Opposite: Female waterbuck in Queen Elizabeth National Park.

More elusive is the **bushbuck**, a common but shy antelope of the forest and riverine woodland. In Uganda, bushbuck can be found in most forests and national parks; it is particularly plentiful in Queen Elizabeth National Park. The male bushbuck is a handsome animal with a dark chestnut coat flecked with white spots and stripes. The female is smaller and lighter coloured and is often mistaken for a duiker, of which there are numerous species in Uganda. Most Ugandan duikers prefer forest as their habitat, but one, the **grey duiker**, is more often seen in woodland and savannah. The **red, Harvey's, blue**, and **yellow-backed duikers** are widespread in the country's forests.

One of the more unusual antelopes resident in Uganda is the **sitatunga**, found in many of the country's papyrus swamps, where the animal's greatly elongated hooves enable it to walk on floating vegetation. It is very shy and hence difficult to see; when confronted, it dives under the water and hides, with only its nose showing.

The medium-sized, yellowish **Bohor reedbuck**, which prefers rank, medium-height grasslands as its home, may be found in Lake Mburo, Queen Elizabeth, and Murchison Falls national parks. Featuring small, crescent-shaped horns, it is often seen in pairs in open country near water.

Look for the smaller, 18-kilo (40-lb) **klipspringer** prancing about on cliffs, rocky hillsides, and mountain screes. It is thought that the klipspringer mates for life; they are often seen in pairs.

Lake Mburo National Park is home to the straw-coloured **oribi**, readily identified by a large black mark, a gland, below each ear. Very much a grassland animal, it lives in small herds.

Other herbivores

In addition to the antelopes, elephant, rhino (if it indeed exists in the country), and buffalo, several other herbivores occur in Uganda.

One of these is the world's tallest animal, the giraffe. The variety that occurs in Uganda is the **Rothschild's giraffe**, an intermediate

between the blotchy-spotted Maasai giraffe and the reticulated giraffe, which has a more defined pattern to its coat. Found in Kidepo Valley and Murchison Falls national parks, in general the giraffe is an animal of open woodland and acacia savannah, but there are curious gaps in its distribution. In Uganda, for example, despite suitable habitats, none are found between the Victoria Nile and Kagera River. Seemingly, such large rivers are difficult to cross.

The **common**, or **Burchell's, zebra** is the only species of this member of the horse family to occur in Uganda. Although always within daily reach of water, the zebra avoids wetter areas where grasses are uniformly higher than one metre (three feet) and too tough and rank. Mature stallions gather small harems of mares and, even when they congregate in their hundreds, it is easy to spot these basic social units.

Branching out as a distinctive form just over 10 million years ago, the **hippopotamus** derives from the pig lineage. One of the largest land animals, a big male hippo may weigh up to 3,200 kilos (7,000 lbs). A grazer, it mows grass — not with its teeth, but with its sharp-edged horny lips. Though it sometimes walks a long way from water — usually in cool, wet weather — it normally spends its non-grazing hours partially submerged.

Because water is a separate habitat from that of humans, and hippo graze at night, the two often live close together. Even in Uganda, hippo continue to persist in the midst of human settlement, even when other wildlife have moved away. As a result, human and hippo meet fairly frequently. Since hippo are short tempered and armed with huge, cutting canine teeth, the outcome is that they cause more human deaths than any other herbivore in Africa. In some places, the toll they take exceeds that of the great cats and crocodile combined.

Hippo are strongly territorial, herds of 10 or more being presided over by a dominant male. Although they occur throughout the country, the most auspicious places to see them are in Lake Mburo, Queen Elizabeth, and Murchison Falls national parks — particularly on a launch trip in the latter two.

Top: Common or Burchell's Zebra.
Middle: The ubiquitous warthog.
Above: Hyrax are found throughout Uganda.
Opposite: Hippo graze near the Kazinga Channel in Queen Elizabeth National Park.

239

Above: Just another rock? Look closer . . . a well-camouflaged crocodile at Murchison Falls.
Opposite: Baby chimpanzee looks curiously out at the world around it.

All three East African members of the pig family — warthog, giant forest hog, and bushpig — are present in Uganda, but you are likely to see only the ubiquitous warthog, as the other two are more nocturnal and prefer the thick, dense cover of forest as their habitat.

Turning up wherever grasses grow in highlands and lowlands, the **warthog** lives in an underground den, which it always enters backwards so that any animal following it faces its sharp tusks. Warthogs are often seen in family groups, running determinedly with their tails high in the air.

The **giant forest hog** is a true forest animal and the largest African pig, weighing up to 275 kilos (600 lbs). It is actually a West African forest fringe species that adapted to highland and lowland forests in East Africa during a wetter era. When the western forests retreated, these hogs stayed in the mountains and in the gallery forests on the lower slopes. They are known to be present in Bwindi Impenetrable and Mgahinga Gorilla national parks, in particular, but are rarely seen. Equally shy is the **bushpig**, a larger, stockier, and hairier version of the warthog. It prefers thicket, forest, and relatively wet areas as its habitat. Inveterate and competent crop raiders, bushpigs are greatly disliked by farmers. Resembling guinea-pigs, both the **tree hyrax** and the **rock hyrax** also occur in Uganda; they are particularly noticeable in the Ruwenzori Mountains National Park, where, if not seen, the tree hyrax in particular makes itself heard with its unmistakable shrieking call at night.

Reptiles and amphibians

A wide variety of **lizards, frogs**, and **toads** make Uganda their home, as do **snakes**, although they are rarely encountered on an average safari. What is encountered, however, is the **Nile crocodile**, often growing to enormous proportions, up to nearly five metres (16 feet) long. These are found throughout the country but are most readily seen on a launch trip in Murchison Falls National Park. Two other West African crocodile species, the **long-nosed** and the **broad-nosed**, also occur in the westernmost regions of Uganda but are rarely seen.

Uganda's Mountain Gorillas

Few of earth's creatures have captured humankind's attention like the gorilla. Although maligned for decades as one of the world's most ferocious and dangerous beasts, gorillas are now described as 'gentle giants teetering on the brink of extinction'. Anatomically, socially, and behaviourally, humans recognize components of themselves in our largest primate cousin's physique and lifestyle. Over the past two decades, in-depth scientific field studies and comprehensive conservation programming have increased our knowledge of the gorilla, and today individuals and governments are battling to preserve the species and its threatened forest homes.

Gorillas occur only in Africa. The species *Gorilla gorilla* is subdivided into three recognized subspecies: the **western lowland gorilla** *(Gorilla gorilla gorilla)*, which occurs in several countries in West Africa; the **eastern lowland gorilla** *(Gorilla gorilla graueri)*, which inhabits remnant forest areas along the eastern border of Zaire; and the **mountain gorilla** *(Gorilla gorilla beringei)*, which occurs only in two separated and extremely small populations on and near the Ugandan, Zairean, and Rwandan borders.

All three subspecies of gorillas are classified as endangered; however, whereas the eastern and western lowland subspecies of gorillas are estimated to have populations of about 40,000 and 8,000 respectively, the world population of mountain gorillas has recently been enumerated at an extremely fragile 600. DNA analysis of hair samples collected from night nests during these recent censuses provided scientific evidence linking the Virunga population of gorillas on the Rwanda/Zaire/Uganda border (309 gorillas) to the Bwindi Impenetrable Forest gorilla population in Uganda (280 gorillas) approximately 32 kilometres (20 miles) away. This link effectively doubled the world count of mountain gorillas overnight and allows Uganda 'boasting rights' to half the world's population of mountain gorillas.

Mountain gorillas are mainly terrestrial and quadrupedal — they walk on the soles of their hind limbs, but pivot on the knuckles of their forelimbs. Gorillas are predominantly herbivorous, feeding mainly on the leaves, stems, and roots of specific plants. Of the great apes, the gorilla shows the most stable grouping patterns.

Groups are strongly bonded; the same individuals typically travel together for years at a time. Groups are led by an adult male or 'silverback'. All males, as they mature, become silverbacks, developing very distinct characteristics, including an impressive silver saddle extending across their back from shoulders to rump. However, not all silver-backs are successful enough to ultimately gain leadership of a group.

The size of a gorilla group varies from two to as many as 35 individuals. Average group size is about nine. In addition to a dominant silverback and occasionally one or two subordinates, the group consists of several adult females, subadults (who will most likely transfer out of their natal group upon reaching sexual maturity), juveniles, and infants.

Female gorillas mature sexually at about nine years. Gorillas do not have a distinct breeding season; females cycle about every 28 days (comparable to a human female). Gestation is about eight-and-a-half to nine months. Newborn infants weigh 1.8 to 2.2 kilos (four to five pounds) and are totally dependent on their mother.

Infants are weaned at about three-and-a-half years of age and females, who mature at six to nine years, typically give birth at four- to five-year intervals.

Male gorillas mature at 10 to 12 years, but because of competition for mates, few will start to breed before 15 years.

Opposite: Young mountain gorilla.

Above: An encounter with a male silverback and his family is long to be remembered.

Group daily activity patterns follow a relatively simple routine. Awaking in their night nests after daybreak, gorillas begin foraging and continue to feed slowly and selectively until a mid-morning rest period, during which individuals sleep, groom each other and, if younger, play. The rest period may last more than an hour, after which feeding once again begins. An afternoon rest period follows several additional hours of feeding. The group wraps up the day with another feeding bout, and just before dusk, each gorilla — excluding infants — begins constructing a nest in which

it will sleep throughout the night. Unweaned infants sleep with their mothers.

The gorilla tourism programme that has become such an integral component of mountain gorilla conservation programmes complements the daily activity patterns of the gorillas. Beginning in the early morning, tourists hike to that point in the forest where a gorilla group was contacted the day before. Following a trail through dense forest and over rough terrain, the previous night's nests are discovered and a fresh trail is pursued. If lucky, the tourists will find the gorilla group during the mid-morning or early afternoon

become increasingly successful and rewarding, the gorillas remain shy. They are approachable to within four or five metres (15 feet), but they take full advantage of the dense forest vegetation and may be difficult to see and photograph. Viewing will undoubtedly become better and better as gorilla individuals become more comfortable with daily visits.

Mountain gorillas inhabit and are protected in two of Uganda's newest national parks — the Bwindi Impenetrable National Park, formerly known as the Impenetrable Forest, and Mgahinga Gorilla National Park, located on the northern slopes of two of the Virunga volcanoes adjacent to Volcano National Park in Rwanda and Virunga National Park in Zaire. The Ugandan gorilla conservation programmes are modelled after Rwanda's innovative Mountain Gorilla Project and have received monetary and technical assistance from the International Gorilla Conservation Programme, a consortium funded by the African Wildlife Foundation, the World Wide Fund for Nature, and the Fauna and Flora Preservation Society. The programme integrates sound park management policy, anti-poaching patrols, conservation education programming, gorilla tourism, and community revenue sharing to produce a product of improved forest and gorilla protection.

The **Bwindi Impenetrable National Park** is a 331-square-kilometre (128-square-mile) tract of lower altitude montane forest ranging between 1,100 and 2,600 metres (3,600 and 8,530 feet) elevation. This is Uganda's most accessible and dependable gorilla viewing park. Two gorilla groups are visited on a daily basis by no more than six tourists in each group.

The forest hike to see the gorillas is spectacular, as Bwindi has some of the richest forest flora and fauna in Africa. In addition to mountain gorillas, nine other primate species occur. These include **red-tailed** and **L'Hoest's monkeys**, **black-and-white colobus**, and common **chimpanzees**. Bwindi's **bird** list totals 334 species and includes nearly 40 regional endemics — an impressive statistic indicative of the forest's overall biodiversity.

rest period, and will be able to observe a wide variety of gorilla social interactions and behaviours. Tourists stay only one hour with a gorilla group; the gorillas are then left to pursue their continuous nomadic lifestyle within their established home range, which averages 10 to 15 square kilometres (four to six square miles).

Gorilla tourism in Uganda is relatively in its infancy. Gorilla visiting programmes in nearby Rwanda and Zaire have been operational for almost 15 years; the Ugandan National Parks Service began habituating groups of gorillas for tourism only a few years ago. Tourists began visiting gorilla groups regularly in Uganda in late 1993. Although contacting gorilla groups has

Above: A rare sight – gorilla family crosses a path near the Bwindi park headquarters.

Mgahinga Gorilla National Park is small — 33.7 square kilometres (13 square miles), set in a high-altitude montane forest that protects the Ugandan portion of the Virunga Mountains, which form the country's border with Rwanda and Zaire. The park is located on the slopes of Mount Muhabura (4,127 metres, 13,540 feet) and Mount Gahinga (3,475 metres, 11,400 feet), two of the ancient cones of the Virunga Volcanoes. Gorilla viewing there is less dependable, as groups frequently cross the border into neighbouring Zaire and cannot be followed. Viewing possibilities are determined on a day-to-day basis and cannot be assured. Nonetheless, there are other natural history oriented activities available, including day hikes to the peaks of the two volcanoes. The higher reaches of both mountains are covered in lovely afro-alpine vegetation; the lower slopes include bamboo and hypericum/hagenia forests. A very unusual high-elevation bog tops Mount Gahinga, while Mount Muhabura is capped by a small crater lake.

The gorilla-viewing opportunities in both Bwindi and Mgahinga are extremely well regulated. The national parks staff and their technical advisers diligently enforce the rules. A maximum of six tourists a group a day are allowed to visit the gorillas. Given that two gorilla groups have become habituated for tourists at Bwindi, and one group at Mgahinga, 12 and six permits a day respectively are available at the parks.

Gorilla permits for Bwindi Impenetrable National Park can be purchased at National Park headquarters or through reputable agents in Kampala. Demand is high and therefore permits should be sought well in advance. For adventuresome travellers who don't have set travel schedules, two permits per day are available at Bwindi park headquarters at Buhoma. However, the waiting list may be long, and people who attempt to obtain permits in this manner may have to wait days. Several camping possibilities are available at Buhoma park headquarters; they range from clean but relatively simple (you need to supply almost everything) to a well-furnished luxury tented facility. Prices vary accordingly. A limited supply of food and drink is available for purchase at Buhoma.

Permits for gorilla viewing at Mgahinga are purchased through the park headquarters, located in Kisoro, approximately 15 kilometres (nine miles) away from the park. (The dirt road to the park entrance is extremely rough and can be reached only with a four-wheel-drive vehicle.) Since the habituated gorilla at Mgahinga sometimes ranges into Virunga National Park in Zaire, and therefore cannot be followed, gorilla viewing at Mgahinga is not nearly as dependable as at Bwindi, and several days may lapse before the gorilla group returns to Mgahinga and Uganda.

There is a community-operated campground at the park entrance where campers can pitch a tent. As only a limited supply of food and drink is available, they should carry all needed supplies with them.

It should be noted that in both national parks, the primary objective is to protect the gorillas; the tourist experience is of secondary importance. Therefore, tourists are monitored at park headquarters for signs of even minor illness. Gorillas are nearly 99 per cent genetically the same as humans and therefore susceptible to the diseases humans transmit but have no immunity to them. Even signs of a common cold may be cause for disallowing someone to visit gorillas.

Before entering the forest, tourists are briefed by their guides in appropriate gorilla etiquette; the do's and don'ts of acting accordingly after a gorilla group is contacted are clearly outlined.

The hike to see gorillas may be strenuous — both parks are located at relatively high elevation and the terrain is rough. Hikes to contact a gorilla group may take one to three hours or more. Recommended clothing to wear includes a long-sleeved shirt and long trousers. Layering of clothing is a good idea as it is cool in the early morning hours and gets progressively warmer throughout the day.

Wear boots or shoes that supply good traction. Rain at any time throughout the day or year can be expected, so a poncho or other raingear is a good idea. Since the trek may take the better part of the day, a packed lunch with plenty of liquids should be arranged. If you plan to take photographs, you will need faster speed films of 200 and 400 ASA (or even higher), as the forested areas where the gorillas are found are often dark or in shadow.

Gorilla viewing permits for both of Uganda's national parks are expensive (check with Uganda National Parks headquarters as to current prices), and daily park entrance fees have to be paid on top of that.

This limited, well-regulated, expensive, and relatively non-intrusive natural history tourist activity has become a key ingredient in protecting the mountain gorilla. By allowing national governments and local communities to perceive gorillas and their forested homes as important national resources, it is hoped that the future of this extremely endangered species may be insured.

Above: The mountain gorilla – facing an uncertain future.

Birdlife: Beautiful and Bounteous

As with most of eastern Africa, Uganda has a large and diverse avifauna. More than 1,000 species, including many migratory species from Europe or Asia, have been recorded. Given the relatively small size of the country, this number is exceptionally high.

Human activities, especially forest clearing, have had a tremendous effect on the abundance and distribution of Ugandan birds. Some ubiquitous, open-country species, like the **common bulbul** (*Pycnonotus barbatus*) and the **mousebird** (*Colius striatus*), have been able to proliferate and to extend their distribution widely, but many forest species are now confined to small relict patches of forest. Until now, no species has become extinct, however, and birds are still abundant in most areas of Uganda. Unlike mammal hunting, bird hunting — except for some trapping of francolins and doves — is rare, and even unknown in most traditional Ugandan cultures.

One of the first impressions of most visitors, even the non-bird watchers, is the abundance of birds around Entebbe and Kampala. Small birds like **sparrows**, bright yellow **weavers**, metallic-blue **starlings**, and colourful **sunbirds** are everywhere. **Woodland kingfisher, broad-billed roller, black-and-white flycatcher, black-headed gonolek,** and **Heuglin's robin chat** are common garden birds. Large fruiting trees in the middle of Kampala attract **black-and-white casqued hornbill, crowned hornbill, great blue turaco,** and **Ross's turaco. Abdim's stork, black-headed heron,** and **hadada ibis** are regular visitors on golf courses. Large birds like **marabou stork, hooded vulture, black kite,** and even **African fish eagle** are rarely absent from the sky. The marabou, the largest of all storks in Africa but also the most repulsive, with its large, fleshy pouch hanging from the neck, even breeds on some trees in the overcrowded city streets of Kampala. Outside towns and villages, birds are mainly distributed according to the occurrence of broad vegetation types.

Most birds of the woodlands and wooded grasslands — the most extensive type of natural or semi-natural habitat in Uganda — have a very broad distribution, both geographically and ecologically. They range widely outside Uganda: some are found all over East Africa; others reach South Africa or West Africa, and still others are found throughout tropical Africa. This is the case with many raptors like the **black kite** and **black-shouldered kite**, the **African cuckoo falcon**, most **vultures**, the **harrier hawk**, the splendid **bateleur eagle, brown snake eagle** and **banded snake eagle, African hawk eagle, tawny eagle,** several **sparrowhawks** and **goshawks, lizard buzzard, long-crested eagle, crowned eagle,** and **martial eagle**. Vultures and large eagles are now mainly confined to the national parks, except for the **hooded vulture** and **palmnut vulture**, which still have a wide distribution.

Many savannah species, however, are more or less restricted to specific vegetation types or eco-climatic conditions: some prefer the moister woodlands, some are only found in dry or very dry habitats. Even if they are distributed widely outside Uganda, their distribution inside the country is often limited.

In the moist savannahs of southern and south-western Uganda occurs the **black-headed olive-back**, a small greenish, finch-like bird with a black head and a narrow white collar. It lives in rank, lush vegetation on edges of swamps, around forests, and in cultivated areas and has a very restricted distribution. In the much drier acacia savannahs of **Lake Mburo National Park** are found other interesting species. The most peculiar is the **red-faced barbet**, a plump, black bird with a stout bill, yellow shafts to the primary feathers, and a bright red

Opposite: Uganda's beautiful national bird, the crowned crane.

face. It is a rare species, restricted to a small area of south-western Uganda, eastern Rwanda, north-eastern Burundi, and north-western Tanzania. A much less spectacular species found in the Lake Mburo area, is the tiny **Tabora cisticola**, a small greyish warbler with a fairly long narrow tail and a russet crown. It is endemic to Uganda.

The bright blue **Abyssinian roller**, the large **Abyssinian ground hornbill** with its blue face wattles, **black-billed barbet**, **white-fronted black chat**, and **black-faced firefinch** occur all over the northern savannahs, from the Zaire border to Kenya.

In the areas around Lake Albert and the **Murchison Falls National Park** are found many species from west and central-west Africa, like the **red-necked buzzard**, which is mainly a non-breeding visitor to the area, **Heuglin's francolin**, **black-bellied wooddove**, **Bruce's green pigeon**, **white-crested turaco**, **long-tailed nightjar**, **red-throated bee-eater**, **piapiac**, **Emin's shrike**, **dusky babbler**, **red-winged grey warbler**, **white-rumped seed-eater**, and **grey-headed olive-back**. This last species closely resembles the black-headed olive-back, but most of the black of the head is replaced by a pale grey.

In the semi-arid areas of Karamoja in the north-east — in and around the **Kidepo Valley National Park** — are found typically dry country species like the **ostrich**, **swallow-tailed kite**, the tiny **pygmy falcon**, **fox kestrel** and **white-eyed kestrel**, **Clapperton's francolin**, **stone partridge**, **kori bustard**, **Hartlaub's bustard**, **white-bellied bustard**, **Abyssinian scimitarbill**, **red-and-yellow barbet**, **red-pate cisticola**, and **Karamoja apalis**.

Compared with other East African countries, Uganda is especially rich in forest birds. They form a very substantial part of the avifauna and are one of the best reasons for a birdwatcher to visit Uganda. Some species have a widespread distribution, occurring in many different forests. Others are restricted to one, two, or three forest blocks, mostly along the wesern Rift — the richest being the Budongo, Kibale, Semuliki, Maramagambo-Kalinzu, and Bwindi forests. These forests harbour many central or west African species, which reach their easternmost limit of distribution in western Uganda.

Especially in the lowland forests of the Semuliki National Park, which are an extension of the forests of the Zaire Basin, there are many species that don't occur elsewhere in East Africa. These include the **spotted ibis**, **Congo serpent eagle**, **chestnut-flanked goshawk**, **long-tailed hawk**, **Bates' nightjar**, **wattled black hornbill**, **red-billed dwarf hornbill**, **black dwarf hornbill** and **white-crested hornbill**, **African piculet**, **Gabon woodpecker**, **yellow-throated nicator**, **black-winged oriole**, **Sassi's olive greenbul**, **bearded greenbul** and **Capuchin babbler**, **northern bearded scrub robin**, **forest ground thrush**, **grey ground thrush**, **red-eyed puffback**, **pale-fronted negrofinch**, and **Grant's bluebill**. **Cassin's spinetail** is known from only Budongo Forest.

Montane forests are poorer in bird species than lowland forests, but harbour more species with a restricted distribution. The high-altitude forests along the western Rift have many species that occur nowhere else: the Kivu-Ruwenzori endemics.

The best places to spot them are the forests of the Ruwenzori range and those of Bwindi. There one can find the **handsome francolin**, **Ruwenzori turaco**, **Ruwenzori batis**, **white-bellied crested flycatcher**, **yellow-eyed black flycatcher**, **Ruwenzori apalis**, **red-faced woodland warbler**, **red-throated alethe**, **Archer's robin chat**, **mountain black boubou**, **stripe-breasted tit**, **purple-breasted sunbird**, **regal sunbird**, **blue-headed sunbird**, **strange weaver**, **dusky crimsonwing**, **Shelley's crimsonwing**, and **dusky twinspot**. The **Tanganyika ground thrush** is restricted to Bwindi and the volcanoes. The **dwarf honeyguide**, **short-tailed warbler**, and

Opposite top left: Abyssinian ground hornbills. Opposite top right: Black-headed heron.
Opposite middle left: African fish eagle. Opposite middle right: Weaver bird.
Opposite bottom left: Little egret. Opposite bottom right: Male ostrich.

Above: Saddlebill stork wades through the waters of Lake Mburo.
Opposite: Unusual-looking shoebill stork in Murchison Falls National Park.

Grauer's warbler are found only in the Bwindi Forest. The rarely seen **green broadbill** is found in only the higher parts of the Bwindi Forest, mainly around Ruhija and the Bwindi swamp.

The extensive and diverse wetlands attract a rich waterbird fauna. Most of the species of **pelicans, cormorants** and **darters**, **herons, storks, ibises** and **spoonbills, ducks** and **geese, plovers, waders** and **gulls, raptors**, and **passerines** known to occur in the eastern and southern African wetlands exist in Uganda. The **African fish eagle** is abundant, and some rare species like the **rufous-bellied heron** are also quite widespread.

Some species typically restricted to papyrus swamps and virtually endemic to the Lake Victoria basin, like the **papyrus gonolek**, the **white-winged warbler**, and the **papyrus canary**, are also widespread. The striking **shoebill stork** is known from the Victoria Nile and the larger swamps around lakes George, Edward, Victoria, and Kyoga. It is a large bird, about the size of a marabou, silver-grey with a conspicuous broad bill. It can stand motionless for hours on floating meadows or on the water's edge, waiting for fish.

In the montane swamps of the Bwindi Impenetrable National Park occurs the very local, unobtrusive and skulking **Grauer's rush warbler**, known from only a few places in south-western Uganda, western Rwanda, and northern Burundi. On the Semuliki River **Hartlaub's duck** has been recorded, and along the edges of swamps north-east of Lake Kyoga lives the only strictly Ugandan endemic species: **Fox's weaver**.

The serious birdwatcher visiting Uganda will obtain some help from *A Field Guide to the Birds of East Africa* by Williams and Arlott (Collins) and from the more recently published *Birds of Kenya and Northern Tanzania* by Turner, Zimmerman, and Pearson (Black). But many birds seen in the western parts of the country, especially forest birds, are not mentioned or depicted in these books.

The only book covering all species of western Uganda is the *Handbook on Birds of West and Central Africa* by Pread and Grant

Above: Uganda's extensive wetlands attract many waterbirds, including cormorants.

(1970–1973), although it is hard to find and somewhat out of date. A checklist with rough distribution is given by Britton (1983), and there are also some local publications, including a list of species found in the Kampala area by Carswell and Pomeroy.

The last word about the birds of Uganda has not been said. A few more species may still be found and mysteries remain to be solved, such as the two birds collected in the Kibale National Park in 1966, both described as **Prigogine's ground thrush**. Since that time, nobody has been able to find another specimen, so some doubt remains as to their identity. This may be a task future observers.

Above: African pied kingfisher, particularly common around Entebbe.

Flora: A Rich Diversity

Compared with the other countries of East Africa, Uganda is green and lush. However, large areas have been heavily modified by human activities: moist areas mainly by subsistence agriculture, dry areas by pastoralism. In some regions, especially in the south-western highlands, all natural vegetation has been cleared, and almost no indigenous trees are left, except for the **fig tree**, the **red-hot poker tree** (*Erythrina abyssinica*), the *Markhamia lutea* with its clusters of large yellow flowers, or an occasional **flame tree** (*Spathodea campanulata*) with its large, red, tulip-like flowers. For the casual visitor it is hard to imagine that these areas once were covered with forests. Elsewhere, natural or semi-natural vegetation survives in more or less protected areas or in areas that protect themselves, like the huge swamplands around lakes Victoria and Kyoga or the highest mountains. Only in the north and north-east are there still extensive tracts of 'wild' land.

Despite this strong human impact, botanically Uganda remains a rich country. Because of its geographical position, astride the equator between east and central Africa, it is a real melting pot of influences.

The vegetation of Uganda can be divided into six principal belts. Four are mainly dependent on the quantity of available moisture: **forest** and its derivatives; **moist savannah**, including evergreen woodlands, open, bushed or wooded grasslands; **dry savannah**, including mainly thorn bushland; and **semi-desert vegetation** with mainly dwarf shrub grassland. A fifth belt includes **aquatic vegetation** and permanent swamps. A sixth one, the **afro-alpine moorland and grassland**, is influenced more by temperature than by rainfall.

The forest belt can be separated into three main areas. Those around the northern and western shores of Lake Victoria have been linked in the past to those along the western Rift. Those occurring on mountains north-east of Lake Victoria, from Mount Elgon to northern Karamoja, seem to have been isolated for a long time.

The forests around Lake Victoria are all intermediate forests, lying at about 1,200 metres (4,000 feet) above sea level. One of the best remnants and the most accessible is Mabira Forest, between Kampala and Jinja, where the Forestry Department is now establishing trails for visitors. Much of this forest is semi-deciduous, with many *Maesopsis, Celtis, Holoptelea, Albizia,* and the handsome *Baikiaea insignis* in wet places. Nearly untouched forests, accessible only by boat, are found also on many of the Ssese Islands. Subject to a much higher rainfall – up to 2,000 millimetres (78 inches) a year – these are largely evergreen. The dominant species here include the tall, flat-crowned *Piptadeniastrum africanum* and *Uapaca guinensis* with its large, spectacular stilt roots.

Most of the mainland forests have been cleared, with others reduced to isolated patches or blocks. Around Entebbe, Kampala, and Jinja, most of the landscape is a mosaic of lush cultivation with relict indigenous trees and heavily disturbed

Above: Colourful bougainvillea adds a bright touch to a Ugandan garden.

255

Above: Nearly untouched forests can be found on many of the Ssese Islands.

remnants of forest along swamps, rivers, or lakeshores. The tall relict trees are typical. Most of them are *mvule* (*Chlorophora excelsa*), **incense tree** (*Canarium schweinfurtii*), and different species of *Albizia*. Some are heavily loaded with epiphytic **orchids**, especially the most beautiful *Diaphananthe fragrantissima*, or **ferns**, including the large *Platycerum elephantotis*.

South of Masaka towards the Tanzanian border, the Sango Bay forests (Kaiso, Malabigambo, Namalala, and Tero) are unique in East Africa. In that area, which is largely inaccessible because of frequent flooding, are various mixed swamp forest communities.

Although they have been heavily logged in the past, they are still among the richest forests of Uganda, with 60 to 70 tree species a hectare. Most unexpected is the fact that several tree species are found there at much lower altitude than anywhere else, such as the indigenous conifers *Podocarpus milanjanus* and *Podocarpus usambarensis*. Obviously these forests are relicts from a period when the climate was much different from today.

The forests of the western Rift escarpment are much more diverse and probably also much better preserved. They range from lowland forests at 600 metres (2,000 feet) to montane forests at 2,600 metres (8,500 feet). That once continuous belt has been strongly fragmented, however.

Some of the largest and richest remaining forests are now totally protected inside the Semuliki, Ruwenzori, Kibale, Queen Elizabeth, Bwindi Impenetrable, and Mgahinga national parks. Other forests still are subject to logging, but in most larger blocks, like the Budongo and Kalinzu forests, the Forestry Department has set aside some parts as strict forest reserves and some for eco-tourism.

Botanists and foresters recognize several forest types. At low and medium altitudes are colonizing forests with much *Maesopsis*; more mature, mixed forests with *Celtis*, *Albizia*, or even **mahoganies** (*Khaya* and *Entandrophragma*); and climax forests with *Cynometra alexandri* or *Parinari* species. In the Semuliki lowlands, close to the hot springs, is the only East African example of an **African oil palm** (*Elaeis*) swamp forest.

Above: Orange-red flowers of the red-hot poker tree, *Erythrina abyssinica.*

Above 2,000 metres (6,500 feet) mixed *Chrysophyllum* and *Macaranga* forests become dominant. Above 2,600 metres (8,500 feet) on the Virungas grows *Hagenia-Hypericum* forest, and, on the Ruwenzoris, *Hagenia-Rapanea* forest. The forests of Mount Elgon and the few isolated mountains of Karamoja are also montane, but much drier. *Aningeria* and *Podocarpus* forests are well developed on Mount Elgon. *Cassipourea* forest is found on Kadam, Elgon, and Imatong. Dry *Juniperus* forest occurs in small, heavily disturbed pockets in northern Karamoja, such as on Morungole at the edge of the Kidepo Valley National Park.

Associated with forest are also thickets of **elephant grass** *(Pennisetum purpureum)* or **montane bamboo** *(Arundinaria alpina).* Elephant grass used to occur in vast areas where lowland or medium-altitude forest had been cleared for cultivation and subsequently abandoned. It could once be found in the Lake Victoria belt, especially in the areas around Jinja and Tororo, and on the eastern slopes of Ruwenzoris, but most of these thickets have again been cultivated. Montane bamboo is found in

sizeable belts on Mount Elgon, the Ruwenzoris, and the Virungas. It occurs mainly between 2,300 and 2,600 metres (7,500 and 8,500 feet) in well-watered areas, where it forms almost pure stands.

In the south-western Kigezi highlands extensive areas of former montane forest are now montane grasslands. These occur mainly on steep hills with shallow soils and evolved after total deforestation and subsequent impoverishment of the soils under high grazing pressure. The dominant grasses are unpalatable **love-grasses** *(Eragrostis).* Locally, white-flowered bushes of *Protea* can be quite abundant.

Outside the forest belt most of Uganda was covered with moist woodlands and wooded grasslands, often forming a mosaic. However, as with forests, large areas have been cleared for agriculture. Along the road from Kampala to Masindi and on the slopes of the escarpment overlooking Lake Albert, including the Sempaya Valley, the Toro Game Reserve, and the southern parts of Murchison Falls National Park, *Combretum-Terminalia* woodland is dominant. More to the east in Lango, Acholi, Teso, and southern

Above: Beautiful amaryllis thrives in a Uganda garden.

Karamoja, **shea butter nut** (*Vitellaria paradoxa*) becomes a dominant tree. Shea butter or oil can be extracted from its fruit, and has been, to some extent, important for the people inhabiting the area.

In the remote north-western corner of the West Nile region are woodlands with *Isoberlinia* and *Afzelia*, typically a more western vegetation type, here reaching its eastern limit. In many of these northern woodlands the **sausage tree** (*Kigelia africana*) is abundant. Its large, dark purple flowers are pollinated at night by bats.

At the onset of the rains, in March/April, these moist woodlands are also rich in flowers: the red, orange, or yellow flowers of *Gladiolus*, the bright red flowers of the **fireball lily** (*Scadoxus*), the large but ephemeral, pink flowerheads of *Ammocharis*, the smaller, deep yellow flowers of *Hypoxis*, the pale or dark pink flowers of some *Eulophia* **orchids**, and many other species.

Associated with these northern woodlands are also extensive stands of **lowland bamboo** (*Oxythaenanthera abyssinica*) in the Acholi and West Nile regions. This species of bamboo grows in more spaced clumps than its montane relative and can be recognized at once by its plain stems, unlike those of the montane bamboo.

South of the forest belt the moist woodlands are quite different. In Queen Elizabeth National Park, areas likely to be flooded are often covered with dense woodlands of *Acacia gerrardii*, easily recognized by its black bark and dense white flowers. It often occurs alongside *Acacia polyacantha*, a much taller species with long, white flower spikes and a trunk covered with hooked, clawlike spines. Along lakes and rivers, the beautiful *Acacia kirkii*, with its light green, vaporous, many layered flat crown, is widespread. It resembles the more widespread fever tree (*Acacia xanthophlea*) of Kenya and Tanzania, and some visitors mistake it for that species.

Inside the moist woodland belt also occur fairly open grasslands or bushed grasslands. Other vegetation types differ from one place to another according to available moisture. In the western Rift area, extensive, moist grasslands occur mainly in and around the two large national parks. These grasslands remain quite open because of the frequent fires and the grazing of both wild and domestic ungulates. Those of Queen Elizabeth National Park are a mosaic of **red oat grass** *(Themeda)* and grasslands with much taller, tufted species like **hood grasses** *(Hyparrhenia)*, **cotton grass** *(Imperata)*, and **lemon grass** *(Cymbopogon)*. The strongly scented, bluish-green lemon grass makes a pleasant tea but is almost totally unpalatable to ungulates. It often becomes dominant in overgrazed areas. In some places these grasslands are well wooded with *Acacia sieberiana* and *Acacia gerrardii*. Elsewhere they are more open. In still other places, especially along the Kazinga Channel, they are heavily colonized by dense thickets of **wooly caper-bush** *(Capparis tomentosa)* and *Euphorbia candelabra*. In the southern parts of the park, near Ishasha, some **desert date** *(Balanites aegyptiaca)* are also found, indicating a drier habitat.

In Murchison Falls National Park, especially north of the Nile, extensive open grasslands are dotted with **borassus palm** *(Borassus aethiopicus)*, which also occurs in the West Nile region and around Lira. On some black cotton soils, and in Queen Elizabeth and Murchison Falls national parks, are open grasslands with **drop-seed grasses** *(Sporobolus)*, **timothy grass** *(Setaria)*, and **pin-hole grass** *(Botriochloa)*, much favoured by most ungulates.

Dry savannah occurs in three regions in Uganda. In southern Uganda, it is found between Mbarara and Masaka and south of the Katonga River. Some dry savannah is protected in Lake Mburo National Park. Dry savannah consists mainly of bushed or wooded grasslands, with most of the trees losing their leaves during the dry season. Several species of *Acacia* are dominant, the most common being the yellow-flowered *Acacia hockii* and the white-flowered *Acacia brevispica*. Along the lake, succulents are abundant, including several species of *Aloe* and a *Sanseviera*. On stony, shallow soils **russet-grass** *(Loudetia)* is dominant. Another narrow strip of very dry grasslands occurs along Lake Albert. There **aloes** and the broad-leaved *Sanseviera dawei* are also abundant. The most important area of

Top: Many flowering trees add bright splashes of colour to Kampala's suburbs.
Above: *Thunbergia grandiflora.*

259

Above: Harvesting papyrus in a Ugandan swamp.
Opposite: Grasses and plants are scarce in the dry northern parts of Uganda.

dry grassland occurs in Karamoja, where *Acacia mellifera* often becomes the dominant shrub.

The central parts of Karamoja between Moroto and Kabong (including the Matheniko Game Reserve) and the extreme north of Karamoja (including Kidepo Valley National Park) are semi-arid bushland. There grasses are sparse, mainly because of over-grazing, but trees and thorny shrub are abundant. The most common species belong to the genera *Commiphora*, *Acacia*, *Euphorbia*, and *Grewia*. *Acacia brevispica*, well known as the **wait-a-bit thorn**, often forms dense, impenetrable thickets. Other typical species of this region are the small tree *Lannea humilis* and several species of succulents in the genus *Caralluma*. In the Narus Valley of Kidepo National Park, thanks to permanent availability of ground water, are extensive groves of **borassus palm**.

Wetlands are perhaps one of the most typical features of Ugandan landscapes. They are found all over the country and cover thousands of square kilometres. The most extensive swamps occur along lakes Victoria and Kyoga, but some large swamps also occur in the western Rift Valley, especially around Lake George, and in some flooded valleys away from those lakes in southern Uganda. One of the main constituents of these swamps is **papyrus** (*Cyperus papyrus*), well known from ancient Egypt and still very abundant throughout the upper Nile Basin in Sudan and Uganda. Attempts have been made to use it for paper, but it seems to be suitable only for very rough brown paper or fibre board. Compressed papyrus has also provided briquettes, which can be used as an alternative to charcoal. Above all, papyrus has an immense ecological role: it is a very intense oxygen producer, and its root system acts as an efficient filter.

Some typical land plants around these extensive swamps include the tall herb *Aframomum sanguineum* of the ginger family, with its bright red, edible fruit; the shrubby *Alchornea cordifolia* with some red-marked leaves; the wild **date palm** (*Phoenix reclinata*), and in more forested places, the

Above: Boy and boat in the midst of water hyacinths, which have become the plague of Lake Victoria.

raphia palm *(Raphia monbuttorum)*, which features some of the longest leaves in the world. The **ambatch** *(Aeschynomene elaphroxylon)* grows more typically on the edge of open water, mainly in areas where there is not much swamp and around islands. It is a fast-growing tree, with large yellow flowers (much appreciated by sunbirds), and very light wood. Open water areas in the swamps are often colonized by blue or purple **water lilies** *(Nymphaea)*, and more recently by the **water hyacinth** *(Eichornia crassipes)*, a pest introduced in the Lake Victoria Basin in the mid-1980s through the Akagera River.

Above 3,000 metres (9,840 feet), forests and montane grasslands are replaced by the distinctive high mountain vegetation, which has as its characteristics remarkable growth forms, rather few species, and a very high percentage of endemism. These features are mainly the result of low mean temperatures, a large diurnal temperature range, and very intense solar radiation. Many of the remarkable growth forms, like the giant rosettes of the **dendrosenecios**

and **lobelias**, seem to be adaptations to these difficult temperature conditions.

Between 3,000 and 4,000 metres (10,000–13,000 feet) the montane forest belt gives way to woodlands and wooded grasslands of **heaths** and heathlike plants, more highly developed on the Virungas and the Ruwenzoris than on any other East African mountain range. On the Ruwenzoris the often twisted and gnarled trunks of *Philippia trimera* reach a height of more than 12 metres (40 feet) and are draped with long curtains of *Usnea* **lichens**. Among the few other trees or shrubs found in that woodland is the high-altitude **St John's wort** *(Hypericum bequaertii)*, with its bright orange-red flowers. In many places, the undergrowth of the woodland is made of a thick layer of mosses, where in some places large colonies of the beautiful, pink-flowered **orchid** *Disa stairsii* become established. The lowest altitudes often feature dense tangles of *Mimulopsis elliotii*, an acanthaceous plant with long spikes of white flowers, mixed with the **Ruwenzori blackberry** *(Rubus runsoricus)*, showing its

Above: Giant lobelia growing on the slopes of the Ruwenzori Mountains.

delicate, pale pink flowers.

At higher altitudes several species of **everlasting** flowers *(Helichrysum)* are common, and in some places the silvery-leaved *Alchemilla* becomes dominant. Above 4,200 metres (13,800 feet), especially on the Ruwenzoris, steep slopes and rocks are often covered by thick scrub of the straw-coloured and everlasting *(Helychrysum stuhlmanni).* Sometimes mosses form a dense cover below the bushes; sometimes shoots of *Lobelia wollastonii* emerge above them.

Where the ground flattens and becomes waterlogged, the woodland gives way to dense stands of *Erica bequaertii* or; at higher altitudes to large tussocks of *Carex runsorroensis.* Another typical plant of these swampy places, characteristic of most of the valley bottoms of the Ruwenzoris, is the tall *Lobelia bequaertii,* perhaps the most handsome of all **giant lobelias**.

From 3,500 metres (11,500 feet) to the upper limit of vegetation, on the Ruwenzoris and the Virungas as well, occur dense woodlands of **giant groundsels** or **dendrosenecious,** which reach a height of about eight metres (26 feet) but may take 100 years or more to do so.

On Mount Elgon, **heaths** are largely replaced by *Stoebe kilimandscharica,* a shrub of the daisy family, which looks very much like a *Philippia.* In many places the woodlands give way to tussock grasslands.

Mount Elgon is very different from the Ruwenzoris and the Virungas, not only because of its drier climate, but also because some pastoralists live there permanently with their cattle and often burn the grasses in the dry season.

Despite this human interference — or possibly because of it — the tussock grasslands of Elgon are more diverse and richer than those of Ruwenzoris. They feature many attractive flowers, including the pink flowers of the beautiful *Dierama pendulua* of the **iris** family and the handsome *Delphinium macrocentrum* of the **buttercup** family, with its erect spikes of dark blue or turquoise flowers.

Rainforests: A Unique Habitat

If Uganda had not been deeply marked by human activity in the last 3,000 years, a continuous belt of dense rainforest would stretch from the hot Semuliki lowlands and the ice-topped Ruwenzoris to the shores of Lake Victoria and the slopes of Mount Elgon. A few thousands of years ago these forests probably covered about 20 per cent of the country. Today only a few isolated blocks remain, more or less protected in national parks and forest reserves.

The forests of Uganda are the eastern extension of the vast forests of the Zaire Basin, the largest single tract of rainforest in Africa. Their history is quite recent. Indeed, each time Europe and northern America were affected by ice ages, tropical Africa experienced long spells of dry and cold climatic conditions, unsuitable for rainforest. So, over a span of thousands or even ten thousands of years the African tropical forests were reduced to tiny refuges. The Ugandan forests seen today started to develop only about 12,000 years ago, when the climate became warmer and wetter. They reached Lake Victoria about 10,000 years ago and attained their maximum expansion around 4,000 years ago. For at least 3,000 years, however, they have been disturbed by human activity — although at the end of the last century they were able to recover a little after rinderpest, sleeping sickness, and warfare chased away human populations in vast areas.

At first glance, tropical rainforests differ from all other forests by their tall, sometimes very tall, trees, many of which have butressed trunks or stilt roots and abundant lianas and epiphytes. They are essentially also a vegetal world: animal biomass is low, only about two to three per cent of the total. The number of animal species resident there, however, is impressive, as these forests are the kingdom of **insects**. Most evident are the colourful **butterflies**, but most abundant are ants and termites. The vertebrate fauna has many species, including some large mammals like **elephant** and **buffalo**, but most are shy, elusive, or nocturnal. Only primates and birds are prominent. Among the bird fauna are several families or genera that don't exist outside Africa, like the **turacos, honeyguides, batises** and **wattle-eyes, helmet-shrikes,** and **cuckoo shrikes**.

Not one Uganda forest looks exactly like another, and even inside each forest there are important differences, according to rainfall, altitude, soil, slope, and history.

Being on the edge of the rainforest biome, most of the Ugandan forests are semi-deciduous, which means that some trees of the upper canopy shed their leaves all at the same time during short dry periods. In a few high rainfall regions trees never lose their leaves all at once, and forests remain evergreen. The only such forests in Uganda are found along the shores and on the islands of Lake Victoria and in a few places along the western Rift.

With regard to altitude, the most typical rainforests are found in the lowland areas of Semuliki National Park, in the Maramagambo inside Queen Elizabeth National Park, and in some parts of Budongo, below 1,000 metres (3,000 feet) above sea level. These forests have the highest biological diversity and the most complex structure.

Vertically, they are divided into a number of well-defined layers, each representing, in fact, a different habitat. Most typically, three principal layers can be distinguished, the main layer being the upper canopy made of the dominant trees — about 20 to 35 metres (65–115 feet) high — and the emergents — up to 50 or even 60 metres (160–200 feet) high. Under this closed overhead canopy is a lower canopy or mid-stratum. The understorey is dark and open, with only a few bushes, saplings, and herbs. The soil, covered with

Opposite: The thick rainforest of Bwindi Impenetrable National Park.

Above: Large stands of forest still exist in Uganda.

dead leaves and fallen wood, is often very shallow and poor.

The forests of Kalinzu, Kasyoha-Kitomi, Kibale, Itwara, large parts of Bwindi Forest, and most of the Lake Victoria forests — including Mabira Forest — are transition forests. They look much like lowland forests, but the temperature is cooler, the trees are smaller, and the diversity is less. The highest parts of Bwindi Forest and the forests of the volcanoes and the Ruwenzori range are definitely montane. They are much less diverse, with smaller trees. Their canopy is considerably more open and simple. Buttresses are virtually absent. Lianas are few, and among the epiphytes, mosses and lichens become dominant. While these forests look somewhat like temperate forests, they never experience winter.

Perhaps more important than altitude are history and succession. Tall canopy trees can be hundreds of years old, sometimes even more than 1,000 years, but at some moment they die. When they fall down, they make huge gaps, and these treefall gaps constitute one of the ways in which a rainforest regenerates itself.

Remember, light is rare in the understorey. So when a gap appears, the sudden intrusion of full sunlight is a powerfull trigger: saplings, waiting for years and years, suddenly start growing; seeds germinate; and a struggle for life develops. In a few months, a tree may make a single tall shoot, 10 or 15 metres (30 to 50 feet) high, before it starts to divide and make lateral branches. Lianas try to cover everything. In two to three years the gap is closed with dense tangles of vegetation, and while the tallest trees grow higher and higher, the understorey again becomes darker and darker.

The first trees to form a new overhead canopy are very different from the previous ones. They are fast-growing species like the **umbrella trees** (*Musanga cecropioides* and *Musanga leoerrerae*) of the fig family. In the shade of their broad, spreading crown other trees grow up. One of the most common secondary forest trees in Uganda is the *muzizi* (*Maesopsis eminii*) of the family Rhamnaceae. It can reach 30 metres (100 feet) and its crown is broad but light. Its fruit looks like olives and is much appreciated by monkeys and by turacos, hornbills, green pigeons, and many other bird species. But *Maesopsis* is still a secondary forest tree, requiring light and not regenerating in the shade, so eventually it, too, will be replaced by other species. After 50 or perhaps 100 years the forest becomes like a mature mixed forest, but evolution goes on, until finally it reaches a climax state.

On poor soils and in difficult conditions climax forests are often dominated by a single tree species. Along the western Rift, **Uganda ironwood** (*Cynometra alexandri*) of the family Caesalpinaceae tends to be the dominant species in the lowlands. This evergreen tree grows up to 50 metres (160 feet). It often has a crooked trunk with a broad-spreading crown and large, thin, and spreading buttresses. Its wood is so hard and heavy that it is difficult to use, although it is suitable for flooring. In some areas of Semuliki and Maramagambo forests this tree represents 80 per cent of the canopy cover.

At somewhat higher altitudes, the **grey plum tree** (*Parinari excelsa*) of the family Chrysobalanaceae seems to be the most successful. It is a beautiful tree, growing up to 45 metres (150 feet), with a golden-green, broccoli-like crown. Its wood is also very hard. The last untouched stands in Kalinzu Forest need urgent protection. *Parinari* is often accompanied by the **Uganda crabwood** (*Carapa grandiflora*) of the family Meliaceae, easily recognized by its bright red young leaves.

On better soils, climax forest seems to be more diverse. There are several African **mahoganies** (of the genera *Khaya* and *Entandrophragma*). These very large trees, grow up to 55–60 metres (180–200 feet), with long trunks, large massive crowns, and often very large, spreading buttresses. Since they produce a valuable red wood, quite similar to true mahogany from Central and South America, they have been intensively harvested but are still abundant in Budongo Forest.

To the occasional visitor, tropical rainforests seem stable, quiet, silent, and perhaps even boring. After their early morning chorus, birds often become silent, and superficially, there is nothing to see. In reality these forests hide an unbelievable struggle for life. When visiting a rainforest you should be patient, take some time, sit down on a fallen trunk, open your eyes, and listen.

Tropical rainforests are unique because of their diversity. African rainforests are not so rich as those of South America and Asia, but they are no less important, since most of their species are not found on other continents. The *Symphonia globuliflora*, a tall forest tree of the family Clusiaceae with bright red, fleshy flowers, common in some parts of Bwindi Forest and on the lower slopes of the Ruwenzoris, is a rare exception, being found in both Africa and South America.

All over the world, tropical forests harbour more than 90 per cent of the existing life forms known on earth. Many families do not even exist outside rainforests, so rainforests have to be considered as the real cradle of life and evolution. But how can such a diversity be explained? The warm, humid, and stable climatic conditions are only a part of the answer. The intense competition also seems to be very important; in some ways tropical rainforests seem to host an endless vicious circle, where diversity triggers competition and competition diversity. In such a diverse habitat survival becomes a big problem, a nightmare: not only is there a need for resources that are often scarce, but there is also a need for defence against predators and other aggressors, and a need to reproduce. Each species, having many enemies, has to develop more and more complex strategies to solve the many, often paradoxical problems.

With regard to plant species, one of these problems is the availability of sunlight. Epiphytes and lianas have solved it by becoming established at higher levels.

Lianas, woody plants with long, slender stems, have found a way to attach themselves to trees, and so be lifted up into the canopy without having their own massive trunk. They are mostly unobtrusive, and their foliage, often on top of the canopy, becomes visible only when they are flowering. In some forests lianas

Above: Lush rainforest vegetation in Bwindi National Park.

are nearly as abundant as trees, both in number of species and in biomass. In addition to contributing significantly to the overall biological diversity of a forest, they are also important structurally. They make strong links between individual trees, and they give more strength to the canopy. However, the down side of this is that when a tall, emergent tree falls, many smaller trees go down with it.

Epiphytes are plants that grow on other plants without being parasites. They are found in forests all over the world, but in tropical forests they are very prominent. They belong to many different families, from bacteria to higher plants — even some trees are epiphytic. African rainforests are less rich in epiphytes than Asian or South American forests. Some families are even virtually absent in Africa, such as the bromelias and cactus. This can perhaps be explained by the fact that the African rainforests have repeatedly been reduced to small refuges, and that in the dry, cold periods many species became extinct. Nonetheless, up to 45 species of epiphytes have been counted on a single tree in Uganda. In lowland forests, ferns and orchids are dominant.

Water is not a problem in rainforests, except in the highest layers of the canopy, where for short periods it can be rare. Large trees shed their foliage, and many epiphytes develop specialized structures not unlike desert plants, with small or succulent leaves, stems, or roots. In the understorey water is often too abundant, and plants have had to develop strategies to get rid of it.

The major problem facing plant life there is nutrient availability. Nutrients are provided by the decaying vegetation and are found in the most superficial layers of the soil. Consequently, most trees have a superficial but dense root network. Despite poor soils, however, the primary production is quite high, because most of the life cycles in the rainforest go on independently from the soil — just at its surface, or even in the canopy. Thanks to a strong collaboration of trees and fungi, organic matter is promptly recycled. As defence strategies, many plants have developed repulsive or toxic chemicals in their leaves or bark, but predators have found ways around them. Some break down the toxins; others incorporate them, thus

Above: Treading carefully, trekkers explore a Uganda rainforest.

becoming specialists on particular plant species. This chemical war is partly responsible for the growing diversity in tropical rainforests. Over millions of years, millions of molecules have been synthetized, with complex and unexpected effects. People living in these forests have learned to use some of these molecules for hunting or medicinal purposes. Outsiders have only just begun to discover this fantastic world.

The most important problem with regard to production is rarity, the counterpart of diversity. Except for a few dominant species, most of the rainforest species, including plants and animals, are rare indeed. Some are so rare that one cannot understand how they are able to reproduce.

Animals face a paradox: they have to be unobtrusive as much as possible to escape predators, but at the same time they have to make themselves visible or audible to others of their species. They do this by using all kind of signals, including bright colours, strong odours, or particular noises. For plants, including trees, the problem is even more complex: they are not mobile, and often they flower only sporadically at intervals of 2 to 10 years. Their survival thus depends largely on the good relations they establish with animal species.

Most rainforest plants are pollinated only by insects, birds, or bats. To attract these often very specific pollinators, some flowers are large, some are brightly coloured, some are strongly fragrant; others are dark and malodorous, to attract flies and other insects. Many flowers produce nectar.

For the dispersal of their seeds, some species of the upper canopy rely on wind. Orchids produce myriad small seeds, while some lianas have winged seeds. Most seeds are heavy and can be dispersed only by animals: birds, primates, bats, and even some ungulates. Frugivory is a complex subject, however: fruits have to be attractive so that they are eaten but seeds have to be protected so that they cannot be crushed or destroyed by digestive ferments. The tropical rainforest is the most complex, most diverse, and most evolved habitat in the world, but also the most vulnerable. Interaction between species is so tenuous and specialized that when one species disappears many others cannot survive.

Camping in Uganda

Camping in Uganda can be a rewarding and unforgettable experience. But make sure you know what you're getting into: here are some useful pointers that may be of help.

- Bring a good first aid kit with the usual essentials, plus sterile needles and syringes.
- Be aware of any environmental impact you may be having, in particular with relation to heating fuel. There are arguments both for and against wood and charcoal. Paraffin stoves are a better alternative. Burn or bury all your waste and take all non-perishables/non-biodegradables with you.
- It is essential to have a good water purifying system or tablets with you. Bottled water is scarce outside the towns and very expensive.
- You must arrive in all national parks before 1800, as park regulations do not allow you to walk or drive after dark. It is also a good idea to book 'hard' accommodation and any meals you may wish park staff to prepare.
- Be considerate to other campers — no loud music, if any!
- When walking, use existing paths. Each time a new route is made, the path gets wider and more vegetation is buried in mud.

There are many opportunities to camp in Uganda, both inside and outside the national parks. It is a very economical way to see the country: in 1996, the camping fees in all the national parks were the same: Ush 10,000 (about US$ 10) for foreign non-residents, Ush 5,000 (about US$ 5) for foreign residents, and Ush 2,000 (about US$ 2) for citizens. Costs for bandas and various other accommodation vary at each location. It is best to check with the national parks headquarters as to current prices. Outside the national parks, camping charges vary, but are still relatively inexpensive.

Listed below is a summary of where you can camp in Uganda, and what you can expect to find there. (For the uninitiated, long-drop toilets are quite simply a hole in the ground — varying in size and quality — with either a wooden or concrete base and a surrounding screen made of either reeds or a more permanent material. The majority do not have lighting or toilet rolls.)

Bwindi Impenetrable National Park

This is the most popular place to stay if you wish to trek the gorillas. Permits are available from the Uganda National Parks headquarters, but they are limited to a small number per day and these are often booked months in advance. (See Uganda's Mountain Gorillas, Part Four.)

There is a community-run campground here where visitors can stay in bandas, which can each sleep four people in bunk beds. The price includes bedding and mosquito nets.

Alternatively you can camp using your own tents.

There are long-drop toilets, cold water bucket showers (staff will heat water for you on request), and firewood for sale.

Simple meals, such as omelettes, are available from the canteen across the road, which can also provide something more substantial, such as meat stew or chicken and chips, but staff need a few hours' notice! There is a nearby market on Saturdays where you can buy local produce.

If you wish to cook your own meals, bring all food and equipment with you.

Kibale National Park

There are two private campsites here equipped with tents, each with two beds, bedding, and a hurricane lamp.

There are also three general campsites with cooking areas available, but bring your own tent, food, utensils and cooking equipment. The sites have a long-drop toilet, but no showers. Firewood is available at Kanyanchue. It is quite cold here at night, so come prepared!

In addition, at nearby Crater Valley

Above: Tented camp in Kibale Forest.

Kibale Resort Beach visitors can camp with their own tents in a beautiful setting looking out over the lake. You can buy snacks and sodas there.

Kidepo Valley National Park
The only campsite is a basic facility at Kakine. Water and firewood are provided, but you must bring everything else.

At Apoka Rest Camp there is a students' hostel that has 20 small huts, each with two beds. Park staff will provide bedding, mosquito nets, and hurricane lamps. Guests must bring their own food, which park staff can prepare. A gas stove and cooking utensils are also available if needed.

Lake Mburo National Park
There are three campsites: one at Nshara gate (toilets, bathrooms, firewood, and water available), another site near the Interpretation Centre (toilets and firewood only, bring your own water), and the best of the bunch — if you can withstand the mosquitoes — a campsite overlooking the lake. Firewood is the only thing provided at the last site near the lake. Also, at the

park headquarters in Rwonyo six bandas are available for visitors: three doubles, two singles, and one family unit for four people. Meals can be provided by park staff.

You need to be self-contained at all of these sites, although it is possible to buy food from the Rwonyo rest camp dining area.

Mgahinga Gorilla National Park
Gorilla trekking is possible from this park, but make reservations in advance from the Uganda National Parks headquarters in Kampala. Check in before 1700 on the day before your visit at the park booking office in Kisoro. Here you can check whether the gorilla group is in the park, confirm your booking, pay the fee, and receive your permits.

On the day of your trek, arrive at the park headquarters at Ntebeko camp before 0830. Remember to allow yourself at least one hour travelling time to get from Kisoro to the headquarters in a four-wheel-drive vehicle.

The Uganda National Parks campsites

Above: Come self-contained if you plan on using the campsite at the top of Murchison Falls.

are at Ntebeko and near the departure point for the Muhabura climb. You need to bring everything with you, although water is provided and there is firewood for sale.

There is also the Amajambere/WACU community campground near the entrance to the park, which offers camping in your own tent for Ush 3,000 (about US$ 3) a person a night, or using its tents for Ush 4,000 (about US$ 4) per person a night.

Soap and water are supplied; there are basins and a bathing area available. Food and drinks are available at the canteen.

Mount Elgon National Park
The campsites are very simple. As in the Ruwenzoris, bring everything, including a map. It is possible to rent some camping equipment from the Salem Brotherhood, nine kilometres (five-and-a-half miles) from Mbale on the Kumi road.

Murchison Falls National Park
There are two campsites, one at Paraa and the other — more rustic — at the top of Murchison Falls itself.

At Paraa, a central campfire is provided

upon request. You can cook for yourself or take advantage of food provided by park staff — simple fare such as vegetables and chicken, which the camp staff will catch, kill, pluck, clean, and even cook for you.

There is a shower block with warm water, heated in a large drum over an open fire, and long-drop toilets.

You sleep either in bandas (twin rooms) or in your own tents. Open-sided rondavels can be used as kitchens (bring all your own equipment); they also have tables and chairs.

At the campsite on top of the falls, there are rondavels available (the same as those at Paraa) and long-drop toilets, but nothing else. Who needs sophistication when you can lie in your tent and listen to the roar of the Nile as it cascades into the gorge?

Queen Elizabeth National Park
The main campsite is in a lovely setting on the bank overlooking the Kazinga Channel, which connects lakes George and Edward.

Animals usually wander around the campsite at night — especially hyena bent on raiding the rubbish pit and hippos that come out of the river to graze.

You must be totally self-contained: bring camping equipment, food, and drinks. There are clean shower blocks (cold water only), long-drop toilets, and a rest area where you can cook under cover. From this site, it is possible to eat and drink at the nearby Mweya Lodge: park staff allow you to walk or drive there and back from the campsite at night. But watch out for grazing hippo.

There is a second campsite in the north sector of the park, also on the banks of the Kazinga Channel. This is more private but also more basic. Again, bring everything you need for camping. There are long-drop toilets but no shower facilities.

The lovely Ishasha campsite is in the south sector of the park. There is nothing available here but water and firewood.

In addition, near Mweya Lodge is the Uganda Institute of Ecology Hostel for travellers and a students' camp that normally provides accommodation for educational groups. Moderately priced meals and drinks are available at the students' canteen.

Ruwenzori Mountains National Park

This park features many beautiful places to camp, but you need to bring everything with you. It is also cold and very wet, so even if you're not climbing the mountains, it is advisable to bring a good sleeping bag, rain gear, heavy socks, warm and woollen clothing, gumboots or hiking boots, a water bottle, day pack, first aid kit, warm hat, and gloves.

There is no wood available for cooking, so you will need a paraffin stove or alternative cooking fuel. Sunglasses and sunscreen are advisable if you are hiking.

Semuliki National Park

Water and charcoal are available at the campsite at Ntandi, but bring your own food, tent, and cooking equipment. There is a long-drop toilet but no showers.

The privately run campsite at Sempaya adjacent to the hot springs has small thatched shelters for cooking and eating. You must bring your own tent and food, but it is possible to hire cooking utensils.

At both campsites, it is advisable to bring a mosquito net and repellant, as well as hiking boots and wet weather gear.

Outside the national parks

In 1996 it was not advisable to bush camp or free camp in what may look like a suitable spot. However, there are quite a number of locally run campsites.

Lake Bunyonyi, Kabale

There are three possibilities for camping on and around picturesque Lake Bunyonyi, where you can take rides in dugout canoes on the lake and go for walks, watching for the spectacular birdlife in the surrounding forest and at the water's edge.

The first campsite is just outside Kabale on the Kisoro road. Turn left at the edge of town and drive towards the lake. There is an old ruined building on top of the knoll, and you can camp around it. There is a long-drop toilet but no shower. You must bring everything you need. The cost is US$ 2–3 a person.

About 60 kilometres (37 miles) from Kabale, also on the road to Kisoro, there is another site on the lakeshore where you can pitch your own tents. There is a long-drop toilet, but no water or firewood available. You need to be totally selfcontained. Again, the cost is about US$ 2–3 a person.

Finally, there is Bushara Island Camp. This is, quite simply, a 'top spot'. Set in the middle of the lake, the tree-filled island is about a square kilometre in size. It rises gently in the middle, where three large, stationary tents are situated, each with twin beds and bedding, and a veranda area where you can sit outside and admire the tranquil scene. There are also 20 individual sites dotted around the island where you can pitch your own tents.

There are two toilets: one long-drop and one flushing, Western style. Showers are hot and bucket style. If you don't want to cook yourself, you can eat and drink in the camp's own restaurant/bar, set under a thatched roof. Allow about US$ 10 a person for food (breakfast and evening meal). In 1996, accommodation charges there were US$ 35 a person using the stationary tents, or US$ 15 a tent if using your own.

Above: Huts are provided for shelter on the Ruwenzori trails, but bring EVERYTHING you need.

Mountains of the Moon, Fort Portal

For a small fee, this hotel allows people to camp in its grounds and use the hotel facilities, that is, shower, toilets, bar, and restaurant. There is an occasional water shortage.

Natete Backpackers, Kampala

A favourite haunt of backpackers, this hostel, run by a New Zealander, is three kilometres (two miles) from the city centre on the Masaka road. You can either camp in the compound or sleep inside the hostel, which is set on a one-acre site. Simple meals are available, as well as cold drinks. There are hot-water bucket showers and long-drop toilets. There are also barbecue facilities and a large living room. In 1996, charges were Ush 2,300 (about US$ 2) a person to camp; Ush 4,600 (about US$ 4) a person to stay in the dormitory; Ush 11,500 (about US$ 11) for a single room; and Ush 15,000 (about US$ 15) a room for a double room.

University Inn, Mbarara

This small hotel is on the outskirts of Mbarara just before the turnoff to Fort Portal. The manager allows you to put up your own tents in the pretty gardens for Ush 5,000 (about US$ 5) a tent, and you can also shower in one of the rooms. Meals are available in the restaurant and you can drink in the bar.

Others

If you do find yourself outside a large town or in the middle of nowhere, churches and other missions will often allow you to camp on their grass or inside their compound. A small donation would obviously be appreciated.

Also, if you are going to visit the gorillas at Djombe in Zaire, this is an eight-kilometre (five-mile) walk from the Zaire/Uganda border. Officials will allow you to camp at the border and leave your vehicle there if you do not want to drive into Zaire.

Sporting Uganda

Uganda is a sporting country, with over 20 sports disciplines enjoyed by its people. All are promoted through amateur federations with the backing of government, which provides assistance through the National Council of Sports. Football leads the pack in terms of popularity, followed by boxing, athletics, tennis, golf, motor rallying, and — to a lesser extent — cricket.

More than any other sport, boxing has gained Uganda some titles, with track and field a close second.

Many federations organize successful sports meetings outside Kampala, even in the formerly war-torn regions in the north-east, north, and north-west. Golf, too, is on the upswing, with golfers rehabilitating long-abandoned courses throughout the country.

Soccer

Although it remains the largest crowd-puller in the country, soccer (commonly known as football) has attained little success beyond the borders of the regional Confederation of East and Central Africa Football Associations (CECAFA), where the national team, the Cranes, boast of a record six titles since the inception of the association's cup in 1973.

The other testimony to Uganda's football prowess was in 1978, when the Cranes came second to hosts Ghana in the final of the Africa Cup of Nations. Two clubs have reached the final rounds of continental championships three times: Simba in 1978 and SC Villa in 1991 and 1992.

Soccer in Uganda is run by the Federation of Uganda Football Associations (FUFA). The federation runs two major championships every year under the tutelage of the National Football League Committee.

Uganda is endowed with football talent that has not fully been exploited. But some national footballers have recently been lured to join professional soccer: Magid Musisi, a leading striker, is in Turkey after a stint in France, while Jackson Mayanja plays for an Egyptian division-one side.

FUFA was affiliated to the Confederation of African Football in 1956 and three years later admitted to the Federation of International Football Associations (FIFA). Uganda is now part of CECAFA, which has a membership of over 10 countries in the region, giving Africa one of its strongest competitions every year.

At the moment the country has poorly furnished stadia, with the Nakivubo War Memorial Stadium in Kampala serving as the national ground. Other grounds are the Mbale Municipal Stadium and Bugembe Stadium in Jinja. However, through an interest-free loan of US$ 28.6 million from the Chinese government, the Nelson Mandela complex at Kireka near Kampala was under construction in 1996. The facility will feature a soccer pitch, a running track, facilities for outdoor and indoor games, and a 100-bed hostel. The main stadium, when complete, will seat 45,000 fans — 20,000 more than Nakivubo.

Athletics

With the exception of 1976, Uganda has participated in every Olympics since 1956, mainly in the arena of track and field. However, the country's only major success so far is the sensational 1972 gold that the legendary John Akii Bua won after he set an Olympic record of 47.82 seconds in the 400-metre hurdles in Munich, Germany.

A new executive committee of the Uganda Amateur Athletics Federation is working out a programme to revamp the sport, which has seriously lagged in the last few years.

A number of young athletes have won themselves athletics-related scholarships to the USA, which bring with them the opportunity to train at excellent American facilities. Among these promising athletes are Julius Acon, winner of the 1500-metre final at the World Junior Athletics Championships in Lisbon, Portugal, in 1994, and Francis Ogola, a middle distance runner who finished third in the 400-metre flat in the 1992 World Junior Championship in Seoul.

Above: Popular pastime: league football at Nakivubo Stadium in Kampala.

Boxing

Boxing has earned Uganda more fame than any other discipline. Interestingly, the sport has for decades relied almost solely on recruits from Nagger, a suburb of Kampala. At one time, Nagger residents comprised the entire national team of 12 pugilists, with two brothers acting as captain and assistant captain.

Through boxing, Uganda has won several gold, silver, and bronze medals at the Commonwealth Games. John Mugabi, 'The Beast', won a silver at the 1980 Moscow Olympics, and John Munduga brought home a bronze from the Munich games. Mugabi climbed the professional ranks to become world middleweight champion alongside Cornelius Bbosa Edwards, Ayub Kalule, and Jamil Wasajja.

The sport is quite popular among the youth, particularly among school drop-outs, who believe boxing can give them their start in life. One secondary school, Kololo High School, is trying to lure these drop-outs back — and support the sport — by offering vacancies to boxers.

The school holds the intermediate title in the National School Championships.

Golf

Golf in Uganda is regarded as a game of the elite, although the country's only scratch player, Sadi Onito, is a former caddie employed by a local firm as a middle-level clerk. The game suffered greatly during the days of political turmoil, with most of its patrons either running to exile in the 1970s or keeping to their homes. This unfortunately rendered golf courses across the country unplayable. Local developers even put up houses on some fairways and greens.

Now the trend has changed. Golf courses have been refurbished, others reclaimed, and new ones — like the superb Garuga course on the shores of Lake Victoria near Entebbe town — are springing into existence. Tournaments are now being organized throughout the year, the most popular being the Rex Open, the Rank Xerox Open, and the Jinja Grain Millers Open.

Kitante Golf Club in Kampala is headquarters of the Uganda Golf Union and also serves as the central golf course.

Cricket

Like other sports, cricket suffered heavily after the exodus of the Asian community — leading contributors to the sport — in 1972.

However, the remaining Ugandans struggled and managed to maintain the sport, sustaining it to its present-day popularity. Several clubs have endured over the years, including the Africa Cricket Club, Premier, Wanderers, and Kampala Institute.

The national team has consistently participated in the East and Central Africa Quadrangulars, bringing home the Sir Menzies Trophy in 1966 and 1991.

The diplomatic corps in Kampala formed the White Caps Cricket Club, but it collapsed towards the end of the 1980s. Its downfall, however, prompted the formation of the Nile/Jinja Association of Cricket Clubs and the new Aga Khan.

The Uganda Cricket Association (UCA) recently unveiled a master plan aimed at reviving cricket in the former playing schools of Kings College Buddo, Jinja SSS, Busoga College Mwiri, Ntare School, Kibuli, Kasasa, and Ndejje. Several professionals have also been invited to the country to lead training sessions and play exhibition matches against youth select sides. The UCA has high hopes for success.

Visitors

Uganda is endowed with sports facilities a visitor can utilize while in the country. Sports clubs established during the colonial times exist in most major towns, which cater for various types of outdoor and indoor recreation, such as golf, squash, tennis, darts, snooker, and swimming.

Kitante Golf Club in Kampala and the exclusive Kampala Club are particularly popular. The new Garuga Golf and Country Club near Entebbe also has a fine 18-hole course.

To use a private club's facilities, get a friend or member to introduce you, or you can enquire at the club if temporary membership is available.

Major hotels in the country also have tennis courts and swimming pools open to membership and holiday visitors at a fee. Prominent among these are the Sheraton and Hotel Equatoria in Kampala and the Windsor Lake Victoria Hotel in Entebbe.

Jogging in Uganda — even in Kampala — can easily be done, but remember that you may be running at a higher altitude than you are used to, and the sun can be very hot. Don't overdo it.

For hassle-free running, try the Kampala City Council sports grounds, close to the Sports Council headquarters at Lugogo, three kilometres (two miles) east of the city centre. Even some city streets are good ground for joggers — but naturally it is best to avoid the rush hours.

If you are a horse-riding enthusiast, the only place in the country offering this opportunity in 1996 was the Katatumba Academy and Resort near Mbarara.

If you are not really interested in any particular sport but just want to keep fit while you are visiting Uganda, then try walking up and down the many hills of Kampala for a day.

Above: Golfer prepares to take a swing on the Jinja Golf Club course.

Tastes of Uganda

Visitors who are curious and want to discover the unique traditional dishes of Uganda will not be disappointed. Uganda's fertile soils and abundant freshwater lakes provide a true cornucopia of good things to eat, and visitors are sure to be delighted with what they sample — whether it be the country's unique traditional dishes or even the more familiar Western-style dishes, made special by local ingredients.

From Africa's largest freshwater lake, Victoria, come two mainstays of many a Ugandan's diet: Nile perch and tilapia. Fishermen can often be seen near the lake in the late afternoon, carrying their day's catch of Nile perch — a single specimen of which may weigh more than 80 kilos (176 lbs) — to the market. It is usually served fresh, but small-size perch may be smoked. The much smaller — but equally tasty — tilapia, known locally as *ngege*, is normally consumed fresh and rarely dried.

Uganda's waters are also home to another — perhaps not so conventional — foodstuff: the Nile crocodile. Ugandans are beginning to discover the versatility of crocodile meat, which is much nicer than it would seem, with a flavour variously described as resembling chicken, veal, or fish. As the number of commercially raised crocodiles increases, in a few years' time its meat will undoubtedly be appearing in some supermarkets.

For snacks, local people are somewhat addicted to *muchomo*, charcoal-roasted beef, pork, or chicken. Young men in the urban areas can often be seen selling skewered pieces of meat, which they grill on portable charcoal stoves. Roasted meat can be found at a number of roadside markets along the main roads. While travelling from Kampala to Jinja, you can make a stop-over at Nabiwojjojo — almost at the halfway point of the journey — and enjoy roast chicken meat, gizzards, cow liver, beef, or pork. This can be accompanied by grilled bananas — the sweet speciality locally called *gonja* — or fresh banana wine.

The colourful roadside markets are also the place to buy the incredible variety of fresh tropical fruits and vegetables grown in the country, such as several types of banana, passion fruit, oranges, mangoes, onions, tomatoes, juicy pawpaws (papaya), avocados, potatoes, and many more.

Uganda's traditional ethnic dishes are basic and simple. Beef stew is the staple for the more well-to-do, while ground peanuts (groundnuts) and beans, boiled and seasoned with ginger and cooking oil, are the most popular vegetarian dish.

But what has become the 'national dish' is *matoke* — peeled bananas boiled in water while wrapped in banana leaves. Every visitor should try it at least once, preferably as a guest in a rural home, eating with the fingers. When eaten in a private residence, matoke is often accompanied with a variety of tasty relishes and vegetables not often found in more conventional tourist surroundings. Matoke is eaten in most parts of the country, but particularly in the Buganda, western, and eastern regions.

The special matoke bananas are grown mostly in Buganda and western Uganda on well-watered land: the banana plant requires much rain to yield a good crop.

In the drier, northern parts of the country, millet, sorghum, and cassava are grown as food crops. They are cooked and eaten with a sauce made out of groundnuts, simsim (sesame), different meats and fish, as well as leafy greens.

If you really want to throw all caution to the wind, make sure you try such local delicacies as green grasshoppers, locally called *nsenene* (particularly abundant during the rainy seasons), and white ants (actually, termites). The Bagisu tribe also relish young bamboo shoots, which they call *amaleewa*. If any of these are offered to you, don't let the opportunity pass you by: they are nicer than you might think.

Cultivation of maize has become popular in all regions of the country. Maize, originally meant to be cattle and poultry feed, is now served in local restaurants and

Above: Delicious delicacies from Uganda's lakes and fertile soils.

if cooked well, can be tastier than the more expensive matoke. In most boarding and day schools in Uganda, maize porridge is served at breakfast, with maize meal a regular feature at lunch and dinner. It is often accompanied by a sauce made from groundnuts, simsim, meat, and leafy green vegetables.

To wash everything down, try the locally brewed beers, which are first class if you like light, lager-type beers. Two large breweries produce a variety of beers, each trying to out-market the other with all sorts of gimmicks — but only the true connoisseur will be able to tell the difference between Nile and Bell beers.

The well-known 'national drink' is called *Uganda waragi*, a distillate or gin made out of cassava, banana beer, and brown sugar. The raw material out of which Uganda waragi is made is locally called *enguli* — a potent white stuff that is almost 100 per cent pure alcohol. Some people say enguli can be used to generate electricity or power your car!

There is a Uganda law stating that no one is allowed to consume the crude stuff

before it is refined because it can burn one's lungs out — but no one seems to obey this law, and it isn't very strictly enforced. When the enguli is taken to the commercial distillery, it is purified, its alcoholic potency is drastically reduced (to less than 40 per cent), and it is given different flavours. It is either bottled or packed in small plastic bags. Uganda waragi is sold in almost every supermarket, bar, or restaurant.

Another local brew is banana wine, made in the banana-growing rural areas in a dug-out canoe-like wooden container. It is essentially juice from bananas, which is fermented with sorghum flour. After seven days it is ready to drink and is filtered into gourds or jerrycans and taken to the market.

Making the most of what they grow, the rural people in the north and north-east parts make a similar alcoholic drink out of millet. When it is ready, the drink is put in pots and sucked out through locally made straws or tubes. Hot water is added periodically while three to six people sit around the pot, sucking in the drink, locally called *malwa*.

Arts and Crafts of Uganda

Apart from depicting beauty, the arts and crafts of Uganda have religious, cultural, and psychological significance — as well as a practical use.

Barkcloth

A unique Ugandan craft is the making of barkcloth. According to Buganda folklore, it was during the reign of King Kimera that a hunter in the region invented the art after coming across a species of fig tree while on a hunting trip in the forest. He noticed its bark had criss-crossing fibres, similar to the warp and weft of manufactured cloth.

Barkcloth is made by stripping long lengths of bark from the tree, now known as the 'barkcloth tree'. The strips are first soaked in water and are then beaten on a smooth log with a corrugated wooden mallet called a *nsaamo*. Beating thins out the bark and makes it firmer. The resulting soft material is often painted or decorated. The strips are then sown together to make larger pieces.

Barkcloth decorated with bold patterns in black dye was reserved for the royal family. It was considered a matter of etiquette that all princesses and women of the king's court should wear nothing but barkcloth. For the king, a species of barkcloth tree was grown that produced a white barkcloth, which was used at his coronation ceremony, and seldom at other times.

Barkcloth is in use to this day. Peasants in rural areas who cannot afford to buy a wooden coffin wrap their dead in bark-cloth before they are buried. Barkcloth is also still worn on important cultural events and is used for making beautifully deco-rated tablecloths, curtains, handbags, and floor mats.

Gourds

One of the most useful natural objects in Uganda is the calabash or gourd. It grows well in most parts of Africa and, owing to its diversity of shape, can be put to a large number of uses. The beauty and utility of a well-shaped gourd have been so appreciated by many tribes that artisans have copied it in earthenware.

Large gourds are also used as musical instruments in several parts of northern Uganda.

Basketry

Basketry is possibly the oldest and most highly developed craft in Uganda. There has always been a big demand for baskets all over the country; this type of weaving is a foundation of homemaking, building, and defence. Stockades, enclosure fences, and houses are often woven, as are portable shields. Fences, granaries, reedwork, thatching, traps, and heavy field baskets are made by men. Smaller baskets for storing food in the house are made by women. The delicate fancy baskets, pot lids, and pot stands — whose use is almost more ornamental than functional — are the product of endless hours of concentrated effort.

Pottery

Among Ugandans, potters were a distinct class of workmen. The king had his own potters; many chiefs also had their own earthenware workers.

The land provides potters with many different kinds of clay: red soils for large red earthenware, kaolin for white clay, and black soils for dark bluish clay, a substance much favoured for making certain articles.

An earthenware article is made by rolling clay into long strips and coiling them into the desired shape. The surfaces are smoothed, and the product is then dried and fired.

Earthenware pots are used for carrying and storing water, making and storing beer, and storing grains and other foods. Small pots, called *kibya* in Ganda, are used as drinking vessels or as receptacles for food, vegetables, or gravy.

Several tribes in Uganda use clay to manufacture tobacco pipes and pipes for use in temples and shrines.

Above: Ugandans are known for their fine basketry.

Wood

From the many types of wood found in the country, Ugandans make a wide variety of utensils, including spoons, ladles, beer tubes or straws, mallets used in the making of barkcloth, and long boxes used for jewellery and similar items.

Wooden stools are also popular items. There are two types of stools in the Buganda kingdom: the leg and base stool and the cotton-reel stool.

Namulondo, the sacred stool used in Ganda coronation rites, is of the cotton-reel variety.

Weapons

Before the arrival of Arab traders and European colonizers and missionaries, the weapons found in a typical armoury were shields, sticks, spears, bows and arrows, and simple guns, often made out of wood but occasionally of iron. Miniature shields were sometimes kept near their beds by women as charms.

Wooden clubs shaped like a knobkerry were formerly used in warfare and as a weapon of execution. On their 'walkabouts', men from several tribes held walking sticks in their hands, the end of which was either club-shaped or pointed. In Buganda a ceremonial staff is handed over to the katikiro (prime minister) by the kabaka (king) on the occasion of his inauguration. This is a sort of sceptre and a symbol of the prime minister's authority in the kingdom and is regarded as sacred.

Spears were common among the tribes of ancient Uganda. But even today spears are used in traditional hunting and in poaching wild game.

The spear has a narrow and tapering blade; the widest portion is not at the extreme base, so that the shoulders slope upwards. It usually has burnished edges and often gives the appearance of having two wide, shallow blood courses. The sockets are heavy, with an open split and one nail at the back.

Bows and arrows are common, even today. They are used in defence and hunting wild animals.

Above: Many roadside shops make and sell a variety of traditional musical instruments.

Musical instruments

There are as many types, shapes, and varieties of traditional musical instruments in Uganda as there are tribal groups. The most common musical instrument is the drum, which is made out of wood, with its two hollow ends covered by hides or skins.

Drums are not only used to produce music for entertainment or dancing, but they are also used for communicaing different messages. *Ggwanga mujje*, for example, is beaten to summon all the people residing in an area in case of trouble or the need for communal work.

Fine art

Early Ugandan artists, influenced by the foreigners around them during colonial times, often imitated European statuary and paintings. A good example of this type of art is that of Joachim Basasa Kalange, whose work adorns many churches in the diocese of Masaba. Others of note include Charles Ssekintu, Ignatius Sserulyo, F Musango, and Kivubiro.

An interesting style of representational art evolved from the need the Baganda felt to illustrate their numerous pithy aphorisms. In the mid-1920s, people started writing these short wise sayings in form of riddles, known as *bikokyo*, many of which were printed in the local Gambuze newspaper. Later these sayings were copied on paper, mounted, and hung on many a living room wall as both maxims and decorations. Between 1936 and 1940 artists began adding pictures to illustrate the sayings.

The desire to have clan totems illustrated in pictures was also a big factor in this development. With their roots at Mukono in the Bishop Tucker College, these pictures were later brought to Kampala and finally spread throughout the country.

Gradually the occupation of making 'mottos' became popular and commercially practicable; even today you meet people selling these articles anywhere in the country.

Above: Visitors to the Nommo Gallery in Kampala can see many fine examples of Ugandan art.

Where to find Ugandan arts and crafts

Arts and crafts in Uganda are found everywhere — in everyday use, displayed and being exchanged for money in market places, people's homes, public and private galleries, and museums.

School of Fine Art at Makerere

The School of Fine Art at Makerere University is one of the oldest schools at Uganda's highest institution of learning. It has played a leading role not only in producing some of the country's greatest artists but also in Uganda's cultural and social transformation. A five-minute walk from the centre of Kampala, the Margaret Trowell School of Fine Art (named after the wife of the colonial governor who initiated its establishment) houses a permanent gallery of some of the best works of art left behind by the former students of the school. Outside the gallery are numerous sculptures and statues made out of clay, wood, and metal in all sorts of shapes and sizes. Collectors can easily be put in touch with the artists whose works are on display so that they can see more of their work.

Nommo Gallery

For a long time, Nommo Gallery at Nakasero Hill, near State House in Kampala, has been a regular meeting place for artists, buyers, and admirers of art. Almost every week this public gallery exhibits the work of one or several well-known and up-and-coming artists, and it is the perfect place to get an introduction to Ugandan art.

Sheraton Hotel

For some time now, the Kampala Sheraton has allowed artists to exhibit their works in its spacious public areas — particularly the foyer of the Ruwenzori Ballroom — free of charge. Some of the best paintings, batiks, and sculptures being produced by local artists can be seen here, and the exhibitors or their representatives are often at hand to negotiate prices with serious and potential customers.

Above: Batik painting by well-known Ugandan artist N W Nnyanzi.

National Theatre/Arts and Crafts Village

In addition to hosting performing artists for a long time, the lobbies of the Uganda National Theatre are often adorned with the works of the country's fine artists. In the grounds behind the theatre is the permanent Arts and Crafts Village, where a tremendous variety of crafts and artwork are for sale in various kiosks. It is a fascinating experience to stroll around and talk to the artisans or members of the many self-help groups that run the small shops. They are more than happy to answer your questions and show you their work.

Private galleries and studios

During the past few years, several well-known artists forced into exile during the country's civil unrest have returned to their motherland. A number of these are putting up private galleries and studios where they continue to work, display their creations, and entertain buyers and admirers.

One of the outstanding private galleries is **Nnyanzi Art Studio**, located in the heart of Kampala. The gallery/studio has been put up by a self-made artist, 43-year-old Nuwa Wamala Nnyanzi, who worked in neigh-bouring Kenya for many years while in exile.

Nnyanzi, president of the Uganda Artists Association, is also the minister for local government in the Buganda kingdom government. His original batik paintings, which have become world famous, often depict family life themes and the scourges of modern city life.

Uganda National Museum

The Uganda National Museum, in the north-east section of Kampala on Kitante Hill, is home to many of the country's treasured historical arts and crafts, including fossils and cultural artefacts.

Roadside markets

Many artisans making items such as baskets, drums, or pottery can be found on the roadside markets along the country's main roads. Straw furniture makers, for example, are flourishing on the Nsambya–Kabalagala–Kansanga road, targeting their wares to the rich residents of Muyenga and Bunga. Craftspeople specializing in mats and baskets can be found at Mukono shopping centre along the Kampala–Jinja main road.

Uganda's Music and Dance

To appreciate Uganda's richness in music and dance, you need to understand the difference among the peoples that make up Uganda's population.

While today there is talk of some 33 different tribes with a fathomless repertoire of rhythms, melodies, styles, dances, poetry, crafts, and languages, originally Africa was inhabited by three distinct ethnic groups: the pygmoids (who were derogatorily called bushmen), the negroids, and the Hamites. The interaction and inter-marriage among these peoples resulted in the development of important secondary cultures.

The pygmoids

The pygmoids are rather short and small people who once occupied mainly the forested areas. They survive on hunting and gathering and live a very mobile life. Examples of the pygmies in Uganda are the Batwa in the south and the Bambuti in the west.

Because of their nomadic way of life, the pygmies keep very few, light and basic personal belongings — which explains why they do not keep many musical instruments.

As compensation for that lack, they have developed complex vocal 'music' — a unique kind of *a cappella*. They yodel and interlock their voices to levels that many an ordinary ear may dismiss as merely disor-ganized noise, rather than music.

For rhythmic accompaniment, the pygmies use any available objects. For example, often they slap their cheeks as they change the shapes of their mouths, producing different melodic rhythms.

When they make any tools and imple-ments, they bear music in mind. For example, in making fishing canoes, one side is made thicker than the other, giving the sides different pitches when knocked. Rhythms are, therefore, played on the two different sides of the canoe.

Dances are limited in movement — often small steps made to and fro. This might be as a result of the limited space amongst the vegetation in the forests.

The negroids

The dark and well-built negroids constitute the vast majority of the population. They live a very physical and settled kind of life, tilling the land, growing crops, building houses and granaries. They are considered strong, active, and hard-working.

Because of the vigorous nature of their day-to-day lives, the music of the negroes is very rhythmic.

Several percussive and melodic-percussive instruments like drums, xylophones, and rattles were invented or adopted to provide heavy rhythmic accompaniments to stimulate the frenzied dancing that characterizes some social gatherings.

The lyrics of their songs and melodies are often not coherent; they are simply to stimulate dancing and are often overpowered by loud instrumentation.

The negroes have music for every social function and aspect of work. For example, there is music for birth, for naming a child, for twins, for marriage, and for death. There is music for hunting, fishing, grazing animals — and just about every other activity.

The Hamites

The Hamites are Africa's cattle keepers. They are believed to have originated from the north, coming south in search of water and pastures for their animals. Like the pygmoids, the Hamites live a nomadic life.

Their society is very closely knit. People stay together in groups for long hours, talking and telling stories as they either look after the cattle or do other chores. Stories of wars and heroes, of love and wealth, and of expeditions and adventure are often told.

Most of these stories and poems were originally told in music. The Hamites, therefore, developed a different kind of music — one with very coherent lyrics and deep-rooted meanings. They developed epic poetry *(ebyevugo)*, which some feel is the foundation on which the rap music of North America is built.

Above: Ugandan traditional dancers perform at a political function.

The cattle keepers do not have very vigorous dances. They concentrate more on the meanings of the words in the poems. They have beautiful but complex long-phrased melodies.

The only musical instruments that are typical of the Hamites are flutes, trough zithers *(enanga)*, fiddles, and a one-string bow-like instrument *(egoobore)*. Because of the instruments' small size and number (usually only one instrument exists in a whole community), the music they produce is rather 'thin' and requires attentive listening.

To experience Hamite music, one should visit Busongora County in Kasese District or Kashaari and Nyabushozi counties in Mbarara District.

The role of music and dance

In the absence of the written word, Africans designed a way of record-keeping as well as effective communication and instruction through music, dance, poetry, proverbs and storytelling. These are the great books of Africa. They are the window through which one has to look in order to acquire a reasonable understanding and appreciation of the complex social, economic, political, and religious systems that shape and influence modern trends.

Although there are, of course, dances and songs designed purely for entertainment, many have a purpose or a specific theme.

Teaching

Traditional teaching in Africa was informal, with no organized schools, classrooms, paid teachers, time tables or syllabi. Most teaching, therefore, was done through the performing arts. The language complexity was the graduated syllabus. The older you grew the more capable you became to 'read between the lines' to understand hidden meanings and metaphors.

Messages that were not easy to communicate verbally or even in song — such as sex or marriage education — were danced. The *embaga* (wedding) dance in Buganda, which was used to teach sex to newly wedded virgin couples, is a clear example of how body language

Above: The sheer joy of dancing is evident on the faces of these Ndere Troupe performers.

communicates more effectively than the tongue.

Other fertility dances like *eirongo*, *tamenhaibuga*, and *nalufuka* in Busoga, *bakisimba nankasa* and *muwogola* in Buganda, and *naleyo* in Karamoja also harmlessly 'speak' what nobody dares mention verbally in public.

Dances such as *otole* in Acholi and *entoore* in Kisoro, Rwanda, and Burundi were meant to teach war tactics and instil courage in the young warriors in an interesting and non-scaring way.

Children are exposed to different levels and types of training suitable to their ages and sex. This ranges from physical fitness dances like *embanda* in Ankole to movements like *kibuuka tonkutulakutula* in Buganda, which is meant to soften the waists of girls in order to prepare them to have easy childbirth later.

Of course, folk-songs also provide wonderful opportunities to teach, or criticize system and people without raising tempers. Folk-songs are particularly invaluable to women, who can make all the comments, criticisms, suggestions, and

demands they want about their families and society without risking a beating.

Teaching and criticism that would otherwise be frowned upon are wholly and easily 'swallowed' once they are wrapped up and presented as entertainment.

Courtship/love

African tradition dictates that everyone — especially a girl — was supposed to remain a virgin until marriage. To ensure this, members of the opposite sex did not have much freedom of association. The only time the two came close was in the dance arena, where the young men put on suitably provocative displays in front of their chosen ones. If the girls were interested, they responded accordingly, and equally provocatively. All was done silently, through dance movement.

Everybody present, including the elders, noted the intense interest. Often this resulted in marriage negotiations by the elders.

Examples of such dances are *larakaraka* in Acholi, *runyege* and *ntogoro* in Toro and Bunyoro, *fumbe* in Tororo, *okusooma* in

287

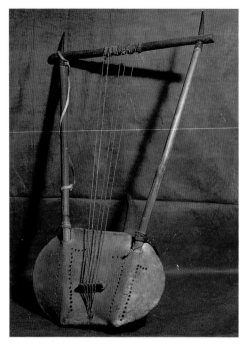

Above: Two examples of Uganda's traditional musical instruments, on display in the National Museum.

Ankole, *kigezi* and *mwaga* in Bugisu, and *akogo* in Teso.

Worship
Dance and music were once the main media used — even to communicate with the supernatural.

Through these means, worshippers were able to meditate to levels of being possessed by spirits. Through these spirits, the living communicated with the living-dead and supernatural beings.

Dances like *ekimandwa* of Ankole and *enswezi* of Busoga were specifically meant to create an ideal atmosphere for worship.

Musical instruments

Uganda has many unique instruments that are often used to provide music to the various dances. Used throughout the country, they can be classified according to how they produce sound.

Membraphones are a type of percussive instruments that produce sound by beating or 'exciting' the membrane or skin stretched on them. They include drums *(engoma)* of different shapes and lengths, such as *embuutu, empunyi, engalabi,* and *namunjoloba.*

Ideophones include simple rhythmic instruments such as rattles, gourds, and wooden blocks, as well as melodic percussion instruments like xylophones *(amadinda).*

Chordophones are stringed instruments that can be plucked, such as harps *(adungu),* zithers *(enanga),* or lyres *(entongoli);* played with a bow, such as fiddles *(endingidi);* or knocked, such as the *egoobole,* which is a one-stringed bow and gourd.

Finally, there are **aerophones**, or wind instruments, which produce sounds by having air blown into them. Examples of these types of instruments are bass trumpets *(agwara),* tenor trumpets *(amakondere),* flutes *(endere* or *emikuri),* pan pipes in sets *(enkwanzi),* and single-stopped pipes *(esheegu).*

Above: Smiling and colourful Ndere Troupe dancers perform to an enthusiastic crowd.

Where to experience Ugandan music and dance

When Christianity was introduced to this part of Africa long ago, traditional dances, instruments, and music were considered evil and a symbol of primitiveness or backwardness. This led to a gradual decline in this creative way of expression, especially among educated people. However, there were those who managed to keep these arts alive, and today the arts are thriving, with more and more people wanting to learn about the traditions and customs of their ancestors.

There are several groups around the country that perform dances and music of a particular region. These include Evaristo Muyinda of Buganda; several groups in Katwe, Buganda; the Acholi cultural group at the Uganda National Museum; the Nebbi community group based in Luzira; the Kasata group, based in Nakisenyi Iganga District, Busoga; and the Watmone group, known for its Acholi music but based in Namuwongo.

But if you want to get an overview of music and dance — and drama — from all regions of the country, make sure you see a performance of the famous Ndere Troupe, who pride themselves on having done thorough research in all regions, training and developing African performing arts. Watching the Ndere Troupe is like going on an exciting tour around the country.

The troupe performs at the Sheraton Kampala Hotel every Thursday in the barbecue area from 1800 to 2000, and at the Nile Hotel International every Sunday from 1745 to 2000.

The troupe is presently constructing a cultural complex 10 kilometres (six miles) outside Kampala on the road to Entebbe, sponsored by the Austrian government. When completed, it will be a mini-Uganda in terms of architecture, artefacts, food, drinks, and — of course — dance, music, and theatre.

Stamps and Coins of Uganda

Uganda's stamps, coins, and paper money are sought after by collectors the world over. All three, in their own way, tell the story of Uganda in a unique and colourful way.

Stamps

The first Ugandan stamps were typewritten by a missionary on simple writing paper in 1895. They were not perforated, and the value was expressed in cowrie shells. These modest, handcrafted stamps are very scarce. Their authenticity can be proven only if they are still stuck on the original envelope.

One year later, values of stamps were expressed in *annas* and were inscribed with the words 'Uganda Protectorate'. In 1898, Uganda issued its own stamps, this time featuring the portrait of Queen Victoria on watermarked paper. From 1903 until 1961, however, Uganda used stamps issued by the postal service common with Kenya (and, later, with Tanganyika).

Until 1922, stamps were inscribed 'East Africa and Uganda Protectorate', changing from 1923 to 1935 to read 'Kenya and Uganda'. From 1935 to 1961 the inscription changed once again, this time to 'Kenya, Uganda, Tanganyika'.

These latter stamps, featuring the portrait of George VI or Queen Elizabeth, are relatively easy to find, are inexpensive, and have the added appeal of that fascinating British African era.

Often the portrait of the reigning monarch is inside an oval, gazing out at the animals or scenery of East Africa.

The East African postal service continued until 30 June 1977, although the last issued stamp of that service is dated 1975. Since its independence in 1962, the country's stamps have been inscribed only with the name 'Uganda'.

When compared with collecting stamps of other countries, collecting Ugandan stamps is a relatively easy and inexpensive hobby — but it requires tremendous patience, because about 1400 different pieces have been issued to date. Most are multicoloured and attractive, and they cover a wide range of subjects.

Commemoratives include innumerable events over the last 30 years; others cover air transport, trains, flowers, birds, animals, fish, Christmas, Walt Disney, World Cups, the British royal family, World Stamp Exhibitions, and more. Undoubtedly the most remarkable — and collectible — issues of Uganda, however, are the ones illustrating the country's abundant natural resources, history, customs, and traditions.

A beautiful example is 'Wildlife at the Waterhole', a set of 20 stamps of 30 shillings value issued in 1989. Printed together in a sheetlet, these stamps form a composite design showing wonderfully illustrated birds and animals found in the national parks of Uganda.

Another beautiful sheetlet showing 'Wildlife in the Wetlands' was issued with 16 stamps in 1991.

From 1979 to 1992, a number of other excellent sets of stamps were issued depicting the country's wildlife and birdlife — the most recent being the set of two stamps issued in 1992 to commemorate the United Nations Earth Summit in Rio de Janeiro, which feature the impala and the zebra.

Many visitors or collectors want a stamp featuring the symbol of Uganda, the crowned crane. Over the years, five stamps have been issued depicting this beautiful bird: two in 1965 (one for the International Trade Fair of Kampala and another in a set of birds), one in 1987 in a 'Birds of Uganda' set, one in the 'Wildlife at the Waterhole' sheetlet of 1989, and the last in another set of birds issued in 1992.

Other remarkable issues are the 1992 set of eight stamps featuring 'Traditional Tribal Musical Instruments', an attractive set of eight issued in 1994 depicting 'The Nation's Fruit and Vegetable Crops', and a

Above: A selection of Uganda's colourful — and collectible — stamps.

colourful 1994 set of eight illustrating the 'Handicrafts of Uganda'.

Even young collectors can find Uganda stamps to their liking: none could pass up the 27 stamps and three sheetlets issued in 1994 illustrating the adventures of Walt Disney's African-based animated film, *The Lion King*.

Kampala's important buildings have also found their way onto the country's stamps — from 1962 to 1987, the Parliament buildings, Namirembe and Rubaga cathedrals, Kibuli Mosque, Mulago Hospital, Makerere University, and the high court building.

Even the massive building on the corner of Colville Street and Portal Avenue had its day in the sun on a 1974 issue of four stamps to commemorate the centenary of the Universal Postal Union.

During Idi Amin's regime, this building was supposed to be the new postal head-quarters of Uganda, but it remained grey and unfinished for almost 20 years. Now completed, it is a shining example of the recovery of the country.

Coins

Effectively, Uganda is a country without coins. Although technically four coins — with denominations of 1, 2, 5, and 10 shillings — are still legal tender, the galloping inflation that affected Uganda has virtually eliminated them from circulation. Today only paper money is in constant use.

The thick, twelve-sided 1- and 2-shilling coins are made of copper-plated steel. One side features the Uganda coat of arms in the centre, with the writing 'Bank of Uganda' above and the value below. On the other side the denomination is inscribed in a circle surrounded by branches of cotton flowers. A small sack of cotton is shown above the date.

The thinner 5- and 10-shilling coins are seven sided and are struck in stainless steel. On the reverse, branches of coffee take the place of the cotton, and a basketful of coffee is shown above the date. Even if today they are no longer used, in the past coins played an important role in Uganda.

Above: Although rarely seen in circulation today, Uganda has had its share of coins in the past.

Before the arrival of the European explorers and missionaries, local people used to barter goods or pay for items using traditional 'currency' like spears, bracelets, hoes, and cowrie shells. In fact, the use of cowries was such a deeply rooted tradition that when the British introduced coin as currency, they were forced to fix an exchange rate of 1,000 cowries to two silver rupees.

The silver rupee, an old Indian coin, was largely used along the Indian Ocean coast. Indian workers brought over to East Africa by the British to build the Mombasa–Nairobi–Kisumu railway were paid in rupees.

The rupee was legal tender in the British territories of East Africa until 1920. But the first coin bearing the words 'East Africa and Uganda Protectorate' was a 10-cent copper nickel dated 1906. In the following years other denominations of one-cent aluminium (1907), half-cent aluminium (1908), and 5-cent copper (1913) were issued.

These coins, which all had a hole in the centre, remained unchanged for about 50 years, until independence. One side of the coins featured a crown above the hole, with the value written below. The name of the reigning British sovereign surrounded the edge. The name of the king followed the chronological list of the British royal family, from Edward VII to Queen Elizabeth II, under whose reign Uganda gained independence.

On the opposite side of the coins, two pairs of elephant tusks and the date were below the hole, with the words 'East Africa' along the border above. Until 1919 the inscription read 'East Africa and Uganda Protectorate'.

Interestingly, among the coinage of the British empire are the 5- and 10-cent coins issued in 1936 with the name of Edward VIII, who was never crowned king.

Also of the same set issued from East Africa were 25-cent, 50-cent, and 1-shilling coins. (This 1-shilling coin, which first appeared in 1921, has remained official currency of Uganda to this date.) Previously minted in low silver, from 1948 they were made of copper nickel. All these coins had a portrait of the British sovereign on one side and a lion with mountains on the reverse. The last coin of this set was struck in 1952 under the rule of George VI. No coins were issued featuring the portrait of Queen Elizabeth.

One East African coin of particular interest to collectors is the low-silver florin, minted only in 1920 with the portrait of King George V.

All the coins of East Africa were struck in the United Kingdom, except the coins issued from 1941 to 1946, which were struck partly in the mint of Bombay, India, and partly in Pretoria, South Africa.

Independent Uganda, through the Bank of Uganda, issued a complete set of coins and paper money in 1966. The set of coins, issued for 10 years, included the 5-cent bronze, 10-cent bronze, 20-cent bronze, 50-cent copper nickel, 1-shilling copper nickel, 2-shilling copper nickel, and 5-shilling copper nickel.

The 5-shilling coin was withdrawn from circulation and almost the entire mintage was remitted.

Although the central hole was eliminated and 'Bank of Uganda' was written on both sides, the 5-, 10-, and 20-cent coins were of the same design as the old East African coins.

More interesting are the 50-cent, 1-shilling, and 2-shilling pieces, which feature the Uganda coat of arms on one side and a crowned crane and mountains on the other.

From 1976 (apart from a short period in 1987), Uganda has become a land of paper money only. True, the Bank of Uganda has issued several coins during this time, but they are purely commemorative issues and do not serve as legal tender in the country, even though the value and 'Bank of Uganda' are written on the coins. These issues, struck in proof condition, are intended for collectors abroad.

Examples of these special coins are the set of 6 silver pieces issued to commemorate the visit of Pope Paul VI to Uganda in 1969, the large gold coin (featuring the portrait of Idi Amin) issued to mark the Organization of African Unity summit in Uganda, and the more recent issuance of two coins to commemorate the visit of Pope John Paul II in 1993 and the World Cup in 1994.

Paper money

In 1905 the government of the East Africa Protectorate at Mombasa introduced the first paper money in the Ugandan territory. These notes, in rupee values, were used until 1919. The florin, with a value of 10 florins to one pound, was legal tender for only one year, 1920. The shilling as a currency, with a value of 20 shillings to the pound, appeared in 1921 under the reign of George V. Denominations of 5-, 10-, 20-, 100-, 1,000-, and 10,000-shilling notes were printed. From 1958 to 1960, parity with the pound was abandoned in the new issue of paper money, which featured Queen Elizabeth's portrait.

All of these banknotes were inscribed in English, Arabic, and Gujarati. Arabic can be found even on the 1964 banknotes issued by the East African Currency Board, but it is supplemented with Swahili. The first paper money issued by the Bank of Uganda was in 1966 in denominations of 5, 10, 20, and 100 shillings.

The 20-shilling note remains to date the most attractive banknote, featuring beautiful illustrations of lion, impala, zebra, and elephant. In 1977 Idi Amin marked his regime with a set of five banknotes featuring himself in a general's uniform. Successive paper money showed the buildings of the Bank of Uganda, a map of Uganda and, later, some notes with the portrait of Milton Obote.

The current set of banknotes has denominations of 5, 10, and 20 shillings (which are no more in circulation), as well as 50, 100, 200, 500, 1,000, 5,000, and 10,000 shillings.

Where to find them

For the more recent stamps, visit the Stamp Bureau on the ground floor of the General Post Office on Kampala road.

Some ancient coins and banknotes can be found in the reception area of the Kasubi Tombs, just outside the city centre.

Only one shop has a wide selection of old stamps, coins, paper money and related curios: Roberto Andreetta Antiques, located at Hotel Equatoria in Kampala.

The Kingdoms of Uganda

Not much is known about the origins of Uganda's five monarchies, mainly because their early history was not written down. Almost the whole vast region between the great lakes of Victoria, Albert, and Tanganyika is occupied by centralized native states headed by monarchies. They are all hereditary monarchies, sometimes with extreme distinctions of class and status.

All the peoples of Buganda, Bunyoro, Ankole, Toro, and Busoga speak related Bantu languages, and it has become usual in ethnographic literature to refer to them collectively as the Interlacustrine Bantu. These monarchies have had a history of contact with Western culture for over 100 years, as well as their own traditional dynastic history that stretches back through the centuries.

They also share the concept of super-ordination and subordination: the notion that some people are always above others — the *abalangira* (royals) — and some are always below — the *bakopi* (peasants). The status destinations are more strongly marked in some kingdoms than in others, but in general they are not rigid, caste-like discriminations. It has always been theoretically possible for able bakopis to rise to positions of high authority in the state.

For the majority of these kingdoms, human history begins with a first family whose head is called *Kintu*, 'the created thing'. A legend shared by them all provides a 'mythical charter' for the social and political order. Nothing is known about the origins of Kintu. The legend maintains that the mythical man, who came from heaven, represents creation itself. Everything concerning the tribes was attributed to Kintu: it is said he must have been the first king of the vast area incorporating all the present five kingdoms and beyond, before they became independent kingdoms.

The Buganda monarchy is one of the best documented of any African monarchy. It has remained almost the only kingdom where extensive historical, political, sociological, and anthropological studies have been carried out. Two important means in which the royal genealogy was kept were the preservation of artefacts inside the royal tombs and the custom of removing and preserving the lower jaw bone of all important people, which goes back to the earliest remembered history of Buganda.

In the case of the royal family, the preservation of such objects was entrusted to an official belonging to a particular clan. For nearly four centuries, the royal tombs did not acquire as great a mystique as the jawbone shrines. These unusual shrines and tombs have been described as Buganda's historical charters, and their locations were known by the families and clans immediately concerned.

Uganda's monarchies evolved out of the clan system. With the gradual unification of the once autonomous clans, it is not unreasonable to suppose that one of the merged heads of clans became the king.

In Buganda, the notables (*bataka*) had a right to present girls to the king, thereby giving every clan the opportunity to provide a successor to one throne.

Such a system ensured their equality and prevented the rise of a ruling clan. Royal children belonged to their mothers' clans, contrary to the otherwise patrilineal clan system of the Baganda. The king was given the title of *sabataka* — chief of the bataka.

Succession to the throne was also modelled on a succession system prevalent in the clans and families. This was generally a brother-to-brother succession, which preserved the unity of the clan or lineage. Primogeniture would have led to

Opposite: Official portrait of Kabaka Ronald Mutebi II, current king of Buganda.

Above: Proud ceremonial guards of the kabaka of Buganda.

individualism at the clan and family levels, and to a hereditary ruling clan at the monarchical level.

No man was considered king unless he had taken part in the accession ceremonies. Before that he was a mere prince. But once he had gone through these ceremonies, he acquired regal qualities and underwent a metamorphosis.

No longer was he an ordinary man; he held powers superior to those of other mortals. Kings showed that they were different by wearing special robes and crowns, and they created among their subjects a sense of awe and reverence. Court etiquette and ceremonies offered another medium for royal display.

Once royal power had been attained and expressed by ceremony and title, no longer could the king be simply a war leader. Nowhere were his powers more forcefully exhibited than in his responsibility for justice and administration of it. Royal officers proclaimed the king's peace wherever they went, using such greetings as *Buganda mirembe, obusiro buladde* — meaning the king meant well.

Winds of change

When Uganda gained its independence in 1962, things were bound to change for the traditional kingdoms — and change they did. In 1966, Ugandan Prime Minister Milton Obote ordered his troops to invade the palace of the kabaka of Buganda, Sir Edward Mutesa II, at Mengo Hill, near Kampala.

A power struggle had been simmering for some time between the kabaka, who had been appointed as ceremonial president of Uganda, and the country's first premier. At independence in October 1962, the various tribes who had been bundled together to form modern Uganda had managed to hammer out a federal constitution that bestowed varied powers to different tribal groups and, for the first time in law, recognized the existence of the five kingdoms of Buganda, Bunyoro, Ankole, Toro, and Busoga.

At the pre-independence negotiations held at Lancaster House in London, the Buganda kingdom — comprising the most self-assertive and biggest tribe in

Above: Prince Mugenyi (left) and Princess Elizabeth Bagaya of Toro attend an official ceremony presided over by the kabaka of Buganda.

the country — were given the best deal. Under the federal constitution, the kabaka was the head of the Buganda kingdom government with a parliament of its own, cabinet ministers, a police force, and powers to tax and spend the kingdom's financial resources.

This gave autonomous status to the centrally located kingdom. It was further stated that in Buganda kingdom the kabaka was above everyone else — including the president of Uganda. Other kingdoms and districts comprising distinctive tribal groups did not enjoy the same privilege. As a result, tribal jealousy and rivalry prevailed.

Obote, as the head of the central government of Uganda, had his hands tied. There was no way his fledgling govern-ment could forge unity and national consciousness by way of the constitution, which gave such powers to tribal leaders at the expense of the national leaders.

The young premier, taking advantage of accusations that the kabaka, together with five cabinet ministers, was plotting to overthrow his government, ordered government troops to invade the kabaka's palace.

Sir Edward Mutesa fled to the United Kingdom and Obote declared himself executive president of Uganda with sweeping powers, abrogated the five kingdoms and reduced them to simple administrative districts, ordered the military to occupy the palaces and other kingdom properties, and declared a state of emergency over Buganda, which restricted its people from carrying out certain political activities.

Although the ancient tribal monarchies had, before the British colonialists and Christians arrived in Uganda, been autocratic, brutal, and ruled by an iron hand, many tribes had come to identify with them as symbols of tribal unity and cultural identity and pride. Therefore, when Obote abolished them in the name of forging unity and national consciousness among Ugandans, many did not like it.

Above: Women in traditional dress await the arrival of their kabaka.

When Idi Amin took over Obote's government in a military coup in 1971, many Baganda royalists and supporters of other abolished kingdoms welcomed his regime, hoping that it would revive the monarchies. The most Amin's government did was to return the remains of the late kabaka of Buganda, who had died of alcoholic poisoning while in exile in London, and accord him a national burial. After that, Amin turned a deaf ear to the pleas by the royalists to revive the kingdoms.

Five successive governments, including Obote's second return to power, did not undo what Obote's regime had done.

When Yoweri Museveni waged a guerilla war against Obote's second regime, he marshalled all aggrieved parties — including the monarchists, who believed the kingdoms would be revived automatically when they got into power. They were not pleased when, as president, Museveni told them that the question whether former kingdoms should be resurrected or not would be dealt with by the Constituent Assembly, which would enact the country's future constitution.

The monarchists, however, did not give up. Although there were advocates for the institution in other former kingdoms, none were as vocal and persistent as those from Buganda.

Museveni and his military defence council eventually relented and, in 1993, announced that former kingdoms that wished to revive their institutions could do so. A law was swiftly passed in the interim legislature to annul Obote's enactment that abrogated the kingdoms. Obote's socialistic law — which said that all Ugandans were equal before the law and that no one could be in a position of leadership on account of blood, tribe, race, or religion except on election through the casting of a popular vote — was removed from the statute books.

However, although the monarchies were revived, there was no return to the independence federal constitution that gave them political and cultural powers. The new law said they were cultural and development leaders who were not expected to participate in partisan politics.

Above: Enthusiastic kabaka supporter does not hide her loyalty.

Thus, 27 years after their abrogation, most Ugandan monarchies — with the exception of Ankole, where there is still some dispute — were restored, amid much celebration.

In Uganda's largest kingdom, Buganda, there was no dispute as to who would take over as king after the monarchy's revival.

The young Prince Ronald Mutebi, who lived with his father in exile in the United Kingdom, was raised as a future king of the Buganda kingdom and, on the death of his father, was declared the heir to the throne. The young king-in-waiting played a part in encouraging his people to back Museveni's guerilla movement during the five-year bush war in the 1980s.

There was, therefore, much jubilation, dancing, and drumming in the Buganda kingdom when Prince Mutebi was officially crowned the 36th kabaka of Buganda in 1993 at the official coronation grounds of Naggalabi, a few kilometres south-west of Kampala. A hand-picked parliament (lukiiko), comprising mainly elderly kanzu-clad heads of the kingdom's 52 clans and a few educated retired civil servants, as well as self-made wealthy gentlemen, has been instituted. It is vocal and influential, and often it feels that it has more powers than the popularly elected central government.

The entire issue of the powers — and the financial upkeep — of the kingdoms (particularly the Buganda kingdom) is a political hotbed. To what extent they will maintain their independence from the central government remains to be seen, but it is certain that the kingdoms of Uganda — an integral part of the country's cultural roots — will remain entities to be reckoned with for some time to come.

Ankole Cattle

Sometime during their stay in Uganda, visitors travelling through the south-west of the country are sure to come across the unique, long-horned Ankole cattle. These hardy, indigenous animals have long been closely associated with the tall, slender, brown-skinned Bahima people of the Ankole kingdom.

There is little information about the origin of the Bantu-speaking Ankole, although they are linked with the Hutu and Tutsi of Rwanda and Burundi and share common physical features, linguisitic types, and interests.

The Bahima are nomadic, walking their cattle long distances every day in search of green pastures and water. How they managed to dominate their longtime adversaries, the settled Bairu agriculturalists, while on their long sojourns is a mystery.

The relationship between the Bahima and the Bairu in Ankole has frequently been misunderstood, exaggerated, and politicized.

Both peoples have similar physical features and speak the same language, but they are devoted to different occupations: the Bahima rear cattle and the Bairu till the land and produce food. Some scholars claim that the two ethnic groups were involved in a caste-like system such as that which exists in India. Others, however, say economic relations between the Bahima and the Bairu were based on the mutual exchange of goods, and their occupations were made mutually exclusive by the environmental conditions rather than by ethnic superiority or inferiority.

The Bahima relationship with their special cattle almost borders on religious. There is a deep friendship, devotion, and comradeship between the two; the cattle are the Muhima man's friends and he treats them as such.

They know his voice and he knows theirs. He gives a different name to each head of cattle; when called by its master each will answer accordingly.

The life of the cattle is the life of a Muhima: what they like, he likes. He will undergo any hardship to ensure their safety, and if one dies, he will mourn its death as he would a friend's.

It was not until modern times that the Muhima looked after his cattle for economic reasons. Rarely could a Muhima trade his cattle for anything. The Bahima, therefore, tended to have large herds of cattle simply because they enjoyed having them around. The larger the herd, the more prestige and honour Muhima received from his fellow Bahima.

Today's Muhima has been forced to change with the times. He is now restricted as to the amount of land he can own and restricted as to the movement of cattle from one area to another for fear of disease.

The Bahima stay in large numbers in a makeshift kraal safe from marauding lions or enemy raids. By custom, women are not allowed to participate in several activities concerning cattle rearing, such as milking, watering, or bleeding them. Although tradition is changing, in the past Bahima families ate virtually no solid foods; they depended solely on the milk and blood of their cattle for sustenance — although cattle are occasionally slaughtered for ceremonial or other reasons.

It is interesting to note that the cattle-rearing Bahima men were usually monogamous. More than one wife was a liability to a nomadic pastoralist, and therefore — more for convenience than for any other reason — monogamy become a custom.

When a Muhima boy had identified the girl he wanted to marry, he had to pay a bride-price to his prospective in-laws. The amount was not specified, but the father-in-law could ask for enough cattle to 'cover his eyesight'. This could mean as many as 10 to 20 head of cattle, if not more, depending on the suitor's ability

Above: Uganda's unique, long-horned Ankole cattle produce superior beef.

to pay and the affection he had for the bride-to-be. In the past, young suitors and their friends often engaged in cattle rustling to acquire a fitting bride-wealth for their future wives.

Interestingly, beef from Ankole cattle has been found to contain less cholesterol and less fat content than any other beef, according to recent studies carried out in the United States in 1993. In another related US study carried out in 1989, Ankole steers were found to be able to survive severe weather. They were subjected to two blizzards and −34°C (−30°F) wind chill factors in the winter, and temperatures to above 32°C (90°F) with high, dry winds in summer. There were no deaths among the 32 Ankole steers involved in the study. Despite the harsh conditions, the steers, which had an average weight of 257 kilos (565 lbs), had doubled their weight in a period of six months.

In view of these findings, it may be that in the future, Uganda's unique Ankole cattle will be reared worldwide for human consumption.

Above: Bahima boy looks after his family's cattle. Overleaf: Bagging sugar, one of the country's most important products, at Lugazi Sugar Factory in Jinja.

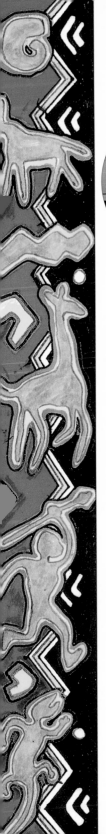

IN THE GARDEN OF AFRICA STAY IN THE GARDENS OF KAMPALA

The luxurious rooms and suites of the Sheraton Kampala Hotel are surrounded by nine acres of lushly verdant greenery yet within easy reach of the city centre.

The gardens contain a lavish outdoor pool, two floodlit tennis courts (the hotel also has two squash courts and Health Club with gym, sauna and steam bath), whilst an 18-hole golf course is just minutes walk away.

With two excellent restaurants, our own English pub and an open-air poolside barbecue, you'll find staying at the Sheraton Kampala is one long garden-party.

Sheraton Kampala
HOTEL

Sheraton

TERNAN AVENUE, PO BOX 7041 KAMPALA.
TELEPHONE: (256) (41) 244590/6
FACSIMILE: (256) (41) 256696

PART FIVE: BUSINESS UGANDA

The Economy

Uganda's economy is dominated by agriculture and remains highly dependent on this sector for its growth. In addition to meeting the food requirements of a growing national population, thousands of refugees who have run away from civil wars and the rising demand for food from neighbouring countries, agriculture has to supply raw materials for rehabilitated and new agro-processing industries. Through exports, agriculture also generates foreign exchange to help meet Uganda's import requirements, as well as service external loans.

The country's chief exports are coffee, cotton, tobacco, cocoa, fish, horticultural and floricultural products, and handicrafts. Imports include petroleum products, textiles and garments, power machinery and switchgear, telecommunication equipment, construction and industrial machinery, motor vehicles and spare parts, office equipment and furnishings, agricultural and textile machinery and spare parts.

Uganda's chief trading partners are Kenya, the UK, Germany, the USA, Japan, Italy, India, Thailand, South Africa, and the Netherlands.

Although Uganda's gross domestic product (GDP) has been dependent on agriculture for many years — with coffee exports responsible for over 70 per cent of the foreign exchange earnings — a concerted effort is being made towards a mixed economy. While the dominance of coffee has declined somewhat over the years (it accounted for over 95 per cent of the country's foreign exchange earnings seven years ago), the recent boom in the world's coffee markets is expected to increase Uganda's coffee export earnings significantly. Coffee, therefore, remains a huge source of foreign exchange that the country can use for development.

In June 1994 the government imposed a coffee stabilization tax on coffee export earnings to protect the exchange rate from destabilization through an upsurge in foreign exchange. It is estimated that this tax alone yielded between US$ 80 and 90 million, which was earmarked by the government for development projects.

The coffee boom, along with the accelerated growth in the economy, has strengthened the country's currency, the shilling, and it is now used as a means of exchange in trade with neighbouring countries. However, as exporters saw their earnings cut back because of the rapidly strengthening currency, the Bank of Uganda had to intervene from time to time to ensure the strength of the shilling did not get out of hand.

Economic recovery

Uganda has now begun to enjoy the results of implementing strong and austere structural adjustment measures in the 1987–88 fiscal year. One of the measures were aimed at the restoration of fiscal and monetary discipline, the improvement of the incentive structure and investment climate for exports and other productive activity, the rehabilitation of the country's social, economic, and institutional infrastructure and the promotion of increased savings and investment, especially within the private sector.

Over the past seven years the programme has emphasized progressive movement towards, and eventual adoption of, a market-determined rate of foreign exchange transactions to strengthen the balance of payments and render the allocation of resources more efficient. On 1 November 1993, the auction system for allocating donor import support that had prevailed since January 1992 was abolished and an interbank market in foreign exchange was introduced, together with the elimination of all restrictions on current international transactions.

In addition, private foreign exchange (forex) bureaux, which deal freely in foreign exchange, were allowed to start operating. To institutionalize the liberalization of the foreign exchange regime, on 5 April 1994, Uganda accepted the obligations the International Monetary Fund's Articles of Agreement to join a select group of African countries that are committed to place no restrictions on current international transactions without prior IMF approval.

Major steps have also been taken to liberalize the external trade system. During the last quarter of 1991, a broadly based import scheme was introduced with only limited restrictions. The import licensing system was replaced by a six-month removable import certificate, which provides the holder permission to import goods not on the restricted list. A similar export certificate system was also introduced.

At regional level, Uganda is also participating in a cross-border initiative, co-sponsored by the World Bank, the African Development Bank (ADB), and the European Union, which aims at facilitating cross-border trade, investments, and payments within eastern and southern Africa and the Indian Ocean region. On 30 November 1993, Uganda, Tanzania, and Kenya signed an agreement setting up a permanent Tripartite Commission to identify areas of cooperation between the three countries. As a member of the Preferential Trade Agreement (PTA) and the Common Market for Eastern and Southern Africa (COMESA), Uganda also accords tariff concessions to goods originating from the 21 other member countries.

At the Paris Donors' Meeting in June 1994, the World Bank, the IMF, and several bilateral donor countries agreed to fund a three-year economic development programme for Uganda totalling US$ 1,498 million. In addition, further financing of some US$ 169 million has been approved by the IMF. A financing gap of about US$ 323 million is projected over the three-year period, which ends with the 1996–97 fiscal year. It is expected that this gap will be filled by a restructuring of US$ 223 million of external arrears and by debt relief from Paris Club creditors and non-Paris Club bilateral and commercial creditors.

Uganda's balance of payments deficit has declined sharply during the last decade, falling from US$ 121.2 million in 1991–92 to US$ 8.2 million in 1992–93, turning into a surplus of US$ 70 million in 1993–94. The country's stock of external debt reached US$ 2.9 million (or 72.6 per cent of the GDP) by the end of June 1994. As part of an overall strategy to deal with its debt-service difficulties, in 1993 and early 1994 the Uganda government bought back its commercial debt at a substantial discount, with the help of the World Bank and other donors. On 20 February 1995 Paris Club donors cancelled US$ 75 million of Uganda's bilateral debt, making Uganda the very first country in the world to benefit from the Naples terms agreed by the group to assist the reduction of the debt burden of least-developed countries. Many economic observers feel this reduction will allow the Uganda government to direct more of its resources to other areas of expenditure, such as social welfare programmes.

In addition to the IMF and the World Bank, Uganda belongs to a number of other international organizations that raise development finance, including the regional East African Development Bank (EADB), PTA/COMESA, the PTA Bank, and the ADB. The country is also a signatory to the Lome II convention grouping the European Union countries with African, Caribbean, and Pacific countries.

Financial and economic pundits feel that the return of political and economic stability has enabled Uganda's war-ravaged economy to recover and progress. The stability has also played an important role in attracting foreign investors to the East African country and the return of thousands of Asian entrepreneurs and other investors who were expelled by the Amin regime in 1972. Major enticements have been the sharply falling money supply growth rates and equally falling inflation, which in 1996 had been reduced to 5.4 per cent a year from over 200 per cent five years ago.

Under a restructuring programme, the civil service has been scaled down considerably and public sector spending reduced. The army also has been pared down, and non-profit-making parastatals are being sold to the highest bidders under a Public Enterprises Reform and Divestiture (PERD) programme.

The government believes in concentrating on doing the things it can do better than anybody else and leaving things it cannot do to the private sector, which can do them more efficiently. The government is also implementing a decentralization programme under which local authorities are being given powers to plan and be responsible for their own development. In addition, the government is actively involved in making sure the all-important infrastructure — electricity, roads, water, and other services — is put in place in both urban and rural areas.

Opportunities

Agriculture
Agriculture is the mainstay of the Ugandan economy. Eighty-nine per cent of the country's 17 million people live in rural areas. Agriculture accounts for about 51 per cent of the GDP and over 90 per cent of exports, and employs 80 per cent of the employed population. Agricultural output comes almost exclusively from some 2.5 million smallholders, 80 per cent of whom have less than 2 hectares (5 acres) each. Only tea and sugar are grown on large estates, which total 40,000 hectares (98,800 acres). The predominance of smallholder farming implies that the benefits from sectoral growth will be fairly distributed.

With its temperate climate, relatively high altitude, and adequate rainfall, Uganda's agricultural potential is good. A large proportion of the country's 241,000 square kilometres (93,000 square miles) could be cultivated, but although over 75 per cent of the country — 18 million hectares (44 million acres) — is classified as arable, only 4 to 5 million hectares (10 to 12 million acres) are under cultivation.

Food crop production carries the agricultural sector in Uganda, accounting for 71 per cent of the agricultural GDP, with livestock products totalling, on average, another 17 per cent. Export crop production is only five per cent of agricultural GDP, while the fisheries subsector accounts for four per cent, and forestry three per cent. Only one-third of food crop production is marketed, compared with two-thirds of the country's livestock production.

The most common food crop is bananas, steamed as the staple food, matoke. Maize is also widely grown, much of it being ground into meal and exported. Drought-resistant sorghum, millet, and cassava have also been grown successfully in drier parts of the country. Coffee is the largest foreign exchange earner in the economy, followed in the agricultural sector by cotton, tea, cocoa, and tobacco — with horticulture and floriculture industries rapidly catching up.

The regional market for food, especially maize and beans, can be expected to increase. Uganda's landlocked status and reliable rainfall provide it with the opportunity to supply food cheaply to several of its neighbours, including Kenya, Tanzania, Rwanda, and Burundi — one of which, in any given year, can be expected to experience drought. However, growth in this market segment depends on the annual import requirements of a client country in a poor agricultural year and may not go beyond 300,000 to 400,000 metric tonnes of food a year.

The coffee industry
During almost two decades of civil wars and political strife, coffee remained Uganda's only export crop, accounting for nearly 95 per cent of the country's foreign exchange earnings. Smallholder peasant farmers abandoned all other traditional cash crops — such as cotton, cocoa, tea, and tobacco — and turned to more rapid-cash crops like maize and beans. When the farmers delivered their crops to the cash-strapped, inefficient and corrupt parastatals, however, they were given promissory notes instead of money — notes that the farmers later discovered weren't worth the paper they were printed on.

Coffee is grown mainly in a 110-kilometre (70-mile) radius around the Lake Victoria Basin. Robusta accounts for 94 per cent of the output, with arabica making up the balance. Robusta is traditionally dry processed. The small arabica output is classified as 'secondary African wild', because of its poor quality and limited availability. The area under production appears to have been reduced, mainly by stumping the coffee trees and intercropping with more lucrative banana and annual food crops. Coffee is estimated to be under cultivation on 272,000 hectares (672,000 acres). Yields have been low and quality has declined since 1980, the output having reached a peak of 213,000 tonnes in 1972 before falling sharply in the late 1970s and early 1980s, to this day still not regaining its former high levels.

Coffee has played such a leading role in Uganda's economic development that its industry has been under tight government control since the colonial era. The passage of the Coffee Marketing Act in 1989 established the Coffee Marketing Board, which had monopoly control over coffee exports. The decline in export value and volume have

led the government to liberalize the industry and to stop fixing prices. The industry is now determined by the market forces of supply and demand.

To restore the proper incentives, in July 1991 the government adopted a new system for pricing and taxing coffee exports that allows the producer price, as well as processor and exporter margins, to be determined by market forces within a competitive environment. A year later, the tax on coffee exports was abolished altogether. The government subsequently removed the Coffee Marketing Board's monopoly on the purchase and marketing of coffee and converted the board into a commercial operation in competition with private exporters. In April 1994, greater flexibility was allowed below the floor price, and the limitations on method of sale (tender only) and means of transport of coffee were removed. These changes have provided the industry with enhanced incentives to increase production and exports, to replace old trees and plant new ones, and to improve the quality of coffee. In addition, international prices improved substantially in 1995 and 1996, further reinforcing incentives for investment by coffee growers.

Hulling and primary processing of coffee in Uganda are done by cooperative unions and private sector processors prior to the delivery to the Coffee Marketing Board or directly to markets abroad. The share of the cooperative unions in this activity has been declining steadily, resulting in an over-investment in hulling capacity. Figures indicate that there are now more than 300 hullery factories and nearly 600 huller machines. On the assumption that annual capacity per huller working one shift a day for 200 days is 800 tonnes of rough hulled coffee, the country has a primary processing capacity of about 450,000 tonnes; therefore hullers are working at only about 35 per cent capacity.

Cotton
Cotton — which used to be of equal importance to coffee in Uganda's economic development during the 1960s and early 1970s, each contributing 40 per cent to the country's foreign earnings — grows well in the northern and eastern regions.

It is a rain-fed annual crop, grown using low input methods. There is little use of fertilizers and pesticides. Cotton is grown at altitudes of less than 1,500 metres (5,000 feet) and requires rain of over 800 millimetres (30 inches) a year. It competes mainly with annual food crops.

The cotton industry in Uganda collapsed when international prices were high. Exports dropped from 65,000 tonnes in 1973 to 10,000 tonnes in 1977. This dramatic decline was caused in part by the dislocation of the ginning and export industries, following the expulsion of the Asians in late 1972, who owned and ran many of the ginneries, and in part to the decline in real prices paid for seed cotton. In addition, financial and managerial difficulties in the ginneries — all of which are owned by cooperatives — have seriously impaired production and marketing. Lint output is currently only a fraction of what it once was. Almost all the union ginneries are heavily in debt and therefore incapable of operating profitably.

The government has taken several actions to resuscitate the industry. After having earlier removed the Lint Marketing Board's monopoly in the export of lint by issuing licences to some cooperatives, a Cotton Development Statute was enacted in January 1994, which abolished the union's monopoly over cotton ginning and the LMB's monopoly over cotton exports, eliminated licensing and other regulatory barriers, and established a new organization, the Cotton Development Organization (CDO) to regulate and organize cotton seed production. The CDO is to be an industry-based entity as soon as the industry is strong enough to carry out the relevant functions. Private operators are now free to purchase, lease, or construct new ginneries, to purchase and gin cotton, and to export lint in competition with the cooperatives and the LMB.

To further restructure the industry, the cooperatives are being given incentives in the form of debt relief to either sell off or lease their ginneries to private operators. In those cases where the union is able to present a business plan sufficiently credible to attract commercial credit, it will also benefit from debt relief in accordance with that plan. When the cooperatives are not able to present such a plan or do not lease or sell their ginnery, the creditor bank will foreclose on the ginnery for the unpaid debts. Under this restructuring plan, the government's target was to have ginning capacity of 100,000 bales — out of a total industry capacity of about 400,000 bales — in private hands by mid-1995. The industry is also being encouraged to integrate vertically, and crop financing is being regularized and placed on a commercial basis, as in the case of coffee.

A key concern now is how to rejuvenate the cotton industry, with a view to winning back the country's position in this market.

Domestic demand for lint comes from five textile firms — Nytil, Ugil, ATM, Pamba, and Rayon Textiles — currently operating at four per cent of capacity. Collectively the firms produced some 8,150 square metres (9,780 square yards) of cloth in 1990, down from 11,750 (14,100) the previous year. Domestic purchase of lint in 1990 totalled about 21,300 bales. Demand from local mills could be a useful, albeit limited, market —

but tapping the regional market for clothing would be even more important to Uganda, although quality needs to improve sufficiently to compete successfully with Kenyan products.

Tea

Tea is grown on good soils at altitudes of over 1,200 metres (4,000 feet) and requires rainfall of more than 1,200 millimetres (50 inches) a year. These conditions can be found in the western districts of Bushenyi, Rukungiri, Kabarole, Hoima, and Masindi, as well as on the northern shores of Lake Victoria. Uganda has the potential to be a low-cost, competitive producer of tea. Since 1987, some rehabilitation of tea fields and factories has taken place, with about half the total planted area back in production. Out of a planted area of 22,000 hectares (54,000 acres), 9,253 hectares (22,800 acres) are in production, and a total of 6,627 metric tonnes (6,500 tons) of made tea were manufactured in 1990. Although there were 24 operating factories, they had a low capacity utilization of 19 per cent.

Processed tea represented between five and six per cent of Uganda's exports in the early 1970s, third in importance behind coffee and cotton. In the peak year of 1972 some 23,000 tonnes of black tea were produced and 21,000 tonnes exported, representing 6.7 per cent of total exports.

Non-traditional agricultural exports

Uganda exports a number of non-traditional crops and commodities, including simsim (sesame seed), hides and skins, maize, beans, and some horticultural crops. In 1990–91 non-traditional agricultural exports totalled a record of US$ 18.8 million, 11 per cent of total exports. Standard measures of comparative advantage, such as the domestic resource cost ratio, show Uganda to be a competitive producer of these crops. Import substitution, as valid as export expansion and diversification in its impact on balance of trade and the national economy, has also been actively pursued through the increased production of sugar and dairy products.

Simsim was the largest single export item after coffee in 1990 and 1991 (US$ 10.7 million), and simsim, maize, and beans accounted for almost half of exports other than coffee, tea, cotton, and tobacco. Exports of pineapple and Asian vegetables to Europe continue — but at very low profit margins, because of air freight costs and relatively low prices. There are other high-value crops with export potential already grown in Uganda, which will require some more product and process development before they can be properly exploited. These include essential oils — especially lemon grass, citronella, and palmarosa — processed cashew nuts, which would require the privatization and rehabilitation of the plant at Soroti; 'apple banana', and fresh ginger (production of the Hawaiian variety, with exports only in November and early December). Other products are spices — especially vanilla, cardamom, dried ginger, and dried chillies — fish, and some textiles. Other essential oil crops that should be seriously considered for export development that could have outstanding export value include patchouli, geranium, chamomile, tuberose and pyrethrum. Vegetable oils are a good example, perhaps, for assessment in an import substitution strategy.

Food production

Food production is the most widespread economic activity in Uganda. It accounts for 74 per cent of the agricultural GDP, which is 60 per cent of the national output. The foods produced in Uganda are high in starch, with bananas accounting for 50 per cent of total tonnage and root crops another 35 per cent. Cereals represent 10 per cent of food production and pulses the remaining 5 per cent. The main food crop, bananas, accounts for one-third of the 3.9 million hectares (9.6 million acres) cultivated for food. Seven other crops each have between seven and 10 per cent of the cultivated land: beans, cassava, groundnuts, maize, millet, sorghum, and sweet potatoes. The market for food is domestic and regional, with the domestic market expected to grow rapidly in the near future.

Sugar

Prior to 1972, sugar processing was the largest industrial venture in Uganda, the country producing enough sugar to satisfy the local market and having surplus for export. However, the 1972 expulsion of the Asian entrepreneurs — including the sugar magnate families, the Mehtas and the Madhvanis — brought that down. Nevertheless, the same families responded positively to the government's call to return and repossess their properties, and they are now growing new sugar cane, rehabilitating their factories and in a few years are expected to produce enough sugar to satisfy local demand and begin exporting.

Climatic conditions for cane cultivation on the northern shores of Lake Victoria are good. Production peaked in 1970 at 154,100 tonnes of processed sugar. By 1985, production had fallen to 1,000 tonnes. Imports increased to 46,000 tonnes in 1986, but per capita consumption has declined dramatically. From levels of around 14 kilograms (31 lbs) a person in the early 1970s (which is comparable to consumption levels in surrounding countries), sugar consumption dropped to below 5 kilograms (11 lbs) a person in the 1980s. The household expenditure survey of 1989–90 shows the average household consumption to be about 3.5 to 4 kilograms (7 to 9 lbs) a person each year. The cost of sugar imports, about US$ 15 million in 1986, declined to US$ 2.4 million in 1988, and US$ 0.8 million in 1990.

There are three sugar factories: Kakira and Lugazi near Jinja, and Kinyala near Masindi. Production in Kakira and Lugazi ran at around full capacity of 140,000 tonnes between 1968 and 1970. Production declined to 69,000 tonnes in 1973 after the expulsion of the Asian owners and continued to drop to 2,400 tonnes in 1980. The slow recovery to about 3,000 tonnes in 1984 and 1985 was frozen in 1986 and 1987 because of civil wars. Since 1988, recovery has been dramatic, assisted by rehabilitation finance from various donors. Output of processed sugar in 1990 and 1991 was about 30,000 tonnes.

Cane is taken mainly from the nucleus estates — around 8,000 hectares (20,000 acres) in Kakira and 10,000 hectares (25,000 acres) in Lugazi — and from outgrowers — 2,600 hectares (6,400 acres) in Kakira. The state-owned Kinyala estate has never performed close to its 35,000-tonne capacity. Completed in the mid-1970s, Kinyala's production peaked at 3,500 tonnes in 1978 before operations were stopped a few years later. The rehabilitation of the Kinyala plant is now under way with funding from international donors. The rehabilitation of Lugazi and Kakira is nearing completion as well. The three factories are expected to restore sugar production capacity to about 170,000 tonnes by 1997.

Uganda's projected demand for sugar over the next decade will eventually outstrip the production capacity of the existing factories. The income elasticity of the demand for sugar is high, especially at the low levels of per capita consumption occurring in Uganda. Projections using consumption levels of the early 1970s implied total demand of about 250,000 tonnes in the mid-1990s, two-thirds greater than the maximum expected output.

Given the high cost of importing sugar into Uganda, which includes transportation from the seaport of Mombasa, an import-substitution strategy makes economic sense.

Animal husbandry

Livestock products contributed 16 per cent to the agricultural GDP in 1990, down from 20 per cent in 1980. Output from this sector has not grown significantly in real terms. Official figures indicate that in 1987 the national cattle herd declined by 25 per cent, and the sheep and goat herd by 36 per cent, as a result of insecurity and cattle rustling in the north-east. As of 1996, however, the strong resurgence of the dairy industry in the south-west caused the livestock subsector of the GDP to grow at 4.9 per cent per year.

The 1990–91 livestock population was estimated to include about 4.3 million pigs and 10 to

12 million fowl, but cattle are the most important type of livestock in both numbers and value.

Both a sign of wealth and a source of livelihood, cattle can be kept throughout Uganda, except in a few places near Lake Victoria where tsetse flies are a hazard. Overgrazing, however, is a serious problem.

The west and south-west of Uganda are the richest in livestock, with about two head of cattle a household, compared with one a household in the rest of the country.

Mixed farming smallholders and pastoralists own over 90 per cent of the national cattle herd. That herd, which once numbered between five and 5.5 million animals, was decimated during the 15 years of civil war and disruption, and was back up to only 4.9 million by 1990. While outright slaughter accounts for some of the decline, the major reason for the reduction in herd size is the resurgence of a series of diseases that had previously been eradicated or controlled.

Commercial dairy farming is based on some 140,000 animals of imported dairy breeds (mainly Friesian) and crosses with indigenous cattle.

Milk production has grown steadily in south-western Uganda, which produces about 90 per cent of marketed processed milk. Milk collected through the formal system has increased from virtually nothing in 1986 to more than 10 million litres (2 million gallons) in 1990, the highest level since 1973 — 50 per cent of processed milk sales. All the milk sold by the state-owned Uganda Dairy Corporation (UDC) in Kampala and other urban areas is locally produced. The number of farmers delivering milk to the UDC increased from less than 400 in 1986 to almost 6,000 in 1991.

The commercial beef ranching sector has suffered heavily from banditry, and only about 50 ranches in the south-west, out of a total of 400 nationwide, remain viably stocked.

Commercial poultry and pig production, almost entirely in small household units, grew steadily from 1950 to 1970. The subsequent decline in those industries has been largely the result of a decline in grain milling and livestock feed.

Natural grass-dominated communal pastures provide almost all feed for indigenous livestock. Exotic and crossbred dairy animals susceptible to tick-borne diseases are usually confined to fenced farms or kept in small enclosures. Some are fed on a cut-and-carry zero-grazing basis.

A study done recently by the Ministry of Agriculture, Animal Industry, and Fisheries indicates that 46 per cent of dairy farmers with exotic or crossbred animals own only one or two cattle; most farmers now practise zero grazing, and most are women. Zebu cattle total some 70 per cent of cattle population, the indigenous Sanga (long-horned Ankole cattle) are 15 per cent, and crosses account for 13 per cent. The remaining two per cent are exotic breeds brought into Uganda since 1960 for the dairy and beef industry.

The prospects for increased demand for meat products, if income per capita continues to grow, are good. The income elasticity for meat is high. With continued problems of disease, Uganda's formal access to overseas export markets will be limited for many years. Demand for livestock will depend on the domestic and regional market. The weakness of domestic demand for livestock products is reflected in very low prices for meat (beef and pork) at present. However, there appears to be substantial demand for goat meat, and the industry should develop on the basis of local demand.

A master plan for the dairy subsector has been prepared by the government with assistance from the Danish aid agency DANIDA. The plan formulates a strategy for development of the dairy subsector, including the domestic market for milk and milk products, regional milk production, efficient artificial insemination, and substitution for imported milk.

Fishing industry

About 42,000 square kilometres (16,000 square miles) of Uganda is water — 18 per cent of the country. Lake Victoria is the largest inland body of water in Africa and the most important source of fish. Lakes Kyoga, Albert, Edward and George — among the most productive of the country's 165 lakes and swamps — are also rich resources, providing fish and irrigation water, while reducing temperature extremes and increasing rainfall. Of the 90 species of freshwater fish found in Uganda, the most important for commercial exploitation are Nile perch and Nile tilapia. Potential sustainable yield from Uganda's waters has not been accurately estimated, although it is thought to be about 300,000 tonnes a year, about 20 per cent above the current catch. The commercial catch has averaged between 170,000 and 220,000 tonnes over the past 13 years. In 1990–91 the catch increased sharply, and an estimated 245,000 tonnes was harvested — worth about US$ 34 million. Lake Victoria, which used to account for 10 per cent of the national fish catch, has been increasing its share rapidly and now provides 50 per cent of the total. This is due to the rise in importance of Nile perch, found principally in lakes Victoria and Kyoga.

The harvesting of fish is regulated by the Fish and Crocodile Act of 1951, revised in 1964. This law sets limitations on minimum fish size and on aspects of fishing technology. Trawling is permitted in Uganda. Regulations are enforced by the Fisheries Department of the Ministry of Agriculture, Animal Industry and Fisheries, which has 500 staff stationed around the country.

Research staff operate the Fish Technology Laboratory in Entebbe and the Uganda Freshwater Fisheries Research Organization in Jinja. Government research, extension, and surveillance have been assisted through funds provided by a number of major donors.

While government monitoring capacity is limited, overfishing in Uganda in general is not yet considered a threat to the overall fish population. The harvest from Lake Victoria, however, is felt to be at its upper limit. The introduction of more intensive fishing techniques could cause catch levels to exceed sustainable limits.

Fishing in Uganda is an attractive business opportunity, and recently a series of private sector and joint venture firms have been established, processing fish for the premium local market and export. Market prospects are good. In 1990 registered exports of fish totalled 1,664 tonnes, worth US$ 1.4 million. Exports of 520 tonnes of frozen or chilled fish were handled by nine companies. Some 818 tonnes of smoked, dried, or salted fish were exported by 23 firms. In 1991 this volume practically tripled, to some 4,700 tonnes worth US$ 5.3 million. The key market for dried, smoked fish is Kenya. Fresh chilled or frozen fish are sent mainly to Gibraltar, Greece, the Netherlands, or the United Kingdom.

Actual export levels are higher than these figures indicate, however. Much of the catch from lakes Albert, Edward, and George is taken into Rwanda, Sudan and Zaire, and much of the trade in fish into Kenya and Tanzania is not monitored. There does not appear to be any limit to the size of the export market. Domestic consumption of fish increased, starting in the early 1970s, and fish is now a significant portion of the national diet. It is estimated that fish consumption is between 8 and 13 kilograms (18 and 29 lbs) a person each year.

Forestry

Forest reserves in Uganda cover some seven per cent of the country, with 700,000 hectares (1.7 million acres) in tropical high forests, 632,000 hectares (1.5 million acres) in savannah forests, and 24,300 hectares (60,000 acres) in plantation forests. The tropical high forests are found in western Uganda, around Lake Victoria, and on Mount Elgon. They include rare plants and animals — some in danger of extinction — and unique ecological systems. Until the early 1970s, the government Forest Department strictly regulated logging, charcoal burning, and revenue collection.

In the mid-1970s, as resources available to the Forest Department declined, the management system of high tropical forests broke down. Indiscriminate logging practices degraded the forest environment and damaged wildlife habitats. Timber resources also have been depleted.

Reserve boundaries have not been respected; both reserves and savannah forest have been subjected to uncontrolled and damaging harvests.

Management of the softwood plantation — first planted in the early 1940s and now totalling 13,400 hectares (33,000 acres) — also deteriorated in the early 1970s, reducing quality and yield. These trees reached maturity after 1971, but the plantations have never been exploited commercially. Their sustainable yield of 90,000 cubic metres (3.2 million cubic feet) of sawn timber a year represents about two-thirds of Uganda's estimated demand for timber in the year 2000. Careful use of the softwood stands could relieve pressure on the ecologically fragile natural hardwood forests.

With the assistance of donors, the government has been working to regain control over the exploitation of the country's forests. The objective of the donor-funded forestry project is to develop forestry management plans that will determine how the country can better manage this resource. The plans would include reducing indiscriminate logging in natural forest areas. The project seeks to improve boundary demarcation and maintenance in high forests and savannah reserves. Areas of natural forest would be reforested and activities of charcoal burners would be controlled. The proportion of natural forest area to be set aside as nature reserves would be increased from five to 20 per cent. A 'protected reserve' category would be applied to another 30 per cent of the natural forest area, under which only limited logging would be permitted.

Environment

Uganda's wildlife, forests, grazing lands, and other natural resources are in danger of being overused, polluted and driven to extinction. Soil erosion is a problem in highly populated, high-rainfall areas, although Ugandan farmers have done a good job in protecting their land under difficult circumstances. Sustainable management practices need to be established in key areas, such as wildlife and forest management, to prevent complete loss. Since there is little commercial incentive to protect these public resources, government intervention and leadership is required.

There has been a clear environmental cost to the years of civil disorder. Natural resource management programmes and policies broke down and have yet to be re-established. Demographic pressures also are having their effect on Uganda's environment. Nowhere is this more apparent than in the loss of tropical high forest, which has declined from 1.2 million hectares (3 million acres) in 1958 to 0.7 million hectares (1.7 million acres) in 1987. Efforts to protect Uganda's forests will have to deal with upwards of 50,000 people who have encroached on forest reserves

— largely since 1970 — and with indiscriminate logging associated with industrial expansion. Pressure on forests also comes from the growing demand for charcoal and building poles, which in turn results from the growth in population, estimated at 3.1 per cent a year.

The establishment of the Ministry of Natural Resources in 1986 indicates that environment issues are of national importance. The United Nations Environment Programme (UNEP) has done a detailed survey of environment problems in Uganda, which was transformed into an operational plan under a donor-supported National Environment Action Plan. The plan was widely debated throughout the country before it was approved by the government in January 1994. It consists of a national environment policy, an institutional framework for environment management, and an environment bill. The adopted policy calls for alignment of sectoral development strategies to address priority environmental concerns to land degradation, deforestation, loss of wetlands, and dwindling fish stocks. Several of these problems are linked to environmental management of the Lake Victoria Basin.

The policy also covers the need to control population growth and enhance security of land tenure. Finally, it advocates environmental education and a system of environmental impact assessment as an essential means of promoting rational resource use. The Environment Bill includes the establishment of a national environment management authority, which would coordinate the implementation of the national environmental action plan and serve as a central environmental policy advisory body.

Industry

Uganda is endowed with rich natural resources that have hardly been tapped. It had developed a sizeable industrial infrastructure during the 1960s, which at one time produced most of Uganda's normal daily requirements. In 1970, for instance, the entire industrial sector was operating at an average capacity utilization of 70 per cent. This steadily dropped over the years; by 1980 it had reached a low of 22 per cent. Uganda's economic ills were triggered by dictator Idi Amin's coup in 1971 and the so-called Economic War in 1972. This was followed by the bizarre exercise in which abandoned industries were allocated to people who had no business acumen and, within a matter of years, there was very little to talk about in the private sector. The state-controlled Uganda Development Corporation, which for years had been spearheading the country's industrial development, was dismantled, and by the time the Amin regime toppled industry was on the brink of complete collapse.

By 1970, manufacturing accounted for 17 per cent of employment in the monetary economy. The sector produced a wide range of consumer and intermediate goods for domestic consumption, with a sizeable surplus for export to Kenya and Tanzania. Agro-industries and food processing, metal products, beverages, tobacco, and textiles were particularly important. During the 1970s industrial production declined through a combination of chronic shortage of foreign exchange for machinery spare parts and all types of production inputs, lack of qualified management resulting in mismanagement of scarce resources, and the proliferation of government entities without the capacity and competence to produce efficiently. Political interference and corruption caused production in many enterprises to come to a halt.

After the removal of Amin's regime in 1979, the expelled Asians and other foreign investors were invited to return to Uganda and repossess their properties and business under an economic recovery programme which the government hopes will bring idle and underutilized assets back to production. More generally, government strategy for the sector has been to reduce the extent of government involvement in industry through divestment and privatization. Emphasis is appropriately given to restoring the capacity of 'core' manufacturing industries such as agro-processing, import-substituting consumer goods, construction materials, and industries with a large impact on government revenue.

Recognizing that the private sector will be the engine of growth for the economy in years to come, Uganda's industrial strategy is designed to promote private sector investment and growth by improving the business climate. In this respect, the government will support local entrepreneurs by strengthening the mechanisms for consulting with the private sector on policy matters and by developing innovative support schemes at the firm level. It also plans to modernize the legislation relating to corporate activities. To guide its strategy, the government has prepared a strategic vision of future manufacturing sector development and how to achieve it, rather than a master plan or blueprint. The plan, prepared in consultation with the business community, identifies specific development strategies, policies and action programmes. Implementation mechanisms that engender wide national involvement, but do not trespass on the commercial interests of individual operators, are now being developed.

The government's forthright and effective resolution of the expropriated properties issue has also contributed strongly to an improved investment climate. Over 2,500 properties have now been returned and the government has embarked on the final phase of the privatization and divestiture programme. This involves a combination of repossession, sale, compensation, and reversion of properties to landlords, all in accordance with the law. By the end of the fiscal year 1994/95 the government began to sell all non-citizen properties that were not claimed or for which compensation had been requested. Every effort is being made to pay valid compensation claims within 90 days of the date of the property's sale.

In 1992 the government also decided to reduce its direct role in the Uganda economy, to promote a greater part for the private sector, and to improve the efficiency and overall performance of those public enterprises that, for short or long term, will remain under government ownership and control. This was done with a view to reducing the financial and administrative burden upon government on account of the large number of public enterprises with problems that included financial losses, corruption, embezzlement, and general poor performance.

Mining

Uganda is endowed with a variety of mineral resources, including gold, diamonds, coal and oil. Uganda was an exporter of copper until 1976 when the mines were closed after the owners were forced to leave the country. Copper exports were third in importance to coffee and cotton as a foreign exchange earner. Since then little commercial mining has taken place in the country.

Little exploration has been carried out in the country to ascertain the quality, quantity, and economic viability of the existing mineral resources. Despite this, inquiries about the country's mineral potential are being made. A French firm, in collaboration with Barclays Metals Limited, recently carried out studies on how to utilize stockpiles of cobalt ore that had been left over during the copper mining operation. A joint venture with Uganda government interests is being floated; a Canadian firm has been granted licences to explore the extent of copper resources in western Uganda; an American company has been granted concessions to invest risk capital in the exploration, mining, and refining of oil products from the shores of Lake Victoria bordering Zaire and an Indian company has signed an agreement to set up a fertilizer industry based on the phosphates in Tororo in eastern Uganda. Other foreign firms been given licences to prospect for gold.

The future of the mining industry in Uganda looks rosy, depending on whether or not the studies show that the country is full of economically viable underground riches.

Transport and communications

Uganda is a landlocked country; therefore a network of transport and communications is critical for the country's survival. Uganda has been dependent on its neighbours, especially Kenya, for the movement of imports and exports, and the related strategic concerns have tended to dominate transport priorities. The availability and quality of transport services deteriorated rapidly during the 1970s as much of the sector's managerial and technical workforce was depleted. Low priority was accorded to the sector in resource allocation, especially for maintenance. In addition, the break-up of the East African Community in the late 1970s had a devastating impact on Uganda's transport system, especially for international trade. Almost overnight, Uganda lost virtually all its railway rolling stock and aircraft, and her part-ownership rights to railway and port facilities in Kenya and Tanzania. Finally, the domestic transport system was adversely affected by the impact of the 1978–79 civil war and subsequent widespread looting.

Since the return of peace and stability in most parts of the country, the government has concentrated on the rehabilitation and maintenance of the transport and communications network, which in the 1960s was one of the best in sub-Saharan Africa.

Uganda has over 27,000 kilometres (16,700 miles) of roads, of which 2,000 kilometres (1,200 miles) are paved. Although the highway network is generally adequate, road conditions deteriorated substantially in the 1970s. The situation was particularly severe for trunk roads serving transit traffic (to Rwanda, Burundi, Zaire, and Sudan), where high volumes and heavy loads showed up numerous structural deficiencies. For the secondary road network, the situation is somewhat better, largely because of the sharp decline in traffic in recent years and the use of a good local road-building material, murram, in construction. Nevertheless, in many areas the secondary road surfaces have become very rough, making travel slow, and on some isolated sections the gravel has worn or washed off, making the roads impassable, particularly during the rainy season. This limits production and marketing of perishable food.

Priority is now the maintenance of the recently rehabilitated main highway network, as well as on the maintenance and rehabilitation of rural feeder roads critical to agricultural development. To achieve this, the government is committed to providing the budget resources needed to execute a roads maintenance programme for the fiscal years 1996–98. Thereafter, the government plans to increase its annual contribution to main road maintenance. Expansion of the network, for which the Ministry of Works, Transport, and Communications is responsible, will be controlled in accordance with the ministry's implementation capacity and the projected availability of resources for maintenance. By making the flow of funds for road maintenance reliable, the government will serve its objective of establishing a sound, experienced road construction capacity in the private sector.

The road vehicle fleet, which was severely depleted in the 1970s, has begun to grow steadily. Public transport service, which until recently was provided by four parastatal bodies, suffered when all four were declared bankrupt and liquidated. The remaining vehicles and scrap were sold to private transporters. With little or no bus transportation available there has been a sharp increase in the number of private passenger 12-seater vehicles (matatus).

Uganda Railways Corporation's (URC) statute enjoins it to operate on commercial principles and to maintain financial viability. To achieve these objectives, on 1 July 1994 URC entered into a performance agreement with the government, which covers rationalization of URC capital structure autonomy. In addition, the agreement defines procedures for establishing effective marketing and debt collection strategies.

Because Uganda remains dependent on Kenya for use of the track to the seaport of Mombasa, cooperation with this neighbour remains a key element in Uganda's overall transport strategy. In recent years, however, Uganda has had to rely on lake transport across Lake Victoria and then by rail through Tanzania as an alternative route to the coast.

This reflects both political concern that Uganda should not be solely dependent on Kenya and economic concerns regarding the impact of congestion and clearance delays at Mombasa port. Uganda operates three ferries, from Port Bell, Luzira, to Mwanza, from which there are connections by rail to the ports of Dar es Salaam and Tanga. Under normal circumstances, the Tanzanian route would be more economical than the Kenya route, as the route across the lake is about 40 per cent cheaper than the route to Mombasa by road. The potential for developing the Tanzania route, however, is limited by the capacity of the Tanzanian railways.

The airport system in Uganda consists of an international airport at Entebbe and 11 domestic airfields. Entebbe Airport has runways capable of handling wide-body jet aircraft. The passenger terminal building has just been refurbished, as have the including navigational aids, meteorological and fire-fighting equipment, and the control tower. The national carrier, Uganda Airlines, has undergone restructuring and is being run strictly on commercial terms, without recourse to government subsidies or contributions, and any expansion of operations is to be tailored accordingly.

Uganda's telecommunications sector has also undergone extensive rehabilitation with assistance from the World Bank. However, the government has decided to privatize the Uganda Posts and Telecommunications Corporation.

Tourism

Following the restoration of peace and stability in most parts of the country, Uganda's tourism industry is recovering steadily. With over 100,000 arrivals in 1993 and an annual income in the region of US$ 40 million, tourism is one of Uganda's most important growth industries.

In the 1960s and 1970s tourism, at 20 per cent, was the fastest-growing industry at the time and had been expected to overtake coffee and cotton in the 1980s and become the country's leading foreign exchange earner. This was shattered by the two decades of civil wars and political turmoil from 1966 to 1986.

Apart from Murchison Falls, which have attracted overseas visitors for many decades, tourism is concentrated in the outstanding national parks and game reserves, the majestic Ruwenzoris (Mountains of the Moon) for mountaineering, the impenetrable forests in southwest Uganda for gorilla viewing, the source of the Nile, and a number of historical and cultural sites, particularly the Kabakas' Tombs at Kasubi in Kampala.

The Uganda Tourist Development Corporation is responsible for coordinating and promoting the entire industry, including hotels, tour and safari operators, travel agents and all tourist areas and attractions. Current government policy is to liberalize and privatize the industry by encouraging investors to build tourist hotels and lodges and manage game reserves on leaseholds. Uganda's tourism industry is at present constrained by lack of adequate accommodation and internationally accepted facilities.

Power

Uganda's power consumption is currently growing at a rate of about 20 per cent each year.

The generation and distribution of electricity is undertaken by the Uganda Electricity Board (UEB), a parastatal. In addition to the domestic market, the UEB exports power to Kenya, Tanzania, and Rwanda. Uganda also hopes in the future to be a major exporter of electricity to other neighbouring countries including Zaire, Sudan, and Burundi.

The UEB has commissioned consultants to prepare important studies that will provide a sound basis for power sector planning and development. The government plans to pursue a low-cost programme for developing the country's abundant hydroelectric potential. A power subsector restructuring study is investigating the merits of abolishing the UEB monopoly on power production and distribution, and establishing regulatory procedures to govern possible private participation in the subsector.

Water resources

With the exception of a few areas in the northeast, Uganda has extensive surface water resources and usually receives adequate rainfall. However, sources of available surface water for human consumption are generally inadequate, unsuitable, or too far from human settlements. The problem is more serious in the rural areas where the groundwater potential is generally poor. During the late 1960s, modern water supply facilities served almost the total urban population and about 70 per cent of the rural population. However, during the 1970s these facilities deteriorated considerably. In 1983, only 40 per cent of the urban population and about 6.5 per cent of the rural population were estimated to have access to drinking water.

The sources of rural water supply consist mainly of boreholes equipped with hand pumps, protected springs, and small dams. Of the 5,000 boreholes existing in 1970, only 10 per cent were functioning a decade later. In both rural and urban areas, this lack of good quality water has led to an increase in waterborne diseases, particularly cholera, bilharzia, and worm infection.

The government gave high priority to the water sector in its rehabilitation and recovery programme. Many of the principal urban water schemes have been rehabilitated by loans and grants from various donors. With the assistance of UNICEF, the government has made substantial progress in rehabilitating the rural water supply. There are major constraints to further improvements in the sector, however, including inadequate local financing, shortage of qualified experienced workers, inadequate local construction capacity and output of building materials, and inadequate institutional and policy framework, particularly regarding cost recovery in the rural water supply.

Uganda's long-term goals for the water and sanitation sector encompass safe water, effective sanitation, and related health education for all who can be practically serviced, under a system of full cost recovery (at least of recurrent costs) for services provided, but with the provision of subsidized safe water and sanitation services to low-income groups. Uganda is also committed to ensure the provision of a reliable supply of water and disposal services to industry.

To accelerate improvements in the sector, the government, through the National Water and Sewerage Corporation, has adopted a new policy whereby the Directorate of Water Development (DWD) will undertake major capital investments, while local user groups will have the main responsibility for system operation and maintenance. Until the financial capacity of local user organizations is developed sufficiently, the government intends to provide supplementary budgetary allocations for the maintenance of the systems in small towns to prevent their further deterioration.

In rural areas, where access to safe drinking water and sanitation is very limited, a cooperative among NGOs, donors, public bodies, and local communities to provide these services has proven effective. The arrangement is being encouraged by the government, which intends to support it by making increased budgetary provisions for field personnel and expenditure on the construction and maintenance of rural systems.

Labour

The development of Uganda's human resources is the responsibility of a number of government ministries, including the Ministry of Education and Sports, the Ministry of Local Government, the Ministry of Finance and Economic Planning, the Ministry of Labour and Social Welfare, the Ministry of Culture and Gender Affairs, the Ministry of Agriculture, Animal Industry, and Fisheries, the Ministry of Justice, the Ministry of Public Service, and the Ministry of Information and Broadcasting. Each takes a direct responsibility in the training and skills of its staff runs training institutions for this purpose.

Training in the public service sector is currently the responsibility of the training division of the Ministry of Public Service and Cabinet Affairs. Training is also provided by the government through overseas scholarships and aid programmes from friendly countries and organizations. On-the-job public service training is also carried out at all levels; senior officers are expected to assist new and younger officers to acquire the skills they need to execute their duties.

Uganda started its own high-level training institution, in the form of the Institute of Public Administration (IPA), in 1968. Apart from the IPA, training has been given for various categories of semi-professionals at the Uganda Technical College, the National Teachers College, the Uganda College of Commerce, and the Law Development Centre on a continuous basis for a long time. In 1974, a recommendation was made to establish a National Training Council within the Ministry of Planning and Economic Development, which would have the overall responsibility of coordinating a national approach to training, covering the civil service and the parastatal bodies. The recommendation was accepted, but it has not been implemented with much success.

The Ministry of Labour and Social Affairs

is expected to ensure that there are healthy industrial and labour relations to enable the industrial sector (and other sectors) to contribute effectively to the development of the country. The ministry has a Department of Labour comprising the labour inspectorate, industrial relations, employment service, the factories inspectorate, occupational health and hygiene, the social security fund (a parastatal), and the industrial court. It also has a directorate of industrial training, which is engaged in identifying training needs for industrial employees, who depend on it to cater for the greater part of their training. It coordinates and directs in-house training, trains industrial organizations, and develops trade testing, guidance, and certification methods and procedures. It also provides guidance services to individuals seeking assistance in industrial career development and to those planning to undergo apprenticeship or institutional training.

The directorate also conducts occupational surveys and analyses for vocational training purposes. It is responsible for designing and improving training and testing systems, methods and techniques, and validation of these standards nationally. It also organizes and maintains technical and professional centres and disseminates research and development results. The centre oversees four vocational training institutes: the Vocational Training Institutes in Nakawa and Lugogo, the YMCA Vocational Training Centre in Jinja and the IDA Vocational Training Institute, also in Jinja.

Education provides skilled labour, an indispensable input for the advancement of the economy. In 1990–91 a significant development in the history of educational policy in Uganda put the future focus on primary education, in terms of both universal access and high quality. The Public Expenditure Review, following on the recommendation of the Educational Policy Review Commission, highlighted the need to orientate the education system towards the needs of the majority of the population by providing vocationally relevant mass education.

This entails shifting resources from secondary and tertiary institutions, particularly where they are being used for non-instructional subsidies, towards the primary level. As a signatory of the World Declaration for the Survival, Protection, and Development of Children in September 1990, Uganda committed itself to the global goal of basic education for all. In 1996 the Ministry of Education and Sports was working on a five-year investment programme to assess the resource requirements needed if universal primary education is to be achieved by 2003.

Investment

Government policy

1. To develop to the full the potential of the agricultural, mining, commercial, and industrial sectors so as to expand their productive capacities, thus promoting growth, generating employment opportunities, and uplifting the standards of living of the people.

2. To restore fiscal and monetary discipline with emphasis on a progressive movement toward, and eventual adoption of, a market-determined rate for foreign exchange transactions to strengthen the balance of payments and render the allocation of resources more efficient. To institutionalize the liberalization of the foreign exchange regime, on 5 April 1994 Uganda adopted the obligations of Article VIII, Sections 2, 3, and 4 of the International Monetary Fund's Articles of Agreement.

3. To develop the private sector, which has a sense of social responsibility alongside the developing public sector.

4. To return properties expropriated by previous regimes to their former owners, thus reinforcing investors' confidence that property rights will be respected.

5. To divest itself of public enterprises that are inefficient and loss making in order to cut down on allocation of subsidies to such enterprises.

6. To liberalize the external trade system. The government has introduced a broadly based import scheme with only a small negative list; a six-month renewable import certificate that provides the holder permission to import goods not on the negative list is now in place.

7. To encourage regional cooperation through the Cross-Border Initiative, cosponsored by the IMF, the World Bank, the ADB, and the European Union, which aims at facilitating cross-border trade, investments, and payments within eastern and southern Africa and the Indian Ocean region.

Foreign investment

Applications for the approval of foreign investment are considered by the Foreign Investment Committee of the Uganda Investment Authority (UIA), a one-stop centre for investors. The government welcomes foreign investment and offers a number of incentives and guarantees. Proposals are considered on their own merit by the UIA against criteria established by the Foreign Investment Committee. A simple and precise form is available at the UIA secretariat (opposite Bank of Uganda offices in Kampala) to guide investors to register for facilities under the Investment

Code, which will leverage the proposed business through at least three years of the start-up investments. Information required includes the legal status of the business; an implementation programme, including a schedule of capital items to be purchased and working capital requirements; sources of funding; environmental aspects; and other considerations.

Release of dividends, branch, and partnership profits
A holder of a certificate of incentives shall be entitled to: (a) exemption from corporation tax, withholding tax, and tax on dividends for a period of three years, in the case of an investment of a value not less than US$ 50,000 and not more than US$ 300,000; and for a period of five years, in the case of an investment of a value greater than US$ 300,000 dollars; (b) exemption from the taxes provided for under paragraph (a), for an additional one year respectively, in the case of an investor operating in any of the priority areas specified.

Priority areas specified include crop processing; processing of forest products; fish processing; steel industry; chemical industry; textile and leather industry; oil milling industry; paper production; mining industry; glass and plastic products industry; ceramic industry; manufacturing of tools, implements, equipment and machinery; manufacture of industrial spare parts; construction and building industry; meat processing; tourism industry; real estate development industry; manufacturing of building materials; packaging industry; transport industry; energy conservation industry; pharmaceutical industry; banking; and high-technology industries.

Incentives

The Investment Code spells out various facilities and incentives that can be enjoyed by Ugandan and foreign investors whose investments have been licensed and received a certificate of incentives. They include:

First arrival privileges
These include exemption from the payment of import duty and sales tax payable on one motor vehicle for personal use and personal and household effects, imported within 12 months from the date of first arrival.

Tax exemption on imported plant, machinery, or construction materials
Any imported plant, machinery or construction material that is not available in Uganda is exempt from import duty and sales tax otherwise payable on those goods, provided the plant,

machinery, or construction material is not more than five years old. Where the new investment involves two or more phases, all those phases shall be treated as forming part of the new investment.

Enterprises that qualify for incentives
An investment to qualify for incentives must contribute to the following objectives:
1. (a) The generation of new earnings or savings of foreign exchange through exports, resource-based import substitution, or service activities;
   (b) The utilization of local materials, supplies, and services;
   (c) The creation of employment opportunities in Uganda;
   (d) The introduction of advanced technology or upgrade of indigenous technology;
   (e) The contribution to locally or regionally balanced socio-economic development; or
   (f) Any other objective that the UIA may consider relevant for achieving the objectives of the Investment Code.
2. (a) In the case of a foreign investor, that investor makes a capital investment or an equivalent in capital goods worth at least US$ 500,000 by way of capital invested; or
   (b) In the case of an investor who is a citizen of Uganda, the value of the investment is at least US$ 50,000.

A foreign investor who engages in any activity specified in the Third Schedule of the Investment Code shall not enjoy the above-named incentives. Activities spelt out in the Third Schedule where a foreign investor is not eligible for investment incentives include wholesale and retail commerce; personal services sector; public relations businesses; car hire services and operation of taxis; bakeries, confectioneries and food processing for the Ugandan market only; postal and telecommunication services; and professional services.

Entitlement to drawback of duties
Investors with certificates of incentive are entitled to a drawback of duties and sales tax payable on imported inputs used in producing goods for export as provided in any law imposing such duties or taxes.

Entitlement to obtain credit from domestic sources
A foreign investor who holds an investment licence may, in relation to the business enterprises to which the licence relates, obtain credit from domestic financial institutions up to the limit established by the Bank of Uganda in consultation with the UIA, having regard to the

amount of foreign capital invested in the business enterprise. The beneficiary of the domestic credit must ensure that the proceeds of that credit are used solely for the purpose of carrying out the activities specified in the investment licence.

Incentives for rural-based investments
During the 1994–95 national budget, the Minister of Finance and Economic Planning announced further incentives for those investors who planned to locate their businesses in the rural areas. This was in the form of accelerated depreciation allowances in the rural area.

Externalization of funds
Foreign investors with certificate of incentives are entitled to externalize their funds for the following purposes:
(a) repayment of foreign loans or interest on those loans;
(b) payment of dividends of shareholders who are not citizens of Uganda and reside abroad;
(c) payment of royalties or fees in respect of an agreement for the transfer of foreign technology or expertise;
(d) payment of emoluments and other benefits to foreign personnel employed in Uganda in connection with the business enterprise; or
(e) externalization of profits or proceeds on disposal of assets.

Investment protection
Protection of investments, both local and foreign, is contained in the constitution. The constitution provides for the protection from deprivation of property. It requires that property may be expropriated only in terms of law and that such a law must require that reasonable notice of intention to acquire the property is given to the owners; that the acquisition is reasonably necessary on one or other of certain specific grounds such as defence, public safety, or order; and that adequate compensation is paid promptly. In the event that the parties fail to agree on what is adequate compensation, the owner of the property can apply to the courts for judicial arbitration.

Areas where a foreign investor is not eligible for incentives
These include wholesale and retail commerce, personal services sector, public relations businesses, car hire services and operation of taxis, bakeries, confectioneries and food processing for the Ugandan market only, postal and telecommunication services and professional services.

Getting started

Company legislation
The Companies Act provides for the constitution of public and private companies and the registration of foreign companies, as well as both the voluntary and compulsory winding up of companies and the judicial management.

A company incorporated abroad may establish a place of business and carry on its activities in Uganda without having to form a separate locally registered company. Before establishing a place of business, the following must be lodged with the Minister of Justice and the Attorney General:
(i) a certified copy of its memorandum and articles of association;
(ii) a list of directors resident in Uganda and particulars of the person responsible for the management of the business; and
(iii) if the foreign company is a subsidiary company or companies, the particulars of such holding company or companies as the case may be.

New foreign investors who propose to engage in major investments but wish to develop their business plans by exploring the market should obtain an investment licence to facilitate trade in the imported products. One work permit for the resident director is also assured. Only US$ 50,000 in either fixed assets or working capital will qualify the investor for this licence. Within three years, the UIA reviews the investor's progress to determine his or her qualification for full or partial incentives. The special offer is also extended to professional practices, especially those with training programmes for local staff.

Business licences and permits
The Shop Licence Act stipulates that a licence should be held by any person who, in any shop, store, or other fixed place of business, carries on the trade or business of selling or letting for hire any goods.

The licence is issued by the local licensing authority, if it is satisfied that the premises concerned are suitable for the conduct of the trade or business in question. The fee for the issue or renewal of a licence is in the range of between Ush 50,000 and 200,000 (US$ 50 and 200), depending on the zone of that particular urban area.

Work permits
Foreign recruitment is a temporary policy adopted by the government to resolve the skilled workforce problem.

Before the employer embarks on a foreign recruitment exercise, permission in principle must be received from the UIA and the Ministry of Finance and Economic Planning. Once a suitable foreign recruit has been identified, the employer must submit an application for work permit to the Immigration Department.

A foreign recruit can be given a temporary pass while his work permit is being processed. The recruit should be able to transfer skills to an identified Ugandan understudy, or undertake a training programme for the company or organization concerned.

Work permits are normally valid for up to one year with a possibility of extension upon application. Work permits become invalid if an expatriate worker changes employers without obtaining prior approval from the Immigration Department.

Import controls and procedures
During the last quarter of 1991, a broadly based import scheme was introduced with only a small negative list, and the import licensing system was replaced by a six-month renewable import certificates, which provides the holder permission to import goods not on the negative list. A similar export certificate system was also introduced.

Customs duties
The customs duty-free allowance is US$ 100 worth of goods without an import licence. The goods under a traveller's personal allowances include limited amounts of wines and spirits; perfume and toilet water; and cigarettes or cigars. These allowances are only applicable to air passengers who are 17 years old or over, for their own use and not for resale. These allowances are applicable only to those passengers whose length of stay outside Uganda has exceeded 24 hours on any journey.

What is needed to import
An import certificate is obtainable from the Department of Trade, Ministry of Trade and Industry, at Farmers' House in Kampala. Form E can be obtained from any commercial bank or private forex bureau. An SGS clean report of findings is required for goods whose value is above US$ 10,000, issued by the SGS from the country of exportation.

Import taxes should be paid to the nearest customs office of the Uganda Revenue Authority (URA). They include an import duty (10–30 per cent), an excise duty (30–50 per cent), a withholding tax (4 per cent), and an import commission (2 per cent).

What is needed to export
An export permit obtainable from the Department of Trade, Ministry of Trade and Industry, at Farmers House in Kampala, is required. A CD3 form is also obtainable from any commercial bank. Euroforms are needed for export to the European Union.

Other than on coffee, there are no taxes on exports, except on re-exports out of customs-bonded warehouses at two per cent of FOB value.

During the 1994–95 national budget speech, the government reintroduced a coffee stabilization tax on exports aimed at controlling the strength of the local currency as well as the exchange rate of the US dollar.

The tax is as follows:
* Earnings below Ush 1,100 per kg: no tax.
* Earnings above Ush 2,200 per kg: 20 per cent.
* Earnings above Ush 2,200 per kg: 40 per cent.

Foreign exchange operations
Over the past several years, Uganda has been carrying out a policy of liberalizing the foreign exchange market. It plans eventually to adopt a market-determined rate for foreign exchange transactions aimed at strengthening of the balance of payments and rendering the allocation of resources more efficient.

On 1 November 1993 the auction system for allocating donor import support that had prevailed since January 1992 was abolished, and an interbank market in foreign exchange was introduced, together with an elimination of all restrictions on current international transactions.

To institutionalize the liberalization of the foreign exchange regime, on 5 April 1994 Uganda accepted the obligations of Article VIII, Sections 2, 3, and 4 of the IMF's Articles of Agreement. By attainment of Article VIII status, Uganda joins a select group of African countries that are committed to place no restrictions on current international transactions without prior IMF approval.

Trade liberalization
Major steps have also been taken to liberalize the external trade system. During the last quarter of 1991 a broadly based import scheme was introduced with only a small negative list, and the import licensing system was replaced by a six-month renewable import certificate, which provides the holder permission to import goods not on the negative list. A similar export certificate system was also introduced.

Finance
Non-resident-owned companies are free to borrow from the local banking and credit institutions if they have the necessary credentials and collateral.

The Kampala Stock Exchange

For the last three years, the Ugandan business community has tried to establish an independent Kampala Stock Exchange. However, to ensure that players in the stock exchange are not cheated, the government introduced a Capital Markets Bill in 1995.

Local stock brokerages have been licensed and are currently dealing in the buying and selling of stocks and shares of some companies under the off-the-counter (UTC) system.

Taxation

Income tax

The tax assessment year runs from 1 March to 28 or 29 February in the succeeding year. Employees' salaries or wages are normally subject to Pay As You Earn (PAYE) deductions.

Several years ago, Uganda abolished different tax rates for married and single persons. The main change is the adoption of a separate taxation system that involves a single rate structure over seven bands of income, from a zero rate band up to 60 per cent rate band.

Individuals earning Ush 840,000 or more a year from employment are subject to PAYE. Taxable income includes income from employment rentals, taxable interest currently at four per cent, and business profits.

Tax rates

The rates of tax are fixed annually after the Minister of Finance and Economic Planning presents the annual budget to parliament, which is usually during the month of June.

Revenue authority

The Uganda Revenue Authority (URA) was set up under an Act of Parliament on 1 August 1991 and was inaugurated on 5 September 1991. It is an executing organ of government charged with the responsibility of improving tax administration and raising revenue collection. Thus, in essence the URA has been charged with the responsibility and challenge of providing the foundation for development through revenue mobilization to finance current and capital development activities of the government.

The URA comprises the commissioner general's office, the board secretariat, internal audit and management services, internal revenue, customs, excise and sales tax, and district offices. There are also customs offices at strategic border points, which are in charge of levying and collecting taxes on imports and exports.

Uganda's revenue collection efforts as a proportion of the GDP are one of the lowest in sub-Saharan Africa. According to a World Bank report of 1991, the 'Challenges of Development', the total current revenue as a percentage of the GNP of Kenya is 23.3 per cent and Ghana 13.8 per cent, while that of Uganda is only 5.3 per cent. The URA's mission is to raise the revenue: GNP ratio to comparable levels. With the above mission in mind, the URA has witnessed increasing revenue collection since it was set up. Before the authority was in existence, collections were about Ush 9 billion per month. In 1991–92, the URA recorded an average monthly collection of about Ush 20 billion, in 1992–93 about Ushs 23 billion, and about Ush 36 billion in the 1993–94 financial year. It is the URA's goal to raise this figure further so that Uganda's budget is totally funded by locally generated resources.

Value-added-tax (VAT)

In the 1994–95 budget, the Minister of Finance and Economic Planning announced the introduction of the value-added-tax (VAT) with a target commencement date of mid-1996. VAT will not be an additional new tax; rather it will substitute for two existing taxes, the sales tax and the commercial transactions levy (CTL). These two taxes will terminate with the effect from the date VAT commences. While many important details of Uganda's VAT arrangements have yet to be announced, the minister has indicated that VAT will have to yield the same revenue as previously given by the sales tax and the CTL. He also announced that export transactions will be outside the scope of the VAT system.

VAT is a tax on the supply of goods and services. It applies to all stages of the importation (supply of raw materials right through to the purchase by the consumer of the finished product or service).

For further information, please contact the VAT Information Officers in the Excise and Sales Tax Division of the URA in Kampala.

Tax identification numbers (TIN)

A tax identification number (TIN) is a unique 12-digit number that is personal to each holder and usable in part of Uganda. Anybody above the age of 18 years qualifies for a TIN. Anybody who transacts business — companies and individuals, charitable organizations, NGOs, parastatals, diplomats, and anyone employed and earning income — needs a TIN.

There are three categories of TINs: business, personal and diplomatic. Applicants obtain forms from the nearest URA Internal Revenue Office, which is supposed to issue them within one week. The TIN is one of the prerequisites in the introduction of VAT.

If an importer has no TIN, no goods will be cleared. No import licence will be issued. No payment will be processed for a supplier without the TIN.

Stamp duty

Stamp duty is a direct tax levied on various instruments or documents. It is collected by the URA under the Stamp Duty Act of 1994. There are over 60 items on which stamp duty is payable, but the most common are transfer of land, mortgage, company registration, lease, and bonds.

In case of land transfer, URA staff must determine the tax due by demanding the consent from the taxpayer on which the consent value of the land is determined by the chief government valuer and confirmed by the commissioner of lands and surveys. The duty payable is one per cent of the consent value (the value of the land and property being transferred).

The duty payable for mortgage, lease, bonds is one per cent of the value in most cases. However, the duty for company registration is determined by the registrar general of companies. The owner of the instrument or the interested party pays stamp duty. Every instrument chargeable with duty that is executed by any person in Uganda shall be stamped within 30 days of the execution. If the instrument is executed outside Uganda, it shall be stamped within 30 days of being received in Uganda.

For further information, contact the Stamp Duty office in Kampala.

Commercial transaction levy

The commercial transaction levy (CTL) is a levy on the sale and rendering of services. The current rate is 15 per cent on the gross amount, except with regard to construction and to motor vehicle repairs, where it is on all costs other than the cost of construction materials and spare parts respectively.

CTL is payable by the receiver of service but is collected and remitted by the renderer of service. Should the renderer of service fail to collect it from the receiver, then the renderer pays.

United Nations offices, high commissions, embassies, and other such bodies should pay CTL when commercial services are rendered to them.

Payment of the levy should be done through the bank. Bank payment forms are given to the taxpayers, who pay cash in the specified Uganda Commercial Bank. The levy is due at the time an invoice or debit note is made out in case of service performed on credit, or at the time cash is paid. The levy must paid every two weeks for small and medium businesses and every month in case of big corporations and hotels. The penalty for late payment of the levy is 2.5 per cent per month compounded and retrospective in case of arrears. Records are supposed to be kept for seven years. Authorized officers are empowered to enter any premises and inspect documents, seize relevant documents, and make extracts from any books or documents.

Services subject to CTL include accommodation, advertising, clearing and forwarding, construction, dry cleaning, electricity, soccer, entertainment, legal practice, motor vehicle repairs, other repairs, printing, professionals, consultancy, tailoring, hairdressing, photography, telephone, postal/courier, insurance, banking, renovation, restaurants, drinks, transport hire, tour operator, and water and sewage.

Private use of motor vehicles

The Traffic and Road Safety Act 1970 provides that no person shall possess a motor vehicle or trailer unless such a motor vehicle or trailer is registered under the provisions of the act. Registration involves the issuing of number plates, road licences and registration cards to motorists. Registration and re-registration is carried out centrally in Kampala Custom's Long Room by the motor vehicle registration unit.

Application for registration of a motor vehicle is done by filling in Traffic Form 1, accompanied by the prescribed fees.

Licence charges vary for private cars, motorcycles, public service vehicles, or commercial vehicles.

Before any motor vehicle is registered it must have a certificate of fitness obtained from the inspector of vehicles, and it must have been lawfully imported. The vehicle owner must be able to produce the import licence, the bill of lading or airway bill, the registration card from the country of origin if a used vehicle, the supplier's invoice, the certificate of origin, and the insurance certificate as well as the SGS report on goods above US$ 10,000 in value.

Before registration, the vehicle owner must have paid any tax or duty applicable, such as import duty, excise duty, sales tax, import licence charges, and withholding tax.

Any person under the age of 18 years and any person with a mental disability or any other chronic disease should not apply to the licensing officer for registration of a motor vehicle.

Re-registration occurs when the owner of a tax-free vehicle decides to pay taxes (such as customs duty and sales tax) or decides to sell off such vehicles, in which case the new owners have to pay the taxes. In this case, the old registration book has to be surrendered and replaced by a new one; tax-free registration number plates have to be surrendered and replaced by new ones, and a certificate of fitness has to be obtained from the inspector of motor vehicles.

When there is a change of ownership of a motor vehicle from one party to another, a transfer fee of two per cent on the value of the vehicle to be transferred must be paid.

To drive, motorists must obtain a driving permit. There are six classes, depending on the size and capacity of the vehicle. The fee paid to obtain a driving permit for one year is about Ush 5,500 (US$ 5.50).

Sales tax and import tax
The rate of sales tax on local purchases and import tax on imported goods, other than those exempted, such as basic foodstuffs, is 10 per cent on all general goods and 30 per cent on certain listed goods. Orthopaedic appliances and other appliances to compensate for a defect or disability, invalid carriages, literature for the blind, Braille typewriters, and Braille watches are exempt from sales tax.

Airport tax
In 1996, an airport tax of Ush 20,000 for each passport was payable by residents embarking on international flights. Non-residents pay US$ 20.

Withholding tax
Withholding is paid on virtually all imports, supplies of goods and services to certain persons, and on execution of contracts and some payments like dividends. It is deducted at source. Presently the rate is four per cent of the gross payment. It is an administrative collection, not a separate tax. According to the URA, the benefits of the withholding tax include minimizing the chances of tax evasion, allowing early collection of tax income, and reducing collection costs. The person withholding the tax must submit it to the Internal Revenue Department within 30 days, failure of which is an offence.

Rental income tax
All landlords with rentable properties are required by law to pay rental income tax of 20 per cent per year.

Graduated tax
All persons in Uganda who are 18 years old and above are required to pay a head tax, which is graduated depending on the size of land, the number of crops, or estimated annual income obtained on regular employment. It is payable to the district or town authority where the taxpayer normally resides. It is payable once in a given financial year, but not after the first four to six months of the year. The range is between Ush 10,000 and 80,000, depending on assessed income. Minors, dependants, very old people without income, the blind, and invalids are exempt from paying graduated tax. In addition, districts or town local authorities sometimes charge a fixed amount of money for certain projects, such as an education tax.

Duty-free shops
Duty-free shops are shops authorized to sell goods on which taxes have not been paid to specific categories of persons entitled to duty-free purchases. These shops are mainly to be found at Entebbe International Airport and in Kampala. At Entebbe Airport, entitled persons include those departing by aircraft to a destination outside Uganda. These are served by the departure lounge duty-free shops. All persons arriving into the country by aircraft from a destination outside Uganda are served by the arrival lounge duty-free shop and entitlement is restricted to the duty-free allowances for passengers arriving from outside Uganda.

In the Kampala Duty-Free Shops persons entitled include diplomats (upon certification of diplomatic status by the Ministry of Foreign Affairs), technical assistance personnel, consular representatives, and persons other than Uganda nationals who are on a bilateral arrangement with the government and whose contacts specifically indicate this entitlement. Diplomats and technical assistance personnel are entitled to duty-free shop privileges upon first arrival in Uganda and entitlement is for the first six months of stay but does not apply to consumables such as cigarettes, wines, spirits, beer, and food.

The president of the Republic of Uganda is also entitled to duty-free shop facilities. Tourists and visitors in Uganda are not entitled to duty-free purchases.

For further information, please contact the URA Excise and Sales Tax Division in Kampala.

Tax relief schemes
Tax relief schemes are incentives to the taxpayers whereby a trader may be relieved of a significant amount in tax liability. They include a tax credit system and a duty draw back.

The tax credit scheme provides for a refund when inputs (raw materials) imported by a trader are satisfactorily accounted for in production of finished goods. In most cases a tax credit equivalent to the amount of sales tax paid on raw materials in any period will be allowed to the taxpayer against the liability on the finished goods. Any taxpayer entitled to a tax credit may claim it on the next return (in writing), but it must be claimed within 12 months from the date of payment of the sales tax on the raw materials.

In the case of imported raw materials, applications should have a customs bill of entry and an original copy of the receipt; in case of locally produced raw materials, government delivery notes, invoices or cash sale receipts, and authorized forms from the Commissioner of Customs and Excise. All these documents must be original and no photocopies will be accepted.

Under duty drawback, traders already registered for sales tax can get a reimbursement of customs duty paid on raw materials used in the manufacture of goods that are to be exported. To qualify for duty drawback, a manufacturer must have stock records maintained and input/output ratios calculated in sufficient detail to allow customs to verify the declared imported content of each product exported. A copy of the export entry to include a request for drawback and marked 'Notice to Pack' is to be lodged with the nearest customs office at least seven days before the goods are packed for exportation, stating the time when such packing will take place.

The Excise and Sales Tax Division will process the claim within one month and may visit the manufacturer to verify the claim. If satisfied the tax division will send the exporter the duty draw back credit voucher (DDCV), which is to be used by the exporter to claim the duty.

Double taxation agreement

Uganda has double taxation agreements with the United Kingdom. Except where they are income effectively connected with the permanent establishment on fixed base in Uganda of a resident in the UK, the following types of income are subject to a Ugandan tax, including branch profit tax and withholding tax at the following restricted rates, which are calculated on the gross amount of the income.

Type of income	Maximum rate
Interest	15 per cent
Technical fees	15 per cent
Royalties	15 per cent

Relief from double taxation

Where income from sources in a country other than Uganda is taxed in both countries, relief is granted against Ugandan tax regardless of whether there exists an agreement with the country of origin for the avoidance of double taxation. Double taxation agreements are being considered with the Netherlands, Mauritius, and Kenya. The reasons for such agreements are to facilitate exchange of qualified technical personnel without the person being burdened with heavier taxation due to double taxes, to facilitate the exchange of technology in commerce and industry without the investors being overburdened with the tax in both countries, and to grant the taxpayer relief where the two countries operate different tax regimes or rates.

PART SIX: FACTS AT YOUR FINGERTIPS

Visa and immigration requirements
Visa applications may be obtained at Uganda diplomatic missions located in Brussels, Belgium; Ottawa, Canada; Beijing, China; Havana, Cuba; Hellerup, Denmark; Cairo, Egypt; Addis Ababa, Ethiopia; Paris, France; Bonn, Germany; New Dehli, India; Rome, Italy; Tokyo, Japan; Nairobi, Kenya; Tripoli, Libya; Abuja, Nigeria; Moscow, Russia; Kigali, Rwanda; Riyadh, Saudi Arabia; Khartoum, Sudan; Dar es Salaam, Tanzania; London, United Kingdom; Washington DC, USA; and Kinshasha, Zaire.

Two photos are required for visas which are usually issued within 24 hours. Visas are also available at the country's entry points and you probably won't need photos.

Visas are required for visitors to Uganda, with the exception of nationals of Antigua and Barbuda, Angola, Australia, Austria, Bahamas, Bahrain, Barbados, Belgium, Belize, Botswana, Burundi, Canada, Comoros, Cyprus, Denmark, Djibouti, Eritrea, Ethiopia, Fiji, Finland, France, Gambia, Germany, Greece, Grenada, Hong Kong, Ireland, Israel, Italy, Jamaica, Japan, Kenya, Kuwait, Lesotho, Libya, Luxembourg, Madagascar, Malawi, Malaysia, Malta, Mauritius, Mozambique, Namibia, Netherlands, New Zealand, Norway, Oman, Portugal, Rwanda, Saudi Arabia, Seychelles, Sierra Leone, Singapore, Solomon Islands, Somalia, South Korea, Spain, St Lucia, St Vincent and Grenadines, Sudan, Swaziland, Sweden, Switzerland, Taiwan, Tanzania, Tonga, Tuvalu, United Arab Emirates, United Kingdom, USA, Vanuatu, Zambia, and Zimbabwe.

Any visitor intending to take up work or residence in Uganda must have a work permit from the Immigration Department. Work permits are normally valid for up to one year with a possibility of extension upon application. A visitor on a tourist visa cannot take up work or get a work permit. It is best to have all formalities cleared before you enter Uganda on a working visa.

Health requirements
Visitors from areas infected with yellow fever and cholera require certificates of inoculation.

Malaria and bilharzia are endemic. All visitors are advised to take an antimalarial prophylactic beginning two weeks before their arrival and continuing for six weeks after their departure. Bilharzia (schistosomiasis) is common throughout Uganda but is easily avoided by drinking treated water and by simply avoiding swimming or bathing in streams, rivers and lakes (although fast-flowing mountain streams are of low risk).

Doctors also recommend that visitors take sensible precautions against tetanus, polio, cholera, typhoid, and paratyphoid. A gamma globulin injection provides some protection against possible infection by hepatitis and is well worth taking. The incidence of these diseases and infections is not high, however.

International flights
Uganda is served internationally by Air Burundi, Air France, Air India, Air Rwanda, Air Tanzania, Alliance, British Airways, EgyptAir, Ethiopian Airlines, Gulf Air, InterAir, Kenya Airways, Royal Swazi, Sabena, and Uganda Airlines. Uganda Airlines has offices in Kampala and its headquarters near Entebbe. They have a good record for punctuality and offer fully automated passenger services.

Uganda's main point of entry by air is Entebbe International Airport, about a 30-minute drive south of the capital, Kampala. Although modest, the modern airport does provide automated passenger facilities, currency exchange, postal services, banking facilities, telephones, duty-free shops, gift shops and a restaurant and bar.

Taxis and rental cars are available at the airport for transport into Kampala.

Air fares
The usual range of fares is available: first, business, and economy class; excursion fares, bookable any time for stays of between 14 and 45 days; an APEX fare, bookable one calendar month in advaance, allowing for stays of between 19 and 90 days. The price of cheaper APEX fares varies according to the season. Stopovers en route are possible when arranged with the airline for all but APEX fares. Reductions are available for children.

In Europe, the best place to find cheap air tickets to Africa is London. Check with an agency that specializes in Africa; there are several.

Departure tax
As of mid-1996, the airport departure tax was Ush 20,000 for residents embarking on international flights. Non-residents pay US$ 20. Although in theory, you should be able to pay the

equivalent in any convertible currency, to be safe have US dollars on hand — and the correct change. Traveller's cheques are not acceptable.

Arrival by rail

The sole point of entry into Uganda by rail is from Kenya by taking the Nairobi–Kampala train (which runs every Tuesday). Arrivals undergo full customs and immigration checks. With the renewal of ties between the East African countries, plans are to expand this line, and in 1996 it was hoped that travel by rail all the way from Mombasa to Kasese would soon be possible.

Arrival by road

There are several 'official' points of entry by road into Uganda from the country's neighbours. Check first, however, before coming in via the Rwanda or Sudan borders. Although situations can change quickly, in the 1990s borders between Uganda and both those countries were either closed or difficult to cross because of instability.

The main border crossing into Uganda from Sudan is at Nimule, while from Rwanda there are two border posts: one at Cyanika, 10 kilometres (six miles) from Kisoro, and one at Gatuna, south of Kabale.

From Kenya, Uganda can be entered at the two main border posts of Malaba and Busia. There are also border points at Suam (near Mount Elgon), Karita, and Amudat, although they are rarely used. The Tanzania border crossings are at Mutukula and Kikagati.

The two main crossing points from Zaire are at Bunagana (between Rutshuru and Kisoro) and Kasindi (between Beni and Katwe) in the south, although the Ishasha border post is also open. Further north, there are crossing points at Goli and Vurra, although they are little used.

Arrival by lake

Although there were no passenger boat connections between Uganda and Kenya in 1996, it is possible to travel across Lake Victoria from Tanzania, using the Port Bell ferry, which connects Mwanza to Port Bell (Kampala) on its regular once-a-week service.

Customs

Besides personal effects, a visitor may import duty-free spirits (including liquors) or wine up to one litre, perfume and toilet water up to half a litre, and 250 grams (half a pound) of tobacco (up to 250 cigarettes).

Other imported items, not exceeding US$ 100 in total value, may also be brought in duty free and without an import licence, provided they are not prohibited or restricted goods, are for personal use, and are not for resale.

Currency declaration forms are not required.

Domestic air services

Uganda has a well-developed domestic air network. There are several air charter companies operating domestic flights to almost any part of the country from Entebbe International Airport.

Road services

There are some 22,100 kilometres (13,730 miles) of secondary and dirt roads throughout Uganda and some 6,230 kilometres (3,870 miles) of tarmac roads.

Major towns are linked by frequent, cheap, and scheduled 'luxury' bus services. These up-country buses depart from the *Baasi za Baganda* in Kampala, behind the main taxi park.

Taxi services

Taxis are immediately available at Entebbe International Airport. They can also be found outside most hotels in Kampala and at most of the country's major centres. They don't have meters, so make sure the fare is negotiated in advance. There are also the ubiquitous *matatus*, which are generally minibuses, pick-ups, or station wagons that ply the routes in the country not otherwise served by public transport. These private, licensed vehicles have developed a bad reputation for overcrowding and speeding, but nevertheless provide an economical means of getting around for a majority of the population.

Car rental

Several firms operate car hire services in Kampala. Vehicles may be hired with or without driver. For trips outside the city it is possible to hire insured cars appropriate for the trip (a four-wheel-drive vehicle with a driver–translator is recommended).

Driving

Driving is on the left. If you have a recognized and valid licence you can drive up to 90 days without applying for an international or Ugandan licence.

Rail services

Uganda has approximately 1,300 kilometres (800 miles) of railway track, once considered to be one of the best rail services in Africa. However, the rail network is notoriously slow and unreliable and rarely used by travellers. In 1996 the Uganda Railways Corporation operated one passenger train a week to western Uganda up to Kasese and three a week from Tororo north-west to Pakwach via Mbale, Soroti, Lira, and Gulu. Expect frequent delays, breakdowns, and spartan third-class carriages.

Climate
Although situated on the equator, Uganda's relatively high altitude tempers the heat, and humidity is generally low.

Throughout the year sunshine averages about 6 to 10 hours a day. Day temperatures range between 25° and 34°C (77°–93°F). In January, the hottest month, temperatures may be in the region of 35°C (95°F). Even during the rainy seasons, the temperatures can be high, which causes heavy tropical thunderstorms. It is considerably warmer all year round in the remote northern and north-eastern parts of the country.

In general there are two major rainy seasons each year: the main long rains, which start late in February and end in April, and the short rains, which start in October and run until about the middle of December. The region around Lake Victoria, however, receives rain at almost any time of year.

Currency
The local currency is the Uganda shilling, made up of 100 cents. In mid-1996, the exchange rate was approximately Ush 1,000 to one US dollar. The current set of banknotes has denominations of 5, 10, and 20 shillings (which are no more in circulation), as well as 50, 100, 200, 500, 1,000, 5,000, and 10,000 shillings.

Although technically four coins — with denominations of 1, 2, 5, and 10 shillings — are still legal tender, the galloping inflation that affected Uganda has virtually eliminated them from circulation. Today only paper money is in constant use.

Currency regulations
There is no limit to the amount of foreign currency imported to Uganda. Since Uganda's currency was freed in 1991, a large number of foreign exchange (forex) bureaux have opened around the country, where you can freely exchange, for example, US dollars for Uganda shillings and vice versa. You can also change money at banks and hotels, although the forex bureaux usually have better exchange rates.

Banks
There is a wide range of banks in Uganda, particularly in Kampala. Their hours are generally from 0830 to 1400 on weekdays, with some banks open on Saturday mornings as well. Forex bureaux keep longer hours — 0900 to 1800 on weekdays and 0900 to 1300 on Saturdays.

Credit cards
Some credit cards are accepted in the major hotels, with American Express the most widely accepted. There are few other places, however, where international credit cards are accepted.

Government
Uganda is a republic and a member of the Commonwealth. It is a one-party state with an elected president, who is head of state, the government, and the armed forces. The governing National Resistance Council (NRC) is made up of 80 representatives of various political organizations within the country. Integral to the country's political system are the Resistance Committees (RCs), village-based administrations responsible for village matters. In theory, RC members can be elected and pass through the system all the way to the NRC. In addition to improving security at the local level, the RCs provide the government with a direct means of disseminating policy information to the people.

Language
English is the official language and is also the medium of instruction in Uganda's education system, from primary school up to university level. Swahili is also spoken, but not widely. There are also some 30 indigenous languages spoken in the rural areas. The most common of these are Luganda and Luo.

Religion
Nearly half the population (44.5 per cent) is Catholic, while 39.3 per cent belong to the Church of Uganda (Anglican/Protestant). A smaller, but still significant, 10.5 per cent are Muslim. Smaller sects of the Seventh Day Adventist Church, Orthodox Church, Jehovah's Witnesses, and the Pentecostal Church also exist. A small portion of the population still practises animism.

Time
Uganda is three hours ahead of Greenwich Mean Time (GMT). There is no daylight savings time; time remains constant throughout the year.

Daylight
Being on the equator, Uganda has an almost constant 12 hours of daylight. In Kampala, sunrise and sunset are at around 0630 and 1845 respectively.

Business hours
Shops and businesses are generally open from around 0830 to 1730 on weekdays, with a lunch break between 1300 and 1400. Some businesses are open on Saturday, at least until midday. Small, local shops or kiosks on the side of many roads are generally open much later, until about 2130, and on weekends and holidays as well; they stock basic food and household items.

Security
The same rules apply for Kampala as for almost

any city anywhere. Be careful and take the usual precautions to safeguard yourself and your belongings. Do not leave valuables in your car (if you do, lock them away, out of sight, in the boot or glove compartment). Walking at night in all major centres is reasonably safe. There have been a few instances of handbags and wristwatches being snatched, and occasional muggings, so be sensible about what you wear (don't flaunt gold jewellery) and keep your eyes open.

There are isolated areas on the country's borders where rebel groups commit acts of thuggery. In particular, check the security situation before you travel anywhere north of Murchison Falls National Park and Karamoja, as this is the area where the rebels mainly operate.

Communications
Telephone, telex, fax, and airmail services connect Kampala to all parts of the world. Services are available at the General Post Office and its many branches, as well as in the main hotels. International direct dialling is available from all the major centres in the country, which are served by microwave.

Media
A number of English-language publications are available in Uganda.

The daily newspaper is the government-owned *New Vision*. Weeklies are the *Monitor, Financial Times, Uganda Confidential,* and *Weekly Topic.*

Two Kenyan dailies, *The Nation* and the *East African Standard,* are also available on the day of publication, as is the weekly *East African* newspaper.

Many international publications — including *Time, Newsweek, The Economist, International Herald Tribune,* and *USA Today* — are also available at news stands and bookshops.

Several newspapers are published in local languages as well, such as *Munno* and *Ngabo* (Luganda), *Orumuri* (Runyankore/Rukiga), *Rupiny* (Luo), and *Etop* (Iteso).

Uganda Television (government owned), Sanyu Television, and CTV provide three television channels of news and entertainment, although none of them broadcast 24 hours a day. Programmes, for the most part, are in English.

Radio stations include the government-owned Radio Uganda as well as Radio Sanyu and Capital Radio.

Energy
All installations are of British standard and appliances should be fitted with the square, three-pin plugs of British specification. The voltage is 240 volts, 50 Hz for domestic use. The voltage fluctuates continually, however, and power surge protectors are advisable for any expensive equipment. Most large hotels are equipped with generators in the event of power cuts.

Medical services
Uganda has reasonable health services, with some good government and private hospitals and clinics in the major cities. There are some first-class private or missionary-run hospitals in Kampala and Jinja with resident specialists and surgeons. There are also excellent dentists and opticians. Air rescue services are available.

Medical insurance
Medical treatment in Uganda is expensive. Visitors should take out medical insurance cover before their departure. Medical insurance can be obtained in Uganda, but usually at a higher premium than you would pay in Europe or North America.

Visitors may wish to get temporary health cover from the Kenyan-based Africa Air Rescue or Medivac, both of which have offices in Kampala. This guarantees you quick rescue and transportation to any nearby competent hospital.

Chemists/pharmacies
There are many chemists in Uganda, all staffed by qualified pharmacists. However, visitors should carry an adequate supply of all medications they may need with them. Most drugs are available, but many will have unfamiliar brand names. If a specific prescription is unavailable, the pharmacist or doctor will often prescribe a suitable alternative.

Pharmacies are open during normal weekday shopping hours, from about 0900 to 1700 (some, but not all, close for lunch). Selected pharmacies in the main centres of Kampala and Jinja also offer night service.

Liquor
Uganda's locally brewed beers are first class if you like light, lager-type beers. Two large breweries produce a variety of beers, the most popular brands being Nile and Bell.

Imported spirits are also available but can be expensive. Much cheaper but quite potent is the well-known 'national drink', *Uganda waragi*, a distillate or gin made out of cassava, banana beer, and brown sugar. Another local brew is banana wine, made in the banana-growing rural areas. It is essentially juice from bananas, which is fermented with sorghum flour. The rural people in the north and north-east parts make a similar alcoholic drink out of millet, locally called *malwa*.

Tipping
Tips up to 10 per cent are an accepted practice and appreciated, particularly by waiters, who earn very basic salaries. At night, tipping the

guard who is watching your car outside a restaurant is also common practice. Boys who help you with your shopping expect a 50- to 100-shilling tip. Taxi drivers usually calculate their tip in the bill, but if the service has been good, you can tip the driver of a negotiated trip.

Clubs

Clubs are a prominent feature of Ugandan social life, whether it be the local 'social drinking clubs' in the suburbs of the capital or in the rural areas, or the more middle- to upper-class sports and social clubs. Some of the latter may charge a temporary membership fee, but all welcome visitors.

Sports club activities include cricket, golf, soccer, squash, swimming, and tennis.

ENGLISH–KISWAHILI

Simple pronunciation guide:
  a as the a in father
  e as the ay in say
  i as the ee in see
  o as the o in go
  u as the oo in boot

The double vowel in words like *choo* or *saa* is pronounced like the single vowel, but more drawn out. Consonants are basically pronounced the same as they are in English, with the exception that *l* and *r*, as well as *b* and *v*, are often interchangeable and therefore variant spellings of the same word often occur.

Meeting and greeting

Hello	Jambo
Good morning	Habara ya asubuhi
Good afternoon	Habari ya mchana
Good evening	Habari ya jioni
Goodbye	Kwaheri
How are you?	Habari?
I am well (good, fine, etc.)	Mzuri
Thank you (very much)	Asante (sana)
Please come in	Karibu ndani tafadhali
Please sit down	Keti tafadhali
You're welcome	Una karibishwa
What is your name?	Jina lako ni?
My name is . . .	Naitwa or Jina langu ni . . .
Where do you come from?	Umetoka wapi?
I come from . . .	Nime toka . . .
Can you speak Swahili?	Unaweza kuongea kiswahili?
Only a little	Kidogo tu
I want to learn more	Nataka kujifunza zaidi
How do you find Uganda?	Unaonaje Uganda?
I like it here	Hapa napapenda

Useful words

Today	Leo
Tomorrow	Kesho
Yesterday	Jana
Now	Sasa
Quickly	Upesi
Slowly	Pole-pole
Mr	Bwana
Mrs	Bibi
Miss	Bi
I	Mimi
You	Wewe
He, She	Yeye
We	Sisi
They	Wao
What?	Nini?
Who?	Nani?
When?	Lini?
How?	Namna gani?
Why?	Kwanini?
Which?	Ipi?
Yes	Ndio
No	Hapana
Excuse me	Samahani
I am sorry	Pole sana
Good	Mzuri
Bad	Mbaya

Directions/emergencies

Where (Place)?	Mahali gani?
Where (Direction)?	Wapi?
Street/road	Barabara
Airport	Uwanja wa ndege
Where is the hotel?	Hoteli iko wapi?
Where are you going?	Unakwenda wapi?
I am going to . . .	Nakwenda . . .
Turn right	Pita kulia
Turn left	Pita kushoto
Go straight	Enda moja kwa moja
Please stop here	Simame hapa tafadhali
Come	kuja
Go	Kwenda
Stop	Simama
Help	Saidia
Hospital	Hospitali
Police	Polisi

Restaurants/shops/hotels

Hotel	Hoteli
Room	Chumba
Bed	Kitanda
To sleep	Kulala
To bathe	Kuoga
Where is the toilet?	Choo kiko wapi?
In the back	Upande wa nyuma
To eat	Kula
To drink	Kunywa
Where can I get a drink?	Naweza kupata kinywaji wapi?
Coffee	Kahawa
Tea	Chai

English	Swahili	English	Swahili
Beer	Bia *or* Pombe	Five	Tano
Cold	Baridi	Six	Sita
Warm, Hot	Moto	Seven	Saba
Food	Chakula	Eight	Nane
Meat	Nyama	Nine	Tisa
Fish	Samaki	Ten	Kumi
Bread	Mkate	Eleven	Kumi na moja
Butter	Siagi	Twelve	Kumi na mbili
Sugar	Sukari	Thirteen	Kumi na tatu
Salt	Chumvi	Twenty	Ishirini
Pepper	Pilipili	Twenty-one	Ishirini na moja
Shop	Duka	Twenty-two	Ishirini na mbili
To buy	Kununua	Twenty-three	Ishirini na tatu
To sell	Kuuza	Thirty	Thelathini
Money	Pesa	Forty	Arobaini
Shilling	Shilingi	Fifty	Hamsini
Cent	Senti	Hundred	Mia
How much?	Pesa ngapi?	Thousand	Elfu
How much does this cost?	Bei ngani?		
That's quite expensive	Bei kali sana	**Days of the week**	
Wait a minute	Ngoja kidogo	Monday	Jumatatu
		Tuesday	Jumanne
Numbers		Wednesday	Jumatano
One	Moja	Thursday	Alhamisi
Two	Mbili	Friday	Ijumaa
Three	Tatu	Saturday	Jumamosi
Four	Nne	Sunday	Jumapili

In Brief

Uganda national parks

The national parks of Uganda have been set aside by the government as wildlife and botanical sanctuaries that enjoy a high degree of protection and management. The 11,023 square kilometres (4,260 square miles) of national park land serve a conservational, educational, and recreational purpose for Ugandans and overseas visitors and form the mainstay of the country's tourism industry.

Uganda National Parks (UNP) is an organization incorporated under the National Parks Act of 1952. It is managed on behalf of the government by a Board of Trustees. It is structured to provide a degree of autonomy with public accountability. Despite the chaos that ruled Uganda for much of the last 20 years, Uganda National Parks somehow managed to survive as an essentially functional unit.

The government of Uganda has made considerable commitment to conservation and is firmly encouraging projects to reinforce management of the country's 10 national parks, with a plan eventually to merge the Uganda National Parks and the Game Department into one parastatal organization: the National Parks and Wildlife Service.

Until 1991 Uganda had only four national parks, occupying 2.8 per cent of the country's total area. But between May 1991 and October 1993, six new parks were established — a tremendous achievement for the nation. Today, 4.6 per cent of Uganda's total area is designated as national parks.

National parks are valued in Uganda for two principal reasons: they conserve representative samples of the nation's natural heritage, and they provide opportunities to sustain natural ecosystem processes through the conservation of the biodiversity on which these depend.

The Uganda government realizes that these areas not only have tremendous recreational and tourism potential but also, through good management, can generate a number of economic benefits — such as maintaining the environmental stability of the surrounding regions and providing research and complementary rural development opportunities.

The country also has a number of game, forest, and mountain reserves to protect those areas not designated as national parks but still important to the survival of the fauna and flora of Uganda.

Uganda National Parks
PO Box 3530
Kampala
Tel: 530158
Fax: 530159

Uganda Tourist Board
PO Box 7211
Kampala
Tel: 232971/2
Fax: 241247

National Parks

Bwindi Impenetrable National Park
Size: 331 sq km
District: Kisoro
Geographical location: South-western Uganda, 120 km north-east of Kabale
Altitude: 1,160–2,607 m
Physical features: The park is part of the Rukiga Highlands, formed by upsurges of the western Rift Valley. They consist of old, Precambrian rock, much eroded and altered. Bwindi also contains the 2-sq-km Mubwindi Swamp and a number of other, smaller swamps. Several trails cut through the park, one of which follows the Munyaga River as it tumbles down the steep slopes south-east of nearby Buhoma, flowing through a series of waterfalls. Zaire's Parc National des Virungas provides a spectacular backdrop, and on rare clear days Lake Edward and the Ruwenzori Mountains are visible.
Vegetation: Tropical rainforest with a very dense understorey of thick growth. The park has an extensive stand of bamboo (about 6 sq km). There are over 163 species of trees, 10 of which occur nowhere else in Uganda and 16 of which show very limited distribution elsewhere in Uganda.
Fauna: Although the park has at least 120 species of mammals, it is particularly known for its mountain gorillas. Other species present include chimpanzee, bushpig, giant forest hog, and two types of duiker. There are a few elephant.
Birdlife: 346 species, of which 184 are typical forest species. Seven species are listed as endangered. Of particular interest are the Kivu ground thrush, white-bellied robin chat, red-throated alethe, collared apalis, short-tailed warbler, yellow-eyed black flycatcher, Ruwenzori batis, blue-headed sunbird, strange weaver, and Shelly's crimsonwing.
Visitor facilities: In Buhoma, there is a community-run campground, a mid-range lodge, and two or three luxury tented camps. The nearest hotel accommodation is in Kabale, 120 km to the south-east.

Kibale National Park
Size: 766 sq km
District: Kabarole
Geographical location: Western Uganda, 35 km south of Fort Portal
Altitude: 1,110–1,590 m
Physical features: At the foot of the Ruwenzori Mountains, Kibale is a unique moist forest habitat. Guided forest walks lead you through the forest and along the Kanyanchu River.
Vegetation: Predominantly mature tropical rainforest, with some trees reaching heights of 55 m. Dominant tree species include *Parinari*, *Pteragota*, *Piptadeniastrum*, and *Cynometra* (ironwood). In valley bottoms, waterlogged soils support swamp forest characterized by lower tree diversity and an abundance of semi-woody plants. Wild coffee grows in the park, as does a variety of medicinal plants.
Fauna: The park supports a rich mammalian fauna that includes 12 species of primate, most notable of which is the chimpanzee. Other animals present include the bushbuck, red duiker, blue duiker, bushpig, and civet. Rarer species are the buffalo, giant forest hog, and forest elephant.
Birdlife: About 325 species of birds are reported in Kibale, a number of which are endemic.
Visitor facilities: Two private and three general campsites near the Kanyanchu Visitor Centre. There is basic lodging in the nearby trading centres of Bigodi and Nkingo, and the nearest hotel accommodation is in Fort Portal, 35 km to the north.

Kidepo Valley National Park
Size: 1,442 sq km
District: Kotido
Geographical location: In the north of the country, bordering Sudan and Kenya, between Nageya Valley and the hills of Karamoja
Altitude: 914–2,749 m
Physical features: The park consists of two shallow valley systems, with a rugged, dry mountain terrain. In the south-west of the park is the Narus Valley, bordered by the Napore range to the north-west. High ground separates this valley from the Kidepo Valley in the north-east. To the south of the Kidepo Valley is the Morungola range, and to the north is Mount Lotuke in Sudan. There is only one rainy season, which usually begins in April and ends in September.
Vegetation: There is a variety of habitats within the park, including montane forest, grassy plains, open tree savannah, dry thorn bush, thick miombo-like woodlands, borassus palm forest, and koppies (rocky outcrops).
Fauna: 80 species, with a wide diversity. Animals one can expect to see include zebra, large herds of elephant, eland, lesser kudu, dik-dik,

and buffalo. Oribi are abundant, as are the almost-tame Apoka waterbuck. A surprising 28 of these species do not exist in other parks in Uganda, such as the cheetah, greater kudu, and Bright's gazelle.

Birdlife: The official checklist includes 462 species, with koppies and forest patches providing refuge for interesting species. Two birds that are not in other Ugandan parks are the ostrich and kori bustard. Birds of prey include Verreaux's eagle, lammergeyer, and Egyptian vulture.

Visitor facilities: A campsite and basic lodge at Apoka.

Lake Mburo National Park

Size: 260 sq km
District: Mbarara
Geographical location: The southern section of the country, about 243 km south of Kampala off the main tarmac road.
Altitude: to 1,670 m
Physical features: In the west of the park are a series of rugged hills overlooking flat-bottomed, open valleys. In the east are lower, undulating hills broken by rocky outcrops. All is complemented by picturesque Lake Mburo and four smaller lakes, plus several others that lie just outside the southern park boundary.
Vegetation: A combination of acacia woodland, open grassland, and wetland.
Fauna: Animals likely to be seen include impala, buffalo, zebra, eland, topi, duiker, waterbuck, vervet monkey, baboon, klipspringer, rock hyrax, crocodile, and hippo. Also present are sitatunga, leopard, hyena, and jackal.
Birdlife: A wide variety of water and dry land species, including the rare shoebill stork, the Abyssinian ground hornbill, and the saddlebill stork. The forested areas of the park are home to Narina's trogon.
Visitor facilities: Bandas at park headquarters and three campsites.

Mgahinga Gorilla National Park

Size: 33.7 sq km
District: Kisoro
Geographical location: In the south-western corner of Uganda bordering Rwanda and Zaire
Altitude: to 4,127 m
Physical features: Part of the 420-sq-km Virunga Conservation Area, where half of the world's remaining mountain gorillas make their home. The park comprises three extinct volcanic mountains — Muhabura, Gahinga, and Sabyinyo — the peaks of which lie along Uganda's border with Rwanda. Three extensive swamps lie in the saddles between the volcanoes.
Vegetation: A typical afro-montane tropical rainforest, comprising a montane forest belt, a bamboo zone, an ericaceous belt, and an alpine zone.

Fauna: The park supports uniquely adapted animal species exhibiting a fairly high level of endemism. Mammals recorded include the endangered mountain gorilla, golden monkey, buffalo, elephant, black-fronted duiker, bushbuck, leopard, giant forest hog, side-striped jackal, Egyptian mongoose, serval cat, golden cat, and spotted hyena.
Birdlife: At least 185 species of birds have been recorded in the area, including 12 endemics. Among these are the handsome francolin, the Ruwenzori turaco, and the stripe-breasted tit.
Visitor facilities: Two campsites. The nearest hotel accommodation is in Kisoro or Kabale.

Mount Elgon National Park

Size: 1,145 sq km
District: Kapchorwa
Geographical location: Eastern Uganda on the border with Kenya
Altitude: to 4,321 m
Physical features: Mount Elgon is the shell of a volcano, with a large caldera. Jutting westwards from the main mountain extends the Nkonkonjeru peninsula, a ridge about 20 km long, which rises to about 2,350 m.
Vegetation: Four altitudinal belts common to afro-montane systems: afro-alpine, subalpine or heath, bamboo, and montane forest. Intriguing and unique plants include giant groundsel, giant lobelia, and giant heather. Bamboo forests grow in the southern and western parts of the park, and shoots can grow up to 15 m tall. There are also many beautiful wildflowers in the park.
Fauna: Although shy, many animals exist in the park, including buffalo, bushbuck, black-fronted duiker, tree hyrax, and bushpig. Leopard and hyena also live in the park, and elephant have recently been returning to the area from Kenya. Primates include blue monkey, baboon, and black-and-white colobus.
Birdlife: Many birds are present in the park. Particularly interesting and often sighted are Ross's turaco, casqued hornbill, gregarious hornbill, crowned eagle, and lammergeyer.
Visitor facilities: Simple campsites. Other accommodation is available in nearby Mbale.

Murchison Falls National Park

Size: 3,840 sq km
District: Masindi
Geographical location: North-western Uganda, some 300 km from Kampala, directly north of Masindi on the shores of Lake Albert
Altitude: to 1,292 m
Physical features: The Victoria Nile bisects the park from east to west for 115 km. About two-thirds of the way along this stretch of the river are the spectacular falls from which the park derives its name. The park's lush plains and

woodlands are home to growing herds of animals.

Vegetation: The park terrain is dominated by rolling savannah and tall grassland with increasingly thick bush and woodlands in the higher and wetter areas to the south and east. Closed canopy forest is restricted to the Rabongo area, where ironwood predominates, and to certain riparian localities along the south bank of the Nile.

Fauna: The original checklist of mammals in the park includes 55 species. Of these the white and the black rhinos have been wiped out. Other animal populations in the park are rapidly regaining their numbers, particularly elephant. Other resident animals include buffalo, Rothschild's giraffe, Uganda kob, hartebeest, waterbuck, oribi, bushbuck, Bohor reedbuck, sitatunga, bush duiker, warthog, and bushpig. There are six species of primates, including the chimpanzee. Large carnivores are represented by lion, leopard, and spotted hyena. Nile crocodiles often bask on the banks of the Nile within the park.

Birdlife: 424 species, including goliath heron, Egyptian goose, pelican, bee-eater, kingfisher, hornbill, cormorant, and the rare shoebill stork.

Visitor facilities: A rest camp with bandas and two campsites. The old lodges in the park were being renovated in 1996, and new ones were planned.

Queen Elizabeth National Park

Size: 2,000 sq km

District: Bushenyi

Geographical location: Bottom end of the western Rift Valley, between lakes Edward and George

Altitude: approx. 1,000 m

Physical features: The Kazinga Channel between lakes Edward and George physically divides the park into two sections, each of which has its own distinctive attractions. North of the main gate is the crater area, while on the eastern side of the main tarmac road are the wetlands of Lake George. The fascinating Chambura Gorge is also part of the park and offers unique walking opportunities. The south of the park is more heavily forested.

Vegetation: The park is filled with grass savannah, open bush country, riverine forest, lowland rainforest, and wetlands. The south of the park has open grasslands scattered with acacia trees and a remarkable floating fig forest that runs along the bank of Lake Albert.

Fauna: There are large numbers of game in the park, including bushbuck, Defassa waterbuck, banded mongoose, warthog, Uganda kob, elephant, buffalo, lion, hippo, black-and-white colobus, red-tailed monkey, chimpanzee and topi.

Birdlife: Avifauna is particularly rich along the Kazinga Channel, where pelican, saddlebill stork, fish eagle, cormorant, skimmer and kingfisher are often seen. The shoebill stork may be seen in the Lake George wetlands.

Visitor facilities: A lodge, a student's camp, and several campsites in the north sector of the park; there is one campsite in the south.

Ruwenzori Mountains National Park

Size: 996 sq km

District: Kasese

Geographical location: Western Rift Valley at Uganda's border with Zaire

Altitude: to 5,109 m

Physical features: Six peaks carrying permanent snow; three with glaciers. Trails provide excellent hiking possibilities through the afro-alpine areas, traversing mountains streams and circling a number of beautiful lakes.

Vegetation: Giant tree heathers, blackberry, cuckoo flower, everlasting flower, giant lobelia, giant groundsel, and a number of other plants unique to afro-alpine areas.

Fauna: Primates predominate, including chimpanzee, Ruwenzori colobus monkey, black-and-white colobus, and blue monkey. Other mammals present are elephant, bushbuck, giant forest hog, hyrax and leopard.

Birdlife: Some unique birds of the area are the Rwenzori turaco, handsome francolin, olive pigeon and white-necked raven.

Visitor facilities: Hostel at park headquarters; huts along the Central Circuit Trail. Nearest hotel accommodation is in Kasese.

Semuliki National Park

Size: 220 sq km

District: Bundibugyo

Geographical location: Western arm of the Rift Valley just below the northern ranges of the Ruwenzori Mountains.

Physical features: The park lies in the Semuliki Valley, where the land is low and flat. The Semuliki River marks the western boundary of the park and the border with Zaire. Sempaya hot springs and several other, smaller hot springs provide interesting micro-habitats.

Vegetation: The only park in Uganda composed primarily of tropical lowland forest. There are also clearings of grassland, bits of swamp, isolated stands of oil palm, acacia, or ironwood, and glimpses of bamboo swamp.

Fauna: The park contains elephant, buffalo, leopard, civet, scaly-tailed flying squirrel, bushbaby, hippo, and crocodile, as well as eight different species of primates. These include black-and-white colobus, red-tailed monkey, baboon, and vervet monkey.

Birdlife: There are around 400 species of birds in the park.

Visitor facilities: Two campsites. Nearest hotel accommodation is in Fort Portal.

Animal Checklist

Mammals

INSECTIVORES
(Insectivora)
Four-toed Hedgehog
Giant Elephant Shrew
Rufous Elephant Shrew
Short-snouted Elephant Shrew
Short-nosed Elephant Shrew
Ruwenzori Golden Mole
Otter Shrew

BATS
(Chiroptera)
Straw-coloured Fruit Bat
Pale-bellied Fruit Bat
Hammer-headed Fruit Bat
Mouse-tailed Bat
White-bellied Tomb Bat
Hollow-faced Bat
False Vampire Bat
Yellow-winged Bat
Lesser Leaf-nosed Bat
Banana Bat
Yellow-bellied Bat
Angola Free-tailed Bat
White-bellied Free-tailed Bat

PRIMATES
Prosimians
(Prosimii)
Greater Galago
Lesser Galago
Demidoff's Galago
Potto
Apes & Monkeys
(Anthropoidea)
Olive Baboon
Grey-cheeked Mangabey
Red-Tailed Monkey
Patas Monkey
Blue Monkey
Golden Monkey
DeBrazza's Monkey
L'Hoest's Monkey
Black-faced Vervet Monkey
Ruwenzori Colobus
Black-and-white Colobus
Red Colobus
Mountain Gorilla
Chimpanzee

AARDVARKS
(Tubulidentata)
Aardvark

PANGOLINS
(Pholidota)
Long-tailed Pangolin
White-bellied Pangolin
Giant Ground Pangolin
Temmincks Ground Pangolin

CARNIVORES
(Carnivora)
Hunting Dog (possibly)
Side-striped Jackal
Black-backed Jackal
Asiatic Jackal
Bat-eared Fox
White-naped Weasel
Striped Polecat
Ratel or Honey Badger
Zorilla
Spotted-necked Otter
Cape Clawless Otter
Congo Clawless Otter
Small-spotted Genet
Servaline Genet
Large-spotted Genet
Giant Genet
African Civet
Two-spotted Palm Civet
Egyptian Mongoose
Slender Mongoose
Marsh Mongoose
Banded Mongoose
Black-footed Mongoose
White-tailed Mongoose
Eastern Dwarf Mongoose
Pousargue's Mongoose
Striped Hyena
Spotted Hyena
Lion
Leopard
Cheetah
Caracal
Serval
African Wild Cat
Golden Cat

HYRAXES
(Hyracoidea)
Tree Hyrax
Rock Hyrax
Cape Rock Hyrax

ELEPHANTS
(Proboscidea)
African Elephant

HARES & RABBITS
(Lagomorpha)
Cape Hare
Whyte's Hare
Bunyoro Rabbit

ODD-TOED UNGULATES
(Perissodactyla)
Burchell's Zebra
Black Rhinoceros (possibly)

EVEN-TOED UNGULATES
(Artiodactyla)
Bushpig
Giant Forest Hog
Warthog
Hippopotamus
Rothschild's Giraffe
Red-flanked Duiker
Blue Duiker
Peters Duiker
Black-fronted Duiker
Yellow-backed Duiker
Common Duiker
Bates' Dwarf Antelope
Kirk's Dik-dik
Oribi
Klipspringer
Bushbuck
Sitatunga
Lesser Kudu
Greater Kudu
Eland
Defassa Waterbuck
Uganda Kob
Mountain Reedbuck
Bohor Reedbuck
Jackson's Hartebeest
Topi
Impala
African Buffalo

RODENTS   (Rodentia)
Alexander's Bush Squirrel
Boehm's Bush Squirrel
Mountain Tree Squirrel
Unstriped Ground Squirrel
Striped Ground Squirrel
Giant Forest Squirrel
Mountain Sun Squirrel
Gambian Sun Squirrel
Red-legged Sun Squirrel
Cuvier's Fire-footed Squirrel
Thomas's Tree Squirrel
Lord Derby's Flying Squirrel
Little Flying Squirrel
Beecroft's Flying Squirrel
Zenker's Flying Squirrel
African Brush-tailed Porcupine
South African Crested Porcupine
North African Crested Porcupine

Giant Gambian Rat
Emin's Giant Rat
Maned Rat
Cane Rat
Lesser Cane Rat
Kenya Mole Rat

Reptiles & Amphibians

Common Python
West African Python
House Snake
Blanding's Tree Snake
Boomslang
Forest Cobra
Tree Cobra
Jameson's Mamba
Olive-Green Night Adder
Carpet Viper
Gaboon Viper
Puff Adder
House Gecko
Chameleon
Two-striped Skink
Red-headed Agama Lizard
Nile Monitor
Long-nosed Crocodile
Broad-nosed Crocodile
Nile Crocodile
Nile Soft-shelled Turtle
Leopard Tortoise
Eastern Burrowing Bullfrog
Caecilians

Birds

OSTRICH
(Struthionidae)
Ostrich

GREBES
(Podicipidae)
Great Crested Grebe
Little Grebe

PELICANS
(Pelicanidae)
White Pelican
Pink-backed Pelican

CORMORANTS
(Phalacrocoracidae)
White-necked Cormorant
Long-tailed Cormorant

DARTERS
(Anhingidae)
African Darter

HERONS, EGRETS, BITTERNS
(Ardeidae)
Little Bittern
Dwarf Bittern
Night Heron
Squacco Heron
Cattle Egret
Great White Egret
Yellow-billed Egret
Little Egret
Grey Heron
Black-headed Heron
Goliath Heron
Purple Heron

WHALE-HEADED STORK
(Balaenicipitidae)
Whale-headed Stork

HAMERKOP
(Scopidae)
Hamerkop

STORKS
(Ciconiidae)
Abdim's Stork
Woolly-necked Stork
Saddlebill Stork
Openbill Stork
Marabou Stork
Yellow-billed Stork

IBISES & SPOONBILLS
(Threskiornithidae)
Sacred Ibis
Hadada Ibis
Glossy Ibis
African Spoonbill

DUCKS & GEESE
(Anatidae)
Fulvous Tree Duck
Egyptian Goose
Spur-winged Goose
Knob-billed Duck
Pygmy Goose
Hartlaub's Duck
Yellow-billed Duck
Red-billed Duck
Garganey Teal
European Shoveler
Hottentot Teal
African Pochard

SECRETARY BIRD
(Sagittariidae)
Secretary Bird

VULTURES, EAGLES, HAWKS
(Accipitridae)
Ruppell's Vulture
White-backed Vulture
Hooded Vulture
Egyptian Vulture
Lammergeyer
African Marsh Harrier
Harrier Hawk (Gymnogene)
Bateleur
Black-chested Harrier Eagle
Beaudouin's Harrier Eagle
African Goshawk
Western Little Sparrowhawk
Dark Chanting Goshawk
Gabar Goshawk
Long-tailed Hawk
Lizard Buzzard
Grasshopper Buzzard
Augur Buzzard
Red-necked Buzzard
Mountain Buzzard
Long-legged Buzzard
Long-crested Eagle
Crowned Eagle
Martial Eagle
Cassin's Hawk Eagle
Verreaux's Eagle
African Fish Eagle
Black Kite
Black-shouldered Kite
Swallow-tailed Kite

FALCONS   **(Falconidae)**
Red-necked Falcon
European Lesser Kestrel

GAME BIRDS
(Phasianidae)
Coqui Francolin
Nahan's Forest Francolin
Forest Francolin
Ring-necked Francolin
Crested Francolin
Shelley's Francolin
Redwing Francolin
Montane Francolin
Clapperton's Francolin
Heuglin's Francolin
Handsome Francolin
Red-necked Spurfowl
Yellow-necked Spurfowl
European Quail
Stone Partridge
Helmeted Guineafowl
Crested Guineafowl

BUTTON QUAILS
(Turnicidae)
Black-rumped Button Quail
Quail Plover

CRANES
(Balearicidae)
Crowned Crane
Sudan Crowned Crane

CRAKES, RAILS, & COOTS
(Rallidae)
Black Crake
Grey-throated Rail
Nkulengu Rail
Little Crake
White-spotted Crake
Boehm's Crake
Red-knobbed Coot

BUSTARDS
(Otididae)
Kori Bustard
Arabian Bustard
Buff-crested Bustard
White-bellied Bustard
Black-bellied Bustard
Hartlaub's Bustard

JACANAS
(Jacanidae)
African Jacana
Lesser Jacana

STONE CURLEWS
(Burhinidae)
Spotted Stone Curlew
European Stone Curlew
Senegal Stone Curlew
Watter Dikkop

PLOVERS
(Charadriidae)
Long-toed Lapwing
Blacksmith Plover
Spur-winged Plover
White-headed Plover
Senegal Plover
Crowned Plover
Wattled Plover
Kittlitz's Plover
Three-banded Plover
Forbes' Plover
Avocet

SNIPE & SANDPIPERS
(Scolopacidae)
African Snipe

PARROTS
(Psittacidae)
Grey Parrot
Brown Parrot
Rose-ringed Parrakeet
Red-headed Lovebird
Black-collared Lovebird

TURACOS
(Musophagidae)
Black-billed Turaco
White-crested Turaco
Rwenzori Turaco
Ross's Turaco
Great Blue Turaco
Eastern Grey Plaintain-eater
White-bellied Go-away-bird
Bare-faced Go-away-bird

COURSERS & PRATINCOLES
(Glareolidae)
Temminck's Courser
Egyptian Plover
Pratincole
White-collared Pratincole

GULLS & TERNS
(Laridae)
Grey-headed Gull
Whiskered Tern
White-winged Black Tern
African Skimmer

SANDGROUSE
(Pteroclididae)
Lichtenstein's Sandgrouse
Four-banded Sandgrouse

DOVES & PIGEONS
(Columbidae)
Speckled Pigeon
Olive Pigeon
White-naped Pigeon
Afep Pigeon
Bronze-naped Pigeon
Dusky Turtle Dove
Red-eyed Dove
Mourning Dove
Ring-necked Dove
Vinaceous Dove
Laughing Dove
Namaqua Dove
Tambourine Dove
Emerald-spotted Wood Dove
Blue-spotted Wood Dove
Black-billed Wood Dove
Green Pigeon
Bruce's Green Pigeon

CUCKOOS & COUCALS
(Cuculidae)
Red-chested Cuckoo
Black Cuckoo
Emerald Cuckoo
Didric Cuckoo
Klaas' Cuckoo
Yellow-throated Green
 Cuckoo
White-browed Coucal

Blue-headed Coucal
Senegal Coucal

OWLS
(Strigidae)
African Marsh Owl
Abyssinian Long-eared Owl
African Wood Owl
Verreaux's Eagle Owl
Spotted Eagle Owl
Fraser's Eagle Owl
Pearl-spotted Owlet
Red-chested Owlet
African Scops Owl

NIGHTJARS
(Caprimulgidae)
European Nightjar
Fiery-necked Nightjar
Abyssinian Nightjar
White-tailed Nightjar
Bates' Forest Nightjar
Long-tailed Nightjar
Gaboon Nightjar
Standard-winged Nightjar
Pennant-winged Nightjar

SWIFTS
(Apodidae)
Alpine Swift
African Swift
Scarce Swift
Little Swift
White-rumped Swift
Palm Swift
Sabine's Spinetail
Cassin's Spinetail

MOUSEBIRDS
(Colidae)
Speckled Mousebird
Blue-naped Mousebird

TROGONS (Trogonidae)
Narina's Trogon
Bar-tailed Trogon

KINGFISHERS
(Alcedinidae)
Giant Kingfisher
Pied Kingfisher
Shining-blue Kingfisher
Malachite Kingfisher
White-breasted Kingfisher
Pygmy Kingfisher
Dwarf Kingfisher
Woodland Kingfisher
Blue-breasted Kingfisher
Chocolate-backed Kingfisher
Striped Kingfisher
Grey-headed Kingfisher

BEE-EATERS
(Meropidae)
Carmine Bee-eater
Southern Carmine Bee-eater
Little Green Bee-eater
White-throated Bee-eater
Cinnamon-chested Bee-eater
Blue-breasted Bee-eater
Little Bee-eater
Red-throated Bee-eater
Black Bee-eater
Swallow-tailed Bee-eater

ROLLERS
(Coraciidae)
Lilac-breasted Roller
Abyssinian Roller
Rufous-crowned Roller
Blue-throated Roller
Blue-bellied Roller

HOOPOES
(Upupidae)
African Hoopoe
Senegal Hoopoe

WOOD HOOPOES & SCIMITARBILLS
(Phoeniculidae)
Green Wood Hoopoe
White-headed Wood Hoopoe
Forest Wood Hoopoe
Black Wood Hoopoe
African Scimitarbill
Abyssinian Scimitarbill

HORNBILLS
(Bucerotidae)
Grey Hornbill
Red-billed Hornbill
Jackson's Hornbill
Yellow-billed Hornbill
Hemprich's Hornbill
Crowned Hornbill
Pied Hornbill
Red-billed Dwarf Hornbill
Black Dwarf Hornbill
White-crested Hornbill
Wattled Black Hornbill
Black-and-white-casqued
   Hornbill
White-tailed Hornbill
White-thighed Hornbill
Ground Hornbill
Abyssinian Ground Hornbill

BARBETS
(Capitonidae)
Double-toothed Barbet
Black-breasted Barbet
Black-billed Barbet

Red-faced Barbet
Black-collared Barbet
White-headed Barbet
Spotted-flanked Barbet
Hairy-breasted Barbet
Red-fronted Barbet
Grey-throated Barbet
Yellow-spotted Barbet
Western Green Tinkerbird
Speckled Tinkerbird
Yellow-fronted Tinkerbird
Golden-rumped Tinkerbird
Yellow-throated Tinkerbird
Lemon-rumped Tinkerbird
Yellow-billed Barbet
D'Arnaud's Barbet

HONEYGUIDES
(Indicatoridae)
Greater Honeyguide
Lesser Honeyguide
Thick-billed Honeyguide
Lyre-tailed Honeyguide
Least Honeyguide
Chapin's Least Honeyguide
Willcock's Honeyguide
Spotted Honeyguide
Cassin's Honeyguide
Zenker's Honeyguide

WOODPECKERS
(Picidae)
Nubian Woodpecker
Little Spotted Woodpecker
Fine-banded Woodpecker
Brown-eared Woodpecker
Buff-spotted Woodpecker
Cardinal Woodpecker
Uganda Spotted Woodpecker
Gabon Woodpecker
Grey Woodpecker
Olive Woodpecker
Yellow-crested Woodpecker
Elliot's Woodpecker
Bearded Woodpecker
African Peculet

BROADBILLS
(Eurylaimidae)
African Broadbill
Red-sided Broadbill
Grauer's Green Broadbill

PITTAS
(Pittidae)
African Pitta
Green-breasted Pitta

LARKS
(Alaudidae)
Rufous-naped Lark

Redwing Bush Lark
Flappet Lark
Northern White-tailed Lark
Fawn-coloured Lark
Pink-breasted Lark
Red-capped Lark
Crested Lark
Thekia Lark

SWALLOWS & MARTINS
(Hirundinidae)
African Sand Martin
Banded Martin
African Rock Martin
Angola Swallow
Blue Swallow
Wire-tailed Swallow
Ethiopian Swallow
Mosque Swallow
Red-rumped Swallow
Rufous-chested Swallow
Striped Swallow
Grey-rumped Swallow
Black Roughwing Swallow
White-headed Roughwing
   Swallow

WAGTAILS & PIPITS
(Motacilidae)
African Pied Wagtail
Mountain Wagtail
Richard's Pipit
Plain-backed Pipit
Yellow-throated Longclaw

CUCKOO SHRIKES
(Campephagidae)
Black Cuckoo Shrike
Purple-throated Cuckoo Shrike
Red-shouldered Cuckoo Shrike
Petit's Cuckoo Shrike
White-breasted Cuckoo Shrike
Grey Cuckoo Shrike

BULBULS
(Pycnonotidae)
Yellow-vented Bulbul
Little Grey Greenbul
Cameroun Sombre Greenbul
Ansorge's Greenbul
Slender-billed Greenbul
Little Greenbul
Yellow-whiskered Greenbul
Olive-breasted Mountain
   Greenbul
Honeyguide Greenbul
Spotted Greenbul
Yellow-throated Leaflove
Joyful Greenbul
White-tailed Greenbul

Leaflove
Grey-olive Greenbul
Fischer's Greenbul
Xavier's Greenbul
Icterine Greenbul
White-throated Greenbul
Yellow-streaked Greenbul
Bristlebill
Green-tailed Bristlebill
Red-tailed Greenbul
Nicator
Yellow-throated Nicator

HELMET SHRIKES
(Prionopidae)
Straight-crested Helmet Shrike
Curly-crested Helment Shrike
Red-billed Shrike
White-crowned Shrike

SHRIKES
(Laniidae)
Northern Brubru
Black-backed Puffback
Puffback Shrike
Black-backed Puffback
Pink-footed Puffback
Black-headed Tchagra
Brown-headed Tchagra
Three-streaked Tchagra
Blackcap Tchagra
Luhder's Bush Shrike
Black-headed Gonolek
Yellow-crowned Gonolek
Slate-coloured Boubou
Sooty Boubou
Mountain Sooty Boubou
Grey-headed Bush Shrike
Grey Bush Shrike
Doherty's Bush Shrike
Multicoloured Bush Shrike
Yellow-billed Shrike
Emin's Shrike
Fiscal Shrike
Mackinnon's Grey Shrike
Grey-backed Fiscal
Taita Fiscal

THRUSHES, WHEATEARS,
& CHATS
(Turdidae)
Stonechat
Capped Wheatear
Red-tailed or Familiar Chat
Sooty Chat
Cliffchat
White-shouldered Black Chat
Little Rock Thrush
Red-backed Scrub Robin
Brown-backed Scrub Robin
Coll's Forest Robin

Spotted Morning Warbler
Morning Warbler
Brown-chested Alethe
Red-throated Alethe
Equatorial Akalat
Akalat
White-bellied Akalat
Forest Robin
White-starred Bush Robin
Robin Chat
Archer's Robin Chat
Grey-winged Robin Chat
Red-capped Robin Chat
Blue-shouldered Robin Chat
White-browed Robin Chat
Snowy-headed Robin Chat
Red-tailed Ant-thrush
White-tailed Ant-thrush
Rufous Flycatcher-thrush
African Thrush
Olive Thrush
Abyssinian Ground Thush

BABBLERS &
CHATTERERS
(Turdoididae)
Arrow-marked Babbler
Brown Babbler
Black-lored Babbler
Capuchin Babbler
Rufous Chatterer
Hill Babbler
Mountain Illadopsis
Brown Illadopsis
Pale-breasted Illadopsis
Scaly-breasted Illadopsis
Grey-chested Illadopsis

WARBLERS
(Sylviidae)
Cinnamon Bracken Warbler
Little Rush Warbler
Grauer's Rush Warbler
White-winged Rush Warbler
Bamboo Warbler
Broad-tailed Warbler
Greater Swamp Warbler
Lesser Swamp Warbler
Yellow Swamp Warbler
African Reed Warbler
Yellow Flycatcher-warbler
Mountain Yellow Flycatcher-
   warbler
African Moustached Warbler
Brown Woodland Warbler
Uganda Woodland Warbler
Red-faced Woodland Warbler
Singing Cisticola
Red-faced Cisticola
Rock-living Cisticola
Whistling Cisticola

Trilling Cisticola
Hunter's Cisticola
Chubb's Cisticola
Rattling Cisticola
Lynes' Cisticola
Winding Cisticola
Carruther's Cisticola
Stout Cisticola
Foxy Cisticola
Pectoral-patch Cisticola
Zitting Cisticola
Desert Cisticola
Wing-snapping Cisticola
Tawny-flanked Prinia
White-chinned Prinia
Banded Prinia
Redwing Warbler
Black-collared Apalis
Collared Apalis
Black-throated Apalis
Masked Apalis
Black-capped Apalis
Black-breasted Apalis
Green-tailed Apalis
Chestnut-throated Apalis
Grey Apalis
Black-backed Apalis
Karamoja Apalis
Grey-capped Warbler
Black-faced Rufous Warbler
Red-winged Grey Warbler
Grey-backed Camaroptera
Yellow-browed Camaroptera
Olive-green Camaroptera
Grey Wren Warbler
Yellow-bellied Eremomela
Green-cap Eremomela
Green-backed Eremomela
Brown-crowned Eremomela
White-browed Crombec
Green Crombec
Crombec
Red-faced Crombec
Yellow-bellied Hyliota
Southern Hyliota
Yellow Longbill
Grey Longbill
Green Hylia

FLYCATCHERS
(Muscicapidae)
Dusky Flycatcher
Swamp Flycatcher
Ashy Flycatcher
Yellow-footed Flycatcher
Dusky Blue Flycatcher
Sooty Flycatcher
Grey-throated Flycatcher
White-eyed Slaty Flycatcher
Shrike Flycatcher
Black and White Flycatcher

Forest Flycatcher
Black Flycatcher
Yellow-eyed Black Flycatcher
Silverbird
Grey Flycatcher
Chin-spot Flycatcher
Rwenzori Puffback Flycatcher
Wattle-eye Flycatcher
Jameson's Wattle-eye
Yellow-bellied Wattle-eye
Chestnut Wattle-eye
Chestnut-cap Flycatcher
Blue Flycatcher
White-tailed Crested Flycatcher
Blue-headed Crested Flycatcher
Dusky Crested Flycatcher
Paradise Flycatcher
Black-headed Paradise Flycatcher

TITS
(Paridae)
Grey Tit
White-breasted Tit
Black Tit
Dusky Tit
Stripe-breasted Tit
African Penduline Tit
Mouse-coloured Penduline Tit

SUNBIRDS
(Nectariniidae)
Little Green Sunbird
Olive Sunbird
Blue-headed Sunbird
Green-headed Sunbird
Blue-throated Sunbird
Green-throated Sunbird
Scarlet-chested Sunbird
Variable Sunbird
Greater Double-breasted Sunbird
Olive-bellied Sunbird
Tiny Sunbird
Regal Sunbird
Marique Sunbird
Shining Sunbird
Splendid Sunbird
Orange-tufted Sunbird
Northern Orange-tufted Sunbird
Copper Sunbird
Superb Sunbird
Malachite Sunbird
Scarlet-tufted Malachite Sunbird
Bronze Sunbird
Tacazze Sunbird
Golden-winged Sunbird
Purple-breasted Sunbird
Red-chested Sunbird
Beautiful Sunbird
Grey-headed Sunbird
Grey-chinned Sunbird
Kenya Violet-backed Sunbird

Violet-backed Sunbird
Collared Sunbird
Pygmy Long-tailed Sunbird

WHITE-EYES
(Zosteropidae)
Yellow White-eye

BUNTINGS
(Emberizidae)
Golden-breasted Bunting
Brown-rumped Bunting
Cinnamon-breasted Rock Bunting
House Bunting

FINCHES
(Fringillidae)
Yellow-fronted Canary
White-bellied Canary
Yellow-crowned Canary
Yellow-rumped Seed-eater
White-rumped Seed-eater
Brimstone Canary
Black-faced Canary
Papyrus Canary
African Citril
Streaky Seed-eater
Streaky-headed Seed-eater
Thick-billed Seed-eater
Oriole Finch

WAXBILLS
(Estrildidae)
Brown Twinspot
Dusky Firefinch
Green-backed Twinspot
Abyssinian Crimsonwing
Red-faced Crimsonwing
Dusky Crimsonwing
Shelley's Crimsonwing
Black-bellied Seed-cracker
Rothschild's Seed-cracker
Large-billed Seed-cracker
Grey-headed Negro Finch
Pale-fronted Negro Finch
Chestnut Negro Finch
White-breasted Negro Finch
Jameson's Hylia-finch
Grant's Bluebill
White-collared Oliveback
Grey-headed Oliveback
Green-winged Pytilia
Red-winged Pytilia
Orange-winged Pytilia
Yellow-bellied Waxbill
Fawn-breasted Waxbill
Black-crowned Waxbill
Black-headed Waxbill
Crimson-rumped Waxbill
Black-rumped Waxbill
Common Waxbill

Black-faced Waxbill
Purple Grenadier
Red-cheeked Cordon-bleu
Red-billed Firefinch
Black-faced Firefinch
Bar-breasted Firefinch
African Firefinch
Jameson's Firefinch
Black-bellied Firefinch
Zebra Waxbill
Quailfinch
Cut-throat
Silverbill
Grey-headed Silverbill
Bronze Mannikin
Black-and-white Mannikin
Magpie Mannikin

WEAVERS, SPARROWS, & WHYDAHS
(Ploceidae)
Pin-tailed Whydah
Steel-blue Whydah
Paradise Whydah
Indigo-bird
White-footed Indigo-bird
Grosbeak Weaver
Baglafecht Weaver
Stuhlmann's Weaver
Little Weaver
Slender-billed Weaver
Holub's Golden Weaver
Orange Weaver
Northern Brown-throated Weaver
Northern Masked Weaver
Masked Weaver
Vitelline Masked Weaver
Heuglin's Masked Weaver
Fox's Weaver
Black-headed Weaver
Viellot's Black Weaver
Maxwell's Black Weaver
Weyn's Weaver
Yellow-backed Weaver
Golden-backed Weaver
Chestnut Weaver
Compact Weaver
Dark-backed Weaver
Yellow-mantled Weaver
Spectacled Weaver
Black-necked Weaver
Black-billed Weaver
Strange Weaver
Brown-capped Weaver
Red-headed Malimbe
Gray's Malimbe
Red-bellied Malimbe
Crested Malimbe
Red-headed Weaver
Cardinal Quelea

Red-billed Quelea
Yellow-crowned Bishop
White-winged Widowbird
Red-collared Widowbird
Fan-tailed Widowbird
Yellow Bishop
Black Bishop
Black-winged Bishop
Yellow-shouldered Widowbird
Hartlaub's Marsh Widowbird
Yellow-mantled Widowbird
Red Bishop
West Nile Red Bishop
Parasitic Weaver
White-billed Buffalo Weaver
White-headed Buffalo Weaver
White-browed Sparrow Weaver
Chestnut-crowned Sparrow
    Weaver
Grey-headed Social Weaver
Rufous Sparrow
Grey-headed Sparrow
Chestnut Sparrow

Yellow-spotted Petronia
Bush Petronia
Speckle-fronted Weaver

STARLINGS
(Sturnidae)
Redwing Starling
Chestnut-wing Starling
Slender-billed Chestnut-wing
    Starling
Waller's Chestnut-wing Starling
Narrow-tailed Starling
Stuhlmann's Starling
Bristle-crowned Starling
Purple-headed Glossy Starling
Splendid Glossy Starling
Purple Glossy Starling
Bronze-tailed Starling
Ruppell's Long-tailed Starling
Violet-backed Starling
Sharpe's Starling
Magpie Starling
Superb Starling

Wattled Starling
Red-billed Oxpecker
Yellow-billed Oxpecker

ORIOLES
(Oriolidae)
Black-headed Oriole
Black-winged Oriole
Western Black-headed Oriole

DRONGOS
(Dicruridae)
Drongo
Velvet-mantled Drongo
Square-tailed Drongo

CROWS
(Corvidae)
Pied Crow
White-necked Raven
Fan-tailed Raven
Cape Rook
Piapiac

Adult male

Ostrich, *Struthio camelus*

Wildlife Profile

Uganda, where East African savannah meets the West African rainforest, has an amazing diversity of wildlife that reflects these different habitats. More than 50 large mammal species are found in the country, but there are even more smaller species that are equally as fascinating. What follows is an overview of some of the more interesting and commonly seen species and where in the country you are likely to see them.

Mammals

(Swahili name, if any, is indicated in parentheses after the species' Latin name.)

INSECTIVORES

Ruwenzori golden mole, *Chrysochloris stuhlmanni*: Has no tail or external ears and only rudimentary eyes. Found in Ruwenzori Mountains, Mgahinga, and Bwindi national parks, but usually only the edges of its tunnels in the soft forest soil are seen.

Ruwenzori otter shrew, *Micropotamogale ruwenzorii*: Prefers mountain streams in the Ruwenzoris, Mgahinga, and Bwindi. Burrows into stream banks and lines them with grass.

BATS

White-bellied free-tailed bat, *Tadarida limbata*: Roosts in colonies, generally in roofs of buildings, but sometimes in hollow trees and in cliffs.

Straw-coloured fruit bat, *Eidolon helvum*: Sometimes thousands occupy a single roost, usually in a tree. One such colony exists in a eucalyptus plantation within the Kampala city boundary.

Hammer-headed fruit bat, *Hypsignathus monstrosus*: More uncommon. Prefers forested areas. It is found most often at Entebbe, usually seen at dusk when flying to feeding areas.

PRIMATES

Greater galago or **bushbaby,** *Galago crassicaudatus* (Komba): Widely distributed. Gallery highland forests and bamboo thickets. Nocturnal. Can be often heard wailing and

screaming. **Lesser galago** or **Senegal bushbaby,** *Galago senegalensis*, is more gregarious. Found in savannah and woodland trees. Tiny **Demidoff's galago,** *Galago demidovi*, is found in western forests. **Eastern needle-clawed galago,** *Galago inustus*, is in Bwindi and Mgahinga national parks.

Potto, *Perodicticus potto*: Nocturnal, rarely seen. Found in Uganda's rainforests. Bwindi, Mgahinga national parks.

Olive baboon, *Papio anubis* (Nyani): Terrestrial and arboreal. Rocky bush and savannah, acacia woodland, gallery forests. Bwindi, Kibale, Lake Mburo, Mount Elgon, Murchison, Semuliki national parks.

Grey-cheeked mangabey, *Cercocebus albigena*: Rainforest species. Prefers vicinity of lakes, rivers. Kibale National Park.

Red-tailed or **black-cheeked white-nosed monkey,** *Cercopithecus schmidti*: Common in Uganda's forests. Essentially arboreal, gregarious. Long red tail, white nose. Bwindi, Kibale, Semuliki national parks.

Patas monkey, *Erythrocebus patas*: Bush, savannah ground-dweller. Trees and termite hills used as vantage points. More common in east and north of country.

Blue monkey, *Cercopithecus mitis stuhlmanni* (Kima): Overall deep blue-grey; large. Prefers deciduous mountain forests. Often associates with other monkey species. Bwindi, Kibale, Mount Elgon, Ruwenzori national parks.

Golden monkey, *Cercopithecus mitis kandti* (Kima): Rare, very beautiful. Entire back greenish-gold merging to orange on flanks, limbs and end of tail black. In East Africa found only in south-western Uganda's mountain bamboo forests. Mgahinga Gorilla National Park.

DeBrazza's monkey, *Cercopithecus neglectus* (Kalasinga): Rain, mountain, and swampy forests, especially bamboo growths and palm swamps. Bwamba Forest; Mount Elgon National Park.

L'Hoest's monkey, *Cercopithecus l'hoesti*: Semi-terrestrial. Mountain and lowland forests, particularly dense forest with clearings. Favours trees high on mountains for sleeping. Bwindi, Kibale national parks.

Black-faced vervet monkey, *Cercopithecus aethiops centralis* (Tumbili): Common and widespread. Favours acacia woodland along streams, rivers, and lakes. Arboreal and terrestrial. Gregarious, often in large troops. Lake Mburo, Semuliki national parks.

Black-and-white colobus, *Colobus polykomos* (Mbega): Distinctive black-and-white long fur and tail. All types of forest, moist savanna. Several races occur in Uganda, including the **Ruwenzori colobus,** *Colobus polykomos ruwenzorii*. Bwindi, Kibale, Mount Elgon, Murchison, Queen Elizabeth, Ruwenzori, Semuliki national parks.

Red colobus, *Colobus badius:* Reddish-brown coat. Much rarer than black-and-white colobus. All types of forest, in both higher and lower tiers, sometimes also in dense secondary forest undergrowth and on ground. Permanent water nearby necessary. Found almost exclusively in Kibale National Park, at high density.

Mountain gorilla, *Gorilla gorilla beringei* (Makaku): Population greatly threatened, only about 600 animals still remaining. Rainforests with dense herbage and bushy undergrowth, also secondary forest and near plantations. Bwindi, Mgahinga national parks.

Chimpanzee, *Pan troglodytes schweinfurthi* (Soko): Long-haired variety. Forest-dweller. Needs rich, all-year-round food supply. When mountain gorillas present, chimpanzees live at lower levels of forest. Found in Budongo Forest; also Bwindi, Kibale, Murchison, Queen Elizabeth, and Ruwenzori national parks.

CARNIVORES

Hunting dog, *Lycaon pictus* (Mbwa mwitu): Diurnal, gregarious. Rarely seen, if in fact still in existence in Uganda. Open savannahs, plains to semi-deserts, mountains to 3000 m. Possibly Kidepo Valley, Queen Elizabeth national parks.

Side-striped jackal, *Canus adustus* (Bweha): Chiefly nocturnal. Savannahs and plains, with plentiful cover of bush, or open woodland. Found around Lake Victoria and in south-west. Bwindi, Mgahinga, and possibly Lake Mburo national parks.

Black-backed jackal, *Canis mesomelas* (Bweha): Well-defined black back. Open plains, bush country, light woodlands. Diurnal and nocturnal. Mates for life. Lake Mburo, Kidepo Valley national parks.

Asiatic jackal, *Canis aureus* (Bweha): Also known as common or golden jackal. Open country with good cover. Follows human settlements. Diurnal and nocturnal. Found in north of country. Kidepo Valley National Park.

Bat-eared fox, *Otocyon megalotis* (Bweha masigio): Distinctive large ears. Prefers sandy country, grass and bush steppe, savannah. Active mainly at dusk or in night. Mates for life. Widely distributed but rarely seen. Kidepo Valley National Park.

Ratel, *Mellivora capensis* (Nyegere): Also known as honey badger. Normally nocturnal. Solitary or in pairs; terrestrial. All habitats from desert to rainforest, mountains to 3,000 m. Widespread but rarely seen.

Spotted-necked otter, *Lutra maculicollis* (Fisi maji): Widely distributed. Rivers, lake shores, papyrus marshes, reed beds, and quiet backwaters. Especially common around Lake Victoria and Lake Bunyonyi.

Cape clawless otter, *Aonyx capensis* (Fisi maji): Inhabits standing and running water in forests, savannahs, plains, steppes; mountains to 3,000 m. Nocturnal and partially diurnal. Shy and not often seen. Not as common in Uganda as spotted-necked otter.

Small-spotted genet, *Genetta genetta* (Kanu): Long-bodied, spotted, catlike. Long banded tail, dorsal crest. Terrestrial and arboreal. Active at dusk and in night. Most frequent in bush country and acacia woodland.

Servaline genet, *Genetta servalina:* Inhabits dense woodlands and forests. Terrestrial, not arboreal. Found in western Uganda.

Large-spotted genet, *Genetta tigrina* (Kanu): Large spots, no dorsal crest. Melanistic examples frequent. Terrestrial and arboreal. Forest edges, forest clearings, moist savannahs, bush country, agricultural regions, reed thickets, long grass. Favours water and swampy areas. Found in suitable areas throughout Uganda.

Giant genet, *Genetta victoriae:* Largest genet. Long-legged, medium-length spinal crest. Thick ringed tail. Found in dense forest areas such as Bwamba Forest.

African civet, *Viverra civetta* (Fungo): Large, size of medium dog. Ringed tailed; stripes and spots on body. Nocturnal and terrestrial. Found in forest, moist and dry savannah, farmland, plains, and hills. Prefers to be near water. Usually solitary.

Seldom seen. Bwindi, Kibale, Semuliki national parks.

Two-spotted palm civet, *Nandinia binotata:* Genet-like in build, but muzzle shorter and tail longer. Solitary; good climber. Active at dusk or by night. Inhabits rainforests in lowlands and mountains to 2,000 m. Found in the rainforests of western and southern Uganda.

Egyptian mongoose, *Herpestes ichneumon* (Nguchiro): Venerated in ancient Egypt. Predominantly diurnal. Habitat varies from rainforest to semi-deserts, moist and dry savannahs, steppes, and mountains to 2,000 m. Prefers vicinity of water. Found in suitable locations throughout Uganda. Mgahinga Gorilla National Park.

Slender mongoose, *Herpestes sanguineus* (Nguchiro): Hunts by day and at dusk. Inhabits all types of country from desert to rainforest, mountains to 3,000 m. Prefers dense cover and nearby water. Sometime follows settlements. Found in suitable locations throughout Uganda.

Marsh mongoose, *Herpestes paludinosus* (Nguchiro): Active at night, sometimes also by day. Spends much time by or in water. Swamps, marshes, and other wet areas in savannah or forest, up to 2,000 m. Found throughout Uganda in suitable locations.

Banded mongoose, *Mungos mungo* (Gitschiro): Diurnal. Likes sun-bathing in morning. Dry and moist savannahs. Prefers vicinity of water; avoids closed forests. Kidepo Valley, Queen Elizabeth national parks.

Black-footed mongoose, *Bdeogale nigripes jacksoni* (Nguchiro): Mainly nocturnal. Solitary or in pairs. Terrestrial. Voice like a dog baying. Lives in rainforests, up to 2,000 m in mountains. South-east Uganda; Bwindi and Mgahinga national parks.

White-tailed mongoose, *Ichneumia albicauda* (Karambago): Large, thickset. Mainly nocturnal. Moist and dry savannahs, dense bush, forest edges, other areas rich in cover. Often near water, sometimes near villages. Not in rainforests or desert areas. Solitary or in pairs. Found in suitable locations throughout Uganda.

Pousargue's mongoose, *Dologale dybowskii:* Dark brown with bushy tail. Lives in savannahs. Found in northern Uganda. Kidepo Valley National Park.

Striped hyena, *Hyaena hyaena* (Fisi): Generally rare. Black transverse stripes on sides of body. Nocturnal. Favours dry, broken bush country. Possibly Kidepo Valley National Park.

Spotted hyena, *Crocuta crocuta* (Fisi): Mainly active at dusk and by night; also hunt by day in some areas. Semi-desert to moist savannah, not in closed forest. Mountains to 4,500 m. Rarely solitary, often in packs or large troops. Eerie, wailing call at night. Kidepo Valley, Lake Mburo, Mgahinga, Mount Elgon, Murchison national parks.

Lion, *Panthera leo* (Simba): Lazy, rests for about 20 hours in each 24. Where undisturbed may be active by day, where hunted entirely nocturnal. Open country from semi-desert to dry and moist savannah, not in closed forests, in mountains to 4,500 m. Kidepo Valley, Murchison, Queen Elizabeth national parks.

Leopard, *Panthera pardus* (Chui): Where undisturbed, active by day and night; where hunted, very secretive and nocturnal. Likes to sun itself on trees or rocks. Climbs well. Inhabits all types of country from desert to rainforest, from lowland plains to 4,500 m on mountains. Solitary. Lake Mburo, Mgahinga, Mount Elgon, Murchison, Ruwenzori, Semuliki national parks.

Cheetah, *Acinonyx jubatus* (Duma): Diurnal. Chief hunting times morning and late afternoon. Solitary, in pairs, or family parties. Open country from desert to dry savannah, including open bush country. Sometimes moist savannah, highlands to 2,000 m. Kidepo Valley National Park.

Caracal, *Caracal caracal* (Sibamangu): Nocturnal, but sometimes observed by day. Solitary. Mainly terrestrial, but can climb trees. Inhabits open country in lowlands, hill, mountains. In Uganda confined to drier areas, most frequent in Karamoja. Kidepo Valley National Park.

Serval, *Leptailurus serval* (Mondo): Mainly nocturnal and terrestrial, but can climb trees. Solitary. Tawny yellow with black spots and short, black-ringed tail. Found in many different types of country but favours scattered bush, tall grass, and dry reedbeds near streams. Not uncommon on montane moorlands. Mgahinga Gorilla National Park.

African wild cat, *Felis silvestris* (Kimburu): Solitary, nocturnal but sometimes observed by day. Terrestrial; partly arboreal. All types of country from semi-desert to rainforest, mountains to 4,000 m. Often near villages and interbreeds with domestic cats. Found in suitable locations throughout Uganda.

Golden cat, *Profelis aurata:* Forest species, rare in East Africa. Solitary, Mainly terrestrial. Nocturnal. Found on Mount Elgon and the forests of the Ruwenzori Mountains; also south-western

Kigezi. Most frequent on the alpine moorlands of the Ruwenzoris. Bwindi, Mgahinga, Mount Elgon, Ruwenzori national parks.

AARDVARKS

Aardvark, *Orycteropus afer* (Muhanga): Also known as ant bear. Entirely nocturnal. Solitary. Grotesque, thickset, with strong digging claws. Extremely long tongue used for feeding upon ants and termites. Seldom seen. Terrestrial. Found throughout Uganda in areas where termite mounds are present.

HYRAXES

Tree hyrax, *Dendrohyrax arboreus* (Perere): Also known as tree dassie. Usually in pairs. Arboreal, although Ruwenzori race are rock dwellers. Long, soft fur. Mainly nocturnal. Emits ear-piercing shrieks, resembling a child's scream, for short periods at beginning of night and again in early morning to mark territory. Found in all types of forest. Mount Elgon, Ruwenzori national parks.

Rock hyrax, *Heterohyrax brucei* (Pimbi): Also known as Bruce's hyrax. Much shorter-haired than tree hyrax. Often seen sunbathing on rocks and boulders. Gregarious, lives in colonies. Mainly terrestrial, but able to climb trees. Although diurnal, usually feeds at night. Plains, mountains to 2,500 m, forests, savannahs, steppes. Found in suitable locations throughout Uganda.

ELEPHANTS

African elephant, *Loxodonta africana* (Tembo): Gregarious, in small or large herds; bulls often solitary. Two types: forest elephant (*cyclotis*), which is smaller with rounded ears and inhabits rainforest areas, and bush elephant (*africana*) elsewhere in range, which is now confined mainly to dry savannah regions. Occurs in all Uganda national parks except Lake Mburo.

ODD-TOED UNGULATES

Burchell's zebra, *Hippotigris quagga* (Punda milia): Pony-like with broad stripes. Gregarious, in herds. Occurs on open grassy plains, savannah grasslands, and semi-arid grass-bush. In Uganda confined mainly to Karamoja. Kidepo Valley, Lake Mburo national parks.

Black rhinoceros, *Diceros bicornis* (Kifaru): Prehensile upper lip. Browser. Exterminated from much of previous range. Usually inhabits dry thickly bushed country with scattered trees or copses, but also grassland with little cover and thickly wooded areas such as mountain forest up to 3,500 m. May still be a few in Kidepo Valley National Park.

EVEN-TOED UNGULATES

Bushpig, *Potamochoerus porcus* (Nguruwe): Nocturnal. Gregarious or solitary. Relatively short, knife-like tusks. Common but seldom seen. Inhabits highland forest and rainforest, riverine woodlands and dense bush, to 3,000 m. Bwindi, Kibale, Mount Elgon, Murchison national parks.

Giant forest hog, *Hylochoerus meinertzhageni* (Nguruwe): Large, thickset, covered with coarse black hair. Well-developed tusks. Mainly nocturnal. Gregarious or solitary. Highland forests and rainforests to 3,000 m. Bwindi, Kibale, Mgahinga, Ruwenzori national parks.

Warthog, *Phacochoerus aethiopicus* (Ngiri): Large wart-like growths on sides of face. Well-developed tusks. Holds tail straight up when running or about to move. Prefers treeless open plains and light savannahs, avoiding dense cover or steep slopes. Up to 2,500 m in mountains. Likes water for bathing and drinking but can do without. Diurnal. Gregarious, usually in family parties. Kidepo Valley, Lake Mburo, Murchison, Queen Elizabeth national parks.

Hippopotamus, *Hippopotamus amphibius* (Kiboko): Generally gregarious. Inhabits lakes, swamps, and rivers with sufficient water, usually near grassy plains for grazing at night. Lake Mburo, Murchison, Queen Elizabeth, Semuliki national parks.

Rothschild's giraffe, *Giraffa camelopardalis rothschildi* (Twiga): Also known as the Uganda giraffe. Legs usually unmarked below the knees. Open acacia woodland, up to 2,000 m from sparsely wooded grasslands to thickly overgrown savannah. Kidepo Valley, Murchison national parks.

Red-flanked duiker, *Cephalophus rufilatus:* Both sexes with horns, although female's very small. Woodland edges and clearings, gallery forest strips, thickets in open country. Not in closed inner regions of large forests. Found in western Uganda.

Blue duiker, *Cephalophus monticola* (Paa): Also known as Maxwell's duiker. Horns in both sexes but sometimes absent in females. Occurs singly or in pairs. Diurnal and nocturnal. Large and small forests, bush and gallery forest, thickets in open country. Kibale National Park.

Peters duiker, *Cephalophus callipygus:* Also known as Harvey's duiker. Horns in both sexes. Inhabits all types of forest, also bush thickets and grassy savannah jungles, on mountains to 3,000 m. Prefers vicinity of water. Mount Elgon National Park.

Black-fronted duiker, *Cephalophus nigrifrons:* Both sexes horned. Swampy forest lands with dense undergrowth. Bwindi, Mgahinga, Mount Elgon national parks.

Yellow-backed duiker, *Cephalophus sylvicultor:* Similar horns in both sexes. Moist forests with dense undergrowth, gallery forests, sometimes small savannah woodlands. Bwindi Impenetrable National Park.

Common duiker, *Cephalophus grimmia* (Nsua): Also known as grey or bush duiker. Usually nocturnal, sometimes diurnal. Solitary or in pairs. Male with horns, female sometimes. Variety of habitats from alpine moorlands and forest to woodlands, scrub, and bush country. Lake Mburo, Murchison national parks.

Bates' dwarf antelope, *Neotragus batesi:* Hare-sized. Horns only in male. Moist forest regions. Western Uganda.

Kirk's dik-dik, *Rhynchotragus kirkii* (Dikidiki): Horns in male only. Diurnal. Usually in pairs or family parties. Desert grass-bush and scrub, mixed grass-woodland. Found only in northern Uganda. Kidepo Valley National Park.

Oribi, *Ourebia ourebi* (Taya): Diurnal. Horns in males only. Occurs singly, in pairs, or small groups. Grasslands, mixed grass and bush, hill slopes, mountains to 3,000 m. Plentiful in north and west, especially abundant in Murchison Falls National Park. Also Kidepo Valley and Lake Mburo national parks.

Klipspringer, *Oreotragus oreotragus* (Mbuzi mawe): Horns in male only. Occurs on rocky hills and outcrops, singly or in small parties. Thick bush as refuge important. Lake Mburo National Park.

Bushbuck, *Tragelaphus scriptus* (Pongo): Only males with horns. Prefer thicket-rich country of any type, to 4,000 m. Also plantations and gardens. Kibale, Mgahinga, Mount Elgon, Murchison, Queen Elizabeth, Ruwenzori national parks.

Sitatunga, *Tragelaphus spekei:* Horns in male only. Shy and difficult to observe. Inhabits dense papyrus swamps. Occurs singly or in family parties. When alarmed often submerges below surface with only nostrils showing. Most frequent in papyrus swamps surrounding Ssese Islands and other localities fringing lakes Victoria and George. Lake Mburo, Murchison national parks.

Lesser kudu, *Tragelaphus imberbis* (Tandala ndogo): Spiral horns, in male only. Arid bush country. Rare in Uganda, found only in north. Kidepo Valley National Park.

Greater kudu, *Tragelaphus strepsiceros* (Tandala mkubwa): Large, majestic antelope with open spiral horns in male. Gregarious. Woodland and thickets, especially in broken, hilly country in semi-desert bush. In Uganda confined to hills in north-east. Kidepo Valley National Park.

Eland, *Tragelaphus oryx* (Pofu): Spiral horns in both sexes. Large, ox-sized antelope with prominent dewlap, particularly in older males. Open plains country, grassland, and semi-desert grass-bush. Gregarious. Kidepo Valley and Lake Mburo national parks.

Defassa waterbuck, *Kobus ellipsiprymnus defassa* (Kuru): Only males horned. White patch on rump. Gregarious; diurnal. Inhabits grassy areas near water and riverine woodland. Locally common in Uganda, especially in Queen Elizabeth National Park. Also Kidepo Valley, Lake Mburo, Murchion national parks.

Uganda kob, *Adenota kob thomasi:* Horns in male only. Diurnal; gregarious. Open grassy plains and tree-grasslands. Queen Elizabeth, Murchison national parks.

Mountain reedbuck, *Redunca fulvorufula chanleri* (Tohe): Greyish in colour; males have short horns. Diurnal, usually in small groups. Open grasslands on hills and mountains to 3,600 m. Kidepo Valley National Park.

Bohor reedbuck, *Redunca redunca* (Tohe): Horns in male only. Occurs singly or in small groups. Prefers marshy surroundings and areas of lush grass. Murchison Falls National Park.

Jackson's hartebeest, *Alcelaphus buselaphus jacksoni* (Kongoni): Horns in both sexes. Tawny-red. Open plains and grasslands with scattered bush and trees. Kidepo Valley, Lake Mburo, Murchison national parks.

Topi, *Damaliscus lunatus topi* (Nyamera): Similar to hartebeest but blackish patches on limbs. Horns in both sexes. Gregarious. Open grassy plains, tree-grasslands, scattered bush, light woodlands. Lake Mburo, Queen Elizabeth national parks.

Impala, *Aepyceros melampus* (Swala pala): Horns in male only. Diurnal and nocturnal. Gregarious.

Grass-woodland, riverine bush, arid grass-bush. In Uganda found only in Lake Mburo National Park.

African buffalo, *Syncerus caffer* (Nyati): Massive, cattle-like. Gregarious. Variety of habitats from forest to open grassy plains and reed beds bordering rivers and swamps. Kibale, Kidepo Valley, Lake Mburo, Mgahinga, Mount Elgon, Murchison, Queen Elizabeth, Semuliki national parks.

HARES & RABBITS

Cape hare, *Lepus capensis* (Sungura): Also known as African hare. Solitary, nocturnal. Frequents open ground, including grasslands, bush, and sparse woodlands. Found in suitable locations throughout Uganda.

Whyte's hare, *Lepus whytei* (Sungura): Savannah, dry bush, plains, semi-desert, and desert. Open dry, sandy regions in plains and hills preferred. Found in suitable locations throughout Uganda.

Bunyoro rabbit, *Poelagus marjorita*: Also known as Uganda grass hare. Shorter ears and legs than Cape hare. Solitary, nocturnal. Open grass-bush country. Can always be seen on the Masindi–Butiaba road after dark. Murchison Falls National Park.

RODENTS

Unstriped ground squirrel, *Xerus rutilus*: Solitary or in pairs. Terrestrial, diurnal. Sandy, semi-desert bush country. Kidepo Valley National Park.

Striped ground squirrel, *Xerus erythropus*: Terrestrial. White flank stripe. Diurnal. Sandy, arid bush country. Found in the vicinity of Lake Victoria, Mount Elgon, Bunyoro.

Mountain sun squirrel, *Heliosciurus ruwenzorii*: Dark grey, lightly speckled. Mountain forests around lakes Albert and Edward. Ruwenzori Mountains National Park.

Lord Derby's flying squirrel, *Anomalurus fraseri* (Kipepeo): Also known as scaly-tailed flying squirrel. Membrane enables animal to glide from one tree to another. Forests, bush woodland, mountains to 2,400 m. Found in forests in Buganda, Bunyoro, Toro districts. Semuliki National Park.

African brush-tailed porcupine, *Atherurus africanus* (Nungu): Tail ends in tuft of soft flattened bristles. Western Uganda forests.
South African crested porcupine, *Hystrix africae-australis* and **North African crested porcupine,**

Hystrix cristata (Nungu): Overlapping territories near equator. South African species does not occur in rainforests; North African species does. Strictly nocturnal. Solitary, terrestrial. Found in suitable locations throughout Uganda.

Giant Gambian rat, *Cricetomys gambianus* (Buku): Large, terrestrial, nocturnal. Generally occurs singly. Forests, wooded areas, dense bush. Found in northern Uganda.

Cane rat, *Thryonomys swinderianus*: Mainly nocturnal, terrestrial. Solitary or in small parties. Inhabits elephant grass and similar vegetation, including sugar cane cultivation. Found in suitable locations throughout Uganda.

Reptiles & Amphibians

Although many species are seldom seen by the average visitor, Uganda is also rich in snakes, lizards, turtles, frogs, and other reptiles and amphibians. Bwindi Impenetrable National Park alone is home to at least 14 species of snakes, 27 species of frogs and toads, 6 chameleons, and 14 lizards, skinks, and geckos. Listed here are some of the more noteworthy species found in the country.

African python: Also known as the common python. Large and widespread. Common about water and swamps, swimming readily. Specimens up to 6 m have been widely recorded. Regularly take mammals up to the size of a large dog.

West African python: Smaller than the common python. Beautifully coloured. Recorded in western Uganda.

Blanding's tree snake: Back-fanged colubrid with fast-acting venom. Commonly longer than 2.5 m. Black or brown. Widespread in Uganda's forests.

Forest cobra: Also known as the black-and-white-lipped cobra. A species of forests and wetter types of vegetation. Likes water. Shiny black, frequently longer than 2.5 m.

Tree cobra: West African forest species found in the lowland forests of Uganda. Black with cream-coloured sides of face and belly. Arboreal. Dangerously aggressive.

Jameson's mamba: Bright green, arboreal, extremely venomous. Last third of its length is black. West African snake with range extending into Uganda.

Olive-green night adder: Found in Uganda's forests. Head wider than neck. Dull olive-green overall. Terrestrial. Moderately poisonous.

Carpet viper: Also known as the saw-scaled viper. Dull grey-brown with pale diamond pattern down its back. Found in north-eastern Uganda. Extremely toxic venom.

Puff adder: Widely distributed throughout savannah and woodlands below 2,400 m. Broad, flat head. Extremely venomous.

Gaboon viper: Bigger and fatter than the puff adder. Beautifully coloured. Occurs in the warm forests of lowland Uganda.

House gecko: Ever-present in houses throughout East Africa. Harmless; eats insects.

Chameleons: A variety of chameleons occurs in Uganda Six different chameleons have been recorded in Bwindi Impenetrable National Park; many others exists in the other parks, including the **three-horned chameleon**.

Nile monitor: Large, slender-built lizard, up to 2 m long. Olive-green flecked with yellow. Lives near water. Climbs and swims well.

Long-nosed crocodile: A secretive species known from western Uganda. Distinguished from other African species by its long, slender snout. Seldom longer than 2 m.

Broad-nosed crocodile: Dark-coloured; seldom longer than 2 m. Found in extreme western Uganda. Stubby, broad snout and a somewhat upturned nose.

Nile crocodile: Most widely distributed of the three East African species. May grow to 5 m long. Found in most of Uganda's rivers and lakes.

Nile soft-shelled turtle: Occurs in the Nile drainage downstream of Murchison Falls and the Semuliki River. Large; up to 30 kg.

Leopard tortoise: Most common land tortoise in region. Mottled black and yellow carapace.

Eastern burrowing bullfrog: Large and widely distributed. A savannah species, active only during wet seasons.

Insects & Arachnids

As rich in insect life as in any other type of wildlife, Uganda is particularly noted for its beautiful **butterflies** and **moths**. More than 202 species of butterflies have been identified in Bwindi Impenetrable National Park, some 300 in Semuliki, and 144 in Kibale. Of particular note are the **Congo long-tailed blue butterfly** and the huge **'moon moth'**, known from the rainforests and woodlands of the western part of the country.

Among the most conspicuous of all beetles in the region are those of the family Scarabaeidae — the **dung beetles**. Commonly large, of grotesque shape, armed with horns and spikes, these beetles appear with the rains searching for herbivore dung, into which they lay their eggs.

The order Hymenoptera includes all the ants, wasps, and bees. For sheer numbers within a colony, honours must go to the ants — in particular those known as **safari, army,** or *siafu* in the genus *Dorylus*. Renowned the length and breadth of Eastern Africa, these vicious, omnivorous insects instil fear and cause discomfort whenever they appear. A colony of siafu may contain twenty million individuals and weigh 20 kgs. Humans unfortunate enough to cross their path will be bitten, although the bite is only momentarily painful and otherwise harmless.

Probably the best known of all social insects world-wide is the honey bee. **African honey bees** are reputed to be particularly fierce, and are thought to account for more deaths annually in Eastern African than snake bites.

The largest spider in Eastern Africa is *Megalamorphida cithariscius crawshayi*. The female of this vast, hairy species has a body the size of a small pear and thick legs. They are residents of lowland, dry savannahs and live in underground burrows. Also impressive are the **'baboon' spider,** which lives in tunnels in many lawns, and the **'wolf spider'**, which is large, hairy, and aggressive. It bites and is considered highly poisonous.

Some 50 species of **scorpion** occur in Eastern Africa, most in warm, dry areas; shunning forests. They are mostly active at night. Scorpion stings are extremely painful but rarely fatal.

Centipedes and **millipedes** are common, widely distributed, and found in most terrestrial environments. Millipedes are harmless in general, while centipedes can inflict an extremely painful bite.

Birds

Uganda is one of the best countries in Africa for birds, with about 1,000 species recorded in its relatively small area. The country's rainforests are particularly rich in West African species that cannot be found elsewhere in East Africa. The forests, in fact, offer some of the best birding opportunities, but also the most frustrating, as the cover is thick and birds are more often heard than seen. Other species favour the semi-desert of the north, the savannahs, or the waters of Uganda's many lakes and rivers.

Ostrich, *Struthio camelus:* This largest of birds is commonly found in grasslands and lightly wooded areas. In Uganda found only in Kidepo Valley National Park.

Grebes: The **great crested grebe,** *Podiceps cristatus,* is found on Uganda's freshwater lakes; sometimes on relatively small dams. The **little grebe,** *Podiceps ruficollis,* is common on fresh and brackish lakes, dams, ponds, and slow-flowing rivers.

Pelicans: The **great white pelican,** *Pelecanus onocrotalus,* is common on Uganda's large inland waters, while the **pink-backed pelican,** *Pelecanus rufescens,* is found on all the larger freshwater lakes. Both can easily be seen in Murchison Falls and Queen Elizabeth national parks.

Cormorants: Uganda's lake, dams, and larger rivers are home to both the **white-necked cormorant,** *Phalacrocorax carbo,* and the **long-tailed cormorant,** *Phalacrocorax africanus.* Both can be seen in Murchison Falls and Queen Elizabeth national parks.

Darters: The **African darter,** *Anhinga rufa,* occurs on many inland waters, favouring slow-flowing rivers and fresh lakes. Particularly common on lakes in western Uganda.

Herons, egrets, and bitterns: Twelve species of this family occur in Uganda, including the very common **cattle egret,** *Ardeola ibis,* which favours swamps, marshes, and pasture land near water and is usually seen near large mammals from elephants to cattle. Also present is the largest African heron, the **Goliath heron,** *Ardea goliath,* and the **purple heron,** *Ardea purpurea,* which inhabits swamps and reed and papyrus beds bordering large lakes. The latter is common on Lake Kyoga.

Whale-headed stork, *Balaeniceps rex:* Also known as the shoebill stork, this large grey water bird with a gigantic shoe-shaped bill occurs in the heart of many papyrus swamps. In Uganda its main centre of abundance is on Lake Kyoga; it also occurs in swamps around Lake Victoria and in Lake Mburo, Murchison Falls, and Queen Elizabeth national parks.

Hamerkop, *Scopus umbretta:* This dusky brown bird with a thick, hammer-shaped crest occurs on many inland wters, favouring slowly running streams and rivers, lake margins, and marches.

Storks: Six stork species occur in Uganda, including the **woolly-necked stork,** *Ciconia episcopus,* and the **openbill stork,** *Anastomus lamelligerus,* which are seen on several of the country's lakes. The large and colourful **saddlebill stork,** *Ephippiorhynchus senegalensis,* is also frequently seen, particulary in Lake Mburo and Queen Elizabeth national parks; as is the gregarious **marabou stork,** *Leptoptilos crumeniferus,* which is commonly seen nesting in trees along Kampala's main roads.

Ibises and spoonbills: Common throughout the country in swamps, marshes, rivers, pasture and ploughed land are the **sacred ibis,** *Threskiornis aethiopicus;* the noisy **hadada ibis,** *Hagedashia hagedash;* the **glossy ibis,** *Plegadis falcinellus;* and the **African spoonbill,** *Platalea alba.*

Ducks and geese: Approximately 12 members of this family occur in Uganda. Common on many inland waters and regularly seen in Murchison Falls National Park is the **Egyptian goose,** *Alopochen aegyptiaca,* while the **spur-winged goose,** *Plectropterus gambensis,* is seen throughout the western half of the country. The **pygmy goose,** *Nettapus auritus,* is very common on Lake Kyoga, while **Hartlaub's duck,** *Pteronetta hartlaubii,* favours forested streams and rivers and is known in the Bwamba Forest (Semuliki National Park).

Secretary bird, *Sagittarius serpentarius:* Long-legged, terrestrial bird of prey that feeds largely on snakes. Frequents open plains, bush country and farmlands.

Vultures, eagles, and hawks: Some 30 members of this family occur in Uganda. The **hooded vulture,** *Necrosyrtes monachus,* is common throughout the settled parts of the country, while the **Egyptian vulture,** *Neophron percnopterus,* can be seen in Kidepo Valley National Park. The **lammergeyer,** *Gypaetus barbatus,* is also known in Kidepo Valley, as well as Mount Elgon National Park. Most frequent in south-western Uganda is the **African marsh harrier,** *Circus ranivorus,* while the **harrier hawk (gymnogene),** *Polyboroides radiatus,* is fairly numerous in the western part of the country. A rare bird recorded in western Uganda is the **Beaudouin's harrier eagle**, *Circaetus beaudouini.* The Semuliki National Park's Bwamba Forest is home to the **western little sparrowhawk**, *Accipiter erythropus,* and the rare **long-tailed hawk**, *Urotriorchis macrourus,* a forest treetop hawk. The dry northern part of Uganda is home to the **grasshopper buzzard**, *Butastur rufipennis,* and is breeding ground to the **augur buzzard**, *Buteo rufofuscus.* The **crowned eagle**, *Stephanoaetus coronatus,* is a forest bird known in Mount Elgon National Park, while another forest lover, **Cassin's hawk eagle**, *Hieraaetus africanus,* has been recorded in Bwindi Impenetrable National Park. Queen Elizabeth National Park is a good place to see the majestic **African fish eagle**, *Haliaeetus vocifer.*

Falcons: Northern Uganda is home to the **red-necked falcon**, *Falco chiquera,* where it is almost always asociated with borassus palms, in which it nests. The **European lesser kestrel**, *Falco naumanni,* is an abundant winter visitor.

Game birds: There are 17 members of the Phasianidae family, many of which occur in Uganda's forests. These include the **Nahan's forest franolin**, *Francolinus nahani,* and the **forest francolin**, *Francolinus lathami.* The **ring-necked francolin**, *Francolinus streptophorus,* frequents stony hillsides with sparse bush and grass, while **Shelley's francolin**, *Francolinus shelleyi,* occurs in south-western Uganda's grasslands, light woodlands, and mixed areas of bush and grass. **Clapperton's francolin**, *Francolinus clappertoni,* and **Heuglin's francolin**, *Francolinus icterorhynchus,* are found in the north, while the Ruwenzori Mountains and western Uganda are home to the **handsome francolin**, *Francolinus nobilis.* A common bird of the north-east is the **yellow-necked spurfowl**, *Francolinus leucoscepus.* **Button quails:** The **black-rumped button quail**, *Turnix nana,* occurs throughout the country, while the **quail plover**, *Ortyxelos meiffrenii,* is found in the north in areas where the silvery 'Heskanit' grass grows.

Cranes: Uganda's national emblem, the beautiful **crowned crane**, *Balearica regulorum,* is common throughout the country on open plains, marshes, swamps, and cultivated land. The **Sudan crowned crane**, *Balearica pavonina,* also occurs in the northern part of the country.

Crakes, rails, and coots: There are 6 members of this family in the country, the most unique of which is the **grey-throated rail**, *Canirallus oculeus,* a forest species keeping to dense cover. In East Africa it is only known from the Semuliki National Park's Bwamba Forest.

Bustards: The large **Kori bustard**, *Ardeotis kori,* which prefers open plains country, open dry bush, and semi-desert areas, occurs in the Kidepo Valley National Park. The eastern part of the country is home to the **white-bellied bustard**, *Eupodotis senegalensis.*

Jacanas: Both the **African jacana**, *Actophilornis africanus,* and the **lesser jacana**, *Microparra capensis,* are found in Uganda. The former is more often seen as it is less skulking and occurs on open waters where there is an abundance of aquatic floating vegetation, especially water lilies.

Stone curlews: The **spotted stone curlew**, *Burhinus capensis,* is widespread in open bush and lightly wooded areas, as well as dry rocky riverbeds and broken ground. The **water dikkop**, *Burhinus vermiculatus,* is found along rivers and the shores of lakes throughout Uganda.

Plovers: 11 species occur in Uganda, the most unique of which is the **Forbes' plover**, *Charadrius forbesi,* a rare species recorded from the western part of the country. The **long-toed lapwing**, *Vanellus crassirostris,* occurs on lakes and swamps where there is an abundance of floating vegetation. In Entebbe it may also be seen on the shores of Lake Victoria. The **Senegal plover**, *Vanellus lugubris,* is common in Queen Elizabeth National Park, where it is attracted to open grasslands.

Snipes and sandpipers: Uganda's swamps, marshy alpine moorlands, edges of lakes, and flooded areas are home to the **African snipe**, *Gallinago nigripennis.*

Coursers and pratincoles: The **Egyptian plover**, *Pluvianus aegyptius,* can be found on sandbars in rivers and lakes in northern Uganda, usually in pairs. The small **white-collared pratincole**, *Galachrysia nuchalis,* may be seen on rocks off Entebbe, while the **pratincole**, *Glareola pratincola,* frequents lakes and other inland waters.

Gulls and terns: Uganda's many lakes and rivers are home to four members of this family: the **grey-headed gull**, *Larus cirrocephalus,* the **whiskered tern**, *Chlidonia hybrida,* the **white-winged black tern**, *Chlidonia leucoptera,* and the **African skimmer**, *Rhynchops flavirostris,* which, when feeding, flies over the water surface ploughing the water with its projecting lower mandible.

Sandgrouse: Northern Uganda's semi-desert areas are the preferred habitats of the **Lichtenstein's sandgrouse**, *Pterocles lichtensteinii,* and the **four-banded sandgrouse**, *Pterocles quadricinctus.*

Doves and pigeons: 18 species of this family exist in Uganda. One of the rarest is the **white-naped pigeon,** *Columba albinucha,* which is found only in the western part of the country in Semuliki National Park's Bwamba Forest. The grey **afep pigeon,** *Columba unicincta,* is a forest bird known from western and central Uganda often seen in fruiting fig trees, while the **vinaceous dove,** *Streptopelia vinacea,* inhabits savannah woodland and bush in the north and west. Northern Uganda is also home to two colourful members of this family: the **emerald-spotted wood dove,** *Turtur chalcospilos,* and **Bruce's green pigeon,** *Treron waalia,* which has a bright yellow breast and abdomen.

Parrots: Five parrots occur in the country, the most well-known being the **grey parrot,** *Psittacus erithacus.* It is found, usually in flocks, in the tops of forest trees and is common in the forests around Entebbe and on the Ssese Islands. The colourful **rose-ringed parrakeet,** *Psittacula krameri,* is found in open savannah woodland and acacia stands in northern Uganda, while the more West African **black-collared lovebird,** *Agapornis swinderniana,* occurs in the very west of the country, in the Bwamba Forest.

Turacos: There are 8 members of this colourful family in Uganda. The **white-crested turaco,** *Tauraco leucolophus,* is numerous on the lower slopes of Mount Elgon and in the Soroti District, while the **Ruwenzori turaco,** *Tauraco johnstoni,* occurs in mountain forests and can be found in Ruwenzori, Mgahinga, and Bwindi national parks. The large **Ross's turaco,** *Musophaga rossae,* is also known from the Mount Elgon National Park.

Cuckoos and coucals: The most common member of this family to occur in Uganda is the **red-chested cuckoo,** *Cuculus solitarius,* which is often called the 'rain bird, as it frequently utters its distinctive, shrill call immediately before rains break. Although more often heard than seen, the brightly coloured **emerald cuckoo,** *Chrysococcyx cupreus,* mainly inhabits forest tree-tops. The **Senegal coucal,** *Centropus senegalensis,* is found in bush and thick cover mainly in savannah woodlands in the north.

Owls: The moorlands, swamps, and marshes of the Ruwenzori Mountains are home to the **Abyssinian long-eared owl,** *Asio abyssinicus,* one of 9 species of owl to occur in Uganda. **Fraser's eagle owl,** *Bubo peonsis,* has been recorded in forests in the south-west, while the western forests are home to the small **red-chested owlet,** *Glaucidium tephronotum.*

Nightjars: 9 species of this nocturnal, insectivorous family occur in the country, including the **fiery-necked nightjar,** *Caprimulgus pectoralis,* which occurs locally along roads through forest, open woodland, and thick bush country. The **Abyssinian nightjar,** *Caprimulgus poliocephalus,* is more often seen in the highlands, while swamps, marshes, and streams provide habitat to the **white-tailed nightjar,** *Caprimulgus natalensis.* More rare is **Bates' forest nightjar,** *Caprimulgus batesi,* a large, dark bird known in East Africa only from the Bwamba Forest in western Uganda's Semuliki National Park.

Swifts: The large **alpine swift,** *Apus melba,* breeds on cliffs in the Ruwenzori Mountains, which, together with the Kigezi region, also provide habitat to the more uncommon **scarce swift,** *Apus myoptilus.* The rare **Sabine's spinetail,** *Chaetura sabini,* and **Cassin's spinetail,** *Chaetura cassini,* are found in the Budongo and Bwamba forests in western Uganda.

Mousebirds: Both the **speckled mousebird,** *Colius striatus,* and the **blue-naped mousebird,** *Colius macrourus,* occur. The latter prefers bush and arid bush country, while the former inhabits forested and wooded areas, dense scrub, cultivation, and gardens.

Trogons: Lake Mburo National Park is particularly noted for the beautiful **Narina's trogon,** *Apaloderma narina,* but it occurs in rain forest, riverine forest, woodland, and dry highland forest throughout much of the country. Much less common is the **bar-tailed trogon,** *Apaloderma vittatum,* which inhabits damp mountain forests.

Kingfishers: 12 members of this brightly coloured family are found in the country. One of the most common is the **pied kingfisher,** *Ceryle rudis,* which is often seen perched on telegraph wires over water. The **shining-blue kingfisher,** *Alcedo quadribrachys,* is a Zaire forest species found in western and south-western Uganda around thickly-wooded and forested streams, rivers, and lakes. The country's forests are home to the **white-breasted kingfisher,** *Alcedo leucogaster,* and the **dwarf kingfisher,** *Myioceyx lecontei.* The Budongo Forest is particularly noted for the **blue-breasted kingfisher,** *Halcyon malimbicus,* and the **chocolate-backed kingfisher,** *Halcyon badius.*

Bee-eaters: Many of the 10 members of this family that occur in Uganda are found in the north, although the **black bee-eater,** *Merops gularis,* is a West African bird that inhabits the country's western forests. Although mainly a passage migrant, some **white-throated bee-eaters,** *Merops albicollis,* breed in Uganda, frequenting a variety of habitats from forest margins to semi-desert bush country.

Rollers: The most commonly seen member of this thickset, large-headed family is the **lilac-breasted roller**, *Coracias caudata,* which occurs in woodlands and open bush country, especially where there are isolated trees to serve as vantage points. The **blue-throated roller**, *Eurystomus gularis,* inhabits the forests of western Uganda, while the **blue-bellied roller**, *Coracias cyanogaster,* is found in the savannah woodlands of the north-west.

Hoopoes: Bush, savannah woodland, and acacia stands are the favoured habitats of the **African hoopoe**, *Upupa epops africana,* while the drier north is home to the **Senegal hoopoe**, *Upupa epops,* a race of the same species.

Wood hoopoes and scimitarbills: 6 members of this slender, long-tailed family occur in Uganda, including the **green wood hoopoe**, *Phoeniculus purpureus,* which frequents various types of woodlands, and the **white-headed wood hoopoe**, *Phoeniculus bollei,* a forest species. The savannah and acacia woodland of the north are favoured by the **black wood hoopoe**, *Phoeniculus aterrimus,* while the **Abyssinian scimitarbill,** *Phoeniculus minor,* inhabits dry bush country and acacia belts along dry water courses.

Hornbills: 16 different hornbills occur in Uganda, many of them forest species more known to West Africa. These include the **pied hornbill**, *Tockus fasciatus,* the **red-billed dwarf hornbill**, *Tockus camurus,* and the **black dwarf hornbill**, *Tockus hartlaubi.* The Bwamba Forest in the Semuliki National Park is known for several other forest species, such as the **white-crested hornbill**, *Tropicranus albocristatus,* the **wattled black hornbill**, *Ceratogymna atrata,* and the **white-tailed hornbill**, *Bycanistes sharpii.* The **black-and-white-casqued hornbill**, *Bycanistes subcylindricus,* is numerous in most of the country's large forests, while the large **ground hornbill**, *Bucorvus leadbeateri,* is known in Kidepo Valley National Park, and the similar **Abyssinian ground hornbill**, *Bucorvus abyssinicus,* is common in the north and in Lake Mburo National Park.

Barbets: 19 members of this fruit-eating family are found in the country. An uncommon species found in south-western Uganda is the **red-faced barbet**, *Lybius rubrifacies,* while rainforests are favoured by the **hairy-breasted barbet**, *Tricholaema flavipunctatum.* Several West African species occur in Uganda's western forests, including the **western green tinkerbird**, *Pogoniulus coryphaea,* and the **speckled tinkerbird**, *Pogoniulus scolopaceus.*

Honeyguides: These remarkable birds guide humans to wild bees' nests in order to feed upon the honeycomb when the nest is chopped out. 10 species occur in Uganda. Known only in the Bwamba Forest in the west is the **lyre-tailed honeyguide**, *Melichneutes robustus,* which has an amazing aerial display, undulating and spiralling high above the forest and then curving downwards to land in the tree-tops. More common is the **lesser honeyguide**, *Indicator minor,* which occurs in a variety of habitats from forest, savannah woodland, and cultivation to acacia woodland and bush country.

Woodpeckers: With its many forests, Uganda is home to a great number of woodpecker species, including the **Uganda spotted woodpecker,** *Dendropicos poecilolaemus,* and the **Gabon woodpecker**, *Dendropicos gabonensis,* a West African forest species known in East Africa only from the Bwamba Forest. Bwamba and Mpanga forests are also home to **Elliot's woodpecker,** *Mesopicos elliotii,* a slim bird with a bright green back.

Broadbills: Forested areas, bamboo forests, and dense forest and scrub along rivers are the preferred habitat for the **African broadbill**, *Smithornis capensis,* while the **red-sided broadbill**, *Smithornis rufolateralis,* is a West African species that occurs in the forests of western Uganda. **Grauer's green broadbill**, *Pseudocalyptomena graeuri,* is known in East Africa only in Bwindi Impenetrable National Park. It is one of the rarest birds in Africa, occuring in bamboo and mixed bamboo and montane forest.

Pittas: Brilliantly coloured forest birds, both the **African pitta**, *Pitta angolensis,* and the **green-breasted pitta**, *Pitta reichenowi,* occur in Uganda, the latter most frequent in the Budongo Forest.

Larks: 9 members of this ground-living song bird family occur in Uganda. Particularly common are the **rufous-naped lark**, *Mirafra africana,* which inhabits open plains and grassy bush country, and the **red-capped lark**, *Calandrella cinerea,* which frequents open plains, ploughed fields, cultivation, airfields, and country after grass fires have passed. The dry bush country of the north is preferred by the **redwing bush lark**, *Mirafra hypermetra,* and the **pink-breasted lark**, *Mirafra poecilosterna.*

Swallows and martins: The **African sand martin**, *Riparia paludicola,* and the **banded martin**, *Riparia cincta,* are two of the more common of the 14 members of this family that occur in the country. Both are widespread and gregarious. Another local resident is the **white-headed roughwing swallow**, *Psalidoprocne albiceps,* which is found mainly in forested and well-wooded localities.

Wagtails and pipits: The most commonly seen member of this family is the **African pied wagtail**, *Motacilla aguimp*, which is closely associated with human dwelling but also occurs on sand bars in rivers, along lake margins, and sometimes along rocky streams. Also look for the locally common **plain-backed pipit**, *Anthus leucophrys*, found on open plains.

Cuckoo shrikes: 6 members of this forest-loving family occur in Uganda, the most common of which is the **black cuckoo shrike**, *Campephaga sulphurata*. The **red-shouldered cuckoo shrike**, *Campephaga phoenicea*, and **Petit's cuckoo shrike**, *Campephaga petiti*, also inhabit the country's rainforests.

Bulbuls: With Uganda's many forests and woodland, it is no surprise that 26 species of the arboreal bulbul family occur in the country. Many occur only in western Uganda, such as the **white-tailed greenbul**, *Thescelocichla leucopleura*, **Xavier's greenbul**, *Phyllastrephus xavieri*, the **icterine greenbul**, *Phyllastrephus icterinus*, and the **red-tailed greenbul**, *Tricophorus calurus*, which is a West African species that extends eastwards to Uganda. The **yellow-throated nicator**, *Nicator chloris*, occurs both in undergrowth and among the branches of forest trees in the western part of the country.

Helmet shrikes: Of the 4 species of this family to occur in Uganda, the **straight-crested helmet shrike**, *Prionops plumata*, is the most widely distributed in bush country and woodlands. The **red-billed shrike**, *Prionops caniceps*, is a thickset forest-treetops bird that is found in small parties in the western forests, particularly Semuliki National Park's Bwamba Forest.

Shrikes: 25 species. Most common are the **black-backed puffback**, *Dryoscopus cubla*, which inhabits forested areas, woodland, thicket, gardens, scrub, and acacia country, and the **puffback shrike**, *Dryoscopus gambensis*, a forest treetop species. Frequently seen around Entebbe and in Queen Elizabeth National Park is the **black-headed gonolek**, *Laniarius erythrogaster*. The Kazinga Channel is Queen Elizabeth is also home to the **yellow-crowned gonolek**, *Laniarius mufumbiri*,, which inhabits papyrus swamps in the Kigezi area as well. Bwindi Impenetrable and Ruwenzori Mountains national parks are home to the **mountain sooty boubou**, *Laniarius poensis*, which is common in the higher forest. **Doherty's bush shrike**, *Malaconotus dohertyi*, is a colourful bird found in the forests of Mount Elgon National Park.

Thrushes, wheatears, and chats: Of the 32 species of this family to occur in the country, the

brown-chested alethe, *Alethe poliocephala*, is one of the most widespread in the forests, but it is very shy and elusive. Semuliki National Park is home to **Coll's forest robin**, *Erythropygia leucosticta*, and the rarer **akalat**, *Sheppardia cyornithopsis*, is also found in the western forests. The only place in East Africa to see the **white-bellied akalat**, *Cossyphicula roberti*, is in Bwindi Impenetrable National Park. The Kigezi forests and the Ruwenzori Mountains are favourite habitats of **Archer's robin chat**, *Cossypha archeri*. A common garden bird is the **African thrush**, *Turdus pelios*.

Babblers and chatterers: Common throughout Uganda is the **arrow-marked babbler**, *Turdoides jardinei*, which favours papyrus swamps, sugar cultivation, and rank bush as habitats. 10 other species occur, including the **brown babbler**, *Turdoides plebeja*, in bush savannah and the **mountain illadopsis**, *Malacocincla pyrrhopterus*, in forests. A West African forest species that also occurs in Semuliki National Park's Bwamba Forest is the **Capuchin babbler**, *Turdoides atripennis*.

Warblers: 68 species occur. In East Africa, several are found only in Uganda, including **Grauer's rush warbler**, *Bradypterus graueri*, found in forested swamps; the **yellow swamp warbler**, *Calamonastides gracilirostris*, which inhabits swamps around Lake George; the **red-faced woodland warbler**, *Phylloscopus laetus*, a mountain forest bird; the **collared apalis**, *Apalis ruwenzorii*, known in Bwindi Impenetrable National Park and the country's other mountain forests; the **brown-crowned eremomela**, *Eremomela badiceps*, known only in the Bwamba Forest; the **yellow longbill**, *Macrosphenus flavicans*, found in forest undergrowth in the west; and the **grey longbill**, *Macrosphenus concolor*, which also favours western forest undergrowth.

Flycatchers: Uganda's forests are home to many of the 28 species that occur in the country. Bwindi Impenetrable National Park is particularly known for the rare **yellow-eyed black flycatcher**, *Melaenornis ardesiaca*, and the **Ruwenzori puffback flycatcher**, *Batis diops*, which also inhabits Uganda's other mountain forests in the west and south-west. More widespread is the beautiful **paradise flycatcher**, *Terpsiphone viridis*, which frequents wooded areas, forests, thick scrub, acacia country, cultivation, and gardens. The western forests are home to the similar **black-headed paradise flycatcher**, *Terpsiphone rufiventer*.

Tits: Of the 7 species of this family in Uganda, the **dusky tit**, *Parus funereus*, is one of the most common, frequenting forest tree-tops. The stripe-breasted tit, *Parus fasciiventer*, is a mountain forest bird found on the Ruwenzoris and the forested mountains of the south-west, particularly Mgahinga Gorilla National Park.

Sunbirds: Flowering trees attract most of the 33 species of this family occuring in the country, the males of which have brilliant metallic plumage. The **blue-headed sunbird**, *Nectarinia alinae*, the **greater double-collared sunbird**, *Nectarinia afer*, and the **purple-breasted sunbird**, *Nectarinia purpureiventris*, can be found in Bwindi, Mgahinga, and Ruwenzori national parks, while the **northern double-collared sunbird**, *Nectarinia preussi*, is also present in Mount Elgon National Park. A locally common species frequenting forest and forest margins as well as lush bush near swamps is the **olive-bellied sunbird**, *Nectarinia chloropygius*.

White-eyes: The only species to occur in Uganda is the **yellow white-eye**, *Zosterops senegalensis*, which frequents a variety of habitats from open thornbush country, acacia and savannah woodland to Brachystegia woodland, cultivation, forests, and gardens.

Buntings: 5 species of this ground-feeding, finch-like family are present. Most widespread is the **golden-breasted bunting**, *Emberiza flaviventris*, which inhabits dry forest and woodlands, scrub, and acacia country. The dry bush of the north-east is home to the **brown-rumped bunting**, *Emberiza forbesi*.

Finches: Common members of this family include the **yellow-fronted canary**, *Serinus mozambicus*, and the **streaky seed-eater**, *Serinus striolatus*, the former inhabiting woodlands and scrub and the latter preferring moorland bush, forest margins, cultivation, and gardens. The **papyrus canary**, *Serinus koliensis*, is associated with papyrus swamps in the central and southern parts of the country.

Waxbills: 45 species occur in Uganda, one of the most notable being **Shelley's crimsonwing**, *Cryptospiza shelleyi*, a rare and seldom seen species that inhabits dense forest undergrowth in Bwindi and Mgahinga national parks. More abundant is the **common waxbill**, *Estrilda erythronotos*, occuring in flocks in lush grasslands, neglected cultivation, and rank grass and bush, often near water. Also common is the **black-and-white mannikin**, *Lonchura poensis*, which frequents grassy margins and glades of forests in savannah woodland.

Weavers, sparrows, and whydahs: One of the largest bird families in Africa, 64 species are found in the country. These include the **orange weaver**, *Ploeceus aurantius*, is a brilliantly coloured bird found mainly around Lake Victoria and in nearby swamps. Bwindi and Mgahinga national parks are home to the **strange weaver**, *Ploceus melanogaster*, which occurs singly or in pairs in treetops or forest undergrowth. Several species are rare, such as **Fox's weaver**, *Ploceus spekeoides*, found in or near swamps in north-western or central Uganda, and **Maxwell's black weaver**, *Ploceus albinucha*, a tree-top weaver known in East Africa only from the Bwamba Forest. Also rare is **Weyn's weaver**, *Ploceus weynsi*, which is most frequent near Entebbe, where it occurs in both forest and lush waterside vegetation.

Starlings: Two of the more commonly seen of the 19 species occuring in Uganda are the **splendid glossy starling**, *Lamprotornis splendidus*, which is numerous in the country's forests and frequent in Entebbe, and the striking **superb starling**, *Spreo superbus*, which inhabits thornbush and acacia country and the vicinity of human dwellings. Several others are forest tree-top birds, including the **chestnut-wing starling**, *Onychognathus morio*, and the **narrow-tailed starling**, *Poeoptera lugubris*.

Orioles: The Bwamba Forest in Semuliki National Park is home to the **black-winged oriole**, *Oriolus nigripennis*, a lowland forest species, while more common is the **black-headed oriole**, *Oriolus larvatus*, which inhabits acacia and other types of open woodland and highland forest.

Drongos: Common throughout all kinds of woodland is the **drongo**, *Dicrurus adsimilis*, while forest is the preferred habitat for the **velvet-mantled drongo**, *Dicrurus modestus*, and the **square-tailed drongo**, *Dicrurus ludwigii*.

Crows: 5 species of crow occur in Uganda, with the **white-necked raven**, *Corvus albicollis*, particularly known in the Ruwenzori Mountains National Park. Most common is the **pied crow**, *Corvus albus*, which is found in a variety of habitats from open country to areas of human habitation and margins of lakes, rivers, and swamps. The West African **piapiac**, *Ptilostomus afer*, extends its range to western and northern Uganda, inhabiting grasslands near borassus palms and pasture.

Demographic Profile

Although no official census has been taken since 1991, the population of Uganda today is estimated at 18 million. The last official census, taken in 1991, showed Uganda to have a population of 16,671,705, with an annual growth rate of 2.5 per cent a year between 1980 and 1991.

Population density averages 70 people to the square kilometre, with uneven distribution. The Kampala area is by far the most densely populated, with 500 or more people to the square kilometre, follwed by the Mbale and Kisoro regions with between 250 and 499 people to the square kilometre. The north-eastern part of the country is the least populated, with less than 50 people to the square kilometre. The urban areas accommodate 11.3 per cent of the population.

The major religions in Uganda are Christianity, to which about 85 per cent of the people nominally belong, and Islam, of which about 11 per cent are followers. Those who do not fall into these two broad categories practise either the traditional (animist) religions or are atheists.

Language
More than 40 languages are spoken in Uganda, although the indigenous population may be classified into four major language groupings: Bantu, Nilotic (western Nilotes), Nilo-Hamitic (eastern Nilotes), and Sudanic. The Bantu groups occupy most of the southern half of Uganda, with the most populous of these being the Baganda, who account for some 20 per cent of the population. The Nilotic (Luo) speaking groups occupy the central section of northern Uganda, while the Nilo-Hamites live in the north-east and the Sudanic in the north-west.

The official language in Uganda is English. Swahili is spoken and understood by some but has not been accepted as the *lingua franca*.

Population
1996 estimate: 18 million, or 74 persons per square kilometre.
1991 population: 16,671,705, or 70 persons per square kilometre.

Population by ethnic groups (1991)

Acholi, Labwor	734,553
Alur, Jonam	395,420
Baamba	62,900
Bachope	12,087
Badama, Japadhola	247,538
Bafumbira	202,437
Baganda	3,014,364
Bagisu, Bamasaba	751,151
Bagwe	40,068
Bagwere	275,492
Bahororo	141,641
Bakiga	1,388,366
Bakonjo	361,539
Banyankole, Bahima	1,640,762
Banyarwanda	328,991
Banyole	228,856
Banyoro, Bagungu	495,122
Baruli	67,986
Barundi	100,825
Basoga	1,370,371
Batoro, Batuku, Basongora	486,229
Batwa, Pygmy	1,385
Iteso	998,857
Kakwa	86,349
Karimojong, Dodoth, Tepeth, Suk.	346,027
Kumam	112,582
Langi	977,455
Lendu	8,595
Lugbara, Aringa	588,330
Madi	178,455
Nubian	14,708
Samia	185,200
Sebei	109,905
Other	103,920

Population by sex and age (1991)

	0-14	15-34	35-54	55+	Total
Males	3,942,680	2,651,888	1,032,644	558,535	8,185,747
Females	3,937,801	2,905,106	1,086,851	556,200	8,485,958

Region/district populations (1991)

Central	4,843,594
Kalangala	16,371
Kampala	774,241
Kiboga	141,607
Luwero	449,691
Masaka	838,736
Mpigi	913,867
Mubende	500,976
Mukono	824,604
Rakai	383,501
Eastern	4,128,469
Iganga	945.783
Jinja	289,476
Kamuli	485,214
Kapchorwa	116,702
Kumi	236,694
Mbale	710,980
Pallisa	357,656
Soroti	430,390
Tororo	555,574
Northern	3,151,955
Apac	454,504
Arua	637,941
Gulu	338,427
Kitgum	357,184
Kotido	196,006

Lira	500,965
Moroto	174,417
Moyo	175,645
Nebbi	316,866
Western	4,547,687
Bundibugyo	116,566
Bushenyi	736,361
Hoima	197,851
Kabale	417,218
Kabarole	746,800
Kasese	343,601
Kibale	220,261
Kisoro	186,681
Masindi	260,796
Mbarara	930,772
Rukungiri	390,780

Population of major urban centres (1991)

Arua	22,217
Bushenyi	14,195
Busia	27,967
Entebbe	42,763
Fort Portal	32,789
Gulu	38,297
Iganga	19,740
Jinja	65,169
Kabale	29,246
Kampala	774,241
Kasese	18,750
Kitgum	12,978
Lira	27,568
Lugazi	18,828
Masaka	49,585
Masindi	10,839
Mbale	53,987
Mbarara	41,031
Mityana	22,579
Moroto	10,517
Njeru	36,731
Soroti	40,970
Tororo	26,783

Religious affiliation

Catholic	44.5%
Church of Uganda	40%
Other Christian	0.5%
Muslim	11%
Other/None	4%

Gazetteer

Second paragraph indicates kilometre distance between major towns. Populations given are from the 1991 census. n/a: Information not available.

ARUA
Arua district.
Entebbe 538, Fort Portal 590, Gulu 249, Jinja 584, Kabale 888, Kampala 504, Kitgum 356, Masaka 625, Masindi 320, Mbale 533, Mbarara 771, Moroto 594, Soroti 436, Tororo 578.
Alt: 1,310 m (4,298 ft). Pop: 22,217. Post Office. Hospital Tel: 93, 143. Police Tel: Arua 64. Petrol: Day hours. Hotels.

ENTEBBE
Mpigi district.
Arua 538, Fort Portal 356, Gulu 380, Jinja 114, Kabale 464, Kampala 34, Kitgum 487, Masaka 171, Masindi 251, Mbale 284, Mbarara 317, Moroto 508, Soroti 381, Tororo 239.
Alt: 1,146 m (3,760 ft). Pop: 42,763. Airport. Post Office. Hospital Tel: 20719, 20160, 20622. Police Tel: 20222, 20223. Petrol: Day; some night. Hotels. Customs and immigration.

FORT PORTAL
Kabarole district.
Arua 590, Entebbe 356, Gulu 432, Jinja 402, Kabale 298, Kampala 322, Kitgum 483, Masaka 378, Masindi 254, Mbale 572, Mbarara 232, Moroto 796, Soroti 552, Tororo 527.
Alt: 1,539 m (5,049 ft). Pop: 32,789. Post Office. Hospital Tel: 2104/5. Police Tel: 2569. Petrol: Day hours. Hotels.

GULU
Gulu district.
Arua 249, Entebbe 380, Fort Portal 432, Jinja 426, Kabale 739, Kampala 346, Kitgum 107, Masaka 483, Masindi 178, Mbale 364, Mbarara 588, Moroto 321, Soroti 267, Tororo 409.
Alt: 1,110 m (3,642 ft). Pop: 38,297. Airport. Post Office. Hospital Tel: 160, 61, 381, 66. Police Tel: Gulu 64. Petrol: Day hours. Hotels.

JINJA
Jinja district.
Arua 584, Entebbe 114, Fort Portal 402, Gulu 426, Kabale 519, Kampala 80, Kitgum 469, Masaka 217, Masindi 297, Mbale 170, Mbarara 363, Moroto 394, Soroti 267, Tororo 125.
Alt: 1,143 m (3,750 ft). Pop: 65,169. Airport. Post Office. Hospital Tel: 2001/7, 20641, 20643. Police Tel: 21702. Petrol: Day, some night. Hotels.

KABALE
Kabale district.
Arua 888, Entebbe 464, Fort Portal 298, Gulu 739, Jinja 519, Kampala 430, Kitgum 837, Masaka 293, Masindi 552, Mbale 680, Mbarara 147, Moroto 904, Soroti 777, Tororo 635.
Alt: n/a. Pop: 29,246. Post Office. Hospital Tel: 22006. Police. Petrol: Day hours. Hotels.

KAMPALA
Kampala district.
Arua 504, Entebbe 34, Fort Portal 322, Gulu 346, Jinja 80, Kabale 430, Kitgum 453, Masaka 137, Masindi 217, Mbale 250, Mbarara 283, Moroto 474, Soroti 347, Tororo 205.
Alt: 1,155 m (3,789ft). Pop: 774,241. Post Office. Hospital Tel: 554008/554849. Police Tel: 231362/233814. Petrol: Day; some 24 hours. Hotels.

KITGUM
Kitgum district.
Arua 356, Entebbe 487, Fort Portal 483, Gulu 107, Jinja 469, Kabale 837, Kampala 453, Masaka 590, Masindi 285, Mbale 344, Mbarara 695, Moroto 281, Soroti 247, Tororo 389.
Alt: n/a. Pop: 12,978. Post Office. Hospital Tel: 45, 46. Police. Petrol: Day hours. Hotels.

MASAKA
Masaka district.
Arua 625, Entebbe 171, Fort Portal 378, Gulu 483, Jinja 217, Kabale 293, Kampala 137, Kitgum 590, Masindi 354, Mbale 387, Mbarara 146, Moroto 611, Soroti 284, Tororo 342.
Alt: 1,335 m (4,380 ft). Pop: 49,585. Post Office. Hospital Tel: 20018. Police Tel: 20095. Petrol: Day hours. Hotels.

MASINDI
Masindi district.
Arua 320, Entebbe 251, Fort Portal 254, Gulu 178, Jinja 297, Kabale 552, Kampala 217, Kitgum 285, Masaka 354, Mbale 395, Mbarara 486, Moroto 456, Soroti 298, Tororo 422.
Alt: 1,149 m (3,770ft). Pop: 10,839. Airport. Post Office. Hospital Tel: 7. Police Tel: Masindi 254. Petrol: Day hours. Hotels.

MBALE
Mbale district.
Arua 533, Entebbe 284, Fort Portal 572, Gulu 364, Jinja 170, Kabale 680, Kampala 250, Kitgum 344, Masaka 387, Masindi 395, Mbarara 533, Moroto 224, Soroti 97, Tororo 45.
Alt: 1,143 m (3,750ft). Pop: 53,987. Post Office. Hospital Tel: 22213, 2611. Police Tel: Mbale 3123. Petrol: Day hours. Hotels.

MBARARA
Mbarara district.
Arua 771, Entebbe 317, Fort Portal 232, Gulu 588, Jinja 363, Kabale 147, Kampala 283, Kitgum 695, Masaka 146, Masindi 486, Mbale 533, Moroto 757, Soroti 630, Tororo 488.
Alt: 1,473 m (4,833 ft). Pop: 41,031. Airport. Post Office. Hospital Tel: 20007. Police Tel: Mbarara 20158. Petrol: Day hours. Hotels.

MOROTO
Moroto district.
Arua 594, Entebbe 508, Fort Portal 796, Gulu 321, Jinja 394, Kabale 904, Kampala 474, Kitgum 281, Masaka 611, Masindi 456, Mbale 224, Mbarara 757, Soroti 158, Tororo 269.
Alt: n/a. Pop: 10,517. Airport. Post Office. Hospital Tel: 94. Police Tel: Moroto 19. Petrol: Day hours. Hotels.

SOROTI
Soroti district.
Arua 436, Entebbe 381, Fort Portal 552, Gulu 267, Jinja 267, Kabale 777, Kampala 347, Kitgum 247, Masaka 284, Masindi 298, Mbale 97, Mbarara 630, Moroto 158, Tororo 142.
Alt: 1,145 m (3,757 ft). Pop: 40,970. Airport. Post Office. Hospital Tel: 82. Police Tel: 218. Petrol: Day hours. Hotels.

TORORO
Tororo district.
Arua 578, Entebbe 239, Fort Portal 527, Gulu 409, Jinja 125, Kabale 635, Kampala 205, Kitgum 389, Masaka 342, Masindi 422, Mbale 45, Mbarara 488, Moroto 269, Soroti 142.
Alt: 1,183 m (3,881 ft). Pop: 26,783. Airport. Post Office. Hospital Tel: 4515, 4555. Police Tel: 4333, 4856. Petrol: Day hours. Hotels.

Museums and Historical Sites

Bigo Bya Mugenyi, Ntusi
District: Masaka
Features: Large earthwork built by the Bachwezi and related kingdoms. Two concentric earthworks, an outer ditch and an inner royal enclosure. Local people believe the earthworks have supernatural powers.

Kabaka Mwanga's Lake, Kampala
District: Kampala
Features: A large lake excavated in the late 1880s on the whim of Kabaka Mwanga, who intended to link it with Lake Victoria.

Kakoro Rock Paintings, Kabwagasa
District: Pallisa
Features: Rock art paintings generally accredited to the hunter-gatherers who lived in the area more than 2,000 years ago. Ancient rock gong.

Kamukazi, Mbarara
District: Mbarara
Features: The old Ankole capital. Buildings still in existence are in a poor state of repair, although the drum house is still standing.

Kasubi Tombs, Kampala
District: Kampala
Features: Traditional burial site of four former kings of Buganda. Inside the enormous domed building are a variety of artefacts that belonged to the kings.

Masaka Hill, Masaka
District: Masaka
Features: Thought to have been the site of the last capital of the Bachwezi leader Wamara. The hill is surrounded by two concentric ramparts and is topped by a grove of ancient fig trees, which are thought to have some ritual significance.

Mparo Tombs, Hoima
District: Hoima
Features: Burial place of Omukama Kabalega of Bunyoro and several successors. Kabalega's grave is surrounded by many personal effects.

Mubende Hill/Nakaima Tree, Mubende
District: Mubende
Features: Focal point for Bachwezi-related religious cults. At the top is the Nakaima Tree, some 400 years old, still a site of worship.

Munsa Earthworks/Rock Shelters, Mubende
District: Mubende
Features: Earthworks surround three large interconnected rock shelters, said to be able to hold up to 100 people and traditionally linked to a Bachwezi prince. Nearby is an ancient shrine reached by stone stairs in a cave in Semwana Hill.

Namugongo Shrine, Kampala
District: Kampala
Features: Sanctuary commemorating the martyrdom of 22 Christian converts burnt alive on Kabaka Mwanga's order in 1886.

Nkokonjeru Tomb, Mbarara
District: Mbarara
Features: Burial place of the last two kings of Ankole, Kahaya II and Gasyonga II.

Ntusi
District: Masaka
Features: The site of what was once the most large ancient settlement in Uganda. Most notable are two large mounds, containing bones, pottery shards, and other waste material. There are also several scraped depressions around the village, the largest of which lies near one of the mounds and is thought to have once been a dam.

Numagabwe Cave, Mbale
District: Mbale
Features: Rock paintings.

Nyero Rock Paintings, Kumi
District: Kumi
Features: Rock paintings, with some fine examples of geometric work.

Source of the Nile, Jinja
District: Jinja
Features: A picnic site and plaque marking the spot where Speke became the first European to see the Nile's source in 1862.

Uganda National Museum, Kampala
District: Kampala
Features: Displays on Uganda's history, anthropology, and geography, including a unique collection of musical instruments.

Public Holidays

1 January	New Year's Day
26 January	NRM Anniversary Day
February/March*	Idd-ul-Fitr
8 March	Women's Day
March/April*	Good Friday/Easter Monday
1 May	Labour Day
3 June	Martyr's Day
9 June	Heroes Day
9 October	Independence Day
25 December	Christmas Day
26 December	Boxing Day

* no fixed date

Listings

Dialling Codes

Bombo	04182
Buzinga	04184
Entebbe	042
Fort Portal	0493
Iganga	0495
Jinja	043
Kakira	043
Kampala	041
Kasese	0483
Lubowa	041
Lugcazi	044
Masaka	0481
Mbale	045
Mbarara	0485
Mityana	046
Mukono	041
Tororo	045

Air Charter Companies

Entebbe
Bel Air Ltd
Tel: 20516
Fax: 344779

Eagle Aviation
Limited
Airport Bldg
PO Box 7392
Tel: 20601/500
Fax: 20601

Take Air Ltd
2nd Flr
Entebbe Int
Airport
PO Box 393
Tel: 20516
Ext: 3106
Fax: 20668

Kampala
Air Uganda Ltd
Black Lines Hse
2 Colville St
PO Box 11316
Tel: 250105–6

Bel Air Ltd
22 Dewinton Rd
Spear Hse

PO Box 3463
Tel: 345902/
343800
Fax: 344779

CEI Aviation
Services
Metropole Hse
8/10 Entebbe Rd
PO Box 10241
Tel: 255825/
250212
Fax: 236097

Speedbird
Aviation Services
Limited
Suite B02
NIC Bldg
3/5 Pilkington Rd
PO Box 10101
Tel: 230587-9
Fax: 230588

Tropical Charters
and Tours
Limited
Kampala Rd
PO Box 9550
Tel: 230827
Fax: 230829

Airlines

Entebbe
Uganda Airlines
PO Box 187
Entebbe
Tel: 20456/21058/
20546
Fax: 20355

Kampala
Air France
Raja Chambers
3 Parliament Ave
PO Box 21025
Tel: 342907/8
Fax: 342995

Air Tanzania
Corporation
United Assurance
Building
1 Kimathi Ave
PO Box 2160
Tel: 234631/73

Alliance Airlines
Impala Hse
13-15 Kimathi
Avenue
PO Box 2128
Tel: 344011/514
Fax: 344534

Bel Air Ltd
Spear Hse
22 Jinja Rd
PO Box 2469
Tel: 343800/
345902
Fax: 344779

British Airways
23 Kampala Rd
PO Box 3464
Tel: 256695/
257414/255518

Dairo Air
Services Ltd
24 Jinja Rd
PO Box 5480
Tel: 257731/
344241/2
Fax: 259242

Ethiopian Airlines
United Assurance
Building
1 Kimathi Ave
PO Box 3591
Tel: 254796/7
345577/8

Friendship
Airline Ltd
Blacklines Hse
2 Colville St
PO Box 2255
Tel: 344766
Fax: 344836

Kenya Airways
United Assurance
Bldg Kimathi Ave
PO Box 6969
Tel: 256506/
233068

Sabena Airlines
Sheraton Bldg
Ternan Ave
Tel: 234201-2/
259880
Fax: 342790

Sudan Airways
Airlines Building
6 Colville St
PO Box 9010
Tel: 343565/
232990
Fax: 220474

Uganda Airlines
Corporation
Airline Bldg
6 Colville St
PO Box 5740
Tel: 232990
Fax: 257279

Airports

Entebbe Int
Airport
Tel: 20516/9

Art Galleries

Kampala
Nnyanzi Art
Studio
Raja Chambers
3 Parliament
Avenue
PO Box 10580
Tel: 257848/
344818

Nommo Gallery
4 Victoria Ave
PO Box 6643
Tel: 234475

Banks

Entebbe
Uganda
Commercial Bank
2 Kampala Rd
PO Box 48

Hoima
Uganda
Commercial Bank
8 Main St
PO Box 129
Tel: 40022

Jinja
St Mulumba
Friendly Society
Limited
8 Spire Rd
St Ludigo
PO Box 1882

Kampala
Bank of Baroda
18 Kampala Rd
PO Box 7197
Tel: 233680–3
Fax: 258263

Barclays Bank
16 Kampala Rd
PO Box 2971
Tel: 230972/6
232594/7
Fax: 259467

Cairo Int
Bank Ltd
Sure Hse
1 Bombo Rd
PO Box 7052
Tel: 230125/7
Fax: 230142

Centenary Rural
Development
Bank Ltd
Talanta Hse
7 Entebbe Rd
PO Box 1892
Tel: 251276/7

Co-operative
Bank Ltd
9 William/Burton
Street
PO Box 6863
Tel: 258323
Fax: 234578

Crane Bank Ltd
Plot 20/38
Kampala Rd
PO Box 22572
Tel: 34141/20
Fax: 231578

Diamond Trust of
Uganda Ltd
17/19 Kampala
Road
PO Box 7155
Tel: 259331-3
Fax: 342286

Gold Trust Bank
Impala Hse
Kimathi Ave
PO Box 70
Tel: 231784

Greenland Bank
Greenland Twrs
30 Kampala Rd
PO Box 6021
Tel: 342811/9
Fax: 230088

International
Credit Bank Ltd
Kato Plaza
11/13 Nkrumah
Road
PO Box 22212
Tel: 342291/69/
231975
Fax: 341470/
230408

Nile Bank Ltd
Spear Hse
22 Jinja Rd
PO Box 2834
Tel: 3455571/2
231904/257723
Fax: 257779

Orient Bank Ltd
Uganda Hse
10 Kampala Rd
PO Box 3072
Tel: 236012-5
Fax: 236066

Sembule
Investment
Bank Ltd
Cargen Hse
13A Kampala Rd
PO Box 2750
Tel: 236535/6/
233980
Fax: 236537

Stanbic Bank
Uganda Ltd
45 Kampala Rd
PO Box 7131
Tel: 230811/2
Fax: 231116

Standard
Chartered Bank
Uganda Ltd
5 Speke Rd
PO Box 7111
Tel: 258211/7
Fax: 231473

Tropical Africa
Bank Ltd
27 Kampala Rd
PO Box 9486
Tel: 231990/5/
232295/341408
Fax: 232296

Uganda
Commercial Bank
UCB Bldg
12 Kampala Rd
PO Box 973
Tel: 345519
Fax: 259012/
342694

Uganda
Development
Bank
IPS Bldg
Parliament Ave
PO Box 7210
Tel: 230740/5
Fax: 258571

Business Associations

Kampala
Centre for
Business
Promotion
Services
27 Nkrumah Rd
PO Box 9619

Uganda
Investment
Authority
Crescent Hse
Plot 2D
Nkrumah Rd
PO Box 7418
Tel: 334105/9
Fax: 342903

Car Hire

Kampala
City Cars
7 Parliament Ave
PO Box 151
Tel: 232335/
268611
Fax: 232338

LPC Transporters
Limited
16-19 Kampala Rd
PO Box 8601
Tel: 259240
Fax: 259240

Rhino Car Rentals
56-60 Kampala Rd
PO Box 10072
Tel: 234295
Fax: 344636

Casinos

Kampala
Kampala Casino
Pan Africa Hse
3 Kimathi Ave
PO Box 7832
Tel: 343630/28/
341666
Fax: 343632

Tourist Paradise
Uganda Ltd
Kampala Rd
PO Box 7250
Tel: 342142/3
Fax: 342137

Vegas Casino
Hotel Equatoria
37/39 William St
PO Box 7503
Tel: 250780/9
Fax: 250146

Clubs

Entebbe
Alice Springs
8 Kampala Rd
PO Box 63
Tel: 21178

Small World
Night Club
23 Kitoro Rd
PO Box 478
Tel: 20175

Hoima
Kosomoro Youth
Association
Fort Portal Rd
PO Box 6

Jinja
Jinja Club
17/29 Nile Cres
PO Box 687
Tel: 20169

Jinja Sailing Club
Plot 1-5
Pier Rd
PO Box 604
Tel: 20791

KK Resort Beach
and Sailing Club
PO Box 18700
Gaba
Tel: 267160

Mountain Clubs
of Uganda
PO Box 4692

Wildlife Clubs of
Uganda
PO Box 4596
Tel: 256354

Kampala
B M K Health
Club
Hotel Africana
2–4 Wampewo
Avenue
PO Box 10218
Tel: 344461
Fax: 232675

Exifa Sports Club
Byashara St
Wandegeya
PO Box 776

Credit Card Representatives

Kampala
American Express
Express Uganda
PO Box 353
Tel: 236767

Cultural Societies

Iganga
Iganga Uganda
Culture and
Crafts Centre
55A Main St
PO Box 449

Men and Women
Cultural
Association
Guremye Rd
PO Box 168

Kampala
Cultural Council
22 Namirembe Rd
PO Box 12708
Tel: 345030

Ugandan German
Cultural Society
20 Buganda Rd
PO Box 11778
Tel: 259612/
251646
Fax: 259612

Foreign Diplomatic Missions

Kampala
Algeria
6 Acacia Ave
Kololo Hill Drive
PO Box 4025
Tel: 232918/689

Australian
Regional Bureau
for Development
Cooperation
3rd Flr Annex
Crusader Hse
3 Portal Ave
PO Box 7457
Tel: 235103/79
Fax: 235160

Austria
6 Entebbe Rd
Bank Lane
PO Box 11273
Tel: 233002/
250754/235796
Fax: 233002

Belgium
5th Flr
Metropole Hse
8/10 Entebbe Rd
PO Box 7043
Tel: 343060/
233833/259561/
341624
Fax: 233007

Burundi
7 Bandali Rise
Bugolobi
PO Box 4379
Tel: 221697

Canada
4 Ternan Ave
Off Sezibwa Rd
Nakasero
PO Box 20115
Tel: 258141
Fax: 234518

China
37 Malcolm X
Avenue
Kololo
PO Box 4106
Tel: 235087/
259881
Fax: 235087

Cuba
19 Nakasero Rd
PO Box 9226
Tel: 233742

Cyprus
Athina Club Hse
30 Windsor Cres
PO Box 8717
Tel: 235812/
236089/341428
Fax: 236053

Denmark
4th–5th Flrs
Crusader Hse
3 Portal Ave
PO Box 11234
Tel: 256783/687
Fax: 254979

Egypt
33 Kololo Hill
Drive
PO Box 4280
Tel: 254525/
345152
Fax: 232103

Federal Republic
of Germany
15 Philip Rd
Kololo
PO Box 7016
Tel: 256767/8
Fax: 343136

Finland
Standard
Chartered Bank
Building
5 Speke Rd
PO Box 7111
Tel: 258211/7/
251010/341623
Fax: 231473

France
Embassy Hse
9-11 Parliament
Avenue
PO Box 7212
Tel: 342120/176/
344/5
Fax: 341252

Greece
3rd Flr
Diamond Trust
Building
Kampala Rd
PO Box 1790
Tel: 230953/1
Fax: 230952

Holy See
Apostolic Nuclature
Mbuya Hill
Chwa 11 Rd
PO Box 7177
Tel: 221167
Fax: 221774

India
1st Flr
Bank of Baroda
Building
18 Kampala Rd
PO Box 7040
Tel: 254943/
344631/257368

Ireland
12 Acacia Ave
Kololo
PO Box 7791
Tel: 268024
Fax: 344353

Italy
11 Lourdel Rd
Nakasero
PO Box 4646
Tel: 341786/
256416/250450
Fax: 250448

Kenya
41 Nakasero Rd
PO Box 5220
Tel: 258235/7
Fax: 258239

Korea
10 Prince Charles
Drive
PO Box 5885
Tel: 254603/
343424

Libya
The People's
Bureau
26 Kololo Hill
Drive
PO Box 6079
Tel: 344924/5
Fax: 344969

Malta
78/80 Fifth St
Industrial Area
PO Box 2133
Tel: 258516/
341849/257066
Fax: 341807

Netherlands
4th Flr
Kisazi Complex
Nakasero Lane
PO Box 7728
Tel: 231859/
334427/708/802
Fax: 231861

Nigeria
33 Nakasero Rd
PO Box 4338
Tel: 233691/2

Norway
Barclays Bank
Building
Kampala Rd
PO Box 7105
Tel: 230972/6
Fax: 232597

Russian Federal
Republic
28 Malcolm X Ave
PO Box 7022
Tel: 233676/
343808

Rwanda
Adj National
Museum
2 Nakayima Rd
PO Box 2468
Tel: 344045
Fax: 258547

South Africa
9 Malcolm X
Avenue
PO Box 10194
Tel: 342891
Fax: 259156

Spain
9th Flr
Uganda Hse
10 Kampala Rd
PO Box 8695
Tel: 344331/
345967

Sudan
21 Nakasero Rd
PO Box 3200
Tel: 343518/
230001

Sweden
Stanbic Bank Bldg
45 Kampala Rd
PO Box 7131
Tel: 236031

Switzerland
1 Roscoe Ave
Baskerville Rd
PO Box 4187
Tel: 341574
Fax: 236852

Tanzania
6 Kagera Rd
PO Box 5750
Tel: 256272

Thailand
10 Kalitunsi Rd
PO Box 5961
Tel: 236182
Fax: 236148

United Kingdom
10/12 Parliament
Avenue
PO Box 7070
Tel: 257054/301-3
Fax: 257304

United States of
America
British High
Commission Bldg
10/12 Parliament
Avenue
PO Box 7007
Tel: 259792/4
Fax: 259304

Zaire
20 Philip Rd
Kololo
PO Box 4972
Tel: 233777

Hospitals

Arua
Adiofe Health
Centre
PO Box 118

Family Medical
Resort
20B Avenue Rd
PO Box 375

Maracha Hosp
PO Box 59

Bombo
St Kizito Natyole
Health Centre
PO Box 35

Entebbe
Entebbe Health
Centre
Kampala Rd
PO Box 538

Uganda
Community
Based Health
Care Association
PO Box 325
Tel: 20691

Fort Portal
Virika Hospital
PO Box 233

Gulu
Lacor Hospital
PO Box 200

St Mary's Hosp
Lacor
PO Box 180

Hoima
Bujumbura
Health Centre
PO Box 34

Diocesan Health
Centre
PO Box 20

Hoima Islamic
Health Centre
Fort Portal Rd
PO Box 202
Tel: 40143

Jinja
Chinese Medical
Team
3 Ntembe Lane
PO Box 43
Tel: 20117

Islamic Institute
Health Centre
PO Box 662

Nida Medical
Centre
43 Rippon Gdns
PO Box 821
Tel: 22040

Nyenga Hospital
PO Box 24

Vithi Medical
Centre
39 Rippon Gdns
PO Box 2031
Tel: 20576

Kabale
Kabale Medicare
Services
Kabale
Municipality
PO Box 407

Rugalama Health
Centre
PO Box 3

Kakooge
Bukedde Medical
Centre
PO Box 25

Kaliro
Budini Health
Centre
PO Box 133

Kalungu
Jevis Health Care
Services
PO Box 70

Kampala
Kisekka
Foundation Hosp
PO Box 8727

Mengo Hospital
PO Box 7161
Tel: 270222–3/
270083

Mulago Hospital
Complex
Mulago Hill
New Mulago
PO Box 7051
Tel: 554748
Fax: 532571

Nsambya Hosp
PO Box 7146

Rubaga Hospital
PO Box 14113

Kamuli
Kamuli Mission
Hospital
PO Box 99

Kayunga
Kayunga Hosp
PO Box 18069
Tel: 1617

Kisoro
Mutolere Hosp
PO Box 26

Kisubi
Kisubi Hospital
PO Box 40

Kitgum
St Joseph's Hosp
PO Box 31

Lira
Aber Hospital
PO Box 310

Masaka
Kitovu Hospital
PO Box 413

Villa Maria Hosp
PO Box 32

Mbale
Chrisco Hospital
47 Sebei Avenue
PO Box 2074
Tel: 33727

Mbarara
Ibanda Hospital
PO Box 481

Mbarara Hospital
PO Box 40
Tel: 20007

Mityana
Mityana Hospital
PO Box 52
Tel: 2014/2279

Moroto
St Kizito's Hosp
Matany
PO Box 46

Nabusanke
Nkozi Hospital
PO Box 501

Naggalama
Naggalama Hosp
PO Box 22004

Nebbi
Nyapea Hospital
PO Box 62

Nkokonjeru
Nkokonjeru
Hospital
PO Box 20

Otuboi
Lwala Hospital
Via Soroti

Pakwach
Angel Hospital
PO Box 14

Rukungiri
Nyakibale Hosp
PO Box 31

Soroti
Soroti Hospital
PO Box 289
Tel: 82

Tororo
St Anthony's
Hospital
PO Box 132

Tororo Hospital
PO Box 2
Tel: 44515/55

Hotels

Apac
Omodi Hotel
PO Box 52

Arua
The White Rhino
Hotel
PO Box 359
Tel: 20057

Bugiri
Beverly Hills
Hotel Ltd
13 Jinja-Tororo
Kikupya Close
PO Box 77

Entebbe
Botanical Beach
Hotel Ltd
PO Box 90
Tel: 20800
Fax: 20832

Crane Guest Hse
19 Hamu Mukasa
PO Box 33
Tel: 20651

Entebbe Resort
Beach
PO Box 5245
Tel: 20934/21012/
20941
Fax: 21028

Sophie's Motel
3/5 Alice Reef
PO Box 6181
Tel: 20885
Fax: 20139

Stay N'Save
Hotel
24 Kampala Rd
PO Box 7666
Tel: 21044

Victoria Inn
29 Mpigi Rd
PO Box 92
Tel: 20925

Windsor Lake
Victoria Hotel
Circular Rd
PO Box 15
Tel: 20027/20645
Fax: 20404

Fort Portal
Mountains of the
Moon Hotel
PO Box 36

Wooden Hotel
PO Box 560
Tel: 22513

Gulu
Acholi Inn
7/9 Church Hill
Road
PO Box 239
Tel: 108
Fax: 250828

Hotel Roma
16 Coronation Rd
PO Box 779
Tel: 224

Justmor Inn
19 Coronation Rd
PO Box 823
Tel: 285

Hoima
Nsamo Hotel
9/11 Fort Portal
Road
PO Box 131
Tel: 40188

Jinja
Annesworth
Hotel
3 Nalufenya
PO Box 1253
Tel: 20086

Crested Crane
Hotel
PO Box 444
Tel: 21513

Daniel Hotel
PO Box 1213
Tel: 20971

Hotel Triangle
PO Box 515
Tel: 22344

Sunset Hotel
International Ltd
17 Kiira Rd
PO Box 156
Tel: 20115/20575
Fax: 20741

Timton Hotel
5 Jackson
Crescent
PO Box 341
Tel: 22397

Kabale
Highland Hotel
PO Box 95
Tel: 22175

White Horse Inn
PO Box 11
Tel: 22020

Kampala
Antlers Inn
PO Box 7036
Tel: 257120
Fax: 343998

Athina Club Hse
PO Box 8717
Tel: 235812
Fax: 341428

Calendar Rest
House
11 Namasole Rd
PO Box 3796
Tel: 268557

Chez Johnson
Hotel
1011 Bombo Rd
PO Box 30896
Tel: 567372

College Inn
PO Box 3852
Tel: 511763
Fax: 531310

Fairway Hotel
1/2 Kafu Rd
PO Box 4595
Tel: 259571/4
Fax: 234160/
233569

Golden China
Restaurant
1/13 Jinja Rd
PO Box 12020
Tel: 251368
Fax: 255608

Greenland Hotel
and Recreational
Services
PO Box 5245
Tel: 20934
Fax: 230088

Hill Top Hotel
Namirembe Rd
PO Box 2783
Tel: 270924

Hotel Diplomate
Limited
Tank Hill Rd
PO Box 6968
Tel: 267690/55
Fax: 267655/25

Hotel Equatoria
PO Box 9211
Tel: 250780/9
Fax: 250146

Hotel Int Ltd
Muyengo Tank
Hill
Tel: 266924

Hotel Rena
PO Box 5545
Tel: 273504

Lion Hotel Ltd
18 Namirembe Rd
PO Box 6751
Tel: 233934/
343490
Fax: 343682

Missouri Hotel
Missouri Building
Bombo Rd
PO Box 9492
Tel: 567726

Mussy Inn Ltd
Mussy Hse
222 Bombo Rd
Wandegeya
PO Box 30193
Tel: 558899

New Highway
Hotel
46/47 Kampala
Road
PO Box 143
Tel: 272867/
270028

Nile Hotel
International
PO Box 7057
Tel: 258080-9
Fax: 259130

Paris Hotel Ltd
210 Mulago Hill
Road
PO Box 467
Tel: 540427

Pope Paul VI
Memorial
Community
Centre
Nabunya Rd
Lubaga
PO Box 14326
Tel: 272189/
271133

Ranch on the
Lake Protea Hotel
PO Box 6577
Tel: 200147/8
Fax: 244779

Reste Corner
Hotel
PO Box 9153
Tel: 267685
Fax: 267993

Safari Trans-
Afrique Ltd
7 Parliament Ave
PO Box 7666
Tel: 250695
Fax: 233363

Sambiya River
Lodge
28/30 Lumumba
Avenue
PO Box 5187
Tel: 233596
Fax: 232307

Sheraton
Kampala Hotel
Ternan Ave
PO Box 7041
Tel: 344590
Fax: 256696

Shires, The
Tank Hill
Muyenga
PO Box 10377
Tel: 267145
Fax: 267159

Silver Springs
Hotel Ltd
76-78 Old Port
Bell Rd
Tel: 221231
Fax: 236361

Speke Hotel
PO Box 7036
Tel: 250554
Fax: 255200

Sportview Hotel
Jinja Rd
PO Box 7
Tel: 285118

Summer Hotel
Gaba Rd
PO Box 8578
Tel: 268019/357

Terrace Hotel
Hoima Rd
PO Box 5380
Tel: 542990

Tourist Motel
Kampala Rd
PO Box 4246
Tel: 273504

Kasese
Hotel Margherita
Kilembe Rd
PO Box 41
Tel: 44015/44379
Fax: 44380

Saad Hotel Ltd
Stanley Street
Hotel Building
PO Box 70
Tel: 44139

Kayunga
Hotel Atlanta
Ssekanja Rd
PO Box 18281
Tel: 8651

Lake Katwe
Mweya Safari Ldg
Box 22
Tel: 44266

Lira
Lira Hotel
PO Box 350
Tel: 20024
Fax: 235915

Malaba
Malaba
Paradise Inn
Main Rd
PO Box 42
Tel: 42012

Masaka
Laston Hotel Ltd
7 Mutuba Ave
PO Box 243
Tel: 20209

Hotel Aribas
82 Masindi Port
Road
PO Box 56

Masindi
Masindi Hotel
PO Box 11
Tel: 20023
Fax: 235916

Mbale
Mbale Hotel
5 Cathedral Ave
PO Box 101

Mt Elgon Hotel
PO Box 670
Tel: 33454

Mbarara
Agip Motel
PO Box 643
Tel: 20645

Andrew's Inn
47 Muti-Kakiika
PO Box 1310
Tel: 20247

Buhumuriro
Hotel
6 Stanley Rd
PO Box 466

Katatumba Resort
Hotel
PO Box 1177
Tel: 20152

Lake View Hotel
Limited
Fort Portal Rd
PO Box 165
Tel: 21392/8
Fax: 21399

Mayoba Inn
Mayoba Bldg
1 Masaka Rd
PO Box 326
Tel: 283

Motel Agip-Nifra
Links
Motel Agip Bldg
36/48 Masaka Rd
PO Box 643
Tel: 21933

Pan Afric Motel
PO Box 1169
Radio: 251550

Pelican Hotel Ltd
16/20 Bananuka Drive
PO Box 1057
Tel: 21100

Riheka Guest Hse
1 Multi Rd
PO Box 234
Tel: 2131

Sanyu Hotel
5 Masaka Rd
PO Box 266
Tel: 20089

University Inn
9 Kabale Rd
PO Box 1410
Tel: 20334–7

Western Hotel
Bulemba Rd
PO Box 248
Tel: 34464

Mityana
New Highway Hotel
46/47 Kampala Road
PO Box 143
Tel: 2192

Moroto
Moroto Hotel
PO Box 54
Tel: 97
Fax: 235915

Mubende
Nakayima Hotel
34 Old Fort Portal St
PO Box 175
Tel: 4053

Soroti
Oriental Hotel
Old Mbale Rd
PO Box 323

Soroti Hotel Ltd
PO Box 1
Tel: 61269

Tororo
Frontier Club Hotel Ltd
12 Jowett
PO Box 1119
Tel: 44474

Rock Hotel
Osukulu Rd
PO Box 293
Tel: 44654/5

Libraries

Fort Portal
Kabarole Public Library
31 Kaboyo St
PO Box 28
Tel: 22255

Hoima
Hoima Public Library
42 Main St
PO Box 189

Kampala
Kajjansi Reference Library and Geological Information
PO Box 2882
Tel: 200101

Lidia Macchi Youth Centre
PO Box 40181

Olympic Library
3 Pilkington Rd
PO Box 2610
Tel: 342010
Fax: 342010

Media

Kampala
Nation Newspaper Ltd
PO Box 6100
Tel: 232770-2/9
Fax: 232781

Saba Saba Publications Ltd
38 Benedict Kiwanuka St
PO Box 6867
Tel: 341440/ 230170
Fax: 273239

The Monitor
3 Dewinton Rd
PO Box 12141
Tel: 236939
Fax: 251352

The New Vision Printing and Publishing Corporation
4 Third St
PO Box 9815
Tel: 235209/846
Fax: 235221

The People Newspaper Ltd
8/10 Kampala Rd
PO Box 4860
Tel: 232416
Fax: 230675

Uganda Confidential
2 Colville St
PO Box 5576
Tel: 250273
Fax: 250273

Kasese
Kasese Media Centre
Stanley St
PO Box 250
Tel: 44025

Mbarara
Orumuri Newspaper
14 Bananuka Drive
PO Box 1471
Tel: 21265
Fax: 21504

Medical Insurance

Kampala
AAR Health Services
574 Nsambya By-Pass
PO Box 6240
Tel: 267576
Fax: 268780

Medivac Equity Insurance Brokers Ltd
78 Kampala Rd
PO Box 2903

Museums

Kampala
Uganda Museum
57 Kiira Rd
PO Box 365
Tel: 344061

Nightclubs

Kampala
Club Silk
15/17 First St
PO Box 12635
Tel: 250907/ 345362
Fax: 345372

New Victoria Club
KA252 Kireka
PO Box 4552

Theatres

Kampala
Bakayimbira Dramactors
13 Old Kampala Road
PO Box 1075
Tel: 344146

Hollywood Theatre
Entebbe Rd
PO Box 12104
Tel: 249462

Uganda National Cultural Centre
National Theatre Building
4-6 Dewinton Rd
PO Box 3187
Tel: 254567/8

Uganda National Theatre
4-6 Dewinton Rd
PO Box 3187
Tel: 254567/8

Westwood Park Hall
Kyengera
Off Masaka Rd
PO Box 21643
Tel: 272292

Nansana
Jjajja Asinansi Shed Ltd
Hoima Rd
PO Box 6383

Tour Operators and Travel Agents

Entebbe
OK Uganda Ltd
PO Box 166
Tel: 20449
Fax: 20003

Kampala
Abercrombie and Kent Ltd
1253 Muyenga Rd
PO Box 7799
Tel: 266700/3
Fax: 266701

Afri Tours and Travel Ltd
28/30 Lumumba Avenue Nakasero
PO Box 5187
Tel: 233596
Fax: 232307

Africa Travel Ltd
Embassy Hse
9/11 Parliament Avenue
PO Box 21833
Tel: 341330-2
Fax: 250773

African Pearl Safaris
Embassy Hse
Parliament Ave
PO Box 4562
Tel: 233566/7
Fax: 235770

Afrique Voyages Inc Tour and Travel Agents
3 Parliament Ave
PO Box 10805
Tel: 342437/ 251366
Fax: 342437

Air Guide
Services Ltd
Pan Africa
Insurance Hse
3 Kimathi Ave
PO Box 6449
Tel: 250689/
251848
Fax: 250689

Airmasters Tours
and Travel Ltd
2 Colville St
PO Box 5649
Tel: 250267/
342447
Fax: 255288

B L Tours and
Travel Ltd
1 Kafu Rd
PO Box 9976
Tel: 230990/
259571
Fax: 256041

Belex Tours Ltd
Kampala Hotel
Ternan Ave
PO Box 10542
Tel: 234180
Fax: 234180

Blacklines Tours
and Safaris
2 Colville St
PO Box 6968
Tel: 255200/88
Fax: 255200/88

City Cars
7 Parliament Ave
PO Box 151
Tel: 232335/
268611
Fax: 232338

Classic Tours and
Travel Ltd
9 Kampala Rd
PO Box 10983
Tel: 344420/2
Fax: 232910

Connexions
Business Centre
Tours and Travel
William St
PO Box 10947
Tel: 232060/
250780
Fax: 232068

Cradle Tours and
Travel
PO Box 12695
Tel: 268886

Crane Bird Tours
and Safaris
29 Luwum St
PO Box 3415
Tel: 344023/5/
254155
Fax: 236360

Crested Crane
Tours and Travel
4 Johnstone St
PO Box 6036
Tel: 232647
Fax: 232648

Crested Tours
and Travels Ltd
United Assurance
Building
1 Kimathi Ave
PO Box 1029
Tel: 344221-3
Fax: 232977

Crimux Co/
Crimux Tours
and Travel
4 Jinja Rd
PO Box 4458
Tel: 258266
Fax: 250329

Delmira Ltd
15A Clement Hill
Road
PO Box 9098
Tel: 255960/
235494
Fax: 231927

Express Uganda -
American Express
Travel Service
Ternan Ave
PO Box 236767/9
Fax: 236769

F K Tours Ltd
Kimathi Ave
PO Box 11970
Tel: 234744
Fax: 236329

Federico Tours
and Travel
Bureau Ltd
8 Burton St

PO Box 31034
Tel: 258000/44
Fax: 258000

Flyway Ltd
40 Kampala Rd
PO Box 6236
Tel: 233207/
257208

Globespan Tours
and Travel Ltd
1 Kimathi Ave
PO Box 12685
Tel: 343668
Fax: 343668

Gorilland Safaris
72 Kampala Rd
PO Box 12567
Tel: 234914
Fax: 232364

Hertena Tours
and Travel
Bureau
4 Johnstone St
Nr Pioneer Mall
PO Box 8659
Tel: 342833
Fax: 232287

Hippo Tours and
Travel Agencies
Limited
13A Parliament
Avenue
PO Box 3829
Tel: 230727
Fax: 259715

International
Tours and Travel
(U) Ltd
PO Box 6552
Tel: 345121/
232303
Fax: 251145/
250630

JCM Travel
Consultancy Ltd
5 Luwum
Tel: 232044/
540462

Jumbo Tours and
Travel Ltd
2 Parliament Ave
PO Box 11420
Tel: 250732/
230252/6

KMG Tours and
Travel Ltd
3 Portal Ave
PO Box 22465
Tel: 254682
Fax: 254626

MEAG Ltd
3 Parliament Ave
PO Box 4801
Tel: 344526/
345458
Fax: 232716

Nature's Green
Tours and Travel
Limited
13 Buganda Rd
PO Box 21906
Tel: 254648
Fax: 254774

Nile Safaris Ltd
6-8 Parliament
Avenue
PO Box 12135
Tel: 345092
Fax: 345092/967

Pan World Tours
and Travel Ltd
Orient Hse
4A Kampala Rd
PO Box 6750
Tel: 255739/
345956
Fax: 345957

Pearl Afric Tours
and Travel
Bureau Ltd
Pilkington Rd
PO Box 1102
Tel: 232730

Pearl Images
Tours and Travel
Limited
2 Colville St
PO Box 2503
Tel: 342910/3
Fax: 255288

Picnic Safaris Ltd
4A Kampala Rd
PO Box 40379
Tel: 343779
Fax: 234160/
257755

Reachout Safaris
and Travel
Agents
27 Nkrumah Rd
PO Box 5249
Tel: 254487
Fax: 254381

Rwenzori
Mountain Tours
and Travel Ltd
13 Kimathi Ave
PO Box 10549
Tel: 342375/
342055
Fax: 341754

S M Tours and
Travel Ltd
65 Kampala Rd
PO Box 5184
Tel: 254739/8
Fax: 258785

Safari Expeditions
and Car Hire Ltd
56/60 Kampala
Road
PO Box 6686
Tel: 255943/4
Fax: 255944

Saama Tours and
Travel Ltd
15/17 Nasser Rd
PO Box 4309
Tel: 233195
Fax: 254381

Savannah Safaris
Limited
7 Cooper Rd
PO Box 5970
Tel: 232446

Spear Touring
Safaris Co Ltd
1 Kimathi Ave
PO Box 5914
Tel: 232395/
259950/341522
Fax: 341233

Sunshine Tours
and Travel Ltd
Impala Hse
13-15 Kimathi
Avenue
PO Box 5011
Tel: 343255
Fax: 251321

Swift Link Tours
and Travel
2C Kampala Rd
Rainbow Arcade
PO Box 7375
Tel: 234315/
234251
Fax: 234316

Tri-Star Tours
and Travel
Bureau Ltd
72 Sunal Hse
PO Box 12155
Tel: 250276

Value Tours and
Travel Ltd
28 Jinja Rd
PO Box 8316
Tel: 250072
Fax: 342754

Uganda Missions Abroad

Belgium
Ave de Tervuren
317
1150 Brussels
Tel: (02) 762 5825
Fax: (322) 763
0438

Canada
231 Cobourg St
Ontario
Ottawa KIN 8J2
Tel: (613) 233
7797/8
Fax: (613) 232
6689

China
5 San Li Tun
Dong Jie
Beijing
Tel: (00-86-1) 532
1708
Fax: (00-86-1) 532
2242

Cuba
Calle 14
No 125 Esquina
Entre 3RAYIRA
Miramar
Havana
Tel: 332900
Fax: 332985

Denmark
Sofievej 15
DK-2900
Hellerup
Copenhagen
Tel: (31) 620966

Egypt
9 Midan
El Messaha Dokki
Cairo
Tel: 348 5975
Fax: 348 5980

Ethiopia
Africa Ave
H-18, K-36, N-31
PO Box 5644
Addis Ababa
Tel: 513513/088
Fax: 513355

France
13 Ave Raymond
Poincare
75116 Paris
Tel: 47-27-46-80
Fax: 47-55-93-94

Germany
Duerenstrasse 44
PO Box 200227
5300 Bonn-2
Tel: (0228)
355027-9
Fax: (0228) 351692

India
C-6/11 Vasant
Vihar
New Delhi 110-
057
Tel: (91-11) 687
7687
Fax: (91-11) 687
4445

Italy
Via Guiseppe
Pisanelli 1
00196 Rome
Tel: 322 5220
Fax: 322 5220

Japan
5-1-1 Heimajima
Ohta-ku
Tokyo 143
Tel: 768 3511
Fax: 768 3724

Kenya
5th Flr
Uganda Hse
Kenyatta Ave
PO Box 59732
Nairobi
Tel: 330801/814/
834
Fax: 330970

Libya
Bin Ashur
Jaraba St
Tripoli
Tel: 48006/604471

Nigeria
Ladi Kwali Way
Maitama
PMB 143
Abuja F C T
Tel: 523 0225
Fax: 523 1570

Russia
Per Sadovskikh 5
Moscow
Tel: 251 0060/299
3093
Fax: 200 4200

Rwanda
Ave de La Paix
B P 656
Kigali
Tel: 76495
Fax: 73551

Saudi Arabia
West of Salahedin
Hotel
Al-Waroud
District
PO Box 94344
Riyadah 11693
Tel: 454 4910
Fax: 454 9260

Sudan
Hse No 6
Square 42
PO Box 2675
Khartoum
Tel: 78409/78
Fax: 78431

Tanzania
Samora Ave
Extelcom Bldg
PO Box 6237
Dar es Salaam
Tel: 31004/5
Fax: 46256

United Kingdom
Uganda Hse
58/59 Trafalgar Sq
London
WC2N 5DX
Tel: (0181) 839
5783/09
Fax: (0181) 839
8925

United States of
America
5909 16th St NW
Washington DC
20011-2896
Tel: (202) 726
0416
Fax: (202) 726
1727

Zaire
17 Ave Tombalbaye
Ave de Travailure
BP 1086
Kinshasha
Tel: 22740/21326

Zambia
11th Flr
Kulima Tower
Katunjika Rd
PO Box 33557
Lusaka
Tel: 227916/8
Fax: 226078

Bibliography and Further Reading

African Wildlife Safaris, Spectrum Guide to (1989), published by Camerapix Publishers International, Nairobi.

An English Boy's Life and Adventure in Uganda (1912), by CW Hattersley, published by the Religious Tract Society, London.

Baganda at Home, The, by CW Hattersley, published by the Religious Tract Society, London.

Behind God's Back (1940), by Negley Farson, published by Victor Gollanz, London.

Birds of East Africa (1995), by Ber Van Perlo, published by Collins, London.

By the Waters of Africa (1917), by Norma Lorimer, published by Robert Scot, London.

Citizen & Subject (1996), by Mahmood Mamdani, published by James Currey, Oxford.

Changing Uganda (1991), edited by Holger Bernt Hansen & Michael Twaddle, published by James Currey, Oxford.

Chiga of Uganda, The (2nd edition 1996), by May M Edel, published by Transaction.

Conflict In Uganda by E Kumar Rupesinghe, published by James Currey, Oxford.

Designs on the Land (1992), by JMA Opio-Odongo.

Developing Uganda (1997), Edited by Holger Bernt Hansen & Michael Twaddle, published by James Currey, Oxford.

East Africa (1986), published by Time-Life Books, Amsterdam.

East Africa: a travel survival kit (1994), by Geoff Crowther and Hugh Finlay, published by Lonely Planet Publications, Hawthorn, Australia.

East Africa International Mountain Guide (1986), by Andrew Wielochowski, published by West Col Productions.

East African Handbook (1994), by Michael Hodd, published by Footprint Handbooks.

Field Guide to the Birds of East Africa (1985), by JG Williams and N Arlott, published by Collins, London.

Field Guide to the Mammals of Africa (1988), by Theodor Haltenorth and Helmut Diller, published by Collins, London.

From Chaos to Order (1995), edited by Holger Bernt Hansen & Michael Twaddle, published by James Currey, Oxford.

Guide to Uganda (1994), by Philip Briggs, published by Bradt Publications, Chalfont St Peter, Bucks, England.

Horn of My Love (1974), by Okot p'Bitek, published by Heinemann.

Imperialism and Fascism in Uganda, by Mahmood Mamdani, published by East African Publishing House.

Kakungulu and the Creation of Uganda, 1868 - 1928 (1993), by Michael Twaddle, published by James Currey, Oxford.

Kampala Women Getting By (1996), by Sandra Wallman, published by James Currey, Oxford.

Kingship and State, The Buganda Dynasty, by Christopher Wrigley, published by Cambridge University Press.

Mountain People, The (1994), by Colin Turnbull, published by Pimlico.

National Parks of East Africa (1994), by JG Williams, N Arlott, and R Fennessy, published by Harper Collins Publishers, Hong Kong.

Obote: A Political Biography (1994), by Kenneth Ingham, published by Routledge.

Political History of Uganda, A (1980), by SR Karugira, published by Heinemann Educational Books, Nairobi.

Uganda, A Century of Existence (1995), edited by PG Okoth, M Muranga, and EO Ogwang, published by Fountain, Kampala.

Uganda by Pen and Camera (1907), by CW Hattersley, published by the Religious Tract Society, London.

Uganda Now, Between Decay and Development (1988), edited by Holger Bernt Hansen & Michael Twaddle, published by James Currey, Oxford.

White Nile, The (1960), by Alan Moorehead, published by Hamish Hamilton, London.

Index